soviet
foreign policy
and
international
relations

O. B. BORISOV, B. T. KOLOSKOV

Sino-Soviet Relations
1945-1973
A Brief History

PROGRESS PUBLISHERS
MOSCOW

Translated from the Russian by *Yuri Shirokov*

О. БОРИСОВ, Б. КОЛОСКОВ

СОВЕТСКО-КИТАЙСКИЕ ОТНОШЕНИЯ

1945—1973

Краткий очерк

На английском языке

First printing 1975

© Translation into English. Progress Publishers 1975

Printed in the Union of Soviet Socialist Republics

Б $\frac{11102-744}{014(01)-75}$ 89—75

CONTENTS

INTRODUCTION

The history of relations between the Soviet Union and China is more than a history of inter-state relations between two nations. It cannot be separated from the Chinese people's national liberation and revolutionary struggle, and its key element is the Soviet Union's support for and assistance to this struggle. After the Great October Socialist Revolution relations with the Soviet Union were a crucial factor of China's development and the radical change of Chinese society. This mirrored the international import of the Great October Socialist Revolution, which Lenin described as a turning-point in world relations, a new chapter in world history.

Farsighted revolutionary leaders of China were quick to appreciate the immense historic importance of the October Revolution for the destinies of their country. Professor Li Ta-chao, one of the founders of the Communist Party of China, wrote: "The workers' and peasants' state and government were forged in the flames of the October Revolution. This state is the homeland, vanguard and mainstay of the workers and peasants of the world."[1]

Lenin closely followed the development of the Chinese revolution. His theoretical works on the national and colonial question, advice to Communists of the East, discussions

---

[1] Li Ta-chao, *Selected Articles and Speeches*, Moscow, 1965, p. 194 (in Russian).

with Chinese representatives on the Comintern (Third Communist International.—*Tr.*) helped to set the guidelines for the revolutionary strategy and tactics of the Communist Party of China, illumined the path of struggle before the Chinese people.

The Communist Party of China was greatly assisted on matters of theory and practice by the Comintern, which made a valuable contribution to working out the key problems of the revolutionary movement in China, including the building up of the Party, the vanguard role of the working class, the question of its allies, the role of the peasantry in China, the formation of a united anti-imperialist front, the setting up of revolutionary strongholds in rural areas, the formation of the Chinese Red Army, etc.

As early as December 1917, the Soviet Government approached the Chinese Government with the offer to discuss Sino-Soviet relations in the context of the foreign policy principles of the first socialist state. It proposed talks on the annulment of unequal treaties and the establishment of relations based on equality and mutual respect for sovereignty.

Immediately after the Revolution, Soviet Russia allied herself with the national liberation movement in China, and gave it every possible support and assistance. Glorious pages were inscribed in the history of Sino-Soviet relations during the Chinese people's heroic resistance to the Japanese invaders between 1937 and 1945. That period of severe trials for the Chinese nation threw into salient relief the Soviet Union's truly internationalist attitude to China.

The routing in 1945 of Japan's crack Kwantung Army by Soviet troops supported by troops of the Mongolian People's Republic and the Chinese People's Liberation Army contributed decisively to the defeat of militarist Japan and expulsion of the Japanese invaders from China, and proved a crucial factor of international importance for the victory of the Chinese revolution. Manchuria liberated by Soviet forces became a dependable military strategic base of China's revolutionary forces, from which the Chinese Communists led the people to a determined struggle against the corrupt Kuomintang regime.

The formation in October of 1949 of the People's Republic of China, her entry on the socialist path opened a new phase in the development of Sino-Soviet relations. The abolition of the reactionary Kuomintang regime removed the obstacles to the Chinese people's efforts to set up relations of all-round co-operation and friendship with the Soviet Union. The historical trends toward close rapprochement between the two nations could now develop on a broad foundation. People's China found in the Soviet Union a loyal friend and ally in the struggle for overcoming her economic backwardness, consolidating her international positions, building a socialist society.

The first decade of the history of the People's Republic of China demonstrated conclusively that all objective prerequisites were available for the development of Sino-Soviet relations in this direction, and that such development met the vital interests of the working people of the Soviet Union and China, all nations of the world. In pursuing steadily the Leninist internationalist policy vis-à-vis China, the Communist Party and Government of the Soviet Union made untiring efforts to develop and strengthen relations of friendship, alliance and all-round co-operation between the Soviet Union and the People's Republic of China, between the CPSU and the CPC, between the Chinese and Soviet peoples.

In the late fifties, however, Sino-Soviet relations began to deteriorate through no fault of the Soviet Union. For all the efforts made by the Soviet side to check this process, it continued to go from bad to worse. The People's Republic of China was diverging from the policy of friendship and co-operation with the Soviet Union and other socialist countries, and openly taking a stand against them.

To justify their splitting tactics, Chinese leaders lie about the true motives of their hostility toward the Soviet Union and other socialist states. They go to all lengths to obliterate from the minds of the Chinese people whatever good things they know of the Soviet Union, to stir up popular sentiments against it, thereby preparing the ground for an anti-Soviet policy to be pursued for a long period ahead. The anti-Sovietists in Peking grossly distort generally known facts from the history of Sino-Soviet relations, slander the CPSU and the Soviet Government, make an effort to misrepresent the Soviet Union's foreign policy principles and the true role of the CPSU and the Soviet Union on the international scene, to foment mistrust in and hostility toward them among other nations. Small wonder, therefore, that such fabrications are readily caught up by reactionary propagandists who regard them as a very helpful aid to their struggle against socialism. Pamphlets and monumental "research" publications which have of late flooded the book markets in the United States, Britain, the FRG and other capitalist countries present a crudely falsified history of Sino-Soviet relations.

Any attempt to conceal the truth about these relations and to denigrate the Leninist foreign policy of the world's first socialist state is doomed to failure. The history of Sino-Soviet relations is a vivid chronicle of events furnishing incontrovertible proof that the policy of the CPSU and the Soviet Government toward the People's Republic of China has invariably been motivated by a desire to promote fraternal friendship and co-operation between the two countries, to give the Chinese people all-round assistance in their struggle for socialism.

CHAPTER I

THE DEFEAT OF MILITARIST JAPAN, A KEY FACTOR IN THE VICTORY OF THE CHINESE REVOLUTION. SINO-SOVIET RELATIONS IN 1945-1949

The Chinese revolution was a dual product of developments on the international scene and deep-going changes in the country itself rooted in the increasing exacerbation of the class antagonisms and the upsurge of the national liberation movement in China. The essence of these antagonisms, the main motive forces and the objectives of the revolution predetermined its anti-feudal, anti-imperialist and democratic character.

Furthermore, the Chinese revolution has furnished striking evidence that today the success of a revolutionary movement in any country, especially where the working class is relatively weak, and where its party has to lean primarily on the revolutionary sentiments of broad sections of the petty bourgeoisie, is dependent decisively on support from a country where socialism has already triumphed, on the role of socialism in international affairs and on its place in the alignment of forces on the world scene. Without such support, successful development of a revolution and transition to the building of socialism are inconceivable.

Considering the Chinese revolution from this angle, it should be borne in mind that the victory of the progressive peace-loving forces over Nazi Germany and militarist Japan in World War II, the brunt of which had been borne by the Soviet Union, was a key factor of its success.

The years between 1945 and 1949 were a particularly eventful period in the history of the Chinese revolution. China's revolutionary forces could not only take advantage

of the favourable situation following the liberation of Manchuria, one of her main areas, from the Japanese invaders
by the Soviet Army but also to lean on direct Soviet support in their drive to overthrow the reactionary regime of
Chiang Kai-shek. It will be recalled that as far back as
1947, Yenan[1] was surrendered to Kuomintang troops and lost
its importance as the centre of the revolutionary forces. Since then the military revolutionary base in Manchuria was the main bulwark of the Chinese people's struggle
against the Chiang Kai-shek regime and its imperialist supporters.

The period 1945-1949 is also significant as the time when
the foundation was laid for the co-operation between the
two countries, which assumed a comprehensive scale after
1949. Hence the need to give a special review of this period
which served as an important take-off stage for developing
Sino-Soviet relations after the People's Republic of China
was proclaimed, bearing in mind that Soviet historians gave
it an extremely lop-sided and sometimes wrong interpretation.

1. MANCHURIA'S PLACE IN THE ANTI-SOVIET PLANS OF THE JAPANESE MILITARISTS

In planning their policy of war against communism,
against the Soviet Union, against China's revolutionary forces,
the Japanese militarists attached priority importance to
building up a military strategic bridgehead in Manchuria.
In pursuance of this objective they did not stop short of
aggression. In 1932, Japan set up the puppet state of Man-
chukuo and went ahead with feverish work to mobilise the
military economic resources of this region of key importance
both in area (1,100,000 sq km within the borders of 1944-
1945) and in industrial potential (over 20 per cent of China's
total).

The Japanese militarists suppressed with fire and sword
Chinese working people's revolutionary actions in Manchuria. They moved in their crack troops and police forces,

---

[1] The centre of the area liberated from the Japanese invaders in
Northwest China and the seat of the CPC Central Committee.

turning the country into a veritable concentration camp. The Japanese militarists, who were sworn enemies of both the Soviet and Chinese peoples, were hatching up, in a collusion with the German Nazis, plans of a further expansion of aggression against the Soviet Union and China, as well as of the conquest of Singapore, Indochina, Thailand, Malaya, Burma, Indonesia, the Philippines.

When going to war in Southeast Asia, the Japanese High Command anticipated an easy victory. After seizing vast areas there, Japan, far from dropping her plans of making war against the Soviet Union, carried on incessant preparations for it. The Kwantung Army in Manchuria was in combat readiness for a thrust northwards. The Japanese Government was simply waiting for Germany's "decisive victory": first, the "fall of Moscow", and second, the "fall of Stalingrad". The Japanese press openly clamoured for the annexation of the Soviet Far East by Japan. The Trans-Siberian Railway with its neighbouring areas west of Omsk was to be seized by Germany, and the part of it east of Omsk, by Japan.

The Japanese General Staff drew up its "Kan-Toku-En Plan" modelled on the Nazi "Barbarossa Plan" of conquering the Soviet Union. The Japanese High Command in Manchuria was busy with preparations for implementing this plan. The Japanese imperialists believed that their conquests in China and Southeast Asia were insecure unless a defeat was inflicted on the Soviet Union, a country the peoples waging guerrilla warfare against the Japanese invaders looked forward to for support.

The Japanese imperialists frequently violated the Soviet-Japanese neutrality pact, coordinating with Nazi Germany their plans of attacking the Soviet Union. On May 15, 1942, the Foreign Minister of the "Third Reich" Joachim von Ribbentrop, in a cable to Tokyo, said that the Japanese troop concentration on the Soviet-Manchurian border was a substantial aid to Germany, because Russia had at any rate to keep troops in Eastern Siberia to guard itself against a conflict with Japan.

The Japanese High Command hastily set up military bases along the Soviet and Mongolian borders, and went ahead with building strategic railways and highways in Manchuria, pooling rolling stock and storing up fuel. Between 1941 and 1945, the Japanese Navy detained 178 Soviet merchant ships and sunk about a dozen Soviet cargo and passenger vessels in the Far East waters. Groups of saboteurs were frequently infiltrated into Soviet territory from Manchuria. The Japanese intelligence regularly supplied Berlin with espionage information about the Soviet Union.

After the capitulation of Nazi Germany, the Japanese imperialists carried on the war in the Pacific, refusing to accept defeat and lay down their arms. They pinned their main hopes on the Kwantung Army, deployed in Manchuria, which had been fully equipped and reinforced with crack troops by mid-1945. The Japanese militarists expected that, leaning on their military industrial bases in Manchuria, which had not been bombed out by the US Air Force, they would be able to hold out until a more favourable situation developed for the Kwantung Army to go into a decisive battle. They also planned to use bacteriological weapons to achieve a reversal in the course of hostilities. This was proved by incontrovertible evidence in the hearings at the Khabarovsk trial of Japanese war criminals. In the occupied areas of Manchuria, the Japanese General Staff organised mass-scale reproduction of plague, cholera, typhus and other epidemic germ carriers. Germ warfare tests were carried out on the population of large occupied areas.

According to plans of the Supreme Command of the US and British forces, "decisive" operations against Japan were not to be started before 1946-1947. In his statement in the Commons on August 16, 1945, Winston Churchill said that no one could tell how much time it would take to carry out these "decisive" operations.

Early in August 1945, the Kwantung Army included troops of the 1st and the 3rd fronts, the 4th Separate Army and the 2nd Air Force. Later, it was reinforced with troops of the 17th Front and the 5th Air Force. The Kwantung Army had over 1,000 tanks, 5,000 pieces of ordnance, 1,800 planes. Its personnel had for a long time been brainwashed in the militarist spirit of samurai traditions, hatred of the Soviet, Chinese and Mongolian peoples. The Command of the Kwantung Army group also had at its disposal the Man-chukuo army of about 190,000 officers and men and puppet troops of the occupied areas of Inner Mongolia and Suiyuan Province.

2. THE ROUT OF THE KWANTUNG ARMY AND THE CAPITULATION OF JAPAN

The situation which took shape in China during the war against Japan—the division of the nation, the disruption of the united front—was advantageous for Japanese imperialism. China was unable to give an effective rebuff to international reaction threatening her national independence. The Soviet Union, therefore, sought to secure military aid to the embattled Chinese people and their unity under the banner of a united anti-Japanese front.

The Soviet Union viewed the struggle against Japanese militarism as part of the joint struggle of the progressive peace forces against the aggressive plans of the extremist imperialist reactionary circles as expressed in the predatory alliance of the "Axis Powers"—Germany, Italy, and Japan. Even before the total defeat of Nazi Germany, at the Yalta Conference, on February 11, 1945, the Soviet Government had pledged to make war on Japan within two or three months of German surrender in Europe.

By taking this commitment the Soviet Union fulfilled its duty as an ally in the anti-Hitler coalition and demonstrated its genuine internationalism coming unhesitatingly to the aid of the Chinese and other peoples waging a war of liberation against the Japanese invaders. At the Yalta Conference, the Soviet Union declared its willingness to conclude a treaty of friendship and alliance with China and send Soviet troops to help liberate her from the Japanese yoke.[1]

Within three months of Nazi Germany's surrender, the Soviet Union moved large military forces and equipment to the Far East. By the time hostilities were opened against the Japanese army Soviet troops had 1,500,000 officers and men, over 26,000 pieces of artillery and mortars, over 5,500 tanks and self-propelled guns, almost 3,900 combat aircraft.

---

[1] *Foreign Policy of the Soviet Union During the Great Patriotic War*, Documents and Records, Vol. III, Moscow, 1947, p. 112 (in Russian).

The Soviet Pacific Fleet and the Amur Naval Flotilla were placed on the alert.

Command of operations against the Kwantung Army was entrusted to Marshals A. M. Vasilevsky, R. Y. Malinovsky, K. A. Meretskov and other celebrated Soviet generals.

On August 8, 1945, the Soviet Government in a motivated statement to the Japanese Ambassador in Moscow declared that as of August 9 the Soviet Union would regard itself in a state of war with Japan.

On the morning of August 9, Soviet troops launched an offensive simultaneously in three directions: on the Trans-Baikal, the 1st and the 2nd Far Eastern fronts. The rate of their advance was extremely fast. Already on August 12, the main forces of the 6th Tank Army of the Guards operating on the Trans-Baikal Front crossed the Great Khingan Mountains and burst upon the Manchurian Plain.

The Soviet Union's entry into the war against Japan, the first successes of Soviet troops caused a shock to the Japanese ruling elite. On August 9, Premier Suzuki stated at a meeting of Japan's Supreme War Council: "The entry of the Soviet Union into the war against Japan this morning has put us finally in a hopeless situation and made it impossible to carry on the war."

The Chinese people welcomed the Soviet Union's declaration of war on Japan with enormous enthusiasm. In tune with these sentiments, Mao Tse-tung wrote on August 9, 1945: "The Chinese people heartily welcome the Soviet Government's declaration of war on Japan on August 8. The Soviet Union's action will very much shorten the duration of the war against Japan. The war is already in its last stage and the time has come for us to defeat finally the Japanese invaders and all their jackals"[1].

The brilliant victories of the Soviet Army and units of the People's Revolutionary Army of the Mongolian People's Republic, which operated jointly with Soviet troops in Northeast China resulted in a flight of Japanese troops from Inner Mongolia and North China and served as a signal for the offensive launched on August 10 by the 8th Route Army and

---

[1] Mao Tse-tung, "The Last Round with the Japanese Invaders". In: *Selected Works* of Mao Tse-tung, Vol. 4, London, 1956, p. 331.

the 4th New Army under the leadership of the Communist Party of China.

Stunned by the rout of the Kwantung Army, the Japanese surrendered the large towns of Kalgan, Chengtehshih and Che foo to the People's Liberation Army virtually without fighting. As a result, the revolutionary troops entered Manchuria and came into direct contact with Soviet forces. The formidable Japanese fortified lines on the rivers Amur, Ussuri and in the Great Khingan Mountains were burst open all along their length. Japanese pockets of resistance were encircled and bypassed. The operations carried out with lightning speed by all the arms of the Soviet ground forces, the Air Force and the Navy frustrated the Japanese militarists' plans to use bacteriological weapons.[1]

The quick and crushing blows the Soviet Army, Navy and Air Force dealt to Japanese troops compelled them to agree to an unconditional surrender. A day after the Soviet Army went into battle, the Japanese Foreign Minister Togo made this statement to the Soviet Ambassador Y. A. Malik: "The Japanese Government is ready to accept the terms of the Declaration of July 26 of this year (i.e., the Potsdam Declaration.—*Authors*.) to which the Soviet Government is a party. The Japanese Government understands that this Declaration contains no demands infringing the prerogatives of the Emperor as the sovereign of Japan. The Japanese Government requests a definite notification on this question."[2] Japanese troops, however, continued to put up stubborn resistance.

On August 11, 1945, the Governments of the USSR, the USA, China and Britain demanded that Japan should secure the conditions of capitulation necessary for compliance with the Potsdam Declaration and issue orders to Jap-

---

[1] At the Khabarovsk trial, the ex-Commander-in-Chief of Japanese Kwantung Army, General Yamada, testified: "The entry of the Soviet Union into the war against Japan and the rapid advance of the Soviet Army into the interior of Manchuria made it impossible for us to use bacteriological weapons against the USSR and other countries." *Records of the Trial of Ex-Servicemen of the Japanese Army on Charges of Developing and Using Bacteriological Weapons*, Moscow, 1950, p. 99 (in Russian).

[2] *Pravda*, August 11, 1945.

anese armed forces wherever they might be deployed to cease
fire and lay down their arms.

On August 14, the Japanese Government announced that
the Emperor of Japan had issued a rescript on the acceptance by Japan of the terms of the Potsdam Declaration and
that he was ready to secure the signing by his government
and the Imperial General Headquarters of a condition for
the fulfilment of the Declaration.

The "Emperor's Rescript", however, was merely a general
declaration. In fact, the Kwantung Army had not been
ordered to cease fire, Japanese forces continued to fight back
and at places even attempted a counter-offensive.

On August 17, 1945, Marshal Vasilevsky, Commander-in-
Chief of the Soviet forces in the Far East, sent the following radio message to the Kwantung Army Commander: "The
Japanese Kwantung Army headquarters radioed a ceasefire
proposal to the Soviet Army headquarters in the Far East
without saying a word about a capitulation of the Japanese
armed forces in Manchuria. In the meantime, Japanese troops
launched a counter-offensive on several sectors of the Soviet-
Japanese front.

"I propose to the Kwantung Army Commander to end all
hostilities against Soviet forces all along the front at 12:00
hours on August 20, to lay down arms and surrender.

"The above deadline is set for the Kwantung Army headquarters to pass down an order to all its troops to cease fire
and surrender. As soon as Japanese troops start laying down
their arms, the Soviet forces will cease fire."[1]

Between August 9 and 20, the Kwantung Army's losses in
killed and taken prisoner in Manchuria amounted to 700,000
officers and men (including 594,148 POW), not counting
missing in action. These casualties were considerably larger
than the total losses incurred by the Japanese armed forces
in all the theatres of operations over the preceding four years
of World War II. On only two fronts, Soviet troops captured
1,565 pieces of artillery, 2,139 mortars and grenade launchers, 600 tanks, 861 aircraft and other weapons.

It was the crushing defeat inflicted by Soviet troops on the
Kwantung Army, the strongest group of the Japanese land

---

[1] *Pravda*, August 17, 1945.

forces, rather than the American atom bombing of Hiroshima and Nagasaki that brought about the speedy capitulation of militarist Japan.

"...The Soviet Army moved into Manchuria and wiped out the Kwantung Army breaking the backbone of the Japanese militarists and forcing imperial Japan to capitulate,"[1] stated Chu Teh, Commander-in-Chief of China's revolutionary army. The Chinese newspaper *Kwangming jihpao*, in its issue of September 3, 1951, wrote in the same vein: "...when the Soviet Union moved in its forces which licked Japan's Kwantung Army, the Japanese invaders' hope of converting Manchuria into the scene of a battle to the last ditch were dashed. The only way out for them was an unconditional surrender. This is conclusive proof that it was the Soviet Union's entry into the war that forced Japan to agree to an unconditional capitulation, and that the Soviet Army's operations, the liberation of the Northeast provinces and Korea shortened considerably the duration of the Allied war effort against Japan...."

The act of Japan's unconditional capitulation was signed on board the battleship *Missouri* in the Tokyo Bay on September 2, 1945. Favourable prospects opened up before the Chinese people for a continued struggle for their national and social liberation.

On August 14, 1945, the Soviet Union and China signed a treaty, which not only provided support for the Chinese people's national liberation struggle but also enabled direct Soviet aid to be given to China's revolutionary and democratic forces and contributed to the creation of a favourable situation for the activities of the Communist Party of China. The treaty became a definite obstacle to the traditional anti-Soviet policy of the Chiang Kai-shek regime. The newspaper *Chiehfang jihpao* of China's People's Liberation Army wrote on August 27, 1945: "The treaty of friendship and alliance with the Soviet Union is the first equal treaty with a foreign nation in China's history. The Chinese and Soviet peoples have joined in a splendid friendly union. We believe this treaty to be yet another expression of the Soviet Union's invariable policy of equality in relations with us...."

---

[1] *Pravda*, July 21, 1949.

3. THE SITUATION IN MANCHURIA
AFTER THE DEFEAT OF MILITARIST JAPAN

After the capitulation of Japan, China remained divided into two camps. Two-thirds of her territory was still controlled by the Chiang Kai-shek regime. The latter had an enormous army which was being armed by the Americans at a feverish pace. The USA also gave this anti-popular regime other aid: huge financial and material, political and diplomatic support, backed up by direct armed intervention in China's domestic affairs.

Like the whole of China, Manchuria was also divided into two camps. West of Changchun and north of Kirin, as well as on the Liaotung Peninsula, where Soviet troops were stationed under the Treaty of August 14, 1945, the power was virtually in the hands of the people led by China's Communist Party.

In an area with a population of 150 million, people's democratic government bodies were set up by a free election and preparations began for sweeping socio-economic reforms. The rest of Manchuria was under Kuomintang control.

China's revolution entered a stage of building up power in conditions of peace. On the initiative of the Communist Party of China, a joint conference of Communist and Kuomintang representatives held in Chungking between August 29 and October 10 decided to call a political consultative conference of all China's political parties and groups. It was to discuss the problems involved in setting up a democratic state and prepare for convening a National Assembly that would form a coalition government.

Later development, however, showed that the Chiang Kai-shek authorities pursued other objectives. Acting in the guise of advocates of a coalition government and with support from US imperialism, they steered toward the establishment of their dictatorship in China and started repressive actions against the revolutionary and democratic forces. Meanwhile, the United States sought to take advantage of the confused situation in China to turn it into an American semi-colony.

The USA invaded the Kuomintang-held areas with its advisers and emissaries, disembarked in Chinese ports its troops which joined in the hostilities against China's revolutionary forces. American aircraft were used to airlift Kuomintang troops into areas under CPC control.

The Soviet Union undertook vigorous diplomatic action to curb the aggression in China Washington was perpetrating under the veil of assistance to the Kuomintang Government. At the Soviet Government's proposal, the Moscow Conference of Foreign Ministers of the USSR, the USA and Britain in December 1945 took a decision which confirmed the policy of non-interference in China's internal affairs, recognised the need for ending the civil war in China, of uniting and democratising all of her national government bodies.

This conference also reached complete agreement concerning the desirability of withdrawing Soviet and American troops from China at the earliest possible date compatible with the fulfilment of their obligations and with their responsibility.[1] In November 1945, the Soviet Command submitted to the Kuomintang authorities a plan of troop evacuation to be completed by December 3, 1945. In accordance with this plan, Soviet troops withdrew from Yingkow and Hulutao and from an area south of Shenyang. However, the Kuomintang Government itself declared that "it would be in a very difficult situation" in case of withdrawal of Soviet troops from Manchuria within the period indicated because it would not be able to organize its civil administration toward the scheduled date.[2] The Soviet Government agreed to postpone the withdrawal of its troops from the Northeast provinces.

The Soviet decision was welcomed by the local population. The people's democratic forces were consolidating in the Northeast provinces and the very presence of Soviet troops contributed to this process.

After a while, the Chiang Kai-shek Government again requested the Soviet Government to postpone troop withdrawal in an attempt to gain time for regrouping its own and American armed forces with a view to seizing the revolutionary

---

[1] *Foreign Policy of the Soviet Union. 1947,* Documents and Records, Moscow, 1952, Part I, p. 376 (in Russian).

[2] *Izvestia,* November 30, 1945.

stronghold in Manchuria. In the meantime, Kuomintang propaganda raised a provocative clamour about the Soviet
Union's alleged "seizure" of Northeast China.

Soviet troop withdrawal from Manchuria was started in
March 1946 and ended on May 3.[1] The Kuomintang authorities, however, proved unable to take advantage of it to reinforce their positions in Manchuria. Chinese revolutionary
troops and the people's democratic government bodies, which
had won high prestige with the population, took over the
administration of the areas left by Soviet units and established revolutionary law and order there.

After defeating the Kwantung Army, Soviet troops dismantled arms depots, munitions and some other factories
which had worked for it and were, therefore, military tro-
phies. The plans of the Kuomintang military to use them in
the war against the People's Liberation Army, against the
liberated areas were foiled.

Infuriated by the failure of its plans, the Kuomintang
clique raised hue and cry about the alleged "seizure of industrial equipment by the Soviet Union". This slander was
readily taken up by the imperialist mass media. The intrigues
of anti-Soviet forces, however, proved of no avail. The Chinese freedom fighters realised that the measures taken by
the Soviet Army had prevented the Kuomintang regime from
using Japanese war industry in Northeast China against
Chinese people's national interests. After the formation of
the People's Republic of China, the Chinese Communists explained that if equipment had not been dismantled, it would
have been seized by the Chiang Kai-shek army and used for
manufacturing arms and ammunition to prolong its mortal
agony, and that the Chinese people would have shed more
blood in the war of liberation. The Chinese people were clearly aware of the fact that the dismantling of equipment by
the Soviet Army was useful for the Chinese revolution. It
was tantamount to aid for which the Chinese people ought
to be extremely grateful.

After the Soviet forces had pulled out of the Kuomintang-
controlled areas in Southern Manchuria, the Chiang Kai-shek

---

[1] *Foreign Policy of the Soviet Union. 1946*, Documents and Records,
Moscow, 1952, p. 112 (in Russian).

authorities undertook repressive actions against local democratic organisations as well as against Soviet offices—the
consulate and Soviet personnel of the Chinese-Changchun
railway.

On March 20, 1946, the Kuomintang authorities forcibly
debarred the Soviet management and railwaymen from work
on the railway. They seized its warehouses and all its property and started transporting plundered materials to Peking.
In Mukden, Sungkiang, Szeping, Liaoyang, and elsewhere,
houses of Soviet railwaymen were fenced with barbed wire.
Soviet citizens were forbidden to leave their enclosures without a permit from Kuomintang security police. The latter
attempted to force them to wear arm bands and chest tags.
Kuomintang troops broke into their homes, searched and
plundered them, insulted and manhandled their occupants.
Many Soviet railwaymen were evicted and forbidden to take
along even their personal belongings. On March 21, four Soviet employees of a foreign trade organisation were shot dead
by Chiang fascist thugs in Mukden. At the Liaoyang railway
station, Kuomintang troops attacked and tied up six Soviet
citizens, including the station master Gorbachev, the section
foreman Agapov and his wife, engineer Tselikovskaya. They
were marched along the streets, jeered and beaten up. The
protests of Soviet officials of the railway administration to
Kuomintang authorities were left unanswered. What is more,
General Tung Yang-ching, commander of Chiang's Northeast headquarters, stated in the press that he could not guarantee the security of Soviet citizens. This was a direct instigation to new repressions against them. As a result, in Changchun alone, after it had been occupied by Kuomintang troops
on April 20-21, 10 Soviet citizens were shot dead, 5 of them
after brutal tortures, 11 Soviet citizens were reported missing.
The homes of Soviet citizens and property of Soviet business
organisations and the Chinese-Changchun Railway were
plundered.

During the period of Kuomintang rule, a total of 60 Soviet
citizens employed by the Chinese-Changchun Railway were
killed or tortured to death, more than 200 Soviet families
were robbed. Kuomintang authorities perpetrated a number
of terrorist acts against official representatives of the Soviet
Government.

Kuomintang thugs killed and looted with the connivance or under the direction of their American patrons. During the reign of terror against Soviet citizens in Mukden, Liaoyang, Tiehling, Sungchiatung, Szeping and later in Changchun, American officers drove about in jeeps and took pictures of "excesses".

In that situation, normal operation of the Chinese-Changchun Railway as a joint enterprise was out of the question. The Soviet Government had to instruct Soviet citizens employed on the railway to leave for the Soviet Union.

The railway ceased for a time to operate as a joint enterprise. Only a handful of Soviet railway officials headed by the railway General Manager A. F. Zhuravlev remained in China to maintain contacts with the people's democratic authorities in Harbin.

Aided by the US imperialists, the Kuomintang regime sought in every possible way to antagonise China to the Soviet Union. In response to the "cold war" doctrine put forward by Washington, Chiang Kai-shek feverishly handed over to the US imperialists parts of Chinese territory, Chinese ports for setting up a network of US naval and air bases spearheaded against the Soviet Union. On November 6, 1946, the Chiang government concluded with the USA the so-called treaty of friendship, trade and navigation and a number of other agreements which reinforced the alliance of the Kuomintang regime with the US imperialist circles.

Simultaneously, the Kuomintang authorities attempted to blockade the area of Dairen and Port Arthur where Soviet troops were stationed under a treaty. The Chiang Kai-shek authorities were particularly enraged by the Soviet Government's determined opposition to their attempts to transport via the port of Dairen troops from South China to Manchuria for fighting the revolutionary forces. It was stated to the Kuomintang Government that under the Sino-Soviet agreement of August 14, 1945, Dairen was a merchant port to be used for the shipment of goods, not troops. The debarkation of any troops in this port would be a violation of this agreement.

As the collapse of the Kuomintang regime drew nearer, anti-Sovietism in the areas under Chiang Kai-shek's control became increasingly unbridled. In an effort to undermine

traditional Sino-Soviet friendship, the Chinese reactionaries
went ahead with a wanton campaign of slander of the Soviet
Union. Kuomintang propaganda circulated fabrications to
the effect that Soviet railwaymen and other specialists helping to rehabilitate transport and industry in the area under
people's democratic control were disguised Soviet servicemen. Although all Soviet troops had pulled out of Northeast China, the Kuomintang authorities alleged that 50,000
Soviet troops in plain clothes remained in Harbin and that
Soviet forces were still stationed at Kiamusze, Mutankiang,
Yenkishih and the Manchuria station.

The Kuomintang press sought to persuade the Chinese people that the chief enemy of China was not US imperialism
but the Soviet Union which was allegedly pursuing an imperialist policy, etc. The Kuomintang Government described
the Soviet demand for the withdrawal of US troops from
China as interference in her internal affairs.

The Soviet diplomatic offices in China worked in intolerable conditions. Kuomintang authorities staged anti-Soviet
demonstrations in front of the Soviet Embassy in Peking,
where local residents were herded and ordered to call out
anti-Soviet slogans, threaten Soviet diplomats with violence,
attack their cars, etc.

Driven to frenzy by their hatred of the Soviet Union, the
Kuomintang authorities went to the length of open appeals
for a "crusade" against it. They were stirring up war hysteria
by clamouring about the "red aggression against China". One
of the Kuomintang leaders, Chen Li-fu stated, for example,
that in China the "vanguard battles of a third world war
were being fought."[1] The Kuomintang diplomat Li Kang-fu
was even more outspoken. He said that the Kuomintang leaders will exchange space for time and "settle accounts in a
third world war".[2]

At the same time, the Kuomintang regime was stepping up
hostilities against China's revolutionary forces. In March
1947, Kuomintang troops launched a broad offensive against
the CPC-controlled area of Shansi-Kansu-Ningsia with the
centre in Yenan and treacherously opened large-scale opera-

---

[1] *New Times*, Moscow, 1948, No. 47, p. 19.
[2] Ibid., No. 49, p. 16.

tions in Manchuria and other areas of China. The areas controlled by the Communist Party of China and the People's
Liberation Army, above all, the Liaotung Peninsula, Heilungkiang, Kirin and Sinkiang provinces were subjected to an
economic blockade.

In that difficult period, the revolutionary bases in Manchuria became the main strongholds of the Chinese revolution, where its army had gathered up strength before it
undertook in 1948-1949 a liberation march southwards, which
culminated in a complete collapse of the Kuomintang regime.

4. SOVIET ASSISTANCE IN CONSOLIDATING
THE REVOLUTIONARY STRONGHOLD IN MANCHURIA

Despite the tremendous difficulties of its postwar rehabilitation, the Soviet Union made effective efforts to strengthen
the area under people's democratic control in Manchuria
established after the defeat of the Kwantung Army.

The area in Manchuria controlled by the Communists and
the People's Liberation Army was administered by people's
democratic government bodies set up in a free election. Harbin was the seat of the people's democratic Administrative
Committee, the supreme executive body of China's Northeast provinces, as this area was called at the time.

It was also the seat of the Northeast Bureau of the CPC
Central Committee, which directed party activities in Manchuria. It had a large measure of autonomy because the headquarters of the CPC Central Committee were in Yenan. This
autonomy became much greater when Yenan was captured
by Kuomintang troops in March 1947, and the leaders of
the CPC Central Committee who went into hiding were unable to direct the revolutionary struggle effectively on a nationwide scale. The Northeast Bureau of the CPC Central
Committee had among its members Kao Kang, Chen Yun,
Chang Wen-tien, Lin Piao, Li Fu-chun, Peng Chen.

From the early days of their existence, the areas under
people's democratic control were given all-round assistance
by the Soviet Union. This contributed greatly to the consolidation of the United Democratic Army (UDA), as the Communist armed forces in Manchuria were called at the time.

The UDA was equipped with first-class weapons captured by Soviet forces from the Kwantung Army.

Direct contacts between Soviet and Chinese Communist Party leaders were set up in 1945-1949 for promoting co-operation with the people's democratic authorities in Manchuria. For example, a delegation from the people's democratic areas of Manchuria led by Kao Kang and Liu Shao-chi visited the Soviet Union in 1945 and met with Soviet leaders.

From 1945 until the proclamation of the People's Republic of China, a group of Soviet representatives stayed in Manchuria to maintain routine contacts with the CPC, the North-east Bureau of its Central Committee in particular.

Already in that period, the Soviet Union gave wide assistance in training Chinese personnel, shared its experience in state administration and economic development with the people's democratic government bodies.

The presence of Soviet troops in Manchuria was a factor of major importance for its economic development. Soviet specialists helped to rebuild and commission a number of large plants and factories, above all, in the areas crossed by the Chinese-Changchun Railway and in the Port Arthur-Dairen treaty area. Soviet army units in Manchuria gave local authorities every assistance in repairing and building highways, in improving public amenities in populated localities. They helped organise occupational training of workers, advanced training of specialists in various fields. The Port Arthur naval base was radically reconstructed. With its modern coastal artillery, aircraft, and warships, this base became an impregnable fortress on the Yellow Sea, a training centre for Chinese military personnel.

The areas under people's democratic control on the Liaotung Peninsula were quite important for promoting Sino-Soviet co-operation. Liaotung became another bridgehead for the successful offensive launched by the people's democratic forces of China.[1]

The areas under people's democratic control in Manchuria, which were cut off from China's central provinces, ex-

---

[1] *The Leninist Policy of the USSR Towards China*, Moscow, pp. 130-133 (in Russian).

perienced an acute shortage of fuel, motor vehicles, coal, medicines, salt, cotton fabrics, footwear, clothes, sugar and many other goods. The first priority needs of the population and fighting units of the People's Liberation Army were also met with Soviet aid.

On December 21, 1946, the first trade negotiations were completed in Voroshilovsk between Soviet foreign trade organisations and the people's democratic Administrative Committee of China's Northeast provinces. The parties signed a contract under which deliveries were started of Soviet goods for the population and the army, as well as equipment for civilian and military hospitals, schools, etc. In addition, captured equipment and provisions requisitioned by the Soviet Army from the Japanese interventionists were handed over to the people's democratic organisations of the Northeast provinces.

When southern Manchuria had been invaded by Kuomintang troops, the food situation on the Liaotung Peninsula sharply deteriorated. Soviet agencies immediately supplied grain, vegetable oil, sugar, tinned foods from Vladivostok directly to Dairen by sea and by transit via North Korean ports. Food supplied to the port of Dairen was distributed to the population of the Liaotung Peninsula at fixed prices by the local Chinese people's democratic administration aided by civilian personnel of the Soviet Army. The Soviet Union met all the costs of food transportation, storage and distribution as part of free assistance to the Chinese population.

In the summer of 1949, a trade delegation of the people's democratic authorities of China's Northeast provinces led by Kao Kang, member of the Political Bureau of the CPC Central Committee, arrived in Moscow. Successful negotiations resulted in signing an agreement for mutual goods deliveries during one year.

Under the agreement, the Soviet Union undertook to export to the liberated areas of Northeast China industrial equipment, motor vehicles, petroleum products, fabrics, paper, medicines and other goods. The people's democratic administration of the Northeast provinces undertook to supply to the Soviet Union soybeans, vegetable oils, maize, rice and other goods. Trade undoubtedly played a crucial role in consolidating people's democratic government in the Northeast provinces, which became the most important base for preparing a general offensive of the People's Liberation Army against the Kuomintang regime.

The development of trade and economic relations demanded a further improvement in transportation facilities, in particular, on the rivers Amur and Sungari.

In April 1947, piers were prepared at Kiamusze, Fuchin, Sasing, and additional moorages were built in the Harbin river port with assistance from the Harbin branch of the Soviet organisation Dalvneshtrans. The Soviet Amur Shipping Line set aside tugs and barges to be used for regular cargo carriage starting in May 1947 between Chinese ports on the Sungari and the Soviet ports of Khabarovsk, Blagoveshchensk, and Komsomolsk-on-Amur.

Traffic on the Sungari was of exceptional importance for Northeast China's areas under people's democratic control, since Kiamusze was a major rear base of the People's Liberation Army, where military schools, central hospitals and logistical supply depots were located. In the navigation periods of 1947 and 1948, i.e., in the years of determined fight of the people's democratic forces against Kuomintang troops, Soviet foreign trade and transport organisations secured regular supplies of all requisite materials, fuel, medicines, clothes, footwear, etc., to the rear areas on the river Sungari in co-operation with Chinese authorities headed by Chang Wen-tien (known under the name of Lo Fu at the time), member of the Northeast Bureau of the CPC Central Committee, who was in charge of Party, civilian and logistic affairs at this base.

The Soviet Union gave great assistance to the revolutionary stronghold in Manchuria in the restoration and development of railway lines and the economy, which was of crucial importance for developing the general offensive of the people's army against the Chiang regime.

As a result of the hostilities in Manchuria, about 6,000 km of railway lines were destroyed or damaged. By the end of 1945, the length of the railway network was only 10,000 km. The trunk line of this region was the Chinese-Changchun Railway (formerly called the Chinese Eastern Railway) built by Russia in 1897-1903.

Japanese troops retreating in panic under powerful strikes of the Soviet Army caused great destruction all along the length of the 1,500-km western and eastern lines of the Chinese-Changchun Railway. They disrupted communications and signalisation facilities, demolished the communications buildings in Mutankiang, Angangchi, Hailar and at the Manchuria station, destroyed local cable networks, blew up railway bridges and waterworks. At many large stations, the Japanese destroyed roundhouses (at the Hailar, Pokotu, Hangtoohechi, Mutankiang stations, etc.). They dismantled and removed station tracks, demolished service buildings at 57 stations and double-tracks points. At the Mutankiang station, they blew up one of Manchuria's biggest locomotive repair works.

By the time of signing, on September 2, 1945, of the act of Japan's unconditional surrender, regular train traffic had been re-opened by the efforts of Soviet railwaymen and servicemen of the Soviet Army on the eastern and western lines of the Chinese-Changchun Railway. To put into good working order the war-ravaged stations and tracks and increase the traffic capacity of railway lines, train speeds and traffic safety Soviet railwaymen handled a tremendous volume of work within an extremely brief period of time.

On the initiative of Soviet railwaymen, courses were opened at the Chinese-Changchun Railway for training railwaymen mass professions from among the Chinese population. The central courses were attended by 536 trainees, the line branches, by over 900. At the structural engineering, transport economy and electrical engineering departments of the Polytechnical Institute of the Chinese-Changchun Railway, opened in the early days of operation of the railway, 400 students were trained by Soviet specialists. This was of great political and practical importance, since until now Chinese had been employed on railways only as general labourers, while all technical jobs were held by Japanese.

While the training of local Chinese personnel was in progress, all the burden of restoration work and operation of the Railway was shouldered by Soviet railwaymen.

Soviet factories and plants of Siberia and the Far East accepted for repairs worn-out and damaged locomotives and wagons belonging to the Chinese-Changchun Railway. Soviet organisations sent to the zone controlled by the people's democratic administration various materials (railway tracks, beams, metal, tools, etc.). Soviet specialists helped staff all railway services with skilled personnel. With the Soviet people's fraternal assistance by the spring of 1947 many trunk railway lines have been restored in Northeast China, a regular railway service was opened to the Soviet Union via Zabaikalsk and Grodekovo.

Chinese railways experienced great difficulties during the civil war. The retreating Kuomintang troops caused great damage to railway transport to check the advance of the People's Liberation Army.

In June 1948, at the request of the people's democratic administration of the liberated areas the Soviet Government sent another group of Soviet railwaymen to China. It consisted of 50 repair engineers, 52 instructors, 220 technicians and skilled workers. They brought along all requisite equipment, including repair trains, diving outfits, hoisting cranes and other mechanisms.[1] The Soviet Union supplied all materials necessary for restoring railways: metal structures, railway tracks, piles, beams, etc. Restoration work was carried out under the direction of the Soviet engineer F. I. Doronin. Coordination of this work throughout Manchuria was entrusted to I. V. Kovalev.

By the time Soviet specialists arrived, projects were available for the restoration of the two biggest bridges on the Harbin-Changchun and Kirin-Changchun lines, they had been drawn up in Harbin by Japanese engineers. According to their estimates, this work would have taken eighteen months.

A group of Soviet specialists and workers, however, restored the Sungari-II bridge within a record period of two months. This bridge on the Harbin-Changchun line was of crucial importance for the operations planned by the People's Liberation Army. Its restoration enabled the Command of the People's Liberation Army to concentrate troops for an offensive against Manchuria's biggest city of Mukden, which was liberated on November 2, and later to launch an offen-

---

[1] *The Leninist Policy of the USSR Towards China*, p. 135.

sive on the Peking front as well. At the proposal of Soviet
specialists, approved by the Northeast Bureau of the CPC
Central Committee, important organisational measures were
taken to restore railway transport. They included the setting up of the Central Restoration Department at the Main
Railway Administration of Manchuria and other bodies, the
formation of railway troops of four brigades with a total
strength of 30,000 officers and men, the organisation of a
procurement and supply service and a number of specialised
bases, the procurement of sleepers and other basic structural
materials, the establishment in Harbin of a base for the
repair and making of bridge structures and equipment, the
establishment of a military railway park, the training of
railway troops and specialists of the Central Restoration
Department in basic methods of restoration work.

At the request of the Northeast Bureau of the CPC Central Committee, Soviet specialists organised consultations on
questions of compiling the economic and financial plan of
restoring and developing Manchuria's economy.

During these consultations special discussions were held
on the introduction of clearing accounts between state and
co-operative organisations, the levying of a turnover tax on
commercial and industrial enterprises (taxes were not levied
in 1947 and 1948), on the introduction of state monopoly
of sale of strong liquors (distilleries were owned by private
capital, while state distilleries were closed down), on compulsory insurance of real estate and other matters.

Technical surveys of motorways and earth roads of Manchuria were carried out, and a two-year plan of repair of
the key transport routes was drawn up.

The proposals of Soviet specialists were discussed and approved by the Northeast Bureau of the CPC Central Committee.

As a result of the great work performed under the guidance of Soviet railwaymen, toward December 15, 1948, over
15,000 km of main railway lines in Manchuria, 120 large and
medium-sized bridges with a total length of over 9,000 m,
including the biggest bridges Sungari-II, 987 m in length,
and the 320-metre-long bridge on the river Yinma Ho on the
Harbin-Changchun line, the 440-metre-long bridge across
the Sungari on the Kirin-Changchun line, as well as 12 other

large and medium-sized bridges on other lines had been restored.

The restoration of railways was carried out in difficult wartime conditions. Kuomintang aircraft systematically bombed and strafed the areas of restoration work, particularly on the Kirin-Changchun, Tungliao-Sinlitun-Ihsien lines. In these air raids the Sinlitun, Chenchiatun, and Tung-liao stations were destroyed, about 150 locomotives and much of the rolling stock were damaged. There were casualties among Chinese railwaymen and Soviet specialists.

The restoration of the main railway lines in Central and Southern Manchuria made it possible to re-deploy and concentrate People's Liberation Army Units on a wider scale, which helped toward the final defeat of the Kuomintang troops in Manchuria and the complete liberation of Northeast China and secured favourable conditions for a successful advance southwards.

On November 25, 1948, direct railway connections between the Soviet border stations of Otpor[1] and Grodekovo and the cities of Dairen and Port Arthur, which had been interrupted in 1945, were re-opened.

Soviet specialists helped to train railway troops of the People's Liberation Army. In the summer of 1948 alone, more than 4,600 servicemen were trained in various specialities.

A special medical service was organised in Chinese railway troops. In September and October 1948, Soviet medics read lectures to Chinese military surgeons and therapeutists at advanced training courses in Harbin.

As a result of the Soviet Union's disinterested assistance in the construction and restoration of railways and bridges in Manchuria, the conversion of the Chinese-Changchun Railway into a veritable school of experience and know-how the Northeast revolutionary base became a powerful springboard for the great offensive of the revolutionary forces against the Chiang regime in 1948-1949. The CPC leaders expressed their high appreciation of Soviet people's help to the Chinese revolution as a striking manifestation of the

---

[1] Now known as Zabaikalsk.

Soviet Union's proletarian solidarity and sincere friendship with the Chinese people. The Vice-Chairman of the People's Republic of China, Sung Ching-ling, stated as follows: "Among the very first arrivals in China from the Soviet Union were railway technicians. They worked at the complicated questions and rendered support that put the restoration of our rail system months ahead of schedule. They came without benefit or fanfare. They did their job and not one single thing was asked in return."[1]

The Chinese people were also given various aid by Soviet medics.

At the end of 1947, a plague epidemic broke out in the liberated areas of Southern Manchuria and North China. At the request of the people's revolutionary authorities, the Soviet Government flew in epidemic-fighting teams led by Professor O. V. Baroyan assisted by Professor N. I. Nikolayev. These teams fitted out with laboratory equipment, preventive and therapeutic remedies took vigorous measures to check the epidemic, and it was wiped out by mid-1948. As was admitted by leading executives of the people's democratic administration, Soviet doctors saved tens of thousands of residents of Northeast China from imminent death.

In the spring of 1949, another epidemic of plague broke out and spread on a fairly wide scale in the region of Kalgan and other localities of Chahar Province in the liberated areas of Inner Mongolia. At the request of the people's democratic authorities, the Soviet Government flew in by special planes an epidemiological expedition of medics, zoologists and other specialists.

The measures taken to fight the epidemic made it possible to bring it under control in Chahar Province by December 1, 1949 and prevent its spread to other provinces of China. Soviet medical workers handed over to democratic authorities large quantities of special equipment, medicines, and, what was most important, trained Chinese personnel who later took an active part in the liberation struggle waged by the people's army.

---

[1] Sung Ching-ling, "The Difference Between Soviet and American Foreign Policies". In: *People's China*, Peking, 1950, Vol. 1, No. 2, January 16, p. 7.

Four million doses of plague vaccine, 100 litres of plague serum, medicines for the treatment of plague, laboratories for bacteriological analysis, motor vehicles and other materials and equipment of the expedition were handed over to China free of charge. This is what Mme Sung Ching-ling wrote about the disinterested aid given by Soviet medics in fighting the plague epidemic: "We did not have enough doctors and technicians to stem this dangerous disease, so we called on our great neighbour. The medical teams we required were soon on the scene. They came, they gave their help and when they were finished, they went home. There were not even thoughts of repayment or concessions to be sought. They did not ask the right to do anything except to serve the Chinese people."[1]

In October 1949, another epidemic of plague flared up northwest of Peking. A quarantine was introduced in the city. Its supply was disturbed, which caused economic difficulties. At the request of Mao Tse-tung, a few plague-fighting teams with equipment (motor vehicles, disinfection apparatus), medical personnel and medicines were flown in from the Soviet Union within 24 hours. Millions of people were inoculated against plague. The epidemic was quickly stamped out.

The results of the operations carried out by the Soviet plague-fighting teams are illustrated by the following data. In 1947, by the time Soviet medics arrived, 30,326 persons were afflicted with plague in the Northeast provinces; in 1948, their number reduced to 5,947, and in 1949, only 250 fatal cases were reported. In addition, Soviet plague-fighting teams trained a large body of Chinese medical workers in implementing preventive measures against plague epidemics, handed over to the people's government of Northeast China over 260 items of medical equipment and a large quantity of valuable medicines.

Troops of China's People's Liberation Army advancing into the southern provinces, particularly the army under the command of Lin Piao, suffered from malaria. At the request of Lin Piao, about one ton of quinine was delivered by air from the Soviet Union within a matter of two days.

---

[1] Ibid.

This helped his army to maintain its combat efficiency and carry out successful operations against Kuomintang troops.

The Chinese population, servicemen of the revolutionary army regarded with profound gratitude the selfless actions of Soviet people, the more so, as scenes of the recent grim past, atrocities of Japanese and Kuomintang thugs, were still fresh in their memory.

It will be recalled that before the formation of the People's Republic of China, plague epidemics had occurred in Manchuria periodically. The Japanese occupationists fought plague by inhuman methods. A village or town suspected of having been hit by plague was encircled by troops, the houses were sprayed with petrol from fire hoses and set on fire. The residents trying to escape were mowed down by Japanese machine-gunners. Soviet specialists inscribed a vivid page in the history of fraternal assistance to the people's democratic areas in Manchuria.

In August 1949, the CPC Central Committee requested the Soviet Union to send to China large groups of specialists to give aid in matters of organisation and technology for the rehabilitation and development of liberated areas. The Soviet Union promptly commissioned the required numbers of experts to work under people's democratic authorities.

The first group of about 250 specialists sent to China was staffed in accordance with the requests and by agreement with the CPC leadership. Some of them were to outline the structure of government, the functions and status of future ministries and government departments, and take part in practical work to organise and aid management of the national economy. Others were sent directly to the biggest factories and plants to organise restoration work, the management and operation of functioning industries.

Soviet engineers and technicians had a major role to play in rebuilding the shipyards in Dairen. The first batches of Soviet equipment arrived there in 1947. Before the end of the year, the shipyards had in operation about 1,000 units of equipment, including 350 metalworking lathes, 50 items of forging and pressing equipment, 30 units of foundry equipment, 11 casting furnaces, 2 dry docks, tool-making, woodworking and other departments. By the end of 1947, the shipyards already employed 254 engineers and technicians, 261 office workers and over 2,000 operatives.

Reconstruction of the shipyards was carried out on a particularly large scale in 1948-1949 as a result of which it surpassed by far its prewar output towards the end of 1949.

All proposals of Soviet specialists concerning the establishment and structure of management bodies were submitted to the CPC Central Committee and newly-formed government bodies. Many ministries and government departments were headed by former army and guerilla leaders with no specialised education or experience. Guided by their internationalist feelings, Soviet advisers and specialists disinterestedly shared their rich experience with new Chinese personnel and gave them daily training.

In addition to the training of Chinese personnel, Soviet advisers and specialists were directly involved in the planning and management of the national economy as well as in the management of large enterprises.

The aid of Soviet specialists assumed a particularly wide scale after the proclamation of the People's Republic of China.

In reviewing Sino-Soviet relations before the victory of the revolution and in the period of their successful development one cannot but note that even in their best years they experienced definite difficulties, because a part of the CPC cadres, mostly those from petty bourgeois families, were infected with nationalistic and anti-Soviet sentiments.

A part of the CPC leadership headed by Mao Tse-tung overestimated their own possibilities and underestimated those of the enemy. Petty bourgeois views on the Chinese revolution, proneness to rush from one extreme to another were characteristic of Mao Tse-tung already in that period. The Soviet Communist Party, the international communist movement advised the CPC to build up forces, to prepare by diplomatic and political actions the conditions necessary to equip and effectively train the People's Liberation Army for the forthcoming offensive. Mao Tse-tung, however, was obsessed by "revolutionary impatience". This is evidenced by the story he has been circulating for years that it was Stalin who kept back the Chinese revolution and was against the civil war and in favour of collaboration with Chiang Kai-shek, insisting that otherwise the Chinese nation would perish. According to Mao Tse-tung, the Chinese did not follow Stalin's advice, and carried the revolution to victory. This deliberate lie slandering the policy of the CPSU was enthusiastically taken up by anti-Communists. Actually, however, the question in point was the need for diplomatic and political flexibility to preserve the Chinese revolutionary forces, to train them for a future offensive in order to secure a quick victory.

The leading group in the CPC was unable or unwilling to understand that a united front policy not only during the war against Japan but also in 1945-1946, when Chiang Kai-shek and his army were still strong and had powerful support from US imperialism, while the Communist Party forces were scattered, gave an advantage primarily to the Chinese revolution. Combination of political and diplomatic methods of struggle along with the building up of military strength for a decisive onslaught on the enemy were the only correct way at that stage of the Chinese revolution.

Later, on the eve of the victory in 1949, Mao Tse-tung, on the contrary, expressed his doubts about the strength of the Chinese revolutionary forces allied with the Soviet Union, the world's first socialist state. Even during the last stage of the war, when the revolutionary army was rapidly advancing southwards, Mao Tse-tung said that it would take at least two years for the revolution to win, and showed helplessness in working out practical problems in anticipation of people's power being established throughout China.

Mao Tse-tung's views on China's foreign policy in that period were highly indicative. He is known to have said that it would be better for China to have no diplomatic relations either with the Soviet Union or the United States of America. At the same time, claims to control by China of the national liberation movement in all of Asia, above all, Southeast Asia, were already in evidence.

Mao Tse-tung displayed defeatist moods caused by his fear of Kuomintang troops which captured Yenan in 1947 and forced him to escape to China's northern provinces. It is known that after the surrender of Yenan, Mao Tse-tung, roaming from place to place in North China, was far from the centre of the revolutionary struggle which had shifted to Manchuria. On the eve of the decisive battle Yenan lost its importance as the headquarters of the Communist Party of China and its armed forces. Manchuria became the main stronghold of the Chinese revolution.

In other matters, too, Mao Tse-tung's political waverings revealed his petty bourgeois world outlook, his proneness to change from one extreme to another: from efforts to spur on the revolution in 1945-1946 to lack of confidence in 1948-1949 in an early victory of the Chinese revolution.

Hostile feelings towards the Soviet Union were also displayed by a certain group of leaders of the CPC Northeast Bureau. Their nationalistic and anti-Soviet sentiments became so manifest that in 1946-1947 the Bureau had to undertake several inquiries in which serious charges were laid against a group of leading functionaries. The CPC leaders, however, denounced them reluctantly in those days, keeping them in key jobs and conniving at their anti-Soviet fabrications.

Furthermore alarming facts were reported of Manchuria's Party organs obstructing the work of the Sino-Soviet friendship society. In Northeast China the newspaper *Wenhuapao* (Culture) for a long time disseminated anti-Soviet fabrications of its editor Hsiao Chün who called for the expulsion from China of imperialists of all hues, listing the Soviet Union among them. The newspaper was subsidised by the Communists, and it was not before the end of 1948 that the Northeast Bureau of the CPC Central Committee took a decision to close it down.

* * *

It was the steadfast policy of the Soviet Union, the CPSU, supported by other Marxist-Leninist parties, the Chinese internationalists, that made it possible to prevent broad intervention by the US imperialists in China, to strengthen the revolutionary forces, to set up a military strategic bridgehead in Manchuria, to isolate the Chiang Kai-shek regime inside the country, to secure moral and political support for the Chinese revolution from progressive world opinion and thereby to bring about the great victory of the fraternal Chinese people in 1949.

Thus, historical facts evidence that the alliance of China's revolutionary forces with the Soviet Union and, through the latter, with the world revolutionary movement was a key factor of victory for the Chinese revolution. This fraternal alliance of China's working people with world socialism compensated for the relative weakness of China's working class, helped consolidate the internal forces of the revolution, barred the way to foreign intervention, created a favourable international situation for the Chinese revolutionaries to fulfil their historic mission.

CHAPTER II

SINO-SOVIET RELATIONS
IN THE EARLY YEARS OF THE PRC.
1949-1952.

The liberation struggle the Chinese people had been waging for years culminated in an epoch-making victory. On October 1, 1949, China was proclaimed a People's Republic. The Chinese revolution dealt a shattering blow to the positions of imperialism in Asia, contributed to the change in the balance of power on the world scene in favour of socialism, gave a new impetus to the national liberation movement in the colonial regions of the capitalist world.

The victory of the Chinese revolution was made possible by the extremely favourable international situation: the routing of Nazi Germany and militarist Japan was followed by the emergence of the world socialist system—the creation of the world proletariat. The Chinese revolution enjoyed growing support from the fraternal states, the world communist movement, and, above all, from the Soviet Union.

The formation of the People's Republic of China opened a new chapter in the history of Sino-Soviet relations. Broad opportunities for developing co-operation opened up before the peoples of the two countries historically united by the bonds of friendship and brotherhood.

1. THE SIGNIFICANCE OF THE FIRST ACTS IN RELATIONS BETWEEN THE SOVIET UNION AND THE PRC

From the early days of the existence of the People's Republic of China, the CPSU Central Committee and the Soviet Government did everything they could to promote Sino-Soviet friendship and co-operation.

The Soviet Union was the first state to grant recognition to and establish diplomatic relations with the PRC immediately after its proclamation—on October 2, 1949. The note of the PRC Ministry of Foreign Affairs on the occasion of establishing diplomatic relations between the Soviet Union and the PRC said in particular: "The Chinese Government and people feel infinite joy because today the Soviet Union has become the first friendly power to recognise the People's Republic of China."[1]

The Soviet Union attached great importance not only to its internationalist material aid to the Chinese people but also to putting Sino-Soviet relations on a firm basis of international law. The Treaty of Friendship, Alliance and Mutual Assistance between the Soviet Union and the PRC signed on February 14, 1950 was of crucial importance for consolidating the latter's position on the international scene, for promoting Sino-Soviet friendship. The Treaty embodied the supreme principles of full equality, respect for territorial integrity, national independence and sovereignty, non-interference in each other's internal affairs, and was a model for a new type of inter-state relations between fraternal socialist nations. In a message of greetings to Soviet leaders on the occasion of the Treaty's first anniversary, Mao Tse-tung said: "The Treaty of Friendship, Alliance and Mutual Assistance between China and the Soviet Union is a great help to building a new China and a firm guarantee of the struggle against aggression and for the maintenance of peace and security in the Far East and the rest of the world."[2]

In view of the cardinal changes in the Far East situation after the formation of the PRC, the Soviet Government agreed to the request of the Chinese side to establish a firm legal status for the Chinese-Changchun Railway, Port Arthur and Dairen.

In the Sino-Soviet agreement of February 14, 1950, the Soviet Government pledged to hand over to the PRC Government free of charge before the end of 1952 all its rights to the joint operation of the Chinese-Changchun Railway and all its property.

---

[1] *Jenmin jihpao,* October 2, 1949.
[2] *Jenmin jihpao,* February 14, 1951.

Within the same period, as it had been stipulated in relation to the railway, the Governments agreed on Soviet troop withdrawal from the jointly operated naval base of Port Arthur and on the handover of all its facilities to the Chinese Government.

The Soviet Government also agreed to hand over to the PRC Government during 1950 all property in temporary use or held on lease by the Soviet Union on conditions subject to finalising within three months of the agreement coming into effect.

The agreement on a Soviet credit of 300 million US dollars, or 1,200 million rubles to the PRC Government was of equal importance for strengthening friendly ties between the Soviet Union and PRC.[1] Soviet deliveries to the PRC were intended for rehabilitating and modernising the key branches of her national economy. Within five years between 1950 and 1954 the Soviet Union was to supply to China equipment and materials for power stations, metal-smelting and engineering plants, coal mines, railway and motor transport and other sectors of the Chinese economy to the total sum of the credit.

In view of the tremendous damage caused to China's national economy by the long-continued hostilities on her territory, the Soviet Government granted the credit on extremely easy terms—at only one per cent interest, which was without precedent in world practices.

The Soviet Union undertook to assist the PRC in the construction of 50 large industrial projects.

On March 27, 1950, agreements were signed on the institution of the following Sino-Soviet joint-stock companies:

(a) the Sovsinmetal (Chungsuchinshukungssu)[2] to prospect

---

[1] In the agreement, the sum of the credit was not specified in rubles. Conversion into rubles was carried out later after a new rate of exchange—4 rubles to a dollar—had been introduced on March 1, 1950.

[2] Before World War II, at the request of the Chinese authorities of Sinkiang Province, Soviet geologists explored this region for non-ferrous metal ores and oil deposits. On their basis joint Sino-Soviet enterprises were set up for mining and dressing a number of non-ferrous metal ores in Purchuma, for extracting and refining oil in the area of Tushangchi. These enterprises had been in operation until 1943. Later they were closed temporarily by Kuomintang authorities. These enterprises provided the basis for the Sino-Soviet joint-stock companies.

for, extract and process non-ferrous and rare metals in Sinkiang Province;

(b) the Sovsinoil (Chungsushihyukungssu) to prospect for and extract oil, gas and oil by-products, and process them in Sinkiang Province;

(c) the SKOGA company (Chungsuminhangkungssu) to operate air services.

Under these agreements signed for a term of 30 years, Sino-Soviet joint-stock companies were set up on a parity basis with provisions for the parties equally sharing in the capital of the companies and in the management of their affairs. Their activities were to be directed by representatives of both sides alternately.

In addition to handling production problems facing the companies in the early period of restoring the Chinese economy, they undertook to train Chinese technicians and managerial personnel. To cope with these tasks, the companies set up technical schools and courses or sent Chinese citizens to Soviet educational establishments. *Jenmin jihpao* wrote in this connection: "The use of advanced Soviet experience in economic development and first-rate technology has made it possible to resume and expand within a short space of time the operation of the enterprises taken over by these companies; these modern enterprises have contributed effectively to the rehabilitation and development of our economy. The imperialists very often use the export of capital to colonial and semi-colonial countries for economic expansion there. The investments the socialist Soviet Union made in these companies, however, were of a totally different character, pursued totally different goals. These goals were to help by financial means and technology to develop our natural wealth, which we ourselves were unable to develop, or to organise the operation of those existing enterprises it was difficult for us to operate on our own and thereby to help create the conditions for economic independence of our people. . . . The Soviet Government helped us to organise the operation of joint-stock companies, to train personnel, made Soviet know-how available to us and is now to hand over its share in these companies, i.e., the enterprises owned by them are to become China's government enterprises in full. Comparing these facts with the economic expansion of the imperialists in the old China, our people cannot but feel profound gratitude to the Soviet Union for its sincere and noble assistance to our country."[1]

On April 19, 1950 a trade agreement was signed in Moscow which laid down the general legal principles of trade relations between the Soviet Union and the PRC. Under this agreement, the Soviet Union undertook to export to China petrol, kerosene and lubricants, various machinery, tools and equipment, transport vehicles, fuel, cotton and other raw materials necessary for rebuilding and developing her economy.

In 1950, the Soviet Union and China signed a number of other agreements: on postal, telegraph and telephone services, on showing Soviet films in China, on river navigation rules.

Describing the significance of the Sino-Soviet agreements signed in that period, Mao Tse-tung stated at a meeting of the PRC Government: "The new Sino-Soviet agreements have given legal enforcement to the relations of friendship between the great peoples of China and the Soviet Union and provided us with a dependable ally. They have facilitated our work in domestic construction and our joint resistance to imperialist aggression in the name of preserving world peace".[2]

2. SOVIET ECONOMIC AID IN THE EARLY YEARS OF THE PRC

In the difficult years of establishing people's power, assistance and support from the Soviet Union were of crucial importance for the PRC. As a result of the long anti-Japanese and civil wars, as well as open plunder by the imperialist predators China's situation was extremely grave: her industry and agriculture, underdeveloped as they were, were ravaged, the people were famished and poor.

The economic situation of the young republic can be illustrated by these figures: in 1950, the PRC produced 36 million tons of coal, 877,000 tons of pig iron, 584,000 tons of steel. The industrial output was far below its maximum level

---

[1] *Jenmin jihpao*, October 13, 1954.
[2] *Jenmin jihpao*, April 13, 1950.

in 1942-1943. For example, the output of coal was only 61 per cent, pig iron, 46, steel, 63, etc.

Chinese agriculture was in a miserable state, too. The harvest of food crops in 1949 was less than three-fourths of the prewar level, while the cotton harvest fell almost by half.

The people's living standards were extremely low. Towards November 1, 1949 the price of one chin (400 g) of millet grew from its level on April 1, 1949 15.3 times in Peking, 14 times in Tientsin, while the rice price rose 13.8 and 11.5 times respectively. In November 1949 food prices again jumped 200-300 per cent, while manufactured goods prices rose 100-200 per cent since the end of October. The central people's government approved the budget for 1950 with a 18.9 per cent deficit to the total expenditures.

The situation was aggravated by the imperialist embargo imposed on trade with China in 1951. As far back as December 1949, the NATO member countries and Japan set up a Coordinating Committee (COCOM) for control and observation of the export of "strategic" commodities to the socialist countries, including the People's Republic of China. On the basis of the COCOM the Chinese Committee (CHINCOM) was set up later and included additionally representatives of Australia, Latin America and some other states. The committee regularly published lists of "strategic commodities" banned for export to the PRC and neighbouring countries. Therefore, China was unable to buy on the capitalist market materials, machines, equipment and other goods she needed, while trade through mediators involved additional spending of scarce foreign exchange.

Just as in the years of China's liberation struggle, the Soviet people, who had not yet repaired the vast ravages of the war against Nazi Germany, gave a helpful hand to China rendering her all-round assistance in economic rehabilitation and development.

As far back as 1950, under the Treaty of Friendship, Alliance and Mutual Assistance and several agreements, the Soviet Union delivered to China industrial plant and equipment, farm machines, motor vehicles, railway equipment, etc. A large group of Soviet specialists worked in China, sharing Soviet scientific achievements and technical know-how with Chinese personnel, helping restore and develop her economy.

Mme Sung Ching-ling stated in this connection: "The Soviet technicians and workers have brought to China a treasure of know-how in solving practical problems of all sizes. They have brought with them a great knowledge in the application of the highest science. They have brought with them a rich experience of working in behalf of the people. Many of them participated in the early days of reconstruction after the October Socialist Revolution. All of them have done valiant work in the building of Socialism and the preparation for Communism in the USSR. Therefore, the conditions we meet in China and the obstacles we have to face, they have met and overcome before. Their assignment and greatest joy is to help the Chinese people use this experience to build the new China."[1]

Trade with the Soviet Union was of crucial importance for the PRC. In 1948, the Soviet Union held ninth place in Chinese exports, third place in 1949, and moved to first place by the end of 1950. Since 1949, the Soviet Union's share in Chinese imports also grew—from 4.86 per cent in 1949 (fifth place) to 20.4 per cent over the first nine months of 1950 (second place).

In 1951, a number of new agreements were signed between the Soviet Union and the PRC, which evidenced the continued development of Sino-Soviet co-operation.

On March 14, a through railway service agreement was signed to provide for the conveyance of passengers, luggage and freight. On June 1, another agreement set the ruble exchange rate against the yuan. The rate of the ruble was set not against the US dollar but directly against the yuan on the basis of the ruble's gold equivalent and the official price of gold in Peking. Under an agreement signed in Peking on July 28, 1951, a Sino-Soviet ship-repair and building joint-stock company, Sovchinsudstroi, was set up in Dairen on a parity basis for a terms of 25 years. Simultaneously, the contracting parties exchanged notes whereby the Chinese Government assumed an obligation to accept within the first three years Soviet orders in volumes actually handled in the period 1949-1950.

---

[1] Sung Ching-ling, "New China Forges Ahead". In: *People's China*, Peking, 1951, Vol. 3, No. 9, May 1, p. 25.

These agreements helped to stabilise the economy and finances of People's China and strengthened her position on the international scene.

A striking feature of close Sino-Soviet co-operation was the steady growth of trade exchanges. Soviet assistance to China's economic development in 1951 helped strengthen its planning principles and improve planning standards. Aided by Soviet advisers, the PRC Government took decisions and approved documents of great importance for improving and stepping up planning work in the centre and in the provinces. In July 1951, a uniform annual state programme of economic rehabilitation and development was drawn up for the first time in China's history.

Co-operation with the Soviet Union, its all-round assistance and support contributed to the continued consolidation and growth of the socialist sector of China's economy in 1951. This is illustrated by the figures below showing the large share of the socialist sector in industry (in percentage):

Heavy industry	80
Oil	100
Pig iron	98
Coal	72.5
Electric power	76
Engineering	82
Light industry (for number of employees)	33
Cotton industry (for factory-made textiles)	70

Under the agreement of February 14, 1950, the Soviet Union supplied to China large consignments of complete plant and equipment. In 1951 and 1952, 30.9 million and 36.6 million rubles' worth of industrial equipment was supplied respectively.[1]

---

[1] Here and elsewhere data are given in new rubles.

In later years, complete plant and equipment became the main item of Soviet exports to China. Agreements on equipment deliveries also provided for assistance in surveys and design work, in commissioning completed projects, in organising the production of new types of industrial goods not manufactured in China before, in assembling and adjusting equipment, in personnel training, etc.

In the same period, the Soviet Union supplied to China 943,000 tons of ferrous metals, which was equivalent to about 40 per cent of her total output, 1.5 million tons of petroleum products, including 506,000 tons of petrol and 477,000 tons of kerosene.

A large number of Soviet experts assisted in drawing up and fulfilling a programme of hydroengineering construction on China's biggest rivers and in reconstructing railways.

In those years, the Soviet Union's support for People's China against the US aggressive plans assumed special importance.

At those hard times for the new republic the Soviet Union's assistance was not confined to diplomatic actions and all-round co-operation in the economic, scientific, cultural and military fields; direct military actions were also undertaken to oppose the imperialists' aggressive designs.

In 1949-1950, at the request of the PRC Government, a large Soviet air force was assigned to protect the industrial city of Shanghai in East China. Kuomintang air raids proved a failure. Enemy airmen were given a stern lesson by Soviet aces.

In 1950, again at the PRC Government's request, the Soviet Union moved into Manchuria its crack air divisions which effectively protected the industrial centres of Northeast China against air raids and brought down scores of enemy planes in aerial battles.

The Soviet Union and the PRC effectively co-operated in the military field during the Korean war. The Soviet Union regularly supplied the Korean People's Army and Chinese volunteers with arms and ammunition, fuel, provisions, medicines. Soviet military advisers, some distinguished generals among them, stayed in Korea. Soviet airmen took part in fighting the aggressors.

3. SINO-SOVIET RELATIONS
AT THE END OF THE REHABILITATION PERIOD

In the early years of the People's Republic of China, the Soviet Union stimulated various forms of co-operation with China. Personal contacts between leaders of the two countries were of great importance for strengthening their interstate relations.

The ceremony of signing in Moscow of the Treaty of Friendship, Alliance and Mutual Assistance was attended by a Chinese delegation which included Mao Tse-tung, Chou En-lai and other eminent Chinese statesmen and Party leaders. The Soviet Union was repeatedly visited by Liu Shao-chi, who led, in particular, the CPC delegation to the 19th CPSU Congress, and by Marshal Chu Teh. For their part, Soviet leaders often paid friendly visits to China.

A conspicuous event in Sino-Soviet relations was the visit to Moscow by a Chinese Government delegation led by Chou En-lai in September 1952. At the talks that followed the parties agreed to go ahead with measures to implement a free and complete handover by the Soviet Union to China of all its rights to joint operation of the Chinese-Changchun Railway. Simultaneously, the Soviet and Chinese Ministers of Foreign Affairs exchanged notes on prolonging the joint operation of the Chinese naval base of Port Arthur. The results of the talks were highly appreciated by the Chinese Government as an expression of selfless and fraternal assistance from the Soviet Union.

Between 1950 and 1952, the Chinese-Changchun Railway was restored all along its length. Within a stipulated period—on December 31, 1952—the Soviet Government handed over to China free of charge all its rights to joint operation of the railway with all its property.

The agreement covered the trunk lines from the Manchuria station to Pogranichnaya (Suifenho) and from Harbin to Dairen and Port Arthur, with buildings and facilities, rolling stock, power stations, communication lines and other enterprises and offices of the railway.

Mao Tse-tung described it in his message to the Soviet Premier Joseph Stalin as the Soviet Union's great contribution to railway construction in China. Speaking at the ceremony of signing the final protocol on the handover of the Chinese-Changchun Railway, Chou En-lai declared: "The Chinese people will never forget this fraternal assistance from the Soviet people. It should be noted in particular that the cordial and patient bestowal of know-how by Soviet comrades has enabled Chinese personnel of the Chinese-Changchun Railway to assimilate the Soviet Union's advanced experience and helped us raise a large body of specialists for railway construction in the new China." The newspaper *Jenmin jihpao* wrote editorially on December 31, 1952 that the free handover to China of the Chinese-Changchun Railway and the consent to prolong the stipulated period of Soviet troop withdrawal from Port Arthur have demonstrated still more vividly the Soviet Government's respect for the national independence and honour of China.

Commenting on the handover of the Chinese-Changchun Railway to China, *Jenmin jihpao* said: "The Soviet personnel of the Chinese-Changchun Railway by sharing with us in full advanced Soviet know-how with due regard for the specific conditions of China helped stimulate the creativity of the Chinese working class, which was tremendous, invaluable aid in various fields of construction in our country."[1]

There are interesting documents illustrating Soviet people's great assistance to the fraternal Chinese people during the joint operation of the Chinese-Changchun Railway. For example, in the final protocol of the Sino-Soviet commission on implementing the free handover of the Chinese-Changchun Railway signed on December 31, 1952 it was pointed out that during the joint Sino-Soviet operation of the Chinese-Changchun Railway reconstruction had been completed of 455 km of second track, 191 km of automatic block systems, and 2,600 freight wagons had been built. A total of 5,150 freight wagons, 943 coaches, 517 locomotives had been restored or undergone capital repairs, 153,000 sq m of housing had been built or reconstructed and 173,000 sq m of housing repaired. Track measuring established that the track facilities of the railway were in excellent or good condition.

The Chinese representative on the Sino-Soviet commission on the handover of the Chinese-Changchun Railway declared

---

[1] *Jenmin jihpao*, December 31, 1952.

on October 20, 1952: "We are sincerely and cordially thankful to the Soviet Government ... for its great disinterested aid to the People's Republic of China, to the Chinese people. The handover of the Chinese-Changchun Railway even more graphically illustrates the Soviet Government's great respect for the Chinese people's sovereignty and national dignity, as well as the Soviet Government's absolute loyalty to the cause of friendship and alliance between China and the Soviet Union. . . ."

When in 1952 the PRC Government decided to organise natural rubber production in China the Soviet Government granted it 8.55 million rubles in credit to finance the development of caoutchouc plantations on Hainan Island and in the coastal areas of Southeast China. In 1952, trade between the Soviet Union and the PRC grew again.

The total turnover of Sino-Soviet trade increased almost twofold since 1950.

The Soviet Union stepped up considerably its technical aid to the PRC. In 1952, in addition to implementing surveys and design operations, it gave China effective help in mastering the operation of sophisticated industrial equipment, as well as in building new industrial projects. The Soviet Union fulfilled in the main its obligations for technical assistance in 1952. Among the larger projects completed in that year were a flax mill in Harbin, a motor repair works in Urumchi, a 25,000 kw power station at Furhsin. Six motor repair shops and plants commissioned at the end of 1951 were brought up to design capacity. In 1952, about 1,000 Soviet specialists worked in China.

Taking advantage of Soviet know-how, Chinese industry gradually adopted a more efficient organisation of production, introduced modern technology, new types of machines and new lines of products. Soviet production techniques, such as high-speed metal cutting, steel smelting, trouble-shooting, etc., were effectively used at metallurgical plants and ore mines. The application of these production techniques greatly raised the productivity of labour, brought into play latent reserves in industry. For example, the application of high-speed metal-cutting techniques pushed up the productivity of metalworking lathes 300-400 per cent, and in certain cases, even 2,900 per cent.

The use of advanced Soviet know-how enabled great progress to be made in the field of capital construction. At the mines of the Fuhsin ore-mining administration, the team led by Mao Pen-chih using Soviet drilling techniques raised its labour productivity almost threefold. The application of Soviet experience in the construction of the vertical shaft at a colliery of the Sian mining administration cut down by half the planned period of construction, saved 1 million man-days and reduced the costs of construction by 40 per cent. The use of Soviet know-how in the construction of the Anshan steel works made it possible to carry on wide-scale building operations in winter, which greatly shortened the period of work on the project. The study of Soviet experience contributed to the rapid development of communications and transport services. Speaking at a meeting held on the occasion of the 3rd anniversary of the Sino-Soviet Treaty of Friendship, Alliance and Mutual Assistance Po I-po, alternate member of the Politbureau of the CPC Central Committee, described the work of Soviet specialists in these words: "The assistance given us by Soviet specialists is quite varied, and every measure in our economic affairs is carried out under their effective technical direction. It is impossible to estimate all the benefits our country has gained from their assistance. If it were not for the selfless aid of Soviet specialists, it would have been very difficult to make the spectacular progress in the rehabilitation and modernisation of China's national economy over the past three years, beginning from healing the wounds of the war and ending with the radical improvement of the financial and economic situation and the provision of various conditions necessary for implementing the first five-year construction programme."[1]

Soviet specialists were directly involved in reorganising the higher education system, the courts of law and institutions of justice, in setting up new ministries, a system of government planning, etc.

During the first three years of people's power in China, Soviet specialists helped with the publication in Chinese of over 3,100 Soviet books, including 943 books on social sciences, 348 on problems of culture and education. In the autumn

---

[1] *Jenmin jihpao*, February 15, 1953.

of 1952, work was started in China to revise all curricula and instruction programmes to model them on those of Soviet institutions of higher learning and to translate text-books and teaching aids used in Soviet higher schools. In 1952, members of the faculty of the agricultural institute of Northeast China translated into Chinese Soviet curricula on 141 subjects and distributed them to all agricultural higher schools in China.

Soviet experience in various fields of socialist construction was broadly popularised under the motto "Learn from the Soviet Union". This was expressed in particular in the mass movement for the study of Russian in the early years after liberation. During the first two years of people's power in China 12 institutes of the Russian language were opened, which had a total student body of 5,000. In addition, in 1952 there were Russian language departments and courses at 57 institutions of higher learning; Russian was taught at all secondary schools of Northeast China, in 59 schools of Peking and other cities.

Sino-Soviet cultural exchanges developed successfully. A striking manifestation of friendship between the Soviet and Chinese peoples was the Sino-Soviet friendship month in November-December 1952, which grew into a wide political campaign. At the ceremony of opening the friendship month, Chou En-lai declared that the Soviet Government's generous and selfless aid enabled China to strengthen her defence capability, to overcome the economic blockade by the imperialist powers and secured rapid progress in economic rehabilitation.

The delegation of Soviet cultural workers, scientists and artists who had arrived in China to take part in the friendship month was enthusiastically welcomed by the Chinese people during its tour of the country. During their stay in China Soviet performers gave more than 80 concerts which drew 500,000 spectators. The Soviet Army Song and Dance Company gave 60 concerts which were attended by a total of 1 million people.

Owing to Soviet assistance, in 1952 people's democracy was further strengthened and considerable progress was made in administrative, economic and cultural work in China. In the economic field, 1952 was mainly the year of completing economic rehabilitation and developing the key branches of the national economy, as well as of preparing for broad economic construction under the first five-year plan.

In 1952, China's gross industrial output increased 24.7 per cent as compared with its 1951 level, the state sector accounting for over 60 per cent of the gross national product. In agriculture, the agrarian reform was completed and a movement was mounting for boosting production and setting up peasant co-operatives. Under the agrarian reform 44 million hectares of land were shared out among peasants who had formerly paid for these under lease terms to the landlords at least 30 million tons of grain.

During the rehabilitation period, important social and economic changes took place in China. Leaning on all-round economic and political support from and broad military co-operation with the Soviet Union, which reliably guaranteed China's national security, the people's state which had inherited from the old regime economic dislocation and decay drew up and implemented with the aid of Soviet specialists a sweeping programme of social reforms and reconstruction of the national economy.

People's revolutionary government became stronger. A socialist sector emerged in the economy, the state nationalised the basic means of production and could now manipulate the main economic levers, such as credit, raw materials supplies, marketing, etc., with which to control the private capitalist sector. Reforms were also being implemented in agriculture, commerce and other fields. In 1949 the gross output of the state-owned industry accounted for only 26.7 per cent of the country's total industrial production, whereas in 1952, the figure rose to 44.7 per cent. The people's standards of living were improving, science and culture were on the upgrade.

During the rehabilitation period Sino-Soviet relations were a crucial factor since the internationalist support and tremendous aid of the Soviet people enabled China to overcome her difficulties at home and abroad and prepare all the conditions for a successful transition to planned socialist construction.

CHAPTER III

SINO-SOVIET RELATIONS
IN THE FIRST FIVE-YEAR PLAN PERIOD.
1953-1957

1. CONTINUED EXPANSION OF SINO-SOVIET CO-OPERATION
IN 1953-1955

The appreciable progress made in China's economic development and democratisation thanks to the Chinese people's selfless labour and disinterested Soviet aid made it possible for the Communist Party of China to formulate in 1953 a general policy of transition from capitalism to socialism. In 1954, this policy was approved by the National People's Congress and enforced in the PRC Constitution.

China's achievements in various fields of building a new life were based on Soviet people's comprehensive experience and tremendous material aid. The CPC Central Committee, in the political report to the 8th National Party Congress, expressed its gratitude to all friends of the Chinese people for their support and assistance. "The Soviet Union," it said in particular, "has given huge assistance to socialist construction in our country; and the People's Democracies in Europe and Asia have also given us help in various ways. The Chinese people will never forget this comradely assistance from fraternal countries."[1]

The PRC was supplied by the Soviet Union and other fraternal countries with everything necessary for developing her industry, science and technology and could sell her traditional export goods on their markets. Therefore, attempts of the USA and its partners in military blocs to organise an economic blockade of China were a complete fiasco.

---

[1] Liu Shao-chi, "The Political Report of the Central Committee of the Communist Party of China to the Eighth National Congress of the Party." In Supplement to *People's China*, October 1, 1956, p. 47.

The Soviet Union continued its vigorous efforts on the international scene to raise the prestige of People's China and foil the imperialists' plans to isolate and blockade her.

In 1953, China adopted her first five-year economic development plan.

The Communist Party's general line in the transitional period was to convert socialist ownership of the means of production into the economic foundation of China's government and social system. In conformity with this central target, China's socialist industrialisation, sweeping socialist reforms in agriculture, the handicraft industries, private capitalist industry and trade were carried out in the transitional period. It was expected that it would take roughly 15 years to attain these targets.

In that period, CPC leaders and Chinese propagandists had on the whole a correct idea of the proportion of the Chinese people's own efforts to the assistance from the Soviet Union and other fraternal countries to socialist construction in China. In an editorial entitled "We Thank the Soviet Union for Its Great Assistance", *Jenmin jihpao* wrote in September 1953: "Chairman Mao Tse-tung, disproving the mistaken view that the victory of the Chinese revolution was possible without international assistance, pointed out that in the era of imperialism a genuine popular revolution in any country could not be victorious without assistance in various ways from international revolutionary forces and that we needed help not only in the past but also in the present and would need it in the future."[1]

In his address to the fourth session of China's People's Political Consultative Conference in February 1953 Mao Tse-tung, among the three main "historic" tasks, as they were described in the press, pointed out the following: "We must learn from the Soviet Union. We are going to carry on our great national construction. The work facing us is hard and we do not have enough experience. So we must seriously study the advanced experience of the Soviet Union. Whether inside or outside the Communist Party, old or new cadres, technicians, intellectuals, workers or peasants, we must all learn wholeheartedly from the Soviet Union. We must learn not

---

[1] *Jenmin jihpao*, September 16, 1953.

only the theories of Marx, Engels, Lenin and Stalin, but also the advanced scientific techniques of the Soviet Union. There must be a great nationwide upsurge of learning from the Soviet Union to build our country."[1]

In 1953-1954, important work was performed to lay down the constitutional principles of the PRC, which are being attacked with special vehemency by the CPC leadership today. At the request of the CPC Central Committee, the Soviet side made a number of comments which were reflected in the draft Constitution of the PRC officially published on June 15, 1954. By August 25, 1954, the elections to the National People's Congress had been completed. A total of 1,226 deputies had been elected throughout the country.

The first session of the National People's Congress held in Peking from September 15 to 28, 1954 was a milestone event in China's development along democratic lines. The PRC Constitution adopted at the session proclaimed the people's congresses the political foundation of the People's Republic of China. Elected by a universal ballot, these congresses were a step forward from the former institutions of government, because they fully expressed the will of the people. They were truly democratic bodies of popular representation. The State Council and local people's committees as executive agencies of government were under the control of the National and local people's congresses respectively.

The PRC Constitution unanimously adopted by the first session of China's National People's Congress was oriented to the continued development of democracy in China along with the establishment of a united centralised leadership of state.

The PRC Constitution affirmed the Chinese people's desire of friendship and co-operation with the Soviet Union. It reads in particular: "China has already built an indestructible friendship with the great Union of Soviet Socialist Republics and the People's Democracies...."[2] In his report on

---

[1] "Three Important Tasks of the Day. Chairman Mao Tse-tung Addresses the P.P.C.C. National Committee." In: *People's China*, Peking, 1953, No. 5, March 1, p. 3.

[2] "Constitution of the People's Republic of China." In: *Documents of the First Session of the First National People's Congress of the People's Republic of China*, Peking, 1955, p. 135.

the draft Constitution, Liu Shao-chi declared: "... the road we are taking is the road traversed by the Soviet Union. About this we have not the slightest doubt. The Soviet road is the road all humanity will eventually take in accordance with the laws of development of history. To by-pass this road is impossible."[1]

In 1953, China started implementing her first five-year economic development plan. In that period Soviet assistance to China assumed a still wider scope. China's first five-year plan was drawn up with the most active aid of Soviet specialists.

It ensured the republic's rapid and balanced development. In fact, China's first five-year plan, which was fulfilled successfully, had been oriented to all-round Soviet material, scientific and technological assistance.

On March 21, 1953, an agreement was signed in Moscow on Soviet aid to China to enlarge existing and build new power stations.

On May 15, 1953, a Sino-Soviet agreement was concluded on Soviet assistance to China in the construction and modernisation of 141 industrial projects. This included 50 enterprises listed in the agreement of February 14, 1950 and an additional 91 large industrial projects.

The development and extension of Sino-Soviet trade exchanges resulted in a 25.5 per cent increase in the goods turnover in 1953 as compared with the 1952 level. In terms of value Soviet exports to China increased 28.8 per cent, and Soviet imports from China, 21.9 per cent since 1952. China's share in the total turnover of Soviet foreign trade in 1953 was 20 per cent, while the Soviet Union accounted for 55.6 per cent in the total turnover of Chinese foreign trade. In 1953, the Soviet Union continued its technical aid to China in a volume almost twice that of 1952.

The early years of the five-year plan were of fundamental importance for building up the basis for Chinese industry. Therefore, Soviet assistance in strengthening its key sectors was of inestimable value for China's economy.

---

[1] Liu Shao-chi, "Report on the Draft Constitution of the People's Republic of China." In: *Documents of the First Session of the First National People's Congress of the People's Republic of China*, Peking, 1955, p. 41.

In 1954, the CPSU Central Committee took new important steps to further strengthen Sino-Soviet relations. A Soviet Government delegation paid an official visit to China in the autumn of 1954.

The talks between the Soviet delegation and the Chinese Government were held in an atmosphere of frankness and culminated in the signing on October 12 of a number of documents aimed at promoting peace in Asia and throughout the world. Among them were the joint declarations of the Soviet and Chinese Governments on Sino-Soviet relations and the international situation and on relations with Japan; the communique and agreements on the naval base of Port Arthur, on Sino-Soviet joint-stock companies, on scientific and technical co-operation; on the construction of the Lanchow-Urumchi-Alma-Ata Railway; the joint Sino-Soviet-Mongolian Government communique on the construction of a railway line from Tsining to Ulan Bator.

In addition, an agreement was signed on a long-term Soviet credit of 520 million rubles to the Chinese Government and a protocol on Soviet assistance to China in the construction of additional 15 industrial projects and on increasing equipment deliveries to 141 enterprises, provided for in an earlier agreement, the total worth of additional Soviet equipment supplies being in excess of 400 million rubles.

Expressing his high appreciation of the results of the talks, Premier Chou En-lai stated at a Soviet Embassy reception on October 12, 1954: "Nobody can separate us. Such friendly relations continue irresistibly to grow stronger and develop daily; they will invariably develop in the centuries and generations to come."[1]

The joint documents of the Soviet and Chinese Governments emphasised full accord in their views on the development of bilateral co-operation and in their appraisal of the international situation.

On October 16, 1954, after a discussion of Chou En-lai's report on Sino-Soviet talks the Standing Committee of the National People's Congress approved their results. At that time, Chinese leaders spoke highly of the Soviet Union's fra-

---

[1] *Jenmin jihpao*, October 13, 1954.

ternal aid. Referring to the Soviet gift in machines and equipment for setting up a large state grain farm in China Mao Tse-tung declared, for example, that the Chinese people regarded this generous aid from the Soviet people as yet another manifestation of their deep sympathy for the Chinese people, their concern and support for the cause of construction carried out by the Chinese people. Guided by the principles of internationalism, friendship and co-operation with China and taking into account the consolidation of her positions on the international scene and defence potential, the Soviet Government on its own initiative took a decision to withdraw Soviet military forces from the jointly operated Chinese naval base of Port Arthur and to hand it over to China free of charge together with all newly-built military strategic installations.

Under the agreement of October 12, 1954, all Soviet rights and shares in the Sovsinoil and Sovsinmetal Sino-Soviet joint-stock companies, and later the SKOGA Sino-Soviet airline, were also handed over into China's full possession.

The Sino-Soviet joint-stock companies greatly contributed to China's economic rehabilitation. For example, the Sovsinmetal company built 11 non-ferrous and rare metal ore mines. Soviet specialists of the company trained 5,150 Chinese engineers, technicians and skilled operatives in 73 different specialities and about 300 members of administrative and managerial personnel.

The company set up a specialised mining and petroleum secondary school in which 600 Chinese students were enrolled. Sovsinoil helped intensify direct economic exchanges between the two countries, as well as between the Soviet Union, China and Mongolia.

In 1954, the Soviet Union assisted China in the construction of 169 industrial projects. The total volume of Soviet technical aid in 1954 grew almost twofold since 1953. On January 1, 1955, about 800 Soviet specialists worked in China in the field of technical assistance alone. In addition to fulfilling their contractual obligations, Soviet specialists handled much work in the training of Chinese personnel. In particular, they trained 800 power equipment assemblymen and fitters, about 600 mechanical fitters and more than 1,000 skilled workers of different specialities.

According to the agreement of October 12, 1954, the conference on scientific and technical co-operation held in Moscow in December 1954 decided that the Soviet Union would hand over to China free of charge blueprints for the construction of metallurgical, machine-building plants and power stations, working drawings for the production of machines and equipment and process charts, as well as scientific and technical publications. The Soviet Union gave China a large amount of documents and drawings on the technological equipment of various branches of the economy. All in all, from the beginning of 1950 to July 1954 Soviet technical documents on 698 items of equipment were handed over to China. Taking advantage of Soviet documents, Chinese industry started production of building and ore-mining equipment, 10-, 20- and 30-ton gantry cranes, excavators, etc.

The Soviet Government agreed to give China assistance in the peaceful uses of atomic energy. Under the agreement signed on April 27, 1955, the Soviet Union helped China to build her first experimental atomic pile and cyclotron.

The resolution of the PRC State Council of January 31, 1955 stated in this connection that this was a splendid expression of the Soviet Union's foreign policy of peace, a new contribution to the great friendship between China and the Soviet Union, that the Chinese people and Government expressed their heartfelt gratitude to the Soviet Union for its sincere and disinterested aid.

According to evidence of the PRC Ministry of Foreign Trade, the Soviet Union's share in the turnover of China's foreign commerce in 1954 was 51.8 per cent.

The opening in Peking of an exhibition of Soviet economic and cultural achievements was an important event in China's life in 1954. On the very first day, the exhibition drew 80,000 visitors, while the total number of visitors while it was on view ran into about 3 million. Chinese citizens admired Soviet achievements. At that time CPC leaders could not but speak in the same vein. For instance, Mao Tse-tung made this entry in the visitors' book: "We are proud to have such a powerful ally. The Soviet Union's power is an important precondition for the general economic and cultural advance of the countries belonging to the camp of peace and democracy, a crucial factor of struggle for peace throughout the world and of mankind's progress." Specialists of the Soviet exhibition in Peking did much to popularise Soviet achievements. They often visited enterprises and gave about 1,000 lectures and talks, which were attended by a total of over 55,000 listeners. Soviet films were regularly shown in the cinema hall on the exhibition grounds.

In 1954, the Soviet Union and China exchanged numerous public delegations and performers' companies. The Soviet Union played host to 20 Chinese delegations, including a press delegation led by Teng To, editor-in-chief of *Jenmin jihpao,* a delegation of the Sino-Soviet Friendship Society led by its Secretary-General Tsien Chün-jui, a delegation led by the Minister of Agriculture Li Shu-cheng, a delegation of the All-China Society for Dissemination of Scientific and Technical Knowledge, delegations of trade union functionaries, architects, railwaymen, sports delegations, etc. China was visited by 12 Soviet delegations of trade unionists, youth, cultural workers, pressmen, co-operative executives, athletes, etc. At the end of the year, the K. S. Stanislavsky and V. I. Nemirovich-Danchenko Theatre company and the Folk Dance Company under Igor Moiseyev made a guest tour of China.

In 1955, China was visited by a group of Soviet scientists led by I. P. Bardin, Vice-President of the USSR Academy of Sciences, a delegation of medical scientists led by F. G. Krotkov, Vice-President of the USSR Academy of Medical Sciences, and a delegation of nuclear scientists. The broad delegation exchange largely contributed to Sino-Soviet friendship, to the expansion of business ties between individual cultural, scientific and art institutions and workers of the Soviet Union and China.

At the request of the Chinese Government, in 1955 an exhibition of Soviet economic and cultural achievements, which had made quite a hit in Peking, was opened in Shanghai and later in Canton. In Canton it drew about 2.4 million visitors, in particular, over 87,000 from Hongkong and Aomen. The exhibition was visited by 52 delegations from 22 countries of the world.

Soviet specialists who worked at the exhibition again did much to pass on Soviet scientific experience and know-how to their Chinese colleagues. In Canton they read over 400 reports and lectures which were attended by about 60,000 listeners, and made more than 30 visits to Canton's industrial enterprises, as well as to suburban farms and co-operatives for the purpose of technical assistance and advice. The 28 elementary vocational training circles opened on the exhibition grounds for Chinese specialists and workers had a student attendance of 1,170.

At the Chinese Government's request, an exhibition of Soviet economic and cultural achievements was also opened in Hankow.

In 1955, three companies of Soviet performers came to China for a guest tour: the Beryozka Dance Company and two concert troupes of 25 members each.

On July 5, 1956, a Sino-Soviet cultural co-operation agreement was signed in Moscow, which provided for exchanges in the fields of science, technology, education, literature and the arts, public health, the press and publishing business, broadcasting and television, cinematography and sports. This agreement summed up the results of fruitful Sino-Soviet cultural exchanges over many years and laid the groundwork for developing them in the future.

The wide scale of Sino-Soviet cultural co-operation was evidenced by the fact that in 1949-1958 the Soviet Union played host to 134 Chinese performers' companies and released 102 Chinese films. Over the same period, China received 112 companies of Soviet performers and showed 747 Soviet films, which drew a total of about 2,000 million spectators.

A wide programme of training Chinese specialists was under way. In 1956 alone 1,800 Chinese under-graduate and research students went to study in the Soviet Union.

In 1953-1955, the Soviet Union and China closely co-operated on the international scene. The Governments of both countries took a joint stand on many foreign policy issues.

It was precisely in that period that China won broad international prestige as a party to the political settlement of the military conflict in Korea. On July 21, 1954, the DRV, the Soviet Union, the PRC and other countries signed the final declaration of the Geneva Conference on a peace settlement in Indochina. Joint statements made by the Soviet

Union and China on relations with Japan were of major significance. China, India and other Asian countries initiated the historic Bandung Conference and put forward the five principles of peaceful coexistence.

At every crucial moment in her struggle for implementing the socialist principles of foreign policy China invariably had by her side the Soviet Union, a dependable guarantor and defender of her rights.

China's policy of active co-operation with the Soviet Union and other countries, struggle against imperialism and colonialism, actions against aggression and for maintaining peace led to her early recognition by many states, to an expansion of her foreign relations.

At the same time, co-operation with China facilitated the solution of some economic problems in the Soviet Union which imported from China valuable raw materials and other goods required for economic development.

In this, a solid economic foundation of friendly co-operation between China and the Soviet Union was laid in the period of China's economic rehabilitation and first five-year plan. Chinese Communist internationalists, true patriots of their homeland, the masses of China could see with their own eyes that the vital interests of the Soviet Union and China were identical, that co-operation with the Soviet Union on a basis of equality and mutual assistance was a short cut to overcoming China's economic and cultural backwardness and making her a great socialist industrial power. Another basic factor that merits emphasis is that the all-round economic and political co-operation of the young People's Republic of China with the Soviet Union, all the other socialist countries, was of crucial importance not only for creating abroad a favourable political situation for building socialism in China but also for providing favourable social conditions for this at home. It will be recalled that at the beginning of the first five-year plan period the working class accounted for about 1 per cent of China's population and that in 1949 the proportion of industrial workers in the Communist Party of China was about 3 per cent, and in 1953, a little over 6-7 per cent.

In that situation, the relative weakness of China's working class was compensated for by the powerful support of the world proletariat, above all, by the high prestige of the world's first socialist country—the Soviet Union.

The internationalist forces within the Communist Party of China were clearly aware of this. On the other hand, at the time when China was not yet strong enough and was in a state of military, political and economic confrontation against the biggest imperialist powers, the nationalistic elements in the Party had no field for manoeuvring. Therefore, the Maoists stowed away their hegemonistic and anti-Soviet ideas for the time being. In that period, they were also interested in co-operation with the Soviet Union.

2. SINO-SOVIET RELATIONS IN 1956-1957

The 20th CPSU Congress in February 1956 and the 8th National Congress of the CPC in September 1956 were milestone events in the history of Sino-Soviet relations and the world communist movement.

In 1956-1957, the struggle was growing between two lines within the Communist Party of China—the Marxist, internationalist line on the one hand, and the petty bourgeois, nationalistic line on the other. This struggle was complicated by the intrigues of imperialist forces on the international scene, which were expressed in the developments in the Middle East, the counter-revolutionary riots in Hungary, Poland, etc. The situation within the international communist movement as a whole became aggravated, too.

The present leaders of the CPC seek to prove that the differences between the CPC and the CPSU and other Marxist-Leninist parties arose after the 20th CPSU Congress whose decisions they allegedly rejected out of considerations of principle.

It is the historical truth, however, that Mao Tse-tung and his group simply took advantage of the decisions of the 20th CPSU Congress as a pretext for their later attacks on the CPSU and for advancing their special conceptions they had been hatching for quite some time. Characteristically, at one time the leaders of the Communist Party of China firmly declared their support for the 20th CPSU Congress decisions. The Vice-Chairman of the Communist Party of China, Chu Teh, stated at the 20th CPSU Congress: "The Central

Committee of the Communist Party of China is firmly convinced that the 20th Congress of the CPSU will make a still
greater contribution to the cause of building communism in
the Soviet Union and to the cause of preserving peace
throughout the world, and also will give still greater inspiration to the Chinese people in their struggle for building
socialism in their country and for ensuring peace in Asia
and the rest of the world."[1]

At the 1957 Moscow Meeting of Communist and Workers'
Parties, the Chinese delegation led by Mao Tse-tung signed
the Declaration containing the following statement: "The
historic decisions of the Twentieth Congress of the CPSU
are of tremendous importance not only to the CPSU and to
the building of communism in the USSR; they have opened
a new stage in the world communist movement and facilitated
its further development along Marxist-Leninist lines."[2]

It was none other than Mao Tse-tung who stated in his
opening address to the 8th National Congress of the CPC in
September 1956, i.e., half a year after the 20th CPSU Congress: "At its 20th Congress held not long ago, the Communist Party of the Soviet Union formulated many correct policies and criticised shortcomings which were found in the
Party. It can be confidently asserted that very great development will follow on this in its work."[3]

In the political report of the CPC Central Committee to
the 8th National Congress of the CPC, which was attended
by Mao Tse-tung, the decisions of the 20th CPSU Congress
were also given a detailed positive assessment. "The 20th
Congress of the Communist Party of the Soviet Union, held
last February," the report said in particular, "was an important political event of world significance. It not only drew
up the Sixth Five-Year Plan of gigantic proportions, decided
on many important policies and principles for further development of the cause of socialism and repudiated the cult

---

[1] 20th Congress of the Communist Party of the Soviet Union. Steno-
graphic Records, Vol. 1, Moscow, 1956, p. 228.
[2] The Struggle for Peace, Democracy and Socialism, Moscow, 1963,
p. 21.
[3] "Opening Address at the Eighth National Congress of the Communist Party of China." In: Eighth National Congress of the Communist Party of China, Vol. 1, Documents, Peking, 1956, p. 10.

of the individual which had had grave consequences inside the Party. It also advocated further promotion of peaceful coexistence and international co-operation, making an outstanding contribution to the easing of international tensions."[1]

The report on the revision of the Party Constitution delivered at the 8th Congress of the CPC contained this statement: "Leninism demands of the Party that all important questions should be decided by an appropriate collective body, and not by any individual. The 20th Congress of the Communist Party of the Soviet Union has thrown a searching light on the profound significance of adhering to the principle of collective leadership and combatting the cult of the individual and this illuminating lesson has produced a tremendous effect not only on the Communist Party of the Soviet Union but also on the Communist parties of all other countries throughout the world."[2]

At one time, Mao Tse-tung made some clearly worded admissions the Maoists deem it wise not to recall today. For example, in April 1956, he stated that the report on the cult of the individual was very useful, that some of its negative implications stood no comparison with the benefits derived by the Communist parties from the discussion of this problem at the 20th Congress of the CPSU.

The directive article under the heading "Once More on the Historical Experience of the Dictatorship of the Proletariat" published in *Jenmin jihpao* on December 29, 1956 said in particular: "The 20th Congress of the Communist Party of the Soviet Union displayed great determination and boldness in doing away with the cult of Stalin, in exposing the gravity of Stalin's mistakes and in eliminating their after-effects. The Marxist-Leninists and Communist sympathisers all over the world support the efforts of the Communist Party of the Soviet Union to correct these mistakes and wish full success to their Soviet comrades."[3]

---

[1] *Eighth National Congress of the Communist Party of China*, Vol. 1, Documents, p. 86.

[2] Teng Hsiao-ping, "Report on the Revision of the Constitution of the Communist Party of China." In: *Eighth National Congress of the Communist Party of China*, Vol. 1, Documents, Peking, 1956, p. 192.

[3] *Jenmin jihpao*, December 29, 1956.

At the same time, unwilling to renounce the system and methods involving violations of legality and the principles of collective leadership, the anti-Sovietists in the CPC from the very outset took pains to shut off the people and Communists of China from the renovating ideas of the 20th Congress of the CPSU. They gambled on the difficulties within the international communist movement (in connection with the developments in Hungary, etc.) in an effort to undermine the prestige of the CPSU and portray themselves as guardians of revolutionary traditions. They pursued in effect only one goal: to place the CPC in the position of leader of the international communist movement, to depict Mao Tse-tung as the "leader and teacher of all nations".

CPC leaders revealed an extreme nationalistic approach to the assessment of Joseph Stalin's role as well as to other issues. Having decided as far back as the early period of the Chinese revolution to make Mao Tse-tung the herald of what may be described as "Chinese Marxism" they went to all lengths to denigrate Soviet experience, that of the CPSU in particular. Although after the 20th CPSU Congress, the Peking leaders took a demagogic stance of defenders of Stalin, the Maoists are known to have made many extremely offensive comments on his role.

It will be recalled that in Stalin's lifetime CPC leaders, while clamouring about the importance of the "ideas of Mao Tse-tung", did not dare to propagate them openly outside China, to describe them as having universal value for the world communist movement. The denunciation of Stalin's mistakes, however, created, in their opinion, the conditions for extolling Mao Tse-tung, for idolising him as the "greatest genius", "the leader of the world revolution", etc.

The efforts of the CPSU to strengthen the Leninist principles of collective leadership were of major importance for stimulating the healthful internationalist trend within the CPC, encouraging supporters of this trend to act resolutely in defence of Marxism-Leninism, socialist theory and practice.

Towards 1956, as a result of the strenuous efforts of the Chinese working people and assistance from the fraternal countries China had made a veritable breakthrough in the development of her economy, science and culture, in raising the standards of public welfare and building up her defence potential. Over the years of people's government, her industrial output had grown fivefold.

The proclamation of the policy of building socialism stimulated the internationalist trends within the Party and people, gave encouragement to the loyal Marxist forces within the CPC. The appreciable achievements in economic and cultural development, in improving the people's standards of life, the growth of China's international prestige furnished the ground for confidence that China was on the right track. Taking advantage of the experience of the fraternal parties, the CPC was making its contribution to solving the problem of transition of underdeveloped countries to socialism. This created favourable prerequisites for convening the next congress of the CPC. The 8th National Congress held in September 1956 approved the Party's general line towards building socialism in close unity with all the countries of the world socialist system. The 8th National Congress holds a conspicuous place in the history of the Communist Party of China. It was key-noted by the consolidation and growth of the loyal Marxist-Leninist forces within the Party.

The Congress made it incumbent on all Communists to keep strictly in line with the objective possibilities for economic development and avoid overstepping the limits in rates of construction. It drew the conclusion that in the struggle between socialism and capitalism in China the question "who beats who" had already been settled. The Congress advanced the task of raising the people's material and cultural levels, and continued development of democracy in the country and Party.

In the General Programme included in the new Party Constitution adopted by the 8th National Congress of the CPC its theoretical principles were clearly defined as follows: "The Communist Party of China takes Marxism-Leninism as its guide to action.... Marxism-Leninism is not a dogma, but a guide to action. It demands that in striving to build socialism and communism we should proceed from reality, apply the principles of Marxism-Leninism in a flexible and creative way for the solution of various problems arising out of the actual struggle, and thus continuously develop the theory of Marxism-Leninism. Consequently the Party in its activities upholds the principle of integrating the universal truth of Marxism-Leninism with the actual practice of China's revolutionary struggle, and combats all doctrinaire or empiricist deviations."[1]

Thus, the 8th National Congress revised the formulation of the Party's ideological and theoretical principles adopted by its 7th Congress. The documents of the latter said on this matter: "Using Mao Tse-tung's theory of the Chinese revolution—the theory which unites the theories of Marxism-Leninism with the actual practice of the Chinese revolution—as the guide in all its work, our Party has formulated a revolutionary programme and revolutionary policies which fully represent the interests of the Chinese nation and people."[2]

As the main tasks of the Party in the transitional period from the proclamation of the People's Republic of China to the building of a full-grown socialist society, the 8th CPC Congress indicated a gradual completion of the socialist transformation of agriculture, the handicraft industries and capitalist industry and trade, and a steady industrialisation of the country. For implementing industrialisation and a steady advance of the national economy, the General Programme said, the priority development of heavy industry was indispensable.

The main report delivered at the Congress levied criticism on digressions from the Party's general line in the transitional period and denounced, along with the Right, the Left deviation which boiled down to the demand to build socialism overnight, as it were, to the refusal to admit that a transition to socialism should be brought about by a gradual advance, to disbelief in the possibility to attain the goals of the socialist revolution by peaceful means.

The political report of the CPC Central Committee to the Congress indicated that an important role in stimulating the activity of the mass of the factory and office workers was played by the steady improvement of their living standards and pointed out the need for consistent implementation of the principle of remuneration according to work, because "it

---

[1] *Eighth National Congress of the Communist Party of China*, Vol. 1, Documents, Peking, 1956, p. 137.

[2] Liu Shao-chi, *On the Party*, Peking, 1954, p. 2.

is wrong to place a one-sided stress on the national, long-term interests and neglect the individual and immediate interests of the workers and employees".[1]

Formulating the Party's foreign policy line, the 8th National Congress stated in the General Programme that "the Communist Party of China advocates a foreign policy directed to the safeguarding of world peace and the achievement of peaceful coexistence between countries with different systems. ... The Party endeavours to develop and strengthen China's friendship with all other countries in the camp of peace, democracy and socialism headed by the Soviet Union, to strengthen proletarian internationalism and to learn from the experiences of the world communist movement. It supports the struggle of the Communists, progressives and labouring people of the whole world for the progress of mankind, and educates its members and the Chinese people in the spirit of internationalism, as expressed in the slogan 'Workers of all countries, unite!' "[2]

The Party report said: "Without the great internationalist solidarity of the proletariat of various countries, without the support of the world's revolutionary forces our socialist cause cannot advance to victory, nor can that victory be consolidated even when it is won."[3] The Congress appealed for an affectionate and modest attitude to any of the fraternal parties, for a resolute fight against any manifestations of dangerous great-power chauvinism and bourgeois nationalism.

Under the pressure of circumstances, CPC leaders had to conceal their true sentiments and views. In his opening address to the Congress, Mao Tse-tung emphasised the need for stepping up work in learning the Marxist-Leninist theory of socialist construction, warned the Party against conceit and urged it to study Soviet experience. He stated in particular: "In transforming China from a backward, agricultural country into an advanced, industrialised one, we are confronted with many strenuous tasks and our experience is far from

---

[1] *Eighth National Congress of the Communist Party of China*, Vol. 1, Documents, Peking, 1956, p. 54.

[2] Ibid., pp. 140-41.

[3] Ibid., p. 110.

being adequate. So we must be good at studying. We must be good at learning from our forerunner, the Soviet Union, from the People's Democracies, from the fraternal parties in other parts of the world as well as from the peoples the world over. We must never adopt a conceited attitude of great-nation chauvinism and become arrogant and complacent because of the victory of the revolution and some success in the construction of the country."[1]

Mao Tse-tung also made the following statement: "Internationally, our victories are due to the support of the camp of peace, democracy and socialism headed by the Soviet Union and the profound sympathy of peace-loving people throughout the world."[2]

The General Programme included in the CPC Constitution also read: "Democratic centralism demands that every Party organisation should strictly abide by the principle of collective leadership coupled with individual responsibility and that *every Party member* and Party organisation *should be subject to* Party *supervision* [our italics—*Authors.*] from above and from below."[3]

The important results of deliberations at the 8th National Congress were attributable to a number of factors.

First, by that time appreciable progress had been made in the building of socialism in China. The fulfilment of the first five-year plan was nearing completion, the socialist relations of production in town and village were being strengthened. Chinese Communists were learning it from their own experience that by following the path of Marxism-Leninism and taking advantage of the experience in building socialism in the Soviet Union and other fraternal countries, China could overcome her centuries-old backwardness and improve radically the life of the masses.

Second, China's successes on the home and international scene were inseparably linked with the tremendous internationalist assistance of the Soviet Union and other socialist

---

[1] Mao Tse-tung, "Opening Address at the Eighth National Congress of the Communist Party of China." In *Eighth National Congress of the Communist Party of China*, Vol. 1, Documents, Peking, 1956, p. 10.

[2] Ibid., p. 8.

[3] *Eighth National Congress of the Communist Party of China*, Vol. 1, Documents, Peking, 1956, p. 142.

countries. Thus, internationalism in action demonstrated to the Chinese working people that without the great international solidarity of the proletariat of all countries and without support from the international revolutionary forces the victory of socialism in China was impossible.

Third, under the influence of the CPSU, other Marxist-Leninist parties, the 8th National Congress of the Communist Party of China called attention to the major importance of adhering consistently to the principle of collective leadership and of opposing the cult of the individual, revised in the Party Constitution the formulation of the Party's ideological and theoretical principles and emphasised that the Communist Party of China was guided in its activities by Marxism-Leninism.

These decisions, however, sharply contradicted Mao Tse-tung's political concepts and posed a real danger to his autocracy. Seeking to prevent the further development of events in this direction, to regain the initiative, Mao and his following in later years turned to their advantage the atmosphere of national revival that prevailed in the country, the Chinese people's natural desire to advance their country as early as possible to the level of highly-developed socialist states.

The implementation of the resolutions of the 8th National Congress imperatively demanded the elimination of shortcomings in Party and government affairs and in ideological work which had been in evidence during previous years. These decisions barred the way to voluntaristic, petty bourgeois trends in the building of socialism, to adventurist foreign policy decisions.

The new stage in building socialism faced CPC leaders with immediate tasks whose fulfilment was complicated by the different views representatives of different trends within the CPC took of the fundamental decisions of this Congress.

The very first steps to carry into effect the decisions of the 8th National Congress indicated that there was an influential group within the Peking leadership whose approach to their fulfilment was declarative and shallow, to say the least. Attempts were in evidence to carry forward voluntaristic conceptions of the type "let 100 flowers bloom, let 100 schools compete", the "struggle against the Right", which for all their attractiveness and justifiableness were called upon to revive nationalistic, anti-Soviet sentiments in China, i.e., to undermine the decisions of the 8th National Congress objectionable to the nationalists.

It is not accidental that the decisions of the 8th National Congress of the CPC come under especially malicious attacks from the nationalists today. Violent curses are heaped on these decisions by the masterminds of the "cultural revolution". In the days of the Congress, however, the nationalistic forces within the CPC were evidently still unprepared for a crucial battle. They had carefully disguised themselves and waited for an opportune moment to make short shrift of all dissenters, to discard Marxist-Leninist theory, to clear the ground for setting up their special party with its special ideological and organisational platform.

3. SINO-SOVIET POLITICAL CO-OPERATION IN 1956-1957

In 1956-1957, Sino-Soviet co-operation in the field of foreign policy continued to develop. On a number of major international issues, the PRC held a joint stand with the Soviet Union.

On September 14, 1956, the Standing Committee of the National People's Congress adopted a resolution which said that the Soviet proposal (for disarmament.—*Authors.*) met the interests of both the Soviet and Chinese peoples and other nations of the world. Therefore, the Standing Committee expressed its full support for the disarmament proposals put forward in the appeal of the USSR Supreme Soviet to the parliaments of all the countries of the world.

The leaders of the CPC and the PRC correctly assessed the developments in Hungary in 1956. The joint Sino-Soviet statement of January 18, 1957 signed on the occasion of the visit to the Soviet Union of a PRC government delegation led by Chou En-lai said in particular: "The armed rebellion in Hungary was provoked by the aggressive imperialist circles and Hungarian counter-revolutionary elements who took advantage of the discontent of the Hungarian working people and youth with the mistakes of the former leadership. They attempted to destroy the socialist system in Hungary, to restore the fascist dictatorship and thereby to create a hotbed

of war in Europe; by their plot in Hungary they attempted
to make a breach in the alliance of the socialist countries in
order to attain their goal of disuniting and crushing them
one by one.

"The quick defeat of the counter-revolutionary forces by
the Hungarian people led by the Hungarian Socialist
Workers' Party and the Workers' and Peasants' Revolutionary Government and assisted by the Soviet Union is a major
victory for the cause of peace and socialism.

"By helping the Hungarian people to suppress the counter-
revolutionary rebellion, the Soviet Union fulfilled its internationalist duty to the working people of Hungary and
other socialist countries, which is in the supreme interests of
peace throughout the world."[1]

On November 2, 1956, the Chinese Government published
a statement concerning the Soviet Government's Declaration of October 30, 1956 on the principles of development
and further strengthening of friendship and co-operation
between the Soviet Union and other socialist states. The
statement said in particular: "The Government of the People's
Republic of China believes that this Declaration of the Government of the Soviet Union is correct."[2] In 1956-1957, there
was an enlivening of Sino-Soviet inter-governmental contacts.

In November-December 1956, the Soviet Union was visited by a delegation of the National People's Congress led by
the Vice-Chairman of its Standing Committee, Peng Chen.

In January 1957, a Chinese government delegation led by
the Premier of the State Council and Minister of Foreign
Affairs, Chou En-lai, paid a friendly visit to the Soviet Union.
The Soviet and Chinese government delegations had an exchange of views on major international issues, in particular
those involved in the Anglo-Franco-Israeli aggression against
Egypt and the counter-revolutionary uprising in Hungary, as
well as on problems involved in the continued friendly co-
operation between China and the socialist countries.

In April-May 1957, the Chairman of the Presidium of the
USSR Supreme Soviet, K. E. Voroshilov, went on an official

---

[1] *Izvestia*, January 19, 1957.
[2] *Pravda*, November 2, 1956.

friendship visit to China. Mao Tse-tung was invited to visit the Soviet Union. While the Soviet delegation stayed in China, Chinese leaders repeatedly expressed their high appreciation of the Soviet Union's policy towards China, of the internationalist line pursued by the CPSU. On April 15, at the ceremony of welcome to K. E. Voroshilov at Peking airport, Mao Tse-tung said that the Soviet people invariably gave tremendous assistance to and expressed their sympathy with the Chinese revolution and the cause of construction. "Let me express our heartfelt gratitude to you and in your person to the Soviet people, the Soviet Government and the Communist Party of the Soviet Union,"[1] he said, addressing President Voroshilov.

At a Soviet Embassy reception in Peking on May 3, 1957, Mao Tse-tung declared: "In these days, the whole world has again witnessed the massive unity and cohesion, as well as the closest and deep-rooted friendship between the peoples of China and the Soviet Union. These cohesion and friendship are not only a factor contributing to the cause of socialist and communist construction in our countries but they are also an important element of the cohesion of the socialist countries, a reliable guarantee of universal peace and mankind's progress. The Chinese people, just as the Soviet people, will continue to bend every effort in the name of continued strengthening and development of the relations of cohesion, friendship and co-operation between our countries."[2]

In September and October 1957, China was visited by a delegation of the USSR Supreme Soviet, which took part in the celebration of the 8th anniversary of the People's Republic of China.

The setting up of the Soviet-Chinese Friendship Society in Moscow on October 29, 1957 was an expression of the firm and consistent policy of the CPSU to develop and strengthen Sino-Soviet relations.

The tasks formulated by the Society were as follows: promotion of the fraternal friendship and co-operation between the two great nations; expansion of cultural exchanges, as well as an all-round exchange of experience in cultural develop-

---

[1] *Izvestia*, April 16, 1957.
[2] Ibid., May 4, 1957.

ment with the People's Republic of China; wider information
of the Soviet public about the Chinese people's life and experience in building socialism; assistance in comprehensive
information of the Chinese people about the Soviet people's
life and work.

In November 1957, the Soviet people solemnly celebrated the 40th anniversary of the Great October Socialist
Revolution. A party and government delegation of the PRC
led by Mao Tse-tung arrived in Moscow to attend the festivi-
ties. Addressing the jubilee session of the USSR Supreme
Soviet held on the occasion, Mao Tse-tung noted that since
the dawn of history relations between any states had never
been like those that had developed between the socialist
countries, when their peoples shared their joys and sorrows,
had feelings of mutual respect and trust, helped and inspired
each other. "We have a common destiny and breathe at one
with the Soviet Union and the entire socialist camp," Mao
Tse-tung said.

This was a hypocritical statement, because Mao Tse-tung
was already at that time seeking to impose his platform on
the socialist countries.

The gradual reversal of the decisions of the 8th National
Congress of the Communist Party of China was continued
by a definite group within the CPC leadership. A nationalistic, anti-Soviet line was being reanimated. For this,
various forms and methods were used and campaigns were
carried out to undermine the positions of Marxism-Leninism
in China. The developments in 1957 were indicative in this
respect.

At that time, Rightist elements in the Party became active
on a wide scale. As it has been made clear today by the
"cultural revolution", the nationalistic part of the CPC leadership chose a very peculiar tactics of struggle against
them. For a long time, CPC leaders refrained from exposing
slanderous statements of Rightist elements. From the beginning of May till the middle of June 1957, the Rightists were
actually given the floor for broad propaganda of their views
in the press, at public meetings, in broadcasts, etc. What is
·more, CPC leaders in effect encouraged the Rightists to
action, in particular by the slogan "let 100 flowers bloom,
let 100 schools compete".

The Rightists were most active in their anti-Soviet propaganda, for which they were given broad opportunities. For example, the newspaper *Heilungkiang jihpao,* the organ of a CPC provincial committee, lavishly quoted a certain Chin Yu-hai who called for regaining lands allegedly seized by the Soviet Union, for a struggle against it to the last drop of blood under the slogan of "revenge". "If a Soviet man and an American stood in front of me now," this rabid anti-Sovietier said, "and I had only one cartridge, I would not hesitate to shoot the Soviet man." The newspaper *Kangkiang jihpao* quoted another Rightist element, Chung Yu-wen, as saying that Vladivostok and Mongolia were Chinese territories. The CPC leadership, however, continued quite deliberately to pursue its "wait-and-see" policy and made no effort to oppose anti-Soviet fabrications of the Rightists.

With the connivance of Chinese authorities Rightist elements attempted to pass from words to violent actions. In February 1957 in Sian a mob of over 100 people carrying anti-Soviet posters broke into the courtyard of a hotel where Soviet specialists lived. In May 1957, anti-Soviet elements planned a provocation in Kwangchou timed for the visit there by the Chairman of the Presidium of the USSR Supreme Soviet, Kliment Voroshilov.

The Rightists spewed out anti-Soviet slander on the pages of newspapers, issued in large impressions pamphlets interspersed with foul anti-Soviet abuse. CPC leaders criticised such statements, it is true, but in very general words, without disproving them with adequate factual material. The territorial claims to the Soviet Union advanced by the Rightists were not disavowed at all.

This position becomes perfectly clear if one bears in mind that the nationalists in the CPC reiterate in effect the very same calumniatory anti-Soviet fabrications the Rightists spread in 1957. Characteristically, a large proportion of the Rightist authors of anti-Soviet statements was reinstated in later years.

Rightist statements published in pamphlet form were recommended for political instruction. All this indicates that in 1957 the nationalists made the most of the anti-socialist and anti-Soviet statements of bourgeois elements to spread anti-Soviet slander within broad sections of the Chinese people, thereby initiating efforts to undermine Sino-Soviet relations. In doing so, the group led by Mao Tse-tung sought to conceal their involvement.

In that period, the struggle within the CPC leadership itself over the issue of relations with the Soviet Union again came into the open. The positions of the internationalist and realistic-minded forces within the CPC were still so strong and the need for co-operation with the Soviet Union so great that the CPC leadership was compelled to manoeuvre. The denunciation of the Rightists also reflected the struggle between the two lines within the CPC leadership itself.

In his report to the 4th session of the National People's Congress, Chou En-lai stated: "Some object to the study of the Soviet Union's experience and even believe that the shortcomings and mistakes in the cause of construction in our country are also the result of learning from the Soviet Union. These are extremely harmful views.... If one need not study Soviet experience in building socialism, should one study US experience in building capitalism, or what? Indeed, it is precisely because we have made a serious study of the Soviet Union's advanced experience that we have passed far fewer meandering ways in the cause of construction and achieved tremendous successes."[1]

In an article entitled "On Bourgeois Nationalism Exemplified by Criminal Anti-Soviet Actions of Rightist Elements", the Secretary General of the Sino-Soviet Friendship Society, Tsien Chun-jui, pointed out that for the Rightists the key factors in attaining their goal (restoration of capitalism in China.—*Authors.*) were the struggle against the Communist Party at home and opposition to the Soviet Union abroad. "Socialism can be stable and dreams of the restoration of reactionary rule frustrated," he said, "only if there is a Communist party and friendly relations with the Soviet Union."[2] In the years of the "cultural revolution" such statements were condemned as counter-revolutionary and their authors subjected to corporal and moral punishment.

Against the background of the "cultural revolution" in China it became strikingly clear that the campaign under

---

[1] *Druzhba* (Friendship), June 28, 1957.
[2] *Hsuenhsi,* 1957, No. 16.

the slogan "let 100 flowers bloom, let 100 schools compete", the struggle against the Rightists, the way it was waged in China, were a reflection of petty bourgeois, nationalistic views within the CPC. The ulterior motive behind this was to sow suspicion of the policy of the CPSU and the Soviet Government.

However, the PRC's great progress in building socialism, which the Chinese people did not separate from the disinterested aid of the Soviet Union and other fraternal states, continued to be an obstacle to the Maoists' subversion of Sino-Soviet relations, and this made the CPC leadership resort to manoeuvring.

The Maoists' political hypocrisy, their attempts to undermine in an underhand way the prestige of the CPSU and to prepare the ground for open attacks on the CPSU and the Soviet Union were revealed in full at the Moscow Meeting of Communist and Workers' Parties in 1957.

The CPC delegation led by Mao Tse-tung did not stint flattering words and oaths of allegiance to the Soviet Union. This was part of the Maoists' plan to continue soliciting greater economic and military aid from the Soviet Union.

At the same time, there was at the Meeting what may be described as a "second stage" on which CPC leaders were active, preparing ideological positions for their later attacks against Marxism and for its replacement with Mao's self-styled views.

Significantly, the CPC delegation to the Meeting did not declare its views for all to hear but set them forth in its semi-official Theses of Views on the Problem of Peaceful Transition, which were unofficially handed in after the closure of the Meeting to a Soviet functionary attached to the delegation. There is not a grain of truth in the statement of *Jenmin jihpao* to the effect that at the Meeting of Communist and Workers' Parties in 1957 the CPC delegation had a heated debate with the CPSU over the issue of transition from capitalism to socialism,[1] that the Soviet draft of the Declaration contained no mention of the possibility to implement the revolution by other than peaceful means.

---

[1] *Jenmin jihpao*, March 31, 1964.

The special stand taken by the CPC leadership at the Moscow Meeting was also expressed in Mao Tse-tung's attitude to war. He stated literally as follows: "Is it possible to predict the number of human casualties in a future war? Possibly one-third of the world's population of 2,700 million, i.e., only 900 million people will die. I believe this is a small figure in case atom bombs are really dropped. This is, of course, very frightening. But one half would not be so bad either. Why? Because it is not we who desire war, it is they who want to impose it upon us. If there is war, atomic and hydrogen weapons will be used. I personally believe that the world will experience sufferings in which more than half of mankind or even more will perish. I had an argument over this question with Nehru. He is even more pessimistic on this score than I. I told him that if half of mankind were destroyed, the other half would survive, and, moreover, imperialism would be fully liquidated and socialism would triumph throughout the world, and in half-a-century or a full century the population would again grow, perhaps by over a half."[1]

At that time, one had the impression that in taking this stand Chinese leaders were acting in good faith, misguided by their misunderstanding of the actual prospects of modern world development and motivated by a desire to bring nearer, if only by extreme means, the triumph of socialism on a worldwide scale. Later developments demonstrated, however, that the ultra-revolutionary conceptions of CPC leaders, which expressed their nihilistic attitude to the struggle for peace, were in effect a mere camouflage for their true intentions—to provoke a military conflict between the Soviet Union and the United States so as to attain their great-power, nationalistic objectives.

At the Moscow Meeting of 1957, the CPSU delegation objected to including the formulation "the socialist camp led by the Soviet Union" in the text of the Declaration. However, it was none other than the CPC delegation that stubbornly insisted on its acceptance. And this despite the fact that Chinese leaders already believed, as they allege today, that the CPSU was pursuing a revisionist policy. The meaning

---

[1] *Pravda*, September 22, 1963.

of this allegation is this: the CPSU is a leader but with a flaw; therefore, it should be replaced, which the CPC and Mao Tse-tung are in a position to do.

Nevertheless, in that period the Maoists were not prepared for direct attacks on the CPSU, on the general policy line of the world communist movement. In view of this, as well as of the sentiments inside the CPC, the nationalistic part of its leadership continued manoeuvring. In May 1958, the second session of the Eighth National Congress of the CPC discussed the results of the Moscow Meeting of 1957 and in a special resolution unanimously approved its Declaration and Peace Manifesto, stating that they had opened a new chapter in the present-day international communist movement, had given great inspiration to all working people, all forces in favour of peace, democracy and progress the world over.

4. SINO-SOVIET ECONOMIC, SCIENTIFIC AND TECHNICAL CO-OPERATION IN THE CLOSING YEARS OF THE FIRST FIVE-YEAR PLAN

The Soviet Union, as before, sincerely sought to help the Chinese people in building socialism during the five-year plan period despite some alarming facts of unfriendliness towards the CPSU shown by a section of the CPC leadership. The Communist Party of the Soviet Union was aware of the fact that assistance in building up the foundations of socialism in the PRC was above all help to the Chinese people rather than to the leading group in the CPC which was steadily undermining the fraternal union between the two states.

In 1956-1957, Soviet assistance to China increased. In April 1956 she was visited by a Soviet Government delegation led by Anastas Mikoyan. The delegation continued the talks with the Chinese Government started in Moscow on the further development of Sino-Soviet economic co-operation. On April 7, 1956, important documents were signed at the end of the talks: an agreement on Soviet assistance to China in developing several industries, which provided for the construction of 55 new industrial projects in addition to the 156 projects being built under earlier agreements. These

55 projects included metallurgical, engineering and chemical plants, man-made fibres and plastics factories, electrical and radio engineering industry enterprises, a synthetic liquid fuel plant, electric power stations, as well as research institutions of the aircraft industry. The total cost of equipment, design operations and other Soviet technical aid in the construction of these enterprises was to run into 2,500 million rubles (on the old price scale). The agreement also envisaged increased Soviet aid to China in geological surveys.

This was another illustration of the Soviet Union's honest, internationalist attitude to the Chinese people: indeed, the above listed projects were vitally important for China's economy.

A Sino-Soviet communique was also signed on the construction and operation of a through railway line from Lanchow via Urumchi to the Aktogay station in Soviet territory.

Meanwhile the Soviet Union continued to give China large aid in strengthening her defence capability. In fact, until the time the CPC leadership reversed its policy of co-operation with the Soviet Union China's defence potential had been increasing mainly due to Soviet assistance. Thousands of Soviet advisers shared Soviet military experience with China, all her munitions factories were built with Soviet assistance, while the Chinese army was armed with Soviet military equipment.

On July 25, 1956, a Sino-Soviet protocol on additional goods deliveries in 1956 was signed in Peking. The Soviet Union undertook to supply to China machine-tools, hoisting cranes, compressors, pumps, diesel engines, generating sets, motor vehicles, farm machines, tools and other goods. China was to supply to the Soviet Union sulphur, mercury, caustic soda, soda ash, rice, tea, woollens, etc.

On August 18, 1956, the Soviet Union and China signed in Peking an agreement on joint exploration and research in the Amur river basin to reveal its natural resources, the prospects for developing its productive forces, and on carrying out survey and design operations so as to compile a plan of comprehensive uses of the waters of the river Argun and the upper reaches of the Amur.

In 1956-1960, it was planned to carry out joint exploration of the natural conditions in the Amur river basin, geological and hydropower surveys with a view to regulating the run-off, improving the conditions for navigation, building power dams, developing fisheries, etc.

In 1956, the Soviet Union sent to China a large group of scientists who helped draw up an extensive programme of developing Chinese science within 12 years. China was also assisted in organising research into the peaceful uses of atomic energy. In 1956 alone, 1,800 Chinese students and research students came to the Soviet Union for study. The Soviet Union handed over to China free of charge Soviet Red Cross hospitals in Dairen, Innin and Urumchi.

In 1956, a number of other agreements were concluded between the Soviet Union and China. Among them were:

1) the June 15 agreement on co-operation between the Soviet Union, the Democratic Republic of Vietnam, the People's Republic of China and the Korean People's Democratic Republic for fishing surveys, oceanological and limnological explorations in the Western Pacific (on December 15, 1958 it was joined by Mongolia). The agreement was signed for a term of 10 years. It provided for coordinated research in an important fishing area of the Pacific. The pooling of efforts by the socialist countries enabled more complete data to be obtained on the raw materials and sea food reserves of this area;[1]

2) the July 3 government agreement between the Soviet Union, the PRC and the Korean People's Democratic Republic on co-operation in saving human lives and rescuing ships and aircraft in distress at sea;[2]

3) the protocol of March 30 on the free handover to China of the property of the Russian church mission, church and monastery buildings, real estate in various towns and regions of China, a printshop, a dairy farm in Peking, etc.

On March 13, 1957, the Soviet Union handed over to the Chinese Government free of charge the Soviet Red Cross hospital in Peking, which had been set up in June 1952 and

---

[1] On May 21, 1965, China's Ministry of Foreign Affairs in a note to the Soviet Embassy in Peking stated: "The Government of China believes it unnecessary to prolong the term of this agreement, and it will become ineffective as of June 12, 1966."

[2] In 1966, this agreement was also unilaterally denounced by Chinese authorities.

provided medical aid to 500,000 outpatients and over 9,300 inpatients. More than 300 highly qualified Chinese doctors had been trained and over 300 research papers on medicine had been prepared at the hospital under the direction and with the aid of Soviet specialists. A total of 17,000 medical workers from all regions of China had visited the hospital and studied its work.

The sixth session of the Sino-Soviet commission on scientific and technical co-operation held in Peking in July 1957 was of major importance for developing relations of mutual assistance between the Soviet Union and China.

The session decided to further encourage direct contacts between related government departments, ministries, research and design centres of the Soviet Union and China, and to convene in 1957 scientific and technical conferences on the key problems facing industry and agriculture.

The Soviet Union undertook to hand over to China free of charge design documents and process charts for the construction of hydroelectric power stations and building materials factories, the manufacture of equipment for power stations and metallurgical production, as well as machine-tools and mechanisms for the light industry; process charts for the manufacture of steel, and goods in the rubber, tyres, and pulp-and-paper industries, as well as dyestuffs and medicines; seed and seedlings of agricultural crops, as well as various reference material and information.

The Soviet Union expressed its willingness to receive Chinese specialists and acquaint them with the processes of manufacturing electrical equipment, measuring instruments, hydropower units, and research in the production of some important chemicals.

In exchange, China was to hand over to the Soviet Union free of charge process charts for manufacturing some non-ferrous metals and processing raw materials for their production, for the use of natural stone as refractory material, blueprints of some types of equipment used in manufacturing refractories and at coal-agglomeration factories, of grain-processing and tea-sorting machines, descriptions of processes of hydraulic gobbing in coal mines, etc.

On December 11, 1957, an agreement was signed in Moscow, on scientific co-operation between the Academies of

Sciences of the Soviet Union and China, which provided for joint research and expeditions, co-ordination of work on the key problems of science and technology.

On December 21, 1957, the Soviet Union and China concluded an agreement on the rules of navigation on the border and adjoining rivers and lakes.

The study and use of Soviet know-how contributed greatly to China's successes in building socialism. The appeal "Learn from the Soviet Union" was by no means an empty slogan in those years. The Central Committee of the Communist Party of China, often acting against the will of the nationalistic section of its leadership, supported the line towards studying the experience of the first socialist country. As a result, the Chinese people scored important successes in building up the foundations of socialism, in training Chinese personnel. During the "cultural revolution" this line was qualified as one of the "crimes" of Liu Shao-chi and his supporters.

In 1956-1957, however, the importance of Soviet experience was admitted, if only hypocritically, also by Mao Tsetung, as well as by other Chinese leaders. In his speech "On the Correct Handling of Contradiction Among the People" at an enlarged session of the Supreme State Council on February 27, 1957, Mao Tse-tung declared: "It is perfectly true that we should learn from the good experience of all countries, socialist or capitalist, but the main thing is still to learn from the Soviet Union."[1]

In his speech at the jubilee session of the USSR Supreme Soviet dedicated to the 40th anniversary of the October Revolution, Mao Tse-tung declared: "It is perfectly clear that if after the October Revolution proletarian revolutionaries of different countries ignore or fail to make a serious study of the experience of the Russian revolution, the dictatorship of the proletariat and the building of socialism in the Soviet Union, and, also, if they fail to analyse and apply this experience in creative spirit in compliance with the specific conditions of their countries, they will be unable to assimilate Leninism, which is a new stage in the development of Marxism, to solve

---

[1] Supplement to *People's China*, Peking, No. 13, July 1, 1957, pp. 26-27.

correctly the problems of revolution and construction in their countries. In such an event they will either lapse into dogmatic errors or into revisionist errors."[1]

Mao Tse-tung said further in this speech: "The Communist Party of the Soviet Union applying creatively Marxist-Leninist theory to the solution of practical problems has secured for the Soviet people continuous victories in building a new life.

"The programme of struggle for building communism in the USSR advanced by the 20th CPSU Congress is an outstanding example. There is not the slightest doubt that the continued consolidation and development in various fields of life in the Soviet Union will be facilitated by the wise steps the CPSU Central Committee has taken to overcome the cult of the individual, to advance agriculture, to reorganise the management of industry and construction, to widen the rights of the Union republics and local bodies, to defeat the anti-Party group and strengthen the unity of the Party ranks, to improve Party political work in the Soviet Army, Navy and Air Force, and so on.

"The peoples of all the countries of the world see their future in the successes of Soviet people more and more clearly with every passing day."[2]

On November 6, 1957, at the public meeting in Peking on the occasion of the 40th anniversary of the October Revolution, Liu Shao-chi declared on behalf of the CPC: "The Soviet people today are marching ahead along the path of building communism. The mighty Soviet Union has become the strongest bulwark of universal peace." "Over the past forty years," Liu Shao-chi went on, "the Soviet Union has accumulated rich experience in revolution and construction. Until today no socialist country has yet gained such relatively comprehensive experience as is possessed by the Soviet Union. This experience is a precious asset, is a contribution of the Soviet people to the treasure store of all mankind. Not to cherish this asset is impermissible; it would be against the interests of our people, the cause of socialist revolution and socialist construction."

---

[1] *Druzhba* (Friendship), 1957, No. 8, p. 3.
[2] Ibid., p. 3.

The report "On the First Five-Year Plan for Development of the National Economy" by the Vice-Premier and Member of the CPC Political Bureau, Li Fu-chun, contained a special section entitled "The Importance of Aid from the Soviet Union and the People's Democracies for Construction in Our Country". It was said in this section in particular: "It is common knowledge that the high rates of implementing the first five-year economic development plan of our country are directly attributable to the aid of the Soviet Union and the People's Democracies, especially Soviet aid. . . . It is obvious that the assistance given us by the Soviet Union contributes tremendously to the immense scope, high rates and high technological level of our construction as well as to our avoidance of mistakes."

A sober assessment of China's socio-economic situation and keen attention to Soviet experience helped many leading cadres of the CPC to work out a realistic approach to the conditions and key factors of socialist construction in China and an understanding of the immediate and long-term prospects of her development.

In contrast to Mao Tse-tung's later theory that "agriculture is the basis for the entire national economy", it was repeatedly affirmed in China in that period that nationwide industrialisation was the key factor in building up the material and technological basis for socialism. In his work "On the Correct Handling of Contradiction Among the People" published shortly after the 8th National Congress of the CPC, Mao Tse-tung declared: "Heavy industry is the core of China's economic construction. This must be affirmed."[1] Ideas of industrialisation permeated all concrete economic activities of the CPC in the early years after the victory of the revolution. Referring to the tasks of the transitional period between capitalism and socialism in the report on China's first five-year plan, Vice-Premier Li Fu-chun said: "Socialist industrialisation is the central task of our country during the transition period, and the main link in socialist industrialisation is to give priority to the development of heavy industry. . . . Thus we can see that the policy of giving priority to the development of heavy industry is the only

---

[1] Supplement to *People's China*, Peking, No. 13, July 1, 1957, p. 26.

correct policy to make our country strong and prosperous
and to create happiness for our people. . . ."[1]

Answering those who believed that in China's specific conditions there was no need to be in a hurry to industrialise,
Li Fu-chun stressed, "We believe such views to be
wrong."[2]

In contrast to the Leftist, adventuristic aberrations of the
"Big Leap", some Chinese leaders had a sober approach to
setting the rates of socialist construction in China. In the
same report, Li Fu-chun stated: "In building socialism we
must take practical steps based on existing realities in our
country so as gradually to achieve socialist industrialisation
and socialist transformation. In industrial construction it is
necessary to proceed according to the availability of funds
and technical forces and keep to the policy of concentrating
our main efforts on priority projects. . . . Co-operation in
agriculture and handicrafts is also no light task to be done
in a short time. This is a major achievement which entails
revolutionising the mode of production and mode of life of
hundreds of millions of peasants and tens of millions of handicraftsmen. For the labouring peasants and handicraftsmen
to give up finally the way of the individual small producer
and step out on to the new highroad of socialist development
calls for a step-by-step process, a fairly long period of hard
work and certain necessary transitional forms of organisation."[3]

Characteristically, in passing on to China their rich experience, the Soviet people not only selflessly shared their
advanced know-how with the fraternal Chinese people but
also warned the young republic and its cadres against
miscalculations and errors, which had occasionally been
made in the first socialist country. This was truly fraternal,
internationalist aid which gave China concrete material
benefits, enhanced her prestige and evoked among her working people sentiments of profound gratitude to and affection
for the Soviet Union.

---

[1] Li Fu-chun, "Report on the First Five-Year Plan for Development
of the National Economy". In Supplement to *People's China*, Peking,
August 16, 1955, pp. 6-7.

[2] Ibid.

[3] Ibid., pp. 8-9.

Even in those years, however, alarming instances of Chinese unco-operativeness in practical interstate relations were already in evidence.

In the course of implementing the programme of Sino-Soviet cultural exchanges in 1956, Chinese organisations refused to exchange ideological workers: without offering any excuses, they refused to send to the Soviet Union a delegation of art and museum workers for the purpose of exchanging experience.

Since the end of 1956 secondary and higher schools in China began digressing more and more from Soviet curricula, textbooks, etc., they had broadly used before.

Much fewer articles about the Soviet Union were printed in the Chinese press. In 1955 *Jenmin jihpao,* organ of the CPC Central Committee, published 173 such articles, in 1956, only 98. The publication and circulation of Soviet literature in China also began to be curtailed.

In 1957, the CPC Central Committee decided to close down the Russian-language newspaper *Druzhba* (Friendship), organ of the Sino-Soviet Friendship Society, which was published in 70,000 copies, of which 60,000 were circulated in the Soviet Union, about 9,000 in China and slightly over 1,000 in other socialist countries.

* * *

Despite the nationalistic activities of the Mao Tse-tung group, what was of decisive importance in 1956-1957 was the fact that by that time the Chinese people had already seen with their own eyes the advantages of socialism, appreciated the role of international solidarity, and the Soviet people's disinterested aid. It was precisely in that period that China made a veritable breakthrough in her economic and scientific development, in raising the people's standards of living on the Leninist principles of socialist economic management and with internationalist assistance from the fraternal countries. In the meantime, the struggle within the CPC between the two lines—nationalistic and internationalist—tended to intensify, which had a bearing on Sino-Soviet relations.

CHAPTER IV

NATIONALISTIC, ANTI-SOVIET TENDENCIES IN THE POLICY OF THE CPC LEADERSHIP AND THEIR SOURCES

Analysis of Sino-Soviet relations in 1945-1957 shows that they developed steadily towards greater friendship and co-operation between the two countries and their ruling parties.

In the foregoing chapters, the authors described the development of all-round economic, political, diplomatic, cultural and military co-operation between China and the Soviet Union, and showed the crucial importance of the Soviet Union's fraternal internationalist aid at all the stages of the revolution and socialist construction in China.

In the late fifties, however, great-power chauvinistic forces came on China's political scene, and began playing an increasingly notable role in shaping her home and foreign policies. In time, they seized the key positions in the Party and government and suppressed the internationalist tendencies within the CPC. The question is how could it happen that in the past few years a group of Chinese leaders, while professing its loyalty to the communist cause, has put in jeopardy the country's socialist achievements and gone to the length of announcing openly an ideological and political struggle against the Communist parties and the socialist states, of severing relations with the international proletariat? How could it happen that the nationalistic, anti-Marxist tendencies have prevailed among the Chinese leaders and now determine the political situation in China? Indeed, it is well known that the Communist Party of China has a spectacular revolutionary record; it led the heroic revolution of

the great Chinese nation which traversed the long and difficult path of a bloody struggle for liberation.

It would be pertinent, therefore, to dwell on the objective
and subjective factors which explain this intricate historical
zigzag in the policy of CPC leaders.

1. THE SOCIO-HISTORICAL ROOTS
OF THE PETTY BOURGEOIS NATIONALISTIC VIEWS
OF CPC LEADERS

The Communist Party of China, the views of Chinese
Communists formed under extremely complicated conditions.
The CPC emerged in a semi-colonial, semi-feudal country
extremely backward economically, socially, politically and
culturally.

Although the development of the capitalist mode of production and commodity-money relations, which had been in
progress since the late 19th century, speeded up the disinte-
gration of feudalism, agriculture, which was plagued by
numerous survivals of feudalism, still remained the leading
branch of the Chinese economy. In 1949, Chinese industry
accounted for only 17 per cent to the gross national product,
the rest being supplied by agriculture (almost 70 per cent),
manufactories and handicraft industries.

China's backward economy was coupled with her undevel-
oped social structure. In 1949, there were only 2.5-3 million
industrial workers in China. Among urban residents petty
bourgeois elements prevailed. The peasants accounted for
at least 90 per cent of China's population of 475 million. The
bourgeoisie as a class was weak and split into two groups—
the comprador, mostly big bourgeoisie which had emerged
in the process of collaboration with foreign imperialists, and
the national bourgeoisie which consisted mainly of the middle
sections of the bourgeoisie and the most well-to-do stratum
of the petty bourgeoisie.

The ideological life of Chinese society was pervaded by
various trends of a patriarchal and feudal character, elements of petty bourgeois and bourgeois ideology, anarchism
and Utopian socialism and, finally, religious beliefs (Bud-
dhism, Confucianism), etc. Warlike Great Han nationalism
which the ruling classes of feudal China had been implant-

ing for centuries had struck deep roots in China. The long existence of feudalism in China, which had been isolated from the rest of the world for centuries and had a relatively advanced national culture as compared with that of the neighbouring peoples, often in vassalage to China, generated among her people the habit of regarding their own country, her institutions and culture as something unique and of "divine" origin. In antiquity and the Middle Ages, China held a leading position in East Asia. Her large population, relatively high level of civilisation, isolation from other countries tended to create the illusion of her being the hub of the universe. The ruling elite inculcated such views in the minds of the Chinese for centuries. The striking contrast between these views and the actual situation of China which had been turned into a semi-colony in the later period lent extreme keenness to national feeling and generated a striving to revive her bygone grandeur at all costs.

In China archaic political ideology has always been extremely viable. In the minds of both the ruling circles and the educated strata of Chinese society Sinocentrism became the supreme criterion of all values.

Even most members of the progressive revolutionary intelligentsia, to which many of the present Chinese leaders belonged, viewed Marxism and any other foreign progressive revolutionary theory through the prism of traditional Chinese ideology, above all, Confucianism and legism.

The victory of the Great October Socialist Revolution in Russia which ushered in the epoch of revolutionary transition from capitalism to socialism on a worldwide scale produced a tremendous impact on China. It showed the Chinese people the way to liberation, contributed to the spread of Marxism-Leninism, the ideas of scientific socialism in China. With all-round assistance from the Comintern, Marxist circles and later communist groups sprang up in China, on the basis of which the Communist Party of China was founded in 1921.

The transition from circles to the formation of a party was relatively quick. This was facilitated by the activities of various revolutionary democratic organisations, within which the Marxist groups had emerged. These groups included Communists followed by anarchists, peasant socialists, etc. It was this motley assemblage that later led to ideological vacillations within individual groups of Chinese revolutionaries.

The specific socio-economic situation and political life of Chinese society influenced the development of Marxist theory in China, the political views of certain leaders of the CPC, and caused great difficulties for the revolutionary movement. These difficulties were largely due to the weakness of its working-class section. The young Chinese working class which had no record of a long class struggle was like a small island in the vast ocean of petty bourgeois anarchy. China's working-class movement was in fact making its first faltering steps and lacked the necessary experience. For their social origin the majority of Chinese Communists were typical petty bourgeois revolutionaries with all their inherent shortcomings and vacillations. In October 1923, Voitinsky, who represented the Comintern in China at the time, wrote that in the situation prevailing in China the working-class movement was far from being a factor greater enough to lead the entire national movement against imperialism.

Another source of difficulties was the fact that before 1917 Marxism had not been known in China. This hindered the formation of a truly revolutionary vanguard in the country. The Chinese revolutionary democrats and many Communists, particularly among the intellectuals, believed that the central task was the national rather than social liberation of China. Therefore, the ideas of nationalism prevailed in their minds, pushing the ideas of class struggle to the background. As Mao Tse-tung himself wrote, they saw in the Marxist-Leninist teaching and the October Revolution primarily the key to the "national revival" and "salvation" of China.

The weakness of the proletariat, combination of the tasks of the socialist, anti-feudal and anti-imperialist revolutions in a common revolutionary torrent, the complicated ideological situation—all influenced the development of Marxist thought in China and the political views of certain Communist Party leaders. The Communist Party of China and its leadership often admitted to their ranks persons who called themselves Marxists and proletarian internationalists and were really prepared to fight selflessly for the liberation of their country but were, in effect, very distantly related to

Marxism and the working-class movement. This accounts for the fact that CPC leaders who followed in the main the right, internationalist road and fought heroically for the working-class cause, were liable to slip and err.

The plenary meeting of the CPC Central Committee held in November 1927 stated in its resolution: "One of the main organisational shortcomings of the CPC, which has great political implications, is the fact that almost the whole leading body of our Party activists consists not of workers, not even of poorer peasants but of petty bourgeois intellectuals. The CPC emerged as a political movement and as a party when the Chinese proletariat had not yet developed into a class and the class movement of the workers and peasants was still in embryo. The upsurge in China of the national liberation movement in which a tremendous role was played originally by the bourgeoisie, particularly the petty bourgeois intelligentsia, started long before the growth of the class awareness and class struggle of the exploited masses. In that period, the most radical elements of the petty bourgeoisie joined the Party, which was the extreme left wing of the national liberation movement. It was these elements that made up the core of the Communist Party of China. The mass inflow of workers and poorer peasants into the Party began relatively late as the revolutionary class movement of the working people progressed. For this reason, the leading role in the CPC remained in the hands of persons with a petty bourgeois family background. Stirred by the wave of revolutionary upsurge and enthusiasm of the initial period, lacking adequate theoretical knowledge of Marxism-Leninism, the experience of the international proletarian movement, unconnected with the exploited grass-root sections of the Chinese people and standing aloof from the class struggle of the workers and peasants, many of these revolutionary petty bourgeois elements, far from being digested by the CPC and remade into consistent proletarian revolutionaries, introduced into it all the political waverings, inconsistency, indecision, inability for organisation, non-proletarian habits and traditions, prejudices and illusions characteristic of petty bourgeois revolutionaries."

In an article entitled "The Victory of Marxism-Leninism in China" and dedicated to the 30th anniversary of the CPC,

Peng Chen pointed out that in the past the Chinese Communist Party remained for a long time in the rural areas which were split up by the enemy. For this reason, the slackness, subjectivism, sectarianism, bureaucracy, liberalism, adventurism, capitulationism, and other tendencies characteristic of the rural community and petty bourgeoisie are sometimes reflected in our Party.[1]

Among other objective factors which had a negative impact on the shaping of the ideology and policy of the CPC leadership it is necessary to mention such as the absence in China of democratic traditions in political and economic life, the specific role of the army in the revolution and in later party activities and, finally, the cultural backwardness of China's population.

The negative effect of the absence of democratic traditions in China was aggravated by implementing the revolution in conditions of a long guerrilla war and isolation from the country's cultural and political centres. In this war the revolutionary army and the Communist Party practically merged into one. Since the mid-thirties to 1949 servicemen accounted for over 80 per cent of the Party membership. Not only did the army resist the counter-revolution by force of arms but it also conducted on behalf of the Party political work among the population in the liberated areas and directed economic activities. In this way the army provided a direct link between the Party and the masses. It became traditional and habitual for CPC cadres to handle all the problems of the revolution and construction through the army and by military methods. The Party began to be ruled by decree, and army subordination was substituted for democratic centralism.

China's large population created in the minds of her leaders the illusion that her manpower resources were inexhaustible. This led to a drastic depreciation of the importance of the individual in China, indifference to the destinies and conditions of life of the people, the idea that "the people is a blank sheet of paper" permitting and justifying arbitrary action in relation to the masses, gambling with the fate of millions upon millions of people.

---

[1] Supplement to *People's China*, Peking, Vol. 4, No. 1, July 1, 1951, p. 8.

Nevertheless, despite these extraordinary difficulties a nucleus of revolutionary Marxists with a good theoretical background and practical experience, staunch supporters of proletarian internationalism gradually formed within the CPC.

Two trends became more and more salient in the CPC: the Marxist internationalist trend guided by the ideas of the October Revolution, and the nationalistic trend, petty bourgeois in its ideological essence. The course and outcome of the struggle between these two trends were substantially influenced by the brutal reign of terror against the Communist Party after the Chiang Kai-shek coup in 1927. The Communists were persecuted with equal hatred by the central Kuomintang Government, the militarist cliques in the provinces, troops of the Western imperialists and the Japanese invaders. Communists displayed exemplary selflessness and heroism in the battles for the working people's liberation. Most of the time-tested leaders of the Communist Party of China, however, were killed in action. The Party organisations of the working-class centres suffered the heaviest casualties.

Thousands of Communists died at the hands of Kuomintang troops and police. Within the first six months of the Chiang Kai-shek coup, the CPC membership dwindled to one-fifth—from 50,000 to 10,000. In the early thirties, the Party suffered heavy losses caused by the repression of Communists in Shanghai as a result of treachery in which Kang Sheng was implicated.

By the beginning of 1935, the majority of Party veterans including many experienced leaders had been killed, and underground Party organisations in towns destroyed. This was a veritable tragedy for the Communist Party of China.

All Party work was concentrated, in fact, within the army units under the control of the CPC and at several strongholds far away from the country's main political centres and separated from the mass of the Chinese proletariat. For a long time, the Party drew its membership, above all, from the peasantry, the petty bourgeoisie, the people owing their origin to the exploiting classes and from the intelligentsia. The influx of workers into the CPC practically ceased, the influence of the petty bourgeois sentiment in the Party increased.

It was precisely in that period that nationalistic elements consolidated their positions in the Communist Party leadership weakened by the casualties sustained and in the army. They were leaning on the support of the army, on the one hand, and of the petty bourgeois, mostly peasant masses and declassed elements, on the other.

It will be recalled that in the specific situation of that period the nationalistic elements within the CPC had to follow for objective reasons the main stream of the Chinese people's revolutionary struggle. The enthusiasm of the masses, the vital need for international support, above all, from the Soviet Union and all liberation forces, dictated for Chinese Communist Party leaders the only possible way to follow, one of revolutionary struggle. For all their nationalistic ambitions, the Maoists could not but reckon with the fact that the political situation at home and abroad gave them no other alternative.

Needless to say, one should not forget about the dual role of nationalism during the struggle for national liberation: its progressive importance in stirring up patriotic sentiments, uniting the nation for a struggle against foreign invaders, and its conservatism expressed in opposing one's own nation to other nations, in national isolationism. In the latter case, nationalism may grow into chauvinism and even merge with racialism.

This dual role of nationalism in strikingly illustrated by the history of China which has strong traditions of Great Han chauvinism. During the anti-imperialist, democratic revolution, however, nationalism, or rather national factors, provided the ideological basis for uniting the mass of the people, at times pushing to the background even their class differentiation. When the anti-imperialist, democratic revolution was completed, however, nationalism exhausted its progressive potential and became reactionary in full, giving food to chauvinistic survivals, hampering the implantation within the Party of the principles of proletarian internationalism and Marxism-Leninism as the sole ideological foundation of the new type of revolution. Therefore, a bitter struggle between the two lines—the nationalistic and the internationalist—flared up within the CPC and Chinese society as a whole.

The Communist Party of China successfully coped with its role as leader in the struggle against oppression by foreign imperialism and carried the popular revolution in 1949 to victory.

In the early fifties, a vigorous campaign was launched in China for uprooting the vestiges of feudalism; sweeping social reforms were implemented, the tasks of the bourgeois democratic revolution were completed and conditions created for successful construction of socialism. The vast assistance to China from the Soviet Union and other socialist countries, the application of international experience in building socialism—all served to hamper the manoeuvres of the nationalistic elements, to strengthen the internationalist trends in China and within the CPC.

Toward the late fifties, however, the situation changed. More and more facts were reported about the utter disregard for the theory and practice of scientific socialism on the part of Mao Tse-tung and his following. In the light of the past history of Maoism this change was not accidental, although it cannot be considered an inevitable, fatal outcome of earlier developments.

In the conditions of a peasant, petty bourgeois country, Lenin's instructions about how vital it is for a Communist party to plan a correct policy, to win support from the working class, to be able to lead the peasantry without being dissolved in its midst are of special significance. The current developments in China show what may happen when these instructions are ignored and the party allows itself to be swamped by petty bourgeois anarchy, when its international links with other fraternal parties and countries are broken.

In the policy of CPC leaders, nationalism and adventurism characteristic of petty bourgeois revolutionaries gradually took the upper hand.

The possibility of a revival of nationalistic sentiments in China was at one time unequivocally pointed out by the CPC Central Committee. In an editorial entitled "Another Look at the Historical Experience of the Dictatorship of the Proletariat", the newspaper *Jenmin jihpao* stated: "We Chinese ought to remember particularly well that in the period of the Han, Tan, Ming and Chin dynasties our country also was a great empire, and although during approximately one hundred years, since the latter half of the 19th century, our country, which had become an object of aggression, was reduced to a semi-colony, although our country today is still backward economically and culturally, nevertheless, when the conditions change, the tendency toward great-power chauvinism will undoubtedly become a grave danger if it is not averted in every way. It should also be pointed out that at present this danger has already become manifest among some of our functionaries."[1]

The tendencies toward great-power chauvinism increased when China's economic power grew in the course of socialist construction.

The building of socialism requires definite prerequisites: the material, such as advanced industry, and the social, such as the industrial proletariat. A country in which such prerequisites are still taking shape can build socialism successfully only when leaning on all-round political, material, scientific and technological aid from the world socialist system, on its experience as well as on the support of the world working-class movement. China's example has again corroborated the validity of Lenin's instruction to the effect that the task of the Communist party in an economically backward country oppressed in the past consists not only in stimulating in every way the formation and growth of the working class, its political education but also in maintaining the links of the country's working class and all working people with the world working class and uniting with the proletarians of other countries in a common struggle.

Gradually, the petty bourgeois, hegemonistic views of the Maoists became increasingly predominant in the CPC leadership. This became manifest particularly strikingly after the early forties.

Repeated attempts have been made in China to misrepresent the history of relations between the world communist movement and the CPC. Apologists of the cult of Mao, twisting the truth, depict him as the author of all the main principles of the strategy and tactics of the Chinese revolution, declaring that the Comintern and the CPSU only interfered with the CPC shaping a correct policy line. The

---

[1] *Jenmin jihpao,* December 29, 1956.

reason for this crude lie is not only political servility. The Maoist "theoreticians" seek to revise in nationalistic spirit the entire history of the Chinese revolution and the Communist Party of China.

Publications on history brought out in Peking pass over in silence the international and internal factors which secured the victory of the Chinese revolution, play down the role of the world communist movement. At the same time, they deliberately distort the history of struggle between the nationalistic and internationalist trends within the CPC, embellish the political image of the present Chinese leaders, whitewash their foul play in intra-Party struggle. A distinctive feature of such publications is immoderate exaggeration of Mao Tsetung's role at different stages of the Chinese revolution, suppression of all evidence exposing the nationalistic elements who have wormed their way to key positions in the CPC.

2. NATIONALISTIC TRENDS WITHIN THE CPC IN THE EARLY 40s

The 40s hold a special place in the history of the CPC and its relations with the international communist movement. Between 1941 and 1945, a campaign for "adjustment of the work style" was carried out in Yenan, the centre of the liberated areas. It was, in fact, a campaign of doing away with the veteran cadres, primarily those educated in the Soviet Union. The latest "cultural revolution" was, in effect, a replica of this campaign against the communist internationalists in Yenan.

With the progress of the campaign, anti-Soviet, nationalistic sentiments became more manifest among CPC members, the cult of Mao was whipped up, and self-styled "theoreticians" came on the scene to challenge the applicability of Lenin's teachings to the conditions of the Chinese revolution. Mao Tse-tung began to be openly called a Chinese Lenin.

As far back as the early 40s, the thesis that Mao Tse-tung's ideas were allegedly a complete system of views and a special contribution to Marxism-Leninism was widely advertised in propagandist literature of the CPC. It was stated in the CPC report to its Seventh Congress held in 1945 that Mao Tse-tung "...is a creative and talented Marxist, combining as he does the universal truth of Marxism—the highest ideology of mankind—with the concrete practice of the Chinese revolution".[1] And further: "What Comrade Mao Tse-tung has done ... is precisely to unite the theories of Marxism-Leninism with the actual practice of the Chinese revolution, thus giving rise to Chinese communism—Mao Tse-tung's theory of the Chinese revolution."[2] It was stated at the Seventh Congress that Mao Tse-tung transformed Marxism from its European form into Chinese form.

Chinese theoreticians started ever more persistently to advocate the view that the significance of the October Revolution was limited to the imperialist countries of Europe, whereas the Chinese revolution was a model for the colonial and dependent countries.

Wang Ming, a CPC veteran, who was a member of its leadership for years, writing about the campaign in Yenan in the 40s, said that in preparing it and in the course of conducting it, Mao Tse-tung himself repeatedly said that by carrying out the campaign he wanted to achieve three aims: 1) to substitute Leninism by Maoism; 2) to write the history of the Chinese Communist Party as the history of Mao Tse-tung alone; 3) to elevate the personality of Mao Tse-tung above the Central Committee and the entire Party. Why did he have to do that? He himself replied: this would give him two opportunities, first, to capture the chief leading place in the Party leadership and all power in the Party in his own hands; second, if he already has taken the first place in the Party leadership, no one should ever be able to oust him.

The campaign for "adjustment of the work style" proceeded in three stages. The first stage (from the autumn of 1941 to the spring of 1942) consisted in the study of 22 documents—mostly speeches by Mao Tse-tung and his supporters, the task being to portray Mao as a great theoretician and a wellspring of new ideas.

The second stage (from the spring of 1942 to the spring of 1943) was devoted to ideological screening of the cadres—

[1] Liu Shao-chi, *On the Party*, Peking, 1954, p. 9.
[2] Ibid., p. 34.

which boiled down, in effect, to harshly doing away with the Party functionaries detested by Mao. The third stage (from March 1943 to the Seventh Congress of the CPC in 1945) was a campaign of hunting down "spies" and purging the Party.

As it follows from the content and character of the first stage, its central task was to inculcate it in the minds of CPC members that the "ideas of Mao Tse-tung" were the dominating ideology of the Party, to substitute them for Marxist-Leninist theory. In the second and third stages of the campaign, which was rather a wholesale purge, a reign of psychological terror was established in the Party and the liberated areas administered from Yenan, and conditions were provided for the removal and liquidation of persons opposed to Mao Tse-tung and his following.

As Wang Ming recalls, Mao Tse-tung artificially divided the entire Party into two groupings—the "dogmatic" and the "empiristic". He placed all the Communists who had studied in the Soviet Union or engaged in ideological and political work and also those who socially originated from the intelligentsia into the so-called "pro-Soviet and dogmatic" grouping. . . .[1].

The massive repressive measures against those who did not support Mao Tse-tung were carried out as a campaign of exposing "spies" started in March 1943. The witch-hunt organised in Yenan was accompanied by numerous meetings where speakers made threatening statements and demanded confession of anti-Party activities, and repentance.

The usurpers of the key posts in the Party forced its leading executives and rank-and-file members to write confessions of their "sins". The sponsors of this campaign sought, above all, to make the accused slander the CPSU and the Soviet Union. Another standard component of these "confessions" was inordinate extolment of Mao Tse-tung and self-flagellation for support of the views and principles of the Comintern. Such "corrective methods" were intended to undermine the Chinese Communists' faith in genuine Marxism and proletarian internationalism.

---

[1] Wang Ming, *China. Cultural Revolution or Counter-Revolutionary Coup?*, Moscow, 1969, pp. 47-48.

During the 1942-1943 campaign for "adjustment of the work style" Chinese who had visited or studied in the Soviet Union were urged to make statements of "repentance" slandering the Soviet Union and the CPSU. Any pretext was seized upon to sow mistrust in the Comintern and the CPSU. Communists were induced to believe that the Comintern was allegedly giving instructions detrimental to the cause of the Chinese revolution, that Chinese students in the Soviet Union were antagonised to the CPC with the connivance of the Comintern and trained as "foreign lackeys of the comprador type" who would have to "usurp leadership in the Communist Party of China". The statements of "repenters" at the Seventh Congress of the CPC in 1945 were of the same nature. Thus, a suspicious and often openly hostile attitude to the Soviet Union was being implanted already in those years.

Thus, as far back as the early 40s, ideological and organisational prerequisites were created within the CPC for replacing Marxism-Leninism by "Chinese Marxism", and the way was cleared for making "Mao Tse-tung's ideas" the dominating ideology in the Communist Party of China.

As the Maoists consolidated their positions in the CPC leadership their nationalistic sentiments became more and more strikingly manifest. It was only natural, therefore, that they displayed a devil-may-care attitude to their internationalist duties.

In the hardest early period of the war against Nazi Germany and its allies the Comintern and the Soviet Union raised before the CPC leadership the question of co-ordinated action to hold back Japanese forces from an attack on the Soviet Union. On June 27, 1941, the leader of the group of Soviet officials in Yenan reported to Moscow that in accordance with the instructions received he had had a meeting with CPC leaders to discuss the question of aiding the Soviet Union in case of an attack by Japan. The Chinese leaders replied that they had already planned a number of measures, and in conclusion of the meeting Chu Teh assured the Soviet side that in the event of Japan's attack on the Soviet Union, the Eighth Route Army would throw all its forces against the Japanese to give the Soviet Union effective support. On July 3, 1941, CPC leaders reaffirmed this statement.

Actually, however, no practical measures were taken. In July 1941, Yenan was informed that the Japanese were sending regular troops to the mainland and effective measures were requested to prevent their concentration in the direction of Peiping-Kalgan and Pao-tow, i.e., against the Soviet Union, and to disturb normal traffic on the railways leading to these centres. This request, just as others, was ignored by CPC leaders.

As recalled by witnesses of these events, on September 3, 1941, Mao Tse-tung was again approached with the question of possible actions of the CPC in case of Japan making war on the Soviet Union. He responded with confusing and evasive statements interspersed with endless reservations and containing demands to the Soviet Union which were obviously unrealistic in the prevailing situation. When asked to tell frankly, without any "ifs", what the CPC would be able to undertake if Japan attacked the Soviet Union, Mao abruptly wound up the discussion on this crucial question, accusing the Soviet representative of inability for dialectical thinking. All later attempts to agree on co-ordinated action were obstructed, too.

The recommendations of the Comintern to implement the tactics of a united front of the Communist Party of China with the Kuomintang were called upon to greatly promote the struggle against the Japanese militarists and the development of the Chinese revolution. These recommendations derived from the general policy of the Comintern to develop mass movements within the framework of a united international front of struggle in defence of China, the countries enslaved by the German Nazis, in defence of the Soviet Union. They provided for the immediate establishment of a united national front in China, for which it was necessary to set up contacts with all forces opposed to fascism.

The Comintern persistently called on the CPC Central Committee to step up the operations of China's Red Army against the Japanese invaders, to consolidate the united front of the Chinese people, which would greatly contribute to an early defeat of the Japanese militarists. The Maoists, however, while swearing allegiance to their internationalist duty, procrastinated in fact and evaded in every way compliance with advice and requests from the Comintern.

CPC leaders were deeply divided over the issue of the united front. The group of internationalists was opposed by the nationalistic elements who denied the need for a united front, for joint actions with the Kuomintang in organising a nation-wide struggle against the Japanese aggressors. When the absolute necessity of forming such a front had been made clear by developments, Mao Tse-tung pretended to be its active supporter. Today, however, chroniclers of Mao's entourage are seeking to prove that the united front tactics are Mao Tse-tung's greatest personal contribution to Marxism-Leninism.

The narrow-minded, nationalistic policy of a group of CPC leaders led in 1941-1942 to a steady decline in the operations of Chinese communist troops against Japan. Mao Tse-tung explained these tactics by an intention to avoid casualties, defeat the Kuomintang, to seize power in China and, leaning on the assistance of the Soviet Union, Britain and the USA, to liberate China from the Japanese invaders.

The passiveness of the nationalistic wing in the CPC on the issue of war against militarist Japan at a time when the interests of the international proletariat, the joint struggle against fascism required an activation of operations against Japan was yet another example of departure from internationalism.

Mao Tse-tung put forward this principle: ten per cent of the forces available is to be used for the war against Japan, twenty per cent against the Kuomintang, and seventy per cent for building up the forces in being. In accordance with this principle for a number of years the Eighth Route Army and the Fourth New Army abstained from active operations against Japanese troops. The following view was also circulated: why annoy the Japanese and ask for trouble? It is wiser to coexist with the enemy on a live-and-let-live principle. A Soviet war correspondent reported from Yenan in January 1943: "All military units have been ordered to abstain from operations against Japanese troops and to retreat when attacked. A ceasefire should be sought whenever possible. ... All the districts, every unit of CPC troops carry on trade with the Japanese rear; in the headquarters, there is more talk about trade exchanges than military operations."

Thus, in the 40s the Maoists were as little concerned with the internationalist duties of the CPC in general and toward the Soviet Union in particular as they are concerned today with China's fulfilment of her internationalist duty toward the socialist nations.

3. NATIONALISTIC ANTI-SOVIET TRENDS AMONG CPC LEADERS IN 1945-1949

The misguided tendencies in the political line and practices of Chinese leaders became strikingly obvious also on the eve of the victory of the revolution. One example of this is the idea of China's self-isolation from the socialist countries, the Soviet Union, in particular, advanced in the late 40s. This nationalistic approach to assessment of the prospects of the Chinese revolution would greatly delay social changes in China, the development of the democratic revolution into a socialist one.

Mao Tse-tung stubbornly advocated the idea that the transition to building socialism in China was a very distant prospect, that China should go through a fairly long period of a "new democracy" before the question of socialism assumed practical importance. Significantly, Mao Tse-tung saw "favourable conditions" for this, in effect, in China's long-continued self-isolation. He proposed, therefore, that after the victory of the revolution, the Soviet Union and other socialist countries should wait with their recognition of China, because it would be better for her to gain recognition first from the great imperialist powers—the USA, Britain, France, etc.

This plan was based on a narrow nationalistic view of the Chinese revolution. The nationalistic elements within the CPC were already hatching up the idea of making China a third force gambling on contradictions between the two world social systems. It was not before this idea met with a determined rebuff that Mao renounced it at the 2nd Plenary Meeting of the Seventh Central Committee of the CPC held in March 1949.

In his article "On the Democratic Dictatorship of the People", Mao Tse-tung appeared as a zealous advocate of alliance with the Soviet Union, of a line of "keeping to one side".

Other instances of zigzags and waverings of the nationalistic elements are also known. Shortly before the defeat of the Kuomintang, Mao Tse-tung maintained that the CPC should not be in a hurry to capture China's main industrial centres, such as Nanking, Shanghai, and others. He alleged that it was unwise for the CPC to seize large cities because of a shortage of cadres, since most of the Communist Party members were peasants.

Mao Tse-tung did not pay due attention to strengthening the proletarian stratum within the Communist Party and overestimated the role of the peasantry. Characteristically, he stated that in spite of China's backwardness as compared with Russia, the Chinese peasants had more political awareness than all British workers and many American workers.

Such statements aroused legitimate concern. CPC leaders were patiently given competent advice. Efforts were made to persuade Mao Tse-tung of the need to enhance Party influence on China's working class, step up work in the biggest industrial centres, to keep the purity of Party's ranks, to widen Party activities within the trade unions, etc.

The process of infiltration of the Communist Party of China and its leadership by alien elements became particularly intensive during the civil war of 1946-1949, when Kuomintang divisions, corps and whole armies including their headquarters and generals went over to the side of China's People's Liberation Army. At that time, the CPC drew its membership mostly from non-proletarian sections holding the petty bourgeois and nationalistic views of the Kuomintang.

It should be noted that as far back as 1936 the Comintern, in a message to the CPC Central Committee, emphasised its concern about the decision to admit to the Party all applicants, irrespective of their social background, about the Party being unafraid of infiltration of its ranks by careerists, as well as about the reported impending admission to the Party even of Chang Hsueh-liang (a militarist and dyed-in-the-wool reactionary.—*Authors*.). The message also described as an error the indiscriminate admission to the Red Army ranks of students and ex-officers of other armies, the admission of members of the propertied classes to political administration in the liberated areas.

CPC leaders, however, not only showed a lack of concern for keeping pure the ranks of the CPC as a Marxist-Leninist party, but adopted the directly opposite policy line. A mass of people, who had joined the CPC during and after the Yenan period, had gone only through a course of Maoist "re-education" and "repentance" before they became a reserve of personnel for political bodies, editorial offices, the officers' corps of the Red Army, etc. The movement for "adjustment of the work style" in the early 40s was directed exclusively against supporters of the Comintern line who did not share the views of Mao Tse-tung, but it was also, in effect, an amnesty for really anti-Party elements. On the eve of the Seventh Congress of the CPC in 1945, the Maoists granted another amnesty to anti-Party bourgeois elements, declaring that the roots of Left deviations and Right opportunist errors had been torn up and that all comrades who had made mistakes in the past should be encouraged to work for the benefit of the Party without any prejudice, if they had admitted their mistakes and taken steps to remedy them. This amnesty was applied, as a rule, to anti-Soviet elements who accepted "Mao's ideas" without reservation. This was a peculiar precursor of the "cultural revolution" unleashed in China in the latter half of the 60s.

In every period of the Chinese revolution, the international communist movement and the CPSU consistently pursued a policy of all-round support for and assistance to the Communist Party of China. Genuine internationalists could not have another attitude to the Chinese people who had risen to a struggle for their liberation, to the Chinese Communists who led them. Furthermore, for all the serious failures of the leaders of the CPC it was an important ally of the progressive forces fighting imperialism. For its part, the CPC, leaning on the support of the international proletariat, drawing on the experience of the CPSU and tremendous assistance from the Soviet Union, fulfilled its role of leader of the Chinese people's national liberation and revolutionary war and brought the revolution to victory.

4. ANTI-SOVIET ASPECTS OF CPC LEADERS' POLICY IN THE EARLY YEARS OF THE PRC

In that period, the anti-Sovietism of some CPC leaders seemed to be rather an annoying discordance in the general atmosphere of friendship and co-operation; nevertheless, its manifestations were not accidental and merit attention for a more comprehensive analysis of Sino-Soviet relations. For example, even when signing the Sino-Soviet Treaty of Friendship, Alliance and Mutual Assistance CPC leaders displayed some distrust and suspicion towards the Soviet Union. Chinese leaders were dissatisfied with the Soviet loan of "only" 300 million dollars, unwilling to reckon with the difficulties the Soviet Union itself had to overcome to heal the wounds of the war as early as possible.

In later years, too, Chinese leaders sought aid from the Soviet Union without regard for its possibilities. In some years nationalistic elements within the CPC claimed as much as 80 per cent of the Soviet Union's annual output of certain types of machine-tools. In October 1951, Mao Tse-tung, in a talk with the Soviet Ambassador, said that not all Chinese, and not even all of the Party members agreed with the policy of friendship with the Soviet Union. What mattered, however, was the position of Chinese leaders themselves rather than the sentiments of rank-and-file Party members.

Quite a few cases were reported of Chinese leaders conniving, in effect, at the nationalistic sentiments of Party functionaries, reducing the level and scope of activities in educating the Party and people in a spirit of internationalism and Sino-Soviet friendship. Early in 1952, the Sino-Soviet Friendship Society decided to observe a Sino-Soviet friendship week, timing it to the first anniversary of the Sino-Soviet Treaty of Friendship, Alliance and Mutual Assistance. Corresponding instructions were sent to the provinces and preparations for the Sino-Soviet friendship week got under way throughout the country. Seven days before the week was to be opened, however, it was cancelled by the CPC Central Committee under the pretext that Chinese institutions were busy with other political campaigns.

At that time, all such facts seemed to be accidental, but in the light of China's "cultural revolution" they assumed a totally different aspect as deliberate steps by CPC leaders towards an open political struggle against the CPSU.

In 1953-1954, measures were taken to wind up the activities of the Sino-Soviet Friendship Society in disseminating the ideas of internationalism and information about the Soviet Union.

As far back as the early years of people's power, Soviet specialists were sometimes wrongly employed: they were shut off from production, the routine work of ministries and government departments, so that they were unable to give competent advice with due regard for the situation in corresponding sectors of the economy. In some institutions, Soviet specialists were charged with petty routine duties and deprived of the possibility to give recommendations on important problems. Often enough, their advice was ignored, although it had been approved by leading government executives. Managers of institutions and enterprises, who had agreed in words with proposals of Soviet specialists, at times did the exact opposite. Later, in 1958-1959, this line developed into a full-scale campaign of denigrating Soviet know-how. This question will be discussed below.

In the early period after the proclamation of the PRC, great-power chauvinism and adventurism manifested themselves in China's external affairs as well. At the trade union conference of Asia and Oceania held in Peking in December 1949, the Maoists laid claim to leadership of the revolutionary movement in Asia. They maintained that the situation in the countries of Asia and Oceania was largely similar to that in China prior to 1949, and, therefore, the revolutionaries should emulate her experience and operate under the direction of Peking. The Chinese delegates declared that the path chosen by the Chinese people to defeat the imperialists and their henchmen and to establish the People's Republic of China should be followed by the peoples of many colonial and semi-colonial countries struggling for national independence and people's democracy. "This path is the path of Comrade Mao Tse-tung", they declared. Delegates of many countries opposed these views, and the Maoists had to retreat.

In 1950-1951, the Maoists attempted to foist on the Communist Parties of Indonesia and India programmes ignoring their domestic situation and providing for emulation of China's experience in the war of liberation (formation of peasant armies, establishment of liberated areas). Joseph Stalin expressed his determined opposition to this line.

These were so far isolated incidents. China was still an economically backward country and needed great assistance from the socialist states to strengthen her defence capability and develop her economy, so the Maoists did not dare to be too outspoken.

The nationalistic, anti-Soviet tendencies characteristic of Mao Tse-tung and his entourage even in the early period of the Chinese revolution developed on a wider scale after Stalin's death. Mao Tse-tung, who claimed leadership of the communist movement, worked out a definite strategy and tactics, whose meaning became clearly transparent in a later period: to take full advantage of Soviet economic, military and other aid in order to secure the material prerequisites for implementing his policy; simultaneously, to undermine in every way Soviet international prestige, to hinder the fulfilment of plans of building communism in the Soviet Union. His designs were hampered not only by the Soviet Union but also by the Chinese people, Chinese Communists, who were well aware of the Soviet Union's great role in building socialism in China.

Nationalistic elements in the leadership of the CPC sought to prevent intercourse between the Chinese people and Soviet specialists who had come to China to help her build socialism. In May 1954, the State Council, in a special injunction circulated in the provinces, categorically forbid all Chinese except personnel of the foreign relations departments of administrative bodies to have private relations with Soviet citizens coming to China on business.

The Chinese press in the provinces drastically cut down space set aside for articles about the Soviet Union. Because of the small circulation of the national newspapers and the narrow scale of broadcasting services in China, the bulk of the population was inadequately and sporadically informed about the achievements and life of the Soviet people.

In 1953, Mao Tse-tung began removing little by little all those who did not support his nationalistic, anti-Soviet line. Whatever labels may be used today for couching Mao Tse-tung's attacks on Wang Ming, Kao Kang, Peng Te-huai, Chang Wen-tien and others, his harsh dealing with many leading cadres of the CPC had only one goal—to clear away the obstacles to implementing his petty bourgeois, chauvinistic policy. As evidenced by reports on the "cultural revolution" one of the main "crimes" of these leaders of the CPC was their friendly feelings for the Soviet Union and other socialist countries.

As it transpired later, the struggle in the Chinese leadership between the Marxist-Leninists, internationalists on the one hand, and the Maoists, great-power chauvinists, nationalists on the other, became increasingly bitter in the early 50s. The arrest and tragic death in 1955 of Kao Kang, member of the CPC Political Bureau and Vice-Chairman of the PRC was an alarming signal. Various, absolutely unfounded charges were raised against him. His main "offence" was never mentioned—his devotion to friendship with the Soviet Union, persistent struggle against the nationalistic deviation, for the Party's internationalist policy.

Mao was aware, however, that much could still be received from the socialist countries to strengthen China which needed protection by the socialist community. What was most important, the sentiments within the CPC Central Committee and the Party in favour of developing friendly relations with the USSR and pursuing a flexible and reasonable policy were so strong that Mao and his following had to reckon with them. All the more so, as after seizing power the CPC set about tackling the key tasks of the socialist revolution in the political and economic fields.

China had to grapple with the most difficult problems of economic rehabilitation, to organise the machinery of state. These problems were complicated by the shortage of administrative, technical, military and other specialist personnel. China badly needed political support and economic aid from abroad.

It will be recalled that in their nationalistic waverings CPC leaders did not abandon the hopes of finding a way out of their difficulties in leaning on US support. There is more evidence to the effect that in the 40s they made a series of attempts at reaching mutual understanding with the American imperialist circles, but such attempts could not then be successful. Washington still relied on the Chiang Kai-shek regime for preserving American influence in China and looked with suspicion on the advances of CPC leaders. Mao's closest associates took care to avoid any actions likely to alienate the Americans and the British. They opposed, for example, the participation of Japan and India in the trade union conference of Asia and Oceania held in Peking in 1949, fearing irritation on the part of Washington and London. Late in 1949, Chinese leaders declared that Soviet specialists ought not to be sent to Shanghai and Taishan, because large American and British interests were concentrated there.

The Korean war which flared up in 1950 aggravated Sino-American relations, cutting off for a long time the way to a collusion between the nationalistic CPC leaders and the US ruling circles and compelling Chinese leaders to wider co-operation with the Soviet Union.

CPC leaders badly needed Soviet aid and support from the CPSU. An atmosphere of tremendous revolutionary enthusiasm prevailed in China, the ideas of socialism, friendship with the Soviet people spread throughout the multi-millioned mass of her working people. They viewed the Soviet Union as the greatest factor of their victory, liberation from the Japanese yoke, from the reactionary Chiang regime.

Mao Tse-tung and his following also had to reckon with the existence in the Party, its leadership in particular, of forces favouring a union and friendship with the Soviet Union as one of the key prerequisites for the victory of socialism in China.

All these factors delayed to a certain extent the development of nationalistic, anti-Soviet trends within the CPC and its leadership, which became so strikingly manifest later.

In that situation, the Peking leaders were compelled to put off the implementation of their great-power, nationalistic plans. They disguised themselves as friends of the Soviet Union so as to solicit its aid in building up the material and technological base required for attaining their goals.

This circumstance made it extremely difficult to detect the true character and the main purpose of the special policy line of the Maoist leadership of the CPC in the international communist movement.

5. FACTORS OF GROWTH OF NATIONALISTIC TENDENCIES WITHIN THE CPC

The effect of the objective factors responsible for the emergence and development of the nationalistic, petty bourgeois trend within the CPC was aggravated by serious subjective factors connected with the activities of the group of Chinese leaders headed by Mao Tse-tung. The harm caused by these activities was made worse by grave miscalculations and errors in the Party line, crude violations of the Leninist principles of Party work.

Soviet specialists who worked in China described the Right opportunist practices in the CPC, one of whose major aspects was the attitude to the working class. They noted that after the victory of the Chinese revolution, CPC leaders took no radical steps to provide political and economic conditions under which the working class would feel itself the ruling class holding the reins of power. The workers continued to drag out a miserable life of semi-starvation. According to labour legislation, the working day was to last 12 hours. The wages remained as low as under Kuomintang rule. No legislation on labour protection and social security was adopted. The rules regulating relations between labour and capital approved in November 1949, far from developing the main principles laid down in the General Programme, meant, in effect, their renunciation.

The role of the working class in the revolutionary remaking of the country was, as before, underestimated by CPC leaders, who regarded the workers as immature, illiterate, politically backward people who had failed to take an active part in the revolution.

Although for many years the CPC had been leaning on the peasants who were the massive reserve of the People's Revolutionary Army and the source of its logistic supplies, Chinese leaders displayed indecision and fear in carrying out revolutionary reforms in rural areas as well.

On the other hand, the Maoists were obviously favourably disposed toward the bourgeoisie: there was no trade turnover tax, and no vigorous measures were taken against profiteers. The absence of any restrictions even against the big national bourgeoisie encouraged an upsurge of its reactionary activities. As far back as 1949, Soviet specialists reported flirtation on the part of Chinese authorities with foreign capitalist enterprises and commercial firms, which were not subjected to any restrictions by taxation or otherwise. Within the Communist Party the view was circulated that after a full military victory the class struggle would tend to die down, since the new government drew into co-operation all the sections of China's population, including the national bourgeoisie.

Among a certain part of the membership and within the leading circles of the Communist Party the theory was current to the effect that the new rich peasants emerging after the implementation of the land reform were allegedly a revolutionary force supporting the Communist Party and the people's government.

For example, at meetings with representatives of the fraternal parties in 1949, Chinese leaders declared: "The emergence of a new type of rich peasants poses no danger at all, because they have received their wealth from the new government and give it their determined support. These new rich peasants are revolutionary-minded."

Describing the situation within the CPC itself, Soviet specialists noted in 1949 that very few members were admitted to the Party from the working class, and no active work was carried on to increase their numbers in the Party. Local Party organisations were heavily infiltrated by landlords, rich peasants and bourgeois elements, and in some areas new members were admitted to the Party indiscriminately.

Such reports from Soviet specialists were confirmed by evidence given by leading executives of the fraternal parties who visited China in those years. They reported that the new democratic authorities granted too much freedom to the national bourgeoisie in towns. The stratum of private capitalist elements in towns had an extremely fertile ground for growth. The workers at private enterprises were still rightless and fully subordinated to their employers.

China's working class was neglected. The new authorities believed that it was not class-conscious and still failed to understand the Party policy. It was held, therefore, that the working class should not be drawn into active constructive work. As a result of this attitude to the working class, nothing was done to encourage the workers to join the Party and to educate them ideologically.

It was noted with concern that Mao failed to outline clearcut prospects before the people, the working class first and foremost. Therefore, concentration in his hands of all power was a cause for apprehension. The grave danger of complete restoration of capitalism both in town and in village, and the failure of CPC leaders to realise and fight the imminent danger were also mentioned.

Peking leaders repeatedly declared that no class struggle should be permitted in private industries in the new China and that the entrepreneur should be given freedom of action to boost production. China's working class, they said, was illiterate and lacked class awareness, and hence, should not be drawn into the class struggle. In reply to the remark that Lenin had emphasised the need to teach the working class and to advance it to the fore boldly, it was stated that these instructions of Lenin's were known in Peking, but they were still inapplicable to China's specific conditions and were a matter for the future.

Chinese leaders took no steps to strengthen the leading role and organisation of the working class, because they staked primarily on the peasantry, on its rich sections. It is interesting to recall in this connection their statements in a discussion with Academician P. F. Yudin in 1951. In their words, there were sentiments within the CPC in favour of regarding the rich peasant as the main figure in rural areas, and hence the conclusion that it was solely by encouraging rich peasant farms that China could develop the productive forces in rural areas, to boost her grain and raw materials production to meet the needs of towns and industry and, therefore, it was necessary to support in rural areas those Communists whose households were growing into rich farms, to help them develop these farms rather than expel them from the Party, regarding such Communists as a model for all peasants.

The Right opportunist tendency within the CPC was consequent on the failure of the Party leaders to keep the Party ranks in purity, to secure the dominating position of the working class and proletarian ideology in the Party.

The CPC Central Committee failed to pursue a determined policy of raising an intelligentsia from the midst of the workers. For example, CPC leaders decided not to admit workers to Party schools, because they were allegedly immature, politically backward, and had not taken an active part in the revolution.

Of course, the growth of China's economic potential, the increasing aid from the fraternal countries, her successes in socialist construction—all tended to create favourable conditions for gradually overcoming these negative tendencies. Meanwhile, petty bourgeois anarchy sustained by the subjectivist actions of Mao and his following was growing, too.

In the middle of 1953, it became clear that many executives, in China's financial and economic bodies in particular, ignored or failed to realise the prospects for the development of the state, committed Right opportunist distortions in the Party policy towards the bourgeoisie. Such views found support within the CPC leadership as well.

Already in the early years of socialist construction in China, grave violations of the Leninist principles in the CPC's activities interfered with its progress. Plenary meetings of the CPC Central Committee were called irregularly. The Central Committee of about 40 members elected in 1945 failed to reflect in numbers and composition the Party's actual position in China and was unable to cope effectively with its tasks. There were practically no experienced business and Party executives among the Central Committee members, veteran soldiers prevailed. Many leading executives in the provinces, towns, and districts, at enterprises and educational institutions held in their hands all Party and administrative authority; the secretary of the CPC committee of a province simultaneously held the office of chairman of its people's committee; the manager of a large enterprise was also secretary of its Party committee. Grave shortcomings in the work of the Party apparatus and the machinery of state were brought to light between December 1951 and July 1952 during the campaign against "three evils"—corruption, extravagance and red tape—in government offices, the army, government enterprises, public organisations and educational establishments and the campaign against "five evils" directed against the activities of the bourgeoisie, such as tax eva-

sions, misappropriation of public property, careless performance of government contracts, stealing of information on
the economic situation, bribery of government officials.

The campaign against corruption, extravagance and red
tape exposed many elements alien to the socialist system
and the working class, who had heavily infiltrated the Party
apparatus and particularly the government offices. Many
spies, bribe-takers, bureaucrats and embezzlers of public property were discovered in a number of organisations and institutions. Many Party and government executives had not been
vigilant against hostile activities of the class enemy. The
CPC Central Committee stated in its instructions on implementing the above campaigns issued in January 1952 that in
some organisations officials guilty of illegal or immoral acts
accounted for 50 to 60 per cent of the total personnel. An
Tzu-Wen, Minister of Personnel in the central people's government, declared in February 1953 at the fourth session of
the National Committee that during the campaign against
"three evils", among the 3,836,000 workers of government
offices (above district level) screened more than 105,000 had
been exposed as dangerous embezzlers of public property.
Each of them had been found guilty of bribery or theft and
had caused damage to the state to the value of over 10 million yuan.

The purge of the Party and government apparatus carried
out at the time was of great importance, although it had a
measure of inconsistency. Significantly, the nationalistic, anti-
Soviet sentiments of Party and government executives in the
capital and provinces were not given a duly principled assessment. This was a reflection, above all, of similar sentiments among CPC leaders themselves.

Some shortcomings in the social and Party policy of the
CPC, which had emerged in the early years of the revolution
and people's government, became increasingly manifest. The
Party was being inflated out of all proportions, no strict
selection of new members existed, and the cult of Mao was
being fanned more and more. This created a favourable situation for the growth of petty bourgeois, nationalistic tendencies. The Party membership increased particularly rapidly
between 1953 and 1957 when 70 per cent of all members were
admitted. This fast increase in membership had a negative

impact on its ideological level. Commenting on the great shortcomings in matters of admission to the Party, the newspaper *Chekiang jihpao* reported that a proportion of party members had a low level of class consciousness, a vague idea of the Party, and was easily susceptible to the influence of bourgeois ideology. Some Party members were infected with bourgeois ideology themselves, held wrong views and had shortcomings in the work style; they failed to qualify in full for Party membership. The views and style of work of members with a longer Party record were not free from shortcomings either.

On the eve of liberation, the number of factory and office workers in China was very small in proportion to the total population: a mere 8 million. After the proclamation of the PRC their numbers began to grow rapidly, yet the proportion of industrial workers in the Party membership remained the same.

The specific features of the CPC's social composition also contributed to nationalistic tendencies. The Party membership was growing at an unreasonably fast rate owing to an influx of new members from the petty bourgeois strata. According to data for May 1953, of the 6,100,000 members of the CPC only 450,000 were workers, who accounted for only 7.3 per cent of the total. In large industrial centres, prior to their liberation from the Kuomintang regime, CPC organisations operating underground had been very small. In Shanghai, with its 600,000 industrial workers, there were only 6,000 Communists even half-a-year after its liberation. Since the bulk of China's peasantry was illiterate, most of the Party members of peasant extraction were also illiterate, a fact which created objective difficulties in the ideological and political education of the Party cadres. In 1950, of the 1.5 million members of Party organisations in Northeast and North China, 1 million were illiterate.

The newspaper *Tungpei jihpao* reported in its issue of October 28, 1950: "At present, the overwhelming majority of rural and district Party cadres consists of peasant activists who received land plots during the land reform and distinguished themselves in its implementation. Their political level is still very low, as a rule, and some of them are illiterate. Of the total number of 1,099 Party secretaries in Heilongjiang province 269 are illiterate, 717 have a primary or secondary education." Similar facts were reported by the organs of the Party committees of Shandong province and the city of Jinan. The situation in other provinces was similar.

One of the major factors stimulating the growth of nationalistic sentiments in the CPC was the deliberate implantation of the cult of Mao.

Since the early years of liberation, writings of Mao Tse-tung have been published in large impressions in China. By October 1951, the Hsinhua News Agency alone had brought them out in an impression of almost 2.4 million copies. Broad campaigns of study of Mao Tse-tung's writings were organised in China, while works by the founders of Marxism-Leninism were completely ignored. In August 1951, local trade unions submitted to the All-China Federation of Trade Unions their programmes, in which six weeks and more was set aside for the study of Mao Tse-tung's articles. Personnel of government óffices were enjoined to devote at least six hours a week to political training, primarily to the study of works by Mao Tse-tung. University and secondary school students, in addition to regular political subjects, had to study Mao's writings 12-15 hours a month.

In October 1951, *Selected Works* of Mao Tse-tung began to be published by a decision of the CPC Central Committee, which gave another impetus to the movement for the study of the "ideas of Mao Tse-tung". In his report to the Third Session of the National Committee in October 1951, Chou En-lai stated:

"We should ... organise the study of the teachings of Mao Tse-tung on a broad, systematic basis, among active elements in every section of society, among combat heroes and model workers, members of democratic parties, all teachers, specialists and cadres, and we should through them help the masses in their studies. The first volume of the *Selected Works* of Mao Tse-tung has been published during this Session of the National Committee. We must make ourselves responsible for stimulating all sections of the population to organise the study of the *Selected Works* of Mao Tse-tung.

"Let us equip ourselves with the teachings of Mao Tse-tung which unite Marxism-Leninism with the revolutionary practice of China. This is the new task of the Chinese People's Democratic United Front."[1]

Already then Chinese propaganda more and more persistently put forward the thesis that the "ideas of Mao Tse-tung" were a complete doctrine which "contributed to the development of Marxism-Leninism". This thesis had been advanced as far back as 1945 at the Seventh Congress of the CPC.

The thesis of the "ideas of Mao Tse-tung" and his decisive contribution to the victory of the Chinese revolution was supported by several leaders of the CPC in their statements made on the occasion of the 30th anniversary of the Communist Party of China in July 1951. They were interspersed with such epithets, addressed to Mao, as "great", "brilliant", etc.

In addition to the cult of Mao, there were other circumstances which helped the nationalistic elements in the CPC to fight internationalist ideology in the Party and country.

Although in the early years of the PRC, Chinese propaganda occasionally referred to the need for learning Marxist-Leninist theory, in fact CPC leaders were very little concerned with a businesslike and profound elaboration of the problems of socialist construction and foreign policy of China, a thorough study and emulation of the experience of the fraternal parties. The newspaper *Jenmin jihpao* acknowledged this in these words: "It should be noted that quite a few comrades among us still fail to understand or underestimate the tremendous importance of Marxist theory for our practical work, particularly for economic development in our country. . . ."[2] The newspaper pointed out frankly that there were many practical problems of economic development which China's theoreticians had not yet approached seriously.

As long as the CPC followed the trail blazed by the Soviet Union, this disregard for Marxist-Leninist theory did not entail grave consequences. However, as soon as Chinese lead-

---

[1] Premier Chou En-lai's "Political Report to the Third Session of the First National Committee of the Chinese People's Political Consultative Conference". In: Supplement to *People's China*, Vol. IV, No. 10, November 16, 1951, p. 10.

[2] *Jenmin jihpao*, May 5, 1953.

ers began to underestimate and then ignore Soviet experience, the absence of their own thorough Marxist elaboration of the problems of socialist construction led to grave mistakes in the practical activities of the CPC.

As a result of underestimation of the importance of theory, as well as the absence of well-trained cadres the Communist Party of China limited itself to post factum theoretical analyses of events. This is strikingly exemplified by the Chinese theory of wave-like economic development which was invented post factum to justify the unevenness in the development of China's economy.

Reports about the "cultural revolution" in China evidence, indeed, that after her liberation a conflict flared up in the Chinese leadership between two lines on the problems of socialist remaking of China and on her foreign policy. The conflict of views on the home policy of the CPC was reflected in China's foreign policy. Already at that time, Chinese leaders sought to impose their voluntaristic goals on the Party policy. For all their pseudo-revolutionary verbiage, these goals boiled down to preserving capitalist ownership, particularly in towns, maintaining connections with the imperialist powers, a parasitic attitude to the Soviet Union combined with denigration of Soviet experience and prestige.

As soon as they consolidated their positions in the Party and country and completed economic rehabilitation, the Maoists changed over to a determined action to impose their great-power, adventurist goals on China. At first, these experiments of nationalistic elements within the CPC were carried out in the field of home policy and after their failure, in the sphere of world politics.

The sad consequences of the policy of Peking leaders strikingly illustrate the end result of voluntaristic methods of leadership, the cult of the individual alien to Marxism-Leninism if they are not opposed effectively. The developments in China in the late 50s and in the 60s vividly demonstrated the danger of a petty bourgeois, nationalistic policy to the revolutionary movement. These developments serve as a serious warning to all the sections of the world revolutionary movement.

CHAPTER V

SINO-SOVIET RELATIONS IN THE PERIOD OF ADOPTION BY THE CPC LEADERSHIP OF A SPECIAL LINE IN HOME AND FOREIGN POLICIES
(1958-1959)

The period 1958-1959 saw further gains for the policy of peaceful coexistence, an intensified struggle for collective security waged by the Soviet Union and other socialist countries. The Soviet Union continued to uphold with determination the interests of People's China on the international scene. The PRC Government also took a number of measures in accordance with the agreed policy of the fraternal states (proposals for collective peace in the Far East, for setting up an atom-free zone in Asia, etc.).

However, in 1958 and particularly in the subsequent period, the PRC more and more often showed signs of great-power chauvinism and adventurism in her foreign policy, such as interference in the internal affairs of other countries, territorial claims, "theories" of the benefit of a nuclear war for the revolution, the slogan of the "wind from the East" (i.e., Peking.—*Authors.*) prevailing over "the wind from the West". All this caused concern to which the CPSU Central Committee called attention through inter-Party channels. The fraternal parties hoped, however, that the loyal Marxist forces in the Communist Party of China would be able to check these tendencies and that the nationalistic factors would be neutralised in the general torrent of socialist construction in China.

1. SINO-SOVIET CO-OPERATION IN 1958-1959

Loyal to its internationalist duty, the Soviet Union continued to give China wide assistance in developing her economy, science, technology and culture. In January 1958, the visit to the Soviet Union by a Chinese delegation led by President of the PRC Academy of Sciences, Kuo Mo-jo, which had lasted for over three months, was successfully completed. The delegation had discussed the key problems of developing science and technology and extending Sino-Soviet scientific and technological co-operation with the USSR State Committee for Science and Technology, the USSR Academy of Sciences, the USSR State Committee for External Economic Relations, the USSR Ministry of Higher Education, and leading Soviet research institutions. Over 600 leading Soviet scientists and experts took part in the discussions.

During the visit, the Chinese delegation requested Soviet aid in solving major scientific and technological problems outlined in China's long-range programme of developing science and technology until 1968. This aid was to consist in commissioning Soviet scientists and specialists to work in China, education and advanced training of Chinese scientists, engineers and technicians in the Soviet Union, supplies of equipment, instruments, materials, etc.

At the end of the talks in Moscow, on January 18, 1958, the governments of the USSR and the PRC signed an agreement on joint performance of major research in science and technology and on Soviet aid to China in this field.

The agreement provided for joint research during 1958-1962 on 122 key scientific and technological problems of fundamental importance for China, as well as for continued extension of direct contacts between Soviet and Chinese research institutions.

Simultaneously, agreements were signed on co-operation in research in the field of science and technology between the Ministries of Higher Education and the Academies of Agriculture of the USSR and the PRC.

In April 1958, the USSR and the PRC signed a Treaty on Trade and Navigation, by which they undertook to carry out all requisite measures to promote their trade exchanges in a spirit of friendly co-operation and mutual assistance, on a basis of equality and mutual benefit.

This treaty has a supplement on the legal status of the USSR Trade Delegation in the PRC and the PRC Trade

Delegation in the USSR, which are to perform the following functions:

a) to facilitate the development of trade and economic relations between the two states;

b) to represent their respective states in foreign trade affairs;

c) to regulate on behalf of a respective state trade exchanges with the other state;

d) to carry on trade operations between the USSR and the PRC.

On August 8, 1958, an agreement was signed in Moscow between the Governments of the USSR and the PRC on Soviet technical aid to China in the building and expansion of 47 industrial enterprises and power stations.

The agreement envisaged, in particular, that Soviet organisations perform design, research and development work on a number of projects, hand over blueprints of individual departments and installations for repeated use, supply equipment, instruments, cables and some special materials for manufacturing completing equipment on the spot. Soviet organisations undertook to send specialists to China to aid in the assembly and adjustment of equipment and in commissioning completed projects, as well as in training Chinese personnel for work at new enterprises.

The agreement also provided that the Soviet Union hand over to China free of charge licences to manufacture products, as well as blueprints and other technical documents needed to organise production at these enterprises. The Chinese were to repay only the actual disbursements involved in making and handing over technical documents.

Outlays made by Soviet organisations in rendering technical assistance envisaged in the agreement were to be repaid with Chinese exports under the terms of the operating Sino-Soviet trade agreement.

The Soviet Government, which invariably came out in support of the PRC, declared in September 1958 its recognition of the 12-mile zone of territorial waters proclaimed by the People's Republic of China.

The year 1959 was a turning point in Sino-Soviet relations. It was the last year when they were on the upgrade in general. In 1960, a rapid decline in economic, scientific, technical and cultural co-operation between the USSR and the PRC, general deterioration and exacerbation of Sino-Soviet relations were provoked by CPC leaders.

In 1959, they still came out with occasional assurances of loyalty to Sino-Soviet friendship, expressing their high appreciation of the home and foreign policies of the CPSU Central Committee and the Soviet Government, emphasising the crucial importance for China of Soviet assistance and support. Speaking at the 21st Congress of the CPSU, Chou En-lai, who led the Chinese delegation, declared: "The 21st Congress of the Communist Party of the Soviet Union is a great event in contemporary political life. The peoples view this Congress not only as a demonstration of the great might of the Soviet Union—the most powerful bastion of peace throughout the world, but also as a majestic and beautiful prospect for all mankind—communism. This greatly gladdens and inspires the peoples of all countries struggling persistently for peace all over the world and for mankind's progress."[1]

Chou En-lai said that the Communist Party of the Soviet Union and the Soviet people had achieved great successes in strengthening the unity of the international communist movement, in building up the power of the socialist camp, as well as in uniting the forces of peace-loving states and peoples in the struggle for strengthening peace, for easing international tensions and for preventing the danger of war.

"Since the Great October Socialist Revolution," Chou En-lai said, "the Soviet Union has always been ahead of the times and by its brilliant example of socialist and communist construction inspires the proletariat and the working people of all the world. They see their future in the Soviet Union's present day. The existence and development of the Soviet Union has undermined the very foundation of imperialist domination. The Soviet Union invariably gives tremendous support and assistance to socialist countries, the international proletariat and all peace-loving states and peoples of the world."[2]

Chou En-lai read out a message of greetings to the 21st Congress of the CPSU from the Central Committee of the

---

[1] *Pravda,* January 29, 1959.
[2] Ibid.

Communist Party of China signed by Chairman Mao Tse-tung. The message said in particular: "At present, the Communist Party of the Soviet Union has put forward the plan of economic development in 1959-1965 based on the great programme of building communism. The implementation of this plan will lay a firm material and cultural foundation for transition to communism in the Soviet Union and enrich the treasure store of Marxism-Leninism with valuable experience in building communism. Moreover, the implementation of this plan will lead to a further change in the world balance of forces and contribute still more to the noble cause of universal peace and mankind's progress."[1]

"The Soviet people led by the Communist Party of the Soviet Union," the message went on, "have always been a splendid example for the proletariat and progressive mankind of the whole world. We are convinced that the proletariat and progressive mankind of the whole world, inspired by the 21st Congress of the CPSU, will struggle with still greater determination for the great cause of universal peace and mankind's progress."[2]

On February 7, 1959, a new agreement was signed in Moscow on Soviet assistance to China in building 78 big projects of the steel, chemical, coal, oil, engineering, electrical engineering, radio engineering, building materials industries, and power stations.

Under the agreement, Soviet organisations were to perform research and development work on the basis of the latest achievements in science and technology, supply equipment, instruments and some special materials, and also commission a large number of Soviet specialists to give China technical assistance in the assembly and adjustment of equipment, the construction and commissioning of projects and invite large groups of Chinese specialists and workers for occupational training at Soviet enterprises.

As under the earlier agreements, the Soviet Union undertook to hand over to China free of charge licences to manufacture products at these enterprises, as well as technical documents for organising production and for manufacturing

---

[1] *Pravda*, January 29, 1959.
[2] Ibid.

9*

complete plant and equipment in China for the projects envisaged in the agreements.

The total value of Soviet equipment deliveries, design work and other technical assistance neared 5,000 million rubles (in old prices). China was to repay these deliveries and all kinds of Soviet technical assistance with supplies of goods under the terms of the operating Sino-Soviet trade agreement.

It was pointed out in the announcement of signing the agreement that the Governments of the Soviet Union and the People's Republic of China regarded it as a new important contribution to the further development and extension of the relations of fruitful, mutually advantageous economic co-operation and fraternal mutual assistance between the two socialist states.

At that time, leaders of the CPC attached great importance to collective forms of co-operation between socialist countries, expressed their high appreciation of the activities of the Council for Mutual Economic Assistance. Commenting on the results of the Council's 11th Session *Jenmin jihpao* wrote on May 20, 1959: "International division of labour between member-countries of the Council secures for every member rational utilisation of its natural wealth and potential economic resources, strengthens the economic power of the socialist camp and permits combining the national interests of each socialist country with those of the entire socialist camp.

"The development of mutual economic assistance and co-operation between the socialist countries has enabled some of them to rise gradually to the level of advanced states. In this respect the comprehensive selfless aid of the most powerful and experienced first socialist state, the Soviet Union, to the other fraternal countries has been the most important factor. Today when economic co-operation between the socialist countries has advanced to a higher stage the role of the Soviet Union has grown still more."

At the end of 1958, trade negotiations were held in Moscow between government delegations of the PRC and the USSR on completing mutual goods deliveries in 1958 and on continued development of trade between the two countries. The parties agreed on additional Soviet goods deliveries, as a result of which the turnover of Sino-Soviet trade originally envisaged in the protocol for 1958 was exceeded by over 600 million rubles.

The talks on goods turnover between the USSR and the PRC in 1959 also culminated in success. In accordance with their common goals and tasks, the parties agreed to expand the turnover of Sino-Soviet trade considerably.

In addition to a large growth in Soviet deliveries of complete plant and equipment under the earlier agreements, there was a considerable increase in Soviet supplies to the PRC of power-generating equipment, in particular, turbogenerators, diesel generators, power transformers, traction engine power stations and small hydropower stations for use in rural areas. As compared with the 1958 level, there was an increase in Soviet deliveries to China of heavy-duty drilling rigs, transport vehicles, bearings and a number of other Soviet goods needed by China's economy.

China was to deliver to the Soviet Union in 1959, just as in earlier years, tin, tungsten, molybdenum, raw silk, wool, tea, citrus fruits and other goods.

The sides agreed that after the end of the talks on the trade turnover in 1958 they would set about drawing up a long-term trade agreement.

At the April 1959 session of the National People's Congress Chinese leaders noted the great importance of Sino-Soviet economic co-operation. Chou En-lai stated in particular: "The countries of the socialist camp led by the great Soviet Union have given us all-round assistance in socialist construction in our country. The 166 large projects built with Soviet aid during the first five-year plan period have greatly contributed to our economic development. The rich experience accumulated by the Soviet Union during its history is also an important foundation for drawing up and implementing our economic development plans. From this rostrum I convey, on behalf of the Government and people of my country, our profound gratitude to the governments and peoples of the Soviet Union and other socialist countries. To strengthen unity with the Soviet Union and all socialist countries is the main line of our country."[1]

---

[1] *Pravda*, April 19, 1959.

At the end of the talks held in Peking between Soviet and Chinese Government delegations from June 16 to 23, 1959 a consular agreement was concluded on the legal status of consulates and other matters connected with consular services. The agreement helped strengthen and develop Sino-Soviet consular relations.

In 1959, the PRC celebrated its 10th anniversary. Summing up the results of its progress, Chinese leaders acknowledged the great role played in China's construction by the broad development of her inter-state relations with the Soviet Union. "Marking the 10th anniversary of the PRC," Chou En-lai wrote in an article entitled "The Great Decade", "our people express their utmost gratitude to the Soviet Union, which gave our country assistance in the building of 166 projects in the first five-year plan period and again signed this year and last year agreements on rendering aid to our country in building 125 projects; moreover, over the past 10 years, the Soviet Union commissioned over 10,800 specialists in economics, culture and education to work in China."[1]

Assistance and support by the Soviet Union created the necessary prerequisites for successful socialist construction in China, but this progress was hampered by Chinese nationalistic elements holding their specific views and goals.

Toward 1958 China was experiencing a great uplift in all fields of political and economic life. By that time the tasks of the rehabilitation period had been solved and the first five-year plan of developing the national economy had been overfulfilled by far.

In 1957 the production of steel increased as compared with 1952, the last year of the rehabilitation period, by 296 per cent, iron by 208, electricity by 166, oil by 335, coal by 96, metal-cutting lathes by 104, grain by 20, cotton by 26.[2]

Tremendous progress had also been made in the socialist remaking of agriculture. Toward the end of 1957, 98 per cent of peasant households were united in farming co-operatives, 96 per cent of them in co-operatives of a higher type. About 90 per cent of handicraftsmen also joined in co-operatives.

---

[1] *Jenmin jihpao,* October 2, 1959.
[2] Ibid., April 7, 1958.

Socialist transformations had practically been completed also in the field of private capitalist industry and trade. By that time, private industrial enterprises accounted for 0.1 per cent of total industrial output in China, and private trade (mostly small traders) for 3 per cent of the total volume of retail trade.[1]

In the first five-year plan period, China was building with Soviet assistance 135 projects, in particular 12 in the coal industry, 29 in the power industry, 1 in the oil industry, 17 in the ferrous and non-ferrous metal industries, 7 in the chemical industry, 26 in the metal-working industry, 1 in the textile industry, 1 in the pulp-and-paper industry, 2 in the food industry.

All in all, over 900 additional projects were being built in China during the first five-year plan period.[2] However, it was precisely the projects built with Soviet assistance that have formed the backbone of modern industry and secured future possibilities for implementing the entire programme of industrialisation in China. They enabled her not only to build up a number of absolutely new industries—aluminium, instrument-making, mining equipment, metallurgical equipment, synthetic rubber, motor, tractor, aircraft, electrotechnical, radioengineering, defence, etc., but also to increase productive capacities for manufacturing major items of industrial products.

2. REVISION OF THE DECISIONS OF THE EIGHTH CONGRESS OF THE CPC. POLICY OF "THREE RED BANNERS"

China's political and economic achievements provided good prerequisites for the continued development of socialist construction. It was precisely at that time, however, that the struggle within the CPC leadership flared up with renewed intensity. Whereas formerly nationalistic elements had camouflaged their views, compelled to operate in accordance with the historical tasks of the revolutionary movement in China, in the situation of great victories won by the Chinese

[1] *Jenmin jihpao*, April 12, 1958.
[2] Ibid., April 14, 1959.

people with the aid of the USSR and other fraternal countries during the rehabilitation and the first five-year plan periods, the nationalists in the CPC decided to come out openly with their great-power, nationalistic views.

The second five-year plan mapped out by the 8th Congress of the CPC was discarded. In 1958, the course charted by the 8th Congress was revised and replaced by the so-called policy of "three red banners": the general line, the great leap, and the people's communes. Chinese leaders decided to fulfil within a few years the tasks for which three and more five-year plans had been set aside in 1956. It was decided to increase during a five-year period (1958-1962) industrial output 6.5 times (at average annual growth rates of 45 per cent) and the total output of farm produce 2.5 times (at average annual growth rates of 20 per cent!).

These plans were drawn up without any economic substantiation whatsoever, without regard for the country's real possibilities. The people's communes set up in the villages were to secure a "leap into communism" within 3 to 4 or 5 to 6 years.

The adventurist policy of "three red banners" captivated part of the Party's cadres who did not realise immediately the disastrous consequences of this policy. In fact, it meant a complete renunciation of the line adopted in 1953 and confirmed in 1956 by the 8th Congress of the CPC. At the same time CPC leaders ignored friendly advice from Marxist-Leninist parties which viewed the Chinese experiments with concern and warned of their grave consequences.

The policy of "three red banners" was an attempt to speed up artificially the rates of economic growth by extreme exertion of all the strength of the Chinese working people, to outstrip other states of the world and, bypassing the requisite stages in the building of socialist society, "to leap" into communism.

The CPC leadership advertised its policy as a model for development of other countries.

The theory and practice of the "leap into communism" ran counter to the objective realities in China and the rest of the world, to science, the experience of the socialist countries and the international communist movement. It was clear that these voluntaristic objectives were unattainable, that it was impossible to leap over definite stages in socialist construction, that slogans could not substitute for technology and that subjective factors could not be omnipotent either in the field of material production or in the field of social relations. It should be noted that the thesis on the need to adopt the highest possible rates of socialist construction had been advocated, in particular, by Mao Tse-tung for many years.

Later, it was formulated by Mao Tse-tung as a slogan "to build socialism on the principle—more, faster, better, more economically" which became a generally accepted expression of the CPC general line in socialist construction. After criticising during the "campaign for improving the work style" the "Right deviationist, conservative views" the CPC leadership at the second session of the 8th Congress held in May 1958 gave a final and full endorsement to its voluntaristic policy of leap-like economic development.

The possibilities provided by the successful fulfilment and overfulfilment of the first five-year plan really opened before the CPC leadership the prospects of a definite rise in the rates of socialist construction. However, it was not content with this and set the task of not only raising the rates but also of "taking a leap" to make China a powerful, advanced, prosperous nation within the shortest possible space of time. This idea was expressed in Mao Tse-tung's appeals to struggle persistently for three years and to secure a change in the general image of most of China's provinces—"a few years of stubborn work—10,000 years of happiness".

The policy of a "big leap", of a "speedy march to communism" was undoubtedly the result of the nationalistic, hegemonistic aspirations of Chinese leaders, an attempt to find a basis for their great-power claims to the leading position in the socialist community and the world liberation movement. Unwilling to confine themselves to the limits of China, CPC leaders went out of their way to impose their adventurist policy of "big leap" on other socialist countries, the entire world communist movement.

The "big-leap" policy was a grave departure from the principles of the Declaration of the 1957 Moscow Meeting, which indicated that the processes of socialist revolution and so-

cialist construction are based on a number of main laws characteristic of all countries taking the socialist path.

One of such general laws is the planned development of
the national economy directed to building socialism and communism, raising the people's standards of living. Leaving to
oblivion the immutable truths of Marxism-Leninism, Chinese
leaders declared a leap-like development of the economy,
ignoring the proportionality inherent in the planned socialist
economy, disregarding completely the goals of raising the
living standards of working people. The Declaration speaks
of the necessity to build the economic and technological basis
of socialism after the working class wins political power. By
seeking to secure the "big leap" by primitive technical means,
for example, by "backyard steel works" Chinese leaders discarded this provision of the Declaration, too.

The ministries, government departments and local organisations, whipped up by calls for a continued acceleration of
rates, announced new counterplans and pledges, which were
practically unrealisable, almost every day. In a situation of
feverish rates created by the CPC leadership itself it increasingly lost the sense of reality and became more and more
self-deluded.

In a talk with a delegation of Soviet journalists in October
1958, one of the Chinese leaders said, for example: "What
would we have if we always marked time?... The increment
in the annual output of farm produce would be only 4-5 per
cent, in industrial output 10 per cent. If we reconciled ourselves to this, the cause of communism would win in China
evidently in 100 years. Now the popular masses have
prompted us that the increment in farm produce can be not 4
or 5 but more than 100 per cent and in industrial output not
10 but 60 to 70 per cent."

The rapid and, what is most important, unwarranted
growth of rates in planning economic development in China
can be illustrated by these data. In accordance with the proposals for the second five-year plan accepted by the 8th CPC
Congress in 1956 steel output at the end of the five-year plan
period, i.e., in 1962 was set at 10.5-12 million tons; at the
second session of the 8th Congress of the CPC in May 1958
it was declared that steel output would top 7.1 million tons
already in the first year of the second five-year plan period,

i.e., in 1958, and in August 1958 at a meeting of the Political Bureau of the CPC Central Committee, it was decided to bring up steel production to 10,700,000 tons in 1958, i.e., to fulfil the five-year plan for steel within one year.

Whereas under the second five-year plan it was contemplated to produce in 1962 about 500,000 million tsin of grain, about 48 million dan of cotton and to increase the head of swine to 250 million, in 1959 these figures were to reach 1,050,000 million tsin, cotton 100 million dan, and the head of swine 1,000 million.

In 1958, Mao Tse-tung stated during a visit to an experimental people's commune in a rural area: "People's communes are good." This was enough for beginning an unjustified disruption of production relations in the villages.

In August 1958, CPC leaders announced the beginning of a new era in China's history—the era of setting up people's communes. This idea had been called forth by the very same voluntaristic desire to leap immediately into a realm of power and prosperity, bypassing despite everything a long period even of relatively fast development. The setting up of people's communes was a concentrated expression of phenomena existing in China in various fields and in varied degree, such as divorcement from reality, disregard for the laws of social development, departure from the policy of leaning in the struggle for communism on the pooled efforts of all socialist nations.

The reasoning of Chinese authors on the role of people's communes in building communism not only lacked a clearly defined argument on the relationship of successful solution of this task to co-operation with the socialist countries but also suggested that China would come to communism ahead of others. "Evidently, the attainment of communism in our country is no longer a matter for a distant future," emphasised the resolution of the CPC Central Committee "On the Setting Up of People's Communes" of August 29, 1958. This was, above all, the fullest manifestation of nationalistic trends beginning to prevail in the policy of CPC leaders. Since that time they have more and more deviated towards their specific positions in relations with the socialist camp, towards the path of opposition to the CPSU and the international communist movement as a whole.

The "big-leap" spirit with its chase after records, with its departure from realities, etc., affected science, education, literature, the arts—fields in which these phenomena sometimes assumed a simply parodic character. Cultural figures were forced to draw up "leap-like" plans. Here are some examples. In March 1958, the Secretariat of the Chinese Writers' Union put forward a draft plan of a steep rise in literary work, which contained the requirement to achieve within a year a rapid advance in literary art so as to obtain a bumper harvest of socialist literature in the coming 3-5 years. In accordance with this plan, a movement for drawing up individual plans of a steep rise in creative activity developed among prose writers, dramatists, literary critics. These plans were made public, and workers in literature and the arts were compelled to compete for their fulfilment and overfulfilment. The poet Chiang Ko-chia, Editor-in-Chief of the *Shihkan* (Poetry) monthly magazine, pledged to write in 1958 twenty works of poetry, including a historical poem covering a century—from the Taiping Rebellion to date, and 15 works in prose. Besides that, he planned to compose several lyrics for songs.

As noted above, not only in industry but also in agriculture the plans and forecasts of the CPC leadership proved to have been built on sand. For example, the CPC Central Committee had to "adjust" repeatedly the targets for grain harvest set for 1959, reducing them from 1,050,000 million tsin to 550,000 million tsin. In fact, the grain harvest of 1959 was even smaller—540,000 million tsin.

Far from building up grain reserves of 300,000 to 500,000 million tsin, China was compelled in later years, after a 10-year interval, to resume food imports on a vastly increased scale.

The 8th plenary meeting of the CPC Central Committee was held in August 1959. At this meeting a group of Central Committee members opposed the "big leap" policy, qualifying it as petty bourgeois fantasy which cost dearly to the Chinese people. The Maoists cracked down on these leading executives with malicious criticism and curses. The communique of the 8th plenary meeting of the CPC Central Committee said that they were slandering the movement for a "big leap", and the movement for setting up people's communes and describing them as fantastic petty bourgeois movements. Among those who disagreed with the Maoist line were member of the Political Bureau of the CPC Central Committee Peng Te-huai, alternate member of the Political Bureau Chang Wen-tien, many leading executives of provincial Party committees, ministries and government departments.

The 8th plenary meeting had to admit as unauthentic the figures of economic achievements in 1958 and gave new figures: for grain, at 250 million tons instead of 375 million, for cotton at 2.1 million tons instead of 3.35 million, for steel at 8 million tons instead of 11 million.

The 8th plenary meeting could not but take account of obvious failures in the "big-leap" policy. This was reflected in the reduction of the plan for 1959 and in a change of approach to people's communes. The plan was reduced for steel from 18 million tons to 12 million, for coal from 380 million tons to 335 million, for grain from 525 million tons to 275 million, for cotton fibre from 5 million tons to 2.3 million. As for people's communes, the decision of the plenary meeting recommended, in particular, consistent implementation of the principles of management and economic self-sufficiency according to stages: distribution according to labour inputs, greater remuneration for greater inputs, i.e., a return to the socialist principles of distribution which had existed earlier. It was recognised as expedient to base the economy not on people's communes but on production teams comparable in size to the former production co-operatives.

The general policy line expressed in the decisions of the 8th plenary meeting, however, remained the same. These decisions, just as those of the 6th plenary meeting, extolled the "big-leap" policy, and appealed to the Party and people to overcome under the leadership of the Party's Central Committee and Mao Tse-tung the Right opportunist sentiments among certain unstable elements and to struggle for a pre-time fulfilment of the second five-year plan in two years (during 1958-1959).

Although Mao and his following succeeded in suppressing and discrediting their opponents, the CPC leadership was divided on the question of ways of China's further development and, therefore, the ground for a new exacerbation of contradictions remained. This was a dispute on the problem of ways and means to convert China into a mighty world power, and the rates of building socialist society. One group, which at different stages was supported by different people, was for rational methods of economic development with due regard for the experience of other socialist countries. The other group led by Mao Tse-tung flatly rejected international-al experience in building socialism and insisted on voluntar-istic methods of stepping up the rates of economic construc-tion and development. The events after the failure of the "big-leap" policy led to a situation in which those followers of the nationalistic line of Mao Tse-tung who supported him against Peng Te-huai gradually began to disagree with Mao in defining ways and means of achieving great-power objec-tives.

The prestige of Mao Tse-tung and the faith in his infal-libility began to fall within the Party and among the people. In response to this, a policy was adopted towards continued curtailment of intra-Party and state democracy, militarisa-tion of society and enhancement of the role of the army, the fanning of nationalistic passions and a still greater in-flation of the cult of Mao.

The spread of a light-minded approach to the solution of varied tasks of economic, cultural, scientific and technolog-ical development was facilitated to a definite extent by the broad movement launched by the CPC against the "blind faith" in foreign experience, which actually turned into a campaign of discrediting the experience of socialist construc-tion in the Soviet Union.

On the initiative of Mao Tse-tung, a critical attitude to Soviet experience was encouraged. To substantiate this new approach, a thesis was advanced on the need to struggle against mechanical imitation of foreign experience, against disregard for China's specific conditions.

At first Chinese leaders sought to undermine trust in Soviet experience by advertising the thesis on independence, on a critical attitude to advice by Soviet specialists. At the first all-China conference of capital construction workers held be-tween the end of February and the beginning of March 1956, Chou En-lai levied sharp criticism on Chinese workers for their uncritical attitude to proposals by Soviet specialists, for ignoring the experience and conditions of China in carrying them into life. The proposition on creative application of foreign experience, which is correct in itself, gradually assumed monstrous forms with utter disregard for the requirements of science and technology and the experience accumulated.

The Mao group deliberately employed the movement against "blind faith" in foreign experience for heating up nationalistic sentiments.

The fight against "blind faith" had a direct bearing on the application of Soviet experience. Cases of criticism and direct defiance of recommendations by Soviet specialists, a distrustful attitude to the quality of Soviet equipment became increasingly frequent; there appeared signs of underestimation of the importance of Soviet assistance in general and sentiments began to emerge which later resulted in the theory of "leaning on one's own forces", discrediting Soviet experience.

The chauvinistic hysteria in the "big-leap" period and the people's disillusionment which followed its failure were craftily used by the Maoists for continued stimulation of anti-Soviet nationalistic sentiments. A new wave of attacks on Soviet experience was begun. Writing about the application of Soviet experience, *Hsüehhsi* magazine frankly stated that in China's conditions there was no great need to apply the Soviet Union's old methods in industrialisation. Concerning the mechanisation of agriculture, the article pointed out that after completing the remaking of agriculture along co-operative lines China was not obliged to start immediately the mechanisation of agriculture because she had little arable land and a lot of manpower.

As noted above, with the rise of nationalistic, great-power sentiments in China, the contemptuous attitude to Soviet specialists became manifest on an ever increasing scale. Facts of mistrust in Soviet specialists became more and more frequent.

The sharp worsening of the attitude to Soviet specialists working in China on the part of veteran personnel of Chinese enterprises, ministries and government departments had been in evidence from the latter half of 1958.

The slogans of fighting "blind faith" in established technical standards, in foreign experience, the struggle against conservatism, etc., proclaimed in 1958 by CPC leaders were, in effect, directed against Soviet experience and Soviet specialists, against strict implementation of the standards and requirements of technical documents and process charts.

This immediately had a disastrous effect on technological performance and the standards of operation of enterprises and threatened the breakdown of major types of equipment.

Contrary to insistent recommendations by Soviet specialists measures were taken at industrial enterprises in the third and fourth quarter-years of 1958 to close down all technical services (technological departments, departments of chief mechanic, chief power engineer, technical control), requisite instructions and norms were withdrawn from working places. This led to disturbances in manufacturing processes in industry and to tremendous spoilage of products. One example was the situation at the Anshan Steel Complex, one of China's biggest industrial enterprises.

From August 1958 departments of the complex began working without technological instructions, products were not checked properly, because all quality control inspectors had been dismissed. Recommendations by Soviet specialists concerning the observance of technological instructions were ignored by Chinese personnel. Technological instructions were simply removed from departments. As a result, the output of first-grade rails fell from 93 per cent to 42-50. The durability of open-hearth furnace vaults reduced to 50 smeltings from 400-500. In 1959 rejection in the tube-rolling department increased three times as compared with 1958, at blooming mill No. 1, almost 250 per cent, and at blooming mill No. 2, more than 200 per cent.

Chinese building organisations often violated the requirements of Soviet design documents, arbitrarily replaced materials of definite specifications and deviated without good reason from Soviet design standards.

Not infrequently disregard for recommendations by Soviet specialists and crude violations of Soviet technical standards resulted in large accidents and loss of human lives, as was the case, for example, at the Hsinganchiang and Hsinfuchiang hydropower stations.

Soviet specialists resolutely objected to such innovation, which entailed dislocation of industry being built by China's working people with Soviet aid in the face of great difficulties, and recommended factory managers to avoid unjustified deviations from accepted process charts and product quality standards and a revision of time-tested management systems.

Not confining themselves to oral recommendations, Soviet specialists addressed letters to industrial managers and corresponding ministries.

Chinese government bodies were approached not only by individual Soviet specialists but also through official channels. For example, on June 7, 1958, the Minister of Engineering Chao Erh-lu was handed in a memorandum from the Soviet Embassy in China on gross violations of technological performance standards at a number of defence enterprises.

On January 5, 1959, a memorandum was conveyed through the Chief of the Department for Work with Foreign Specialists under the PRC State Council, Yang Fang-chih, on gross violations of manufacturing processes and unjustified closure of technical services at the Fulark heavy machine-building plant, the Harbin electrical engineering plant, and the Anshan Steel Complex. The memorandum also said that all technical documents had been removed from the Anshan Steel Complex in August 1958.

On June 2, 1959, the First Vice-Minister of Water Economy and Power Engineering, Li Pao-hua, was handed in a memorandum about violations of the requirements of Soviet technical documents and process charts in the construction of the Sanmenxia and Taiyuan hydropower projects.

Such letters and complaints were quite numerous. They did not mean any interference in China's internal affairs but were motivated by concern for effective use of valuable Soviet equipment and know-how at Chinese enterprises. Another reason for this concern was the loss of property and human lives due to defiance of advice of Soviet specialists who acted in accordance with agreements and contracts. Chinese authorities sought to create the impression that the responsibility for adventurist fascination with the "big-leap" policy also rested with Soviet specialists working in China at the invitation of her Government.

The CPSU did not share the concepts of Chinese leaders concerning innovation and experiments with the "big leap" and people's communes. However, regarding it as China's internal affair, the CPSU Central Committee confined itself to giving Chinese leaders advice in confidential form.

Chinese leaders acted differently. In fact, even as far back as that time they made public their ideological differences with the CPSU and other fraternal parties, sought to oppose their special line to measures of the CPSU Central Committee in the field of communist construction, and from these positions to challenge the wisdom of the home policy of the CPSU. CPC leaders began to spread the "theory" of three types of socialist countries: countries building communism at an accelerated rate; countries marking time at the stage of socialism; countries going back from socialism to restoration of capitalism. They listed China under the first type, the Soviet Union under the second, and Yugoslavia under the third.

Departure from the principles of internationalism became increasingly obvious in the ideological work of the CPC inside China. This was expressed in the substitution of propaganda of "ideas of Mao Tse-tung" for Marxism-Leninism, in holding back information about the activities of the CPSU, the achievements of the Soviet Union and other fraternal parties and countries, in the growth of chauvinistic trends and sentiments.

The cult of Mao Tse-tung rose to a still higher pitch.

The attitude to the publication and circulation of Soviet literature in China changed from year to year. In 1956, the share of Soviet books in reprinted foreign literature reduced from 94 to 89 per cent for the number of titles, and from 92 to 89 per cent for the number of copies as compared with 1955. In the meantime the rates of growth in the publication of books from the capitalist countries were much higher than those of Soviet books. Publication of books from the capitalist countries grew almost 100 per cent in numbers of copies, of Soviet books, only 42 per cent. As for the number of titles, the increment in the publication of books from the capitalist countries is illustrated by even more striking figures: literature from the capitalist countries, 150 per cent; Soviet literature, only 19 per cent.

While still interested in economic co-operation with the Soviet Union, Chinese leaders were already seeking to prevent ideological intercourse between the Soviet and Chinese peoples, regarding it as a danger to the anti-socialist views and principles they were implanting in China. For example, in 1958, Chinese organisations, referring to the need for "saving funds", considerably curtailed the cultural co-operation programme. In mid-April of 1958, the Secretary General of the PRC Committee for Cultural Relations with Foreign Countries, Chen Chung-ching, during his visit to Moscow, conveyed an official request from Chinese organisations to Soviet authorities to cancel (under the pretext of a great volume of business and financial difficulties) many measures provided for in the programme. This curtailment affected exchanges between professionals and artists: visits to China by Soviet radio and television workers for collecting material and preparing a series of programmes dedicated to the 10th anniversary of the PRC, a visit to the Soviet Union by workers of Chinese radio for an exchange of experience and acquaintance with Soviet radio and television services. Also dropped out of the programme were visits to the Soviet Union by 10 researchers of China's higher educational institutions for holding consultations and reading lectures and a group of specialists in Chinese folk medicine for sharing experience with Soviet medics; some other exchanges, in art and cinematography in particular, were also cancelled.

3. THE SPECIAL FOREIGN POLICY LINE OF CPC LEADERS AND ITS IMPACT ON SINO-SOVIET RELATIONS

Confronted with difficulties on the home scene, the nationalists within the CPC moved the focus of their adventurist policy to the international scene, launching a campaign of slander against the socialist countries and Communist parties, resorting to war provocations to aggravate the international situation, advancing ultra-revolutionary slogans to depict Chinese leaders as the staunchest revolutionaries.

All this pursued quite definite goals: on the one hand, to distract the attention of the Party and people from the difficulties at home, to suppress discontent inside the country, to stir up nationalistic passions and war hysteria; on the other hand, to attain the hegemonistic objectives of Chinese leaders by different means.

10*

Since 1958 China's foreign policy diverged more and more from that of other socialist countries. It manifested with increasing clarity trends running counter to the efforts of the Soviet Union and the entire socialist camp to end the cold war and international tensions.

This policy was gaining ground slowly and was affirmed by the Maoists in a bitter struggle against CPC leaders remaining loyal to the socialist principles in China's foreign policy or at least holding a realistic stand. In China, an acute confrontation continued between the two lines on the issue of her socialist development and foreign policy objectives. Therefore, China continued to ally herself with other socialist countries on certain international issues. For example, on April 13, 1958 her Government made a statement expressing its full support for the Soviet Government's decision to end unilaterally as of March 31, 1958 tests of all types of atomic and hydrogen weapons and proposals on this issue to the United States and Britain.

The statement said in particular: "This action by the Soviet Government is a conclusive demonstration of its consistent peace policy. It has thrown into salient relief the Soviet people's profound concern for a life in peace and happiness for all the peoples and strengthened greatly the faith of all peace-loving states and peoples in the struggle for peace. This is undoubtedly an immense contribution to the cause of defending universal peace and securing a happy life of mankind. The Chinese people welcome enthusiastically this great peace initiative of the Soviet Union."

On the whole, however, negative tendencies were growing in China's foreign policy. They were manifested by a transition from flexible tactics to attempts at a direct offensive and frontal attacks against capitalism, to a hard line and intransigence even in matters of secondary importance involving no questions of principle. Chinese leaders began to display proneness to spurring on developments on the international scene, to speeding up the world revolutionary process. They overestimated China's strength and potentialities for solving international problems, having lost the sense of reality, the ability for a sober assessment of the international situation and the balance of forces on the world arena. China's foreign policy became to be dominated by great-power tendencies, efforts to give her a special role in international affairs.

Characteristically, CPC leaders adopted their new hard line exactly at a time when the Soviet Union was implementing broad measures to carry into life the Leninist policy of peaceful coexistence between the two world social systems.

In keeping with this new line, the Maoists in 1958 undertook a number of military actions in the area of the Taiwan Strait, which resulted in a grave deterioration of the international situation. At the end of August 1958, they shelled the offshore islands of Szeming and Matzu allegedly in retaliation for provocations by Chiang Kai-shek troops. The latter, however, had not desisted from provocations ever since they were expelled from the mainland. It was also known that they were unable to carry out large-scale military operations against mainland China without US consent and support. In fact, the action opened on the initiative of the Mao group in that period played into the hands of the war-like circles in the United States, which sought to obstruct the Soviet policy of easing world tensions. By this action, which was not motivated by any sensible considerations, the Mao group hoped to exacerbate Soviet-American relations, to exploit the mechanism of the Sino-Soviet treaty in order to turn the conflict into a full-scale war in the Far East.

The United States reacted to the shelling of the offshore islands with a concentration of large military forces in Taiwan and declared bluntly that if the PRC attacked Taiwan the US would give every assistance to its ally Chiang Kai-shek. Thus, in September and October 1958 a situation threatening war was created in the Far East. All these actions were undertaken by China without consultations with the Soviet Union, in contravention of her direct commitments under the Sino-Soviet treaty of friendship and mutual assistance.

Chinese leaders had not made their plans known to the Soviet Premier who stayed in Peking early in August 1958, i.e., when the decision to shell the islands of Szeming and Matzu had already been taken and preparations for this were in full swing. What is more, Peking leaders resorted to outright double-dealing. Shortly before the events in the Taiwan Strait they had signed a Sino-Soviet communique declaring an identity of views on the problems of joint struggle for a peaceful settlement of international conflicts and defence of peace throughout the world.

Despite the frankly unfriendly attitude of Chinese leaders, the Soviet Union resolutely came out in defence of China when, as a result of her adventurist policy, her security was threatened by the United States and foiled the attempts of aggressive imperialist circles to take advantage of Peking's actions.

The Soviet Premier's appeal to the US President on September 7, 1958, to show common sense and refrain from steps likely to entail irreparable consequences, proved effective and played the crucial role in preventing dangerous developments.

As soon as they saw that their adventure had failed, the Chinese leaders beat a retreat. China's international prestige was damaged, particularly because of the fuzzy explanations offered for the occasion by Chinese propaganda. At first, it spoke of the intention to liberate the offshore islands, not Taiwan. Later it was declared that the PRC could generally wait with the liberation of Taiwan and the offshore islands until better times. The intensive shelling and blockade of the offshore islands was changed to shelling them every other day—on even-number dates, while action against the United States was limited to giving it "stern warnings". Bourgeois propaganda took advantage of these developments to denigrate the foreign policy of the socialist countries, and prove the wisdom of the policy "from positions of strength". As for the countries of Asia, the events in the Taiwan Strait only increased their concern about the implications of China's foreign policy.

As China's economy was rehabilitated and developed with Soviet assistance and her position on the international arena was consolidated, CPC leaders proceeded to step up their anti-Soviet activities, play down the importance of friendship with the Soviet Union, and seek out pretexts for aggravating Sino-Soviet relations.

Already in that period, a wide difference became manifest between the ways of approach of the CPC and the CPSU to disputes between the two countries.

In its relations with China the Soviet Union invariably sought to avoid even the slightest cause for alienation and mistrust, taking efforts to resolve any, even the most insignificant, differences in a spirit of sincerity and fraternal mutual understanding. In contrast to this, Chinese leaders invariably went out of their way to find whatever pretext they could to aggravate Sino-Soviet relations, juggled and twisted facts, not stopping at deliberate provocative acts.

Regardless of protocol Soviet leaders repeatedly came out for setting up direct contacts at top level and visited China in the period when nationalists within the CPC began to complicate deliberately disputed problems in order to undermine Sino-Soviet friendship. Soviet leaders continued these practices in 1958.

On a Soviet initiative Soviet and Chinese leaders met in Peking in late July and early August 1958. At that meeting the Soviet stand was explained in detail to Chinese leaders, on specific issues in particular.

The communique on the Sino-Soviet meeting declared a full identity of views on vital problems of the contemporary international situation, and the continued development of relations of friendship, alliance and mutual assistance between the Soviet Union and China.

Later, Chinese leaders again turned back to individual problems with a view to exacerbating Sino-Soviet relations. In the light of later developments it became perfectly obvious that the raising of these issues was from the outset a deliberate action of the Maoists seeking out a pretext for attacks on the Soviet Union, for a further deterioration of Sino-Soviet relations.

CPC leaders employed the border conflict between China and India, which flared up in the autumn of 1959, for aggravating Sino-Soviet relations.

Until 1959 China and India had developed friendly relations. Their governments formulated the well-known five principles of peaceful coexistence and initiated the Afro-Asian Conference in Bandung. However, from the spring of 1959 Sino-Indian relations deteriorated, which was in the interest of the reactionary circles of the United States, India and the nationalists in the CPC leadership. All these political forces, which seemed different at first glance, sought to provoke a grave conflict over the Indo-Chinese controversy in this area of Asia, involving the Soviet Union and the United States, and exacerbation of Sino-Soviet relations.

The imperialist forces of the United States and Britain sought to denigrade the foreign policy line of the socialist countries, to undermine the trust of the Third World in them. In pursuing their nationalistic goals CPC leaders were utterly unconcerned for the harmful consequences of their adventurist actions on the international scene for the world revolutionary movement.

In the autumn of 1959, the border conflict between China and India rose to a higher pitch. At the end of August and in October 1959 border clashes took place, resulting in Indian casualties. The PRC published a statement that India was claiming an area of Chinese territory of about 130,000 sq km. Although the Sino-Indian border of over 2,000 km had never been delineated, it was clear from the statement of Chinese leaders that they were laying claims to very vast areas.

The border conflict between the PRC and India caused great damage to the cause of peace and socialism. It placed in a difficult situation India's progressive forces, above all her Communist Party. Repeated appeals of the leadership of the Indian Communist Party to the CPC Central Committee failed to alter the position of Chinese leaders.

Peking leaders claimed that one of the causes of the present Sino-Soviet differences was the Soviet Union's failure to support China's stand on the Sino-Indian border conflict. This statement is slanderous. In reality, the Soviet Union from the very outset took up the only possible and correct stand in relation to the Sino-Indian dispute, although—and this should be specially emphasised—the Chinese side, contrary to its commitments under the treaty between the Soviet Union and the PRC, had failed to consult the Soviet Government in advance. The Soviet position was one of facilitating a peaceful settlement of the conflict and preventing the reactionary forces from using it to undermine Sino-Soviet relations, denigrating a socialist country by accusing her of aggression. Through diplomatic and other channels the Soviet side made its position known to PRC Government in good time and warned it of possible negative implications of this incident.

On September 10, 1959 the Soviet news agency TASS published a statement expressing the Soviet Government's concern about the Sino-Indian border conflict and hope for its speedy settlement.

The TASS statement suggested to the PRC Government realistic ways to settle the dispute. However, CPC leaders, far from appreciating the Soviet position duly, attempted to distort it. On September 13, 1959 Chinese leaders came out with a reproach claiming that the TASS statement had shown to the whole world the different stands of China and the Soviet Union on the Sino-Indian border dispute, which was the cause of joy and jubilation for the Indian bourgeoisie, American and British imperialism.

Without going down to the crux of the matter it should be noted that the allegation of CPC leaders to the effect that the Soviet Union had shown to the whole world its different stand was hypocritical from beginning to end, because since 1956 the nationalists within the CPC had been repeatedly and crudely demonstrating to the whole world their differences with the CPSU and the Soviet Union.

After the TASS statement the imperialist camp, far from being jubilant, as Chinese leaders alleged, on the contrary openly expressed its disappointment. It should be presumed that it would have been truly jubilant if the Soviet Union had been drawn into this conflict, because direct unilateral Soviet support to the PRC in the Sino-Indian dispute would have inevitably resulted in the involvement of the United States, Britain and other imperialist powers. There was every indication that the US ruling circles intended to interfere actively in the conflict between China and India. The Soviet Union's position prevented the emergence of a dangerous hotbed of war and made interference by the imperialist forces impossible.

Despite all these obvious circumstances, however, Chinese leaders continued to distort the Soviet Union's stand on the Sino-Indian border conflict.

While undermining insidiously Sino-Soviet friendship, Chinese leaders camouflaged their true sentiments with statements that by no means expressed their actual views. One of the main strategic objectives of some CPC leaders has been to provoke a war between the United States and the Soviet Union—and have these two nations bleed each other to death to suit China's great-power interests. The motto "to sit on a mountain and watch two tigers fight" was widely current in 1958-1959 as well. Therefore, the Maoists were irritated by the normalisation of Soviet-American relations. To conceal their actual views, however, they made now and then statements couched in favourable terms. For example, commenting on the Soviet Premier's visit to the United States, the 8th plenary meeting of the CPC Central Committee held at Lushan in August 1959 welcomed the news of the forthcoming exchange of visits between the heads of government of the Soviet Union and the United States and expressed its belief that this would contribute to a continued relaxation of international tensions and preservation of peace throughout the world.

At a banquet held on the occasion of the 10th anniversary of the PRC, Chou En-lai declared, commenting on the Soviet Premier's visit to the United States: "We congratulate him on the success he has achieved during his visit to the United States as an envoy of peace and we welcome the communique on his talks with the U.S. President Eisenhower."[1] Later, it was preferred not to recall such statements in China.

In 1958-1959, the struggle between the two lines continued not only within the CPC but also in the sphere of Sino-Soviet relations, where the internationalist policy of the CPSU and the Soviet Government came up against the obstacles put up by nationalistic CPC leaders.

4. SOME RESULTS OF SINO-SOVIET CO-OPERATION IN 1949-1959

The year 1959 was a turning point after which Sino-Soviet economic, scientific, technological and cultural co-operation, through no fault of the Soviet Union, began to be curtailed rapidly; therefore, some end results of this co-operation merit attention.

---

[1] *Druzhba* (Friendship), 1959, No. 43, p. 11 (in Russian).

Between 1950 and 1959, the Soviet Union assumed tremendous obligations to aid China in building, modernising and expanding more than 400 industrial enterprises, individual departments and other projects. Leaning on Soviet assistance, China planned to build 12 metallurgical complexes and plants to produce annually 30 million tons of steel, 28 million tons of cast iron, 25 million tons of rolled stock; three aluminium plants with a total output of 738,000 tons a year; a complex of tin-smelting works near the city of Gejiu with an output of 25,000 tons a year; 7 heavy machine-building plants for manufacturing metallurgical, ore-mining, oil-extracting and chemical equipment with a capacity of 240,000 tons of metal goods a year; 17 works for manufacturing steam, gas and hydroturbines and turbogenerators with an annual output of 11.2 million kilowatts; 100 defence industry projects.

All in all, more than 250 large industrial projects, departments and installations fitted out with the most up-to-date equipment were built in China with Soviet assistance. Among them mention is deserved by the Anshan and the Wuhan steel complexes, the Changchun motor works, the complex of plants in Loyang (tractor, bearing, and ore-mining equipment), the electrical engineering, turbine and boiler plants in Harbin, the synthetic rubber factory and oil refinery in Lanchow (the nitrogen fertilizer plants in Kirin and Taiyuan, the shale-processing plants in Fushun, the heavy machine-building plant in Fulark, a number of large power stations and special projects.

Describing the importance of Soviet assistance to China's economic development, member of the Political Bureau of the CPC Central Committee, Vice-Premier of the PRC, Li Fuchung, stated: "Our assessment, which is a firm assessment, is this: the enterprises designed and built in China with Soviet assistance really embody all that is modern and the best of what the Soviet Union has at its disposal. These enterprises are the backbone of our industry, the backbone not only in volume, but also in levels of modern advanced technology. . . . Facts evidence that all Soviet specialists and design organisations really sought to make these enterprises concentrate Soviet experience and become the best in the world. And they have successfully achieved this."

The Soviet Union helped China to build up whole industries—aircraft, automotive, radio engineering, various branches of the chemical industry, large capacities in the steel, power and other industries. Soviet scientific and technological aid to China in nuclear physics was of great importance, too. The first experimental atomic pile and a cyclotron were built in China with Soviet aid.

The productive capacities of enterprises built and commissioned with Soviet assistance were as follows: 8.7 million tons of cast iron, 8.4 million tons of steel, 6.5 million tons of rolled stock, 17.2 million tons of coal, 7.5 million of agglomerated coal, 38,000 tons of aluminium, 150,000 tons of ammonia, 250,000 tons of sulphuric acid, 60,000 tons of heavy machine-building industry products, 20,000 tons of mining equipment, 40,000 tons of oil-refining and chemical equipment, steam and hydraulic turbines with a total capacity of 1.7 million kilowatts, generators with a total capacity of 0.6 million kilowatts, 42,000 tractors (in conventional units), 30,000 lorries, 3,700 metal-cutting lathes, 7,000 tons of steam per hour for electric power stations. At power stations, turbine sets with a total capacity of 3.9 million kilowatts were commissioned.

In China's total production in 1960, the shares of products manufactured at enterprises built with Soviet technical assistance were as follows: cast iron, 30 per cent; steel, about 40 per cent; rolled stock, over 50 per cent; lorries, 80 per cent; tractors, over 90 per cent; synthetic ammonia, 30 per cent; electricity, 25 per cent; steam and hydraulic turbines, 55 per cent; generators, about 20 per cent; aluminium, 25 per cent; heavy machine-building industry products, more than 10 per cent, etc.

Expressing its high appreciation of Soviet assistance and the importance for China of enterprises built with Soviet aid the newspaper *Jenmin jihpao* wrote in February 1959 that the Soviet Union's assistance to economic development in China was without precedent in history both in quantity and in scope.

Between 1950 and 1960, more than 8,500 highly qualified Soviet technical specialists (not counting military advisers) were commissioned to work in China. Over the same period, about 1,500 Soviet specialists were sent to China to give her aid in the fields of science, higher education, public health, and culture.

Soviet teachers commissioned to work in China played an extremely important role in training Chinese personnel. Between 1948 and 1960, 615 highly qualified Soviet instructors went to China to help set up a modern system of higher and specialised secondary education. They trained a large body of Chinese specialists for work in the economic and educational fields. From 1949 to 1960 a total of 1,269 Soviet specialists from the higher and public education systems worked at China's Ministry of Education and higher educational establishments.

About 2,000 Chinese specialists and about 1,000 scientists stayed in the Soviet Union under a programme of scientific and technological co-operation to study Soviet scientific and technological experience and know-how. The Soviet Union handed over to China a large quantity of scientific, technical and other documents vitally important for her economy. In the total volume of technical documents handed over by the Soviet Union to the socialist countries China accounted for about 50 per cent. Using Soviet documents received before July 1, 1957, China designed 159 projects, and organised the manufacture of over 300 new important production items.

China in turn had handed over to the Soviet Union by January 1, 1961 about 1,500 sets of scientific and technical documents on a variety of subjects.

Since 1949, 66 higher schools of China and 85 of the Soviet Union regularly exchanged research findings and other material. Soviet and Chinese institutions of higher learning carried on joint research on 124 problems.

The work of Soviet specialists in China is a vivid page in the history of the Soviet people's friendship with the people of China. By their selfless assistance they won great prestige and affection among Chinese workers, engineers and technicians, all those they had worked with. "Specialists from the Soviet Union and the People's Democracies working in our country have made an outstanding contribution to our socialist construction," Premier Chou En-lai said in his report to the 8th National Congress of the CPC.

The Soviet Government also organised the training of Chinese research and technical personnel and skilled workers at Soviet enterprises, higher educational establishments, design and research organisations. Between 1951 and 1962, more than 8,000 Chinese citizens received vocational training in the Soviet Union. Over 11,000 Chinese undergraduate and research students studied at Soviet educational establishments. More than 900 workers of various institutions of China's Academy of Sciences underwent advanced training and studied research methods at the USSR Academy of Sciences. In addition, over 1,500 Chinese engineers, technicians and scientists went to the USSR under a programme of scientific and technological co-operation to study Soviet scientific and technological achievements and know-how.

The Soviet Union trained for every industrial project being built with its aid practically all technical personnel, ranging from the general manager and the chief engineer to chiefs of department and section, as well as other workers directly involved in building the project: construction work, assembly of equipment, preparation of individual production sections for commissioning.[1]

Over 10-odd years the Soviet Union handed over to China, practically free of charge, 24,000 sets of scientific and technical documents. In the opinion of foreign experts, such documents, if bought by China on the world market, would have cost her many thousand million dollars. These documents included 1,400 large projects. According to Chinese evidence, between 1952 and 1957, of the 51,000 metal-cutting lathes manufactured in China 43,500, or 85 per cent of the total, were built in accordance with Soviet technical documents. Today, every branch of industry in China manufactures products based on designs, specifications and process charts drawn up and tested in the Soviet Union and handed over to China.

It was a distinctive feature of Sino-Soviet co-operation in the fields of science and technology that the Soviet Union gave China an incomparably larger amount of scientific and technical documents than it received from her in return.

---

[1] Chiang Yan-tsin, "Soviet Technical Assistance—Guarantee of Our Success", *Foreign Trade*, 1959, No. 10, p. 22.

"The importance of Sino-Soviet scientific and technical co-operation for remaking our country along socialist lines and for building socialism is tremendous," the newspaper *Druzhba* (Friendship) wrote in its issue of December 4, 1956. "As a result of this co-operation not only have technical difficulties been overcome in the economic development of our country, but the quality of construction and products has been improved and it is possible to speed up her socialist industrialisation with a minimum of manpower and resources, to raise scientific and technical personnel and push up rapidly her scientific and technological levels."

The great volume of scientific and technical literature made available to China by the Soviet Union was of great importance for rehabilitating her economy and for her planned socialist construction. Between 1949 and 1955, 3,000 Soviet scientific and technical books were published in China in a total impression of over 20 million copies.

The links between the libraries of the Soviet and Chinese Academies of Sciences were further extended. In 1956 alone, the main libraries of the USSR Academy of Sciences sent about 70,000 volumes of varied scientific literature to the Academy of Sciences of China.

To help China's economic effort and strengthen her defence capability, the Soviet Government granted her long-term credits on easy terms. Between 1950 and 1961, the Soviet Union gave China eleven such credits to a total of 2,000 million rubles in foreign exchange.

In addition to economic, scientific and technical assistance, the Soviet Union, ever since the proclamation of the People's Republic of China, helped her to build up her own defence industry and handed over technical documents and process charts for the manufacture of modern weapons and equipment. At the same time, the Soviet Union supplied large quantities of military equipment and materials for the People's Liberation Army.

Trade with the Soviet Union was of vital importance for China. In the conditions of the economic blockade and embargo on trade with People's China imposed by the United States and many other capitalist countries the vast and stable Soviet market was of crucial value for Chinese exports.

From the early years of People's China the Soviet Union was the main importer of Chinese commodities. In 1950, the Soviet share in Chinese exports was 28.7 per cent; and in the first five-year plan period, 59.4 per cent on the average. The Soviet Union was practically the only supplier of modern means of production to China.

It will also be recalled that it was extremely difficult for People's China as a young developing state to operate on the world market in view of the inadequate range and quality of her goods and to compete against even some developing countries, let alone economically developed capitalist states. It was only the close economic ties between China and the socialist countries, primarily the Soviet Union, that enabled her to export large quantities of agricultural and industrial raw materials, as well as other goods at profitable prices.[1] What is more, the Soviet Union often bought or actively helped to market many Chinese commodities in low demand on the world market.

Cultural co-operation with the Soviet Union was also of great practical importance for building socialism in China. Acquaintance with the cultural life of the Soviet people, who had traversed a long road of struggle for socialism, with their science, literature and art helped increase the influence of Marxist-Leninist ideology on the Chinese working people, contributed to the assimilation of socialist ideas by builders of the new China, provided living, graphic examples which helped to find new ways to progress and could be used to stimulate the intellectual life of the multi-million masses of the extremely backward country, semi-feudal and semi-colonial a short time ago.

Progressive people in China, leaders of the CPC loyal to the cause of socialism were well aware of the prime importance of intellectual intercourse between the Chinese and Soviet peoples, and from the early days of the October Revolution sought to develop intensive and all-round Sino-Soviet cultural exchanges. It is necessary to note the great inspiration China's revolutionary circles received on their acquain-

---

[1] Unprocessed and processed agricultural raw materials and products of the peasant handicraft industry accounted for 90.7 and 71.6 per cent of Chinese exports in 1950 and 1957 respectively.

tance with Russian literature before the proclamation of the PRC. This refers to the early 20th century when English and then Chinese translations of Pushkin, Lermontov, Turgenev, Dostoyevsky, Gogol, Chekhov, and Gorky began to appear in China. Describing the importance of Russian literature the eminent Chinese author, Lu Hsin wrote that its influence was a major cause of the literary revolution in China.

After the Great October Socialist Revolution the influence of Russian and Soviet literature became a fairly important stimulus to the development of revolutionary processes in China. Public interest in it became exceptionally wide. Explaining the reasons for this interest, Tsü Chiu-po wrote in 1920:

"The main reason is that the red Bolshevik revolution in Russia has brought about staggering political, economic and social changes; the revolution has shaken the world and influenced the development of ideas in all countries. All are willing to understand the essence of this revolution, to take a closer look at Russian culture—and so mankind's attention has become riveted to Russia, to Russian literature. And since in Chinese society, where so much is sombre and tragic, people were searching for new ways in life, their minds could not but be excited by the reverberations of the unprecedented collapse of the old society. Therefore, everybody in China has taken an interest in Russia, and Russian literature has become a beacon for Chinese writers."[1]

The All-China Association of Workers in Literature and the Arts, in a message to Soviet cultural workers on the occasion of the 32nd anniversary of the Great October Revolution, declared:

"Works of Soviet literature and art created after the Great October Revolution have produced an indelible impression on writers and artists throughout the world. Their influence on China's revolutionary literature and art has been particularly strong. Soviet literature and art have fertilized Chinese revolutionary literature and art."[2]

---

[1] Tsü Chiu-po, *Essays and Articles,* Moscow, 1959, p. 89 (in Russian).

[2] *Jenmin jihpao,* June 12, 1950.

The finest works of Soviet literature dedicated to the Soviet people's heroic exploits during the revolution, the Civil War and the Great Patriotic War inspired millions of Chinese working people in their revolutionary and national liberation struggle. Many works by Soviet authors, in particular *Volokolamsk Highway* by A. Bek, *Days and Nights* by K. Simonov, *Front* by A. Korneichuk and others were included in lists of "compulsory reading" for Chinese Party cadres and army personnel.[1]

Soviet literature had an equally fruitful influence on the intellectual life of Chinese society after the proclamation of the PRC. For example, the well-known literary critic Tsao Ching-hua, in an article entitled "Soviet Literature and Its Chinese Readers" published in 1954, wrote that for those involved in implementing the agrarian reform in China the novel *Virgin Soil Upturned* by Mikhail Sholokhov was a desk book in which they sought answers to many questions.

In 1957 the Chinese Writers' Union, in a message of greetings to the USSR Writers' Union on the occasion of the 40th anniversary of the Great October Socialist Revolution, said: "The Chinese people are regular readers of Soviet books and regard Soviet literature as a guide to life and struggle. . . . Chinese authors have invariably emulated Soviet literature, studied thoroughly its rich experience and are ready to take a determined stand alongside their brothers—Soviet authors—in defence of socialist realism in literature."

Translated literature was published in the Soviet Union and China in huge impressions.

In the period from 1946 to 1960, 976 books by Chinese authors were published in the Soviet Union in a total impression of about 43 million copies in Russian translation and in 50 other languages of the peoples of the USSR. During 1950-1958, more than 13,000 works by Soviet authors were translated in China and published in a total impression of about 230 million copies.

Guided by the principles of socialist internationalism, the Soviet Union over 10-odd years (1949-1960) commissioned for long-term work in China at the request of her government about 2,000 most experienced specialists in the fields of

---

[1] *Hsinhua yüehkan*, Peking, 1950.

culture and education who accounted for approximately 20 per cent of all Soviet specialists working in China.

In the period from 1949 to 1960, about 17,000 instructors, mostly in branches of new technology, were trained in China with the aid of Soviet specialists. Adding to this the number of instructors (about 1,700) trained for China in the Soviet Union, their total will amount to about 19,000, i.e., roughly one-fourth of the total staff of instructors in Chinese institutions of higher learning. In 1951-1962, over 11,000 Chinese undergraduate and research students were enrolled in Soviet higher schools. Fifty per cent of expenditure involved in their training was borne by the Soviet Government.

There were also close cultural exchanges between the USSR and China in the field of cinematography. In 1949-1959, about 750 Soviet films were shown in China, which drew a total audience of roughly 1,900 million spectators. Over the period, more than 100 Chinese films were shown in the Soviet Union.

In whatever field the USSR developed co-operation with People's China, its main guiding principle was to contribute in every way to reinforcing socialism in China and to promoting Sino-Soviet friendship.

CHAPTER VI

THE CHANGEOVER OF THE CPC LEADERSHIP FROM THE POLICY OF SINO-SOVIET FRIENDSHIP TO AN OPEN STRUGGLE AGAINST THE CPSU AND THE SOVIET UNION

The year 1960 was a turning point in Sino-Soviet relations. It marked the beginning of a new period when the key positions in the CPC were taken by forces which imposed a nationalistic policy on the People's Republic of China. Its implementation led to a radical revision of China's foreign policy, the departure of her Communist Party from the principles of proletarian internationalism, the rupture by Peking leaders of the relations of friendship and co-operation with the Soviet Union and other socialist countries, and an open political struggle against them.

The renunciation by the CPC leadership of the Leninist principles of foreign policy of a socialist state was inseparably linked with the internal processes of China's development. It was the direct result of the growth of anti-socialist tendencies in China, the imposition of anti-Marxist, anti-Leninist views on the Communist Party, the departure of Peking leaders from the path of socialist construction.

On the other hand, the home situation in China in that period was characterised by an exacerbation of the class struggle, because the great setbacks in economic development caused by the disastrous voluntaristic policy of the "big leap" and the setting up of people's communes undermined the positions of socialism in China and gave the anti-socialist forces an opportunity for a counter-offensive.

1. CHINA'S HOME SITUATION IN THE EARLY 60s

The situation which had taken shape in China toward the early 60s was characterised by a sharp deterioration of the economic conditions. The failure of attempts by CPC leaders to overcome economic backwardness within a brief space of time by voluntaristic methods, and thereby to provide the internal prerequisites for making their nationalistic aspirations and claims to leadership come true, became strikingly obvious to everybody.

China's economy was completely disorganised. Her industrial and agricultural production fell sharply. By 1962 her gross industrial output had reduced almost by half as compared with 1959, in particular, steel by 46 per cent, electricity by 13 per cent, coal by 48 per cent, iron ore by 66 per cent, coke 72 per cent, cement by 40 per cent, power equipment by 75 per cent, metal-cutting lathes 69 per cent, cotton fabrics by half, edible vegetable oils by 30 per cent, sugar by 12 per cent. The total grain harvest fell by one-third. A large proportion of her productive forces was destroyed. According to expert estimates, the total value of main production assets in industry reduced at least by 33 per cent, in agriculture by 25-30 per cent.

The CPC leadership had to take emergency measures to check the further decline of production. For this purpose, the 9th plenary meeting of the CPC Central Committee held in January 1961 decided to curtail the scope of capital construction and to adjust the rates of development. This implied massive suspension of work at enterprises built mostly in the "big-leap" years, complete closure of "backyard" blast furnaces, and from the middle of 1961, termination of capital construction in industry and the transport services, including that in the stage of completion. Industry, in addition to production of consumer goods, was geared primarily to serve agriculture, although this demanded termination of the manufacture of main products of enterprises which had earlier supplied other sectors of the economy.

Developments forced the CPC leadership to give up the idea of "early communisation". The communes set up in towns disintegrated, and in rural localities communes were reorganised into ordinary agricultural co-operatives which came to be known as teams. Free meals introduced without any justification had to be abolished, subsidiary plots returned to peasants, and the principle of material incentives restored to a definite extent.

Economic development was now based on such principles as "to work for a high level in production, to keep to a low level in life", "to apply firmly a rational system of low wages". To justify the freezing of the living standards of the population, Chinese propaganda put forward the slogan "To defy suffering, to defy death". Villages and enterprises which coped with difficulties leaning on their own resources, without assistance from the state were advertised as a model for emulation. Communes, enterprises, whole towns and provinces were oriented to natural economy.

Outlays for social and cultural development were markedly cut down. In 1959, housing and communal construction, the building of schools and institutions of higher learning was stopped. The student body in higher schools reduced from 695,000 in 1960 to 250,000 in 1964, in secondary schools it fell by 2.7 million and in primary schools, by 8-10 million.

The failure of the "big leap" resulted in unprecedented difficulties in food and consumer goods supplies to the population. Rationing and special coupons were introduced for the purchase of many goods and later rations of grain, fats, sugar were sharply diminished. In 1962 and later years an adult person's monthly ration was 150-200 grams of meat, 100-150 grams of vegetable oil. The annual ration of cotton fabrics was 2-3 metres per person.

The emergency measures taken by the CPC leadership to deal with the consequences of the "big leap" produced a definite effect. By the end of 1962 the economic situation levelled off to a certain extent. Nevertheless, the curtailment of heavy industry, the growth of military spending, the policy of developing natural economy could not secure any appreciable progress.

Of course, many difficulties in China's economic development were due to objective causes. Suffice it to recall that China with her huge population accounts for only 4 per cent of the world industrial output. The people's government inherited from pre-revolutionary times primitive agriculture, backward industry, poverty and economic dislocation. The difficulties inevitable under such conditions were multiplied tenfold by mistakes of Mao Tse-tung and his followers, their renunciation of fraternal co-operation with the socialist countries, disregard for the laws of economic development.

It should be emphasised that when correcting their blunders and errors, Chinese leaders withheld the truth from their people. They repeated over and over again that the policy of "three red banners" was the only correct course to victory.

It was revealed during the "cultural revolution" that in those years the Maoists' adventurist policy on the issues of China's internal development, in which the Chinese people were assigned the role of a mere "scrap of blank paper", was censured in the Party ranks, in the CPC leadership in particular. Besides that, nationalistic elements did not yet hold dominating positions, therefore the controversy within the leading bodies of the CPC assumed the form of a compromise: on the one hand, it was alleged that the policy of "three red banners" was infallible, on the other hand, measures to adjust the former policy, i.e., its revision, were being implemented.

It was not fortuitous that Mao Tse-tung who had led the country during the "big-leap" years to a deep crisis and the people to starvation, allowed Liu Shao-chi, Teng Hsiao-ping and other members of the CPC Central Committee to save the situation, while he himself concentrated on theoretical studies. It was precisely in that period, in 1958, that he stepped down as Chairman of the PRC. When the country had recovered from these "experiments", Mao Tse-tung went out of his way during the "cultural revolution" to dispose of witnesses of his blunders.

Failures in the home policy, chronic economic difficulties, increasing violations of legality and the democratic principles of social life, caused growing discontent in all the strata of Chinese society, including the Party and government apparatus.

As far back as August 1959, at the 8th plenary meeting of the CPC Central Committee, a group of Central Committee members came out against the "big-leap" policy, quali-

fying it as a petty bourgeois phantasy, which cost dearly to
the Chinese people. Among those opposed to the Maoists'
policy were Political Bureau member Peng Te-huai, alternate member of the Political Bureau, Chang Wen-tien, many
leading executives of provincial Party committees, ministries and government departments.

In the early 60s, discontent with the policy of the nationalists within the CPC became even more manifest. Doubts
about the correctness of their special line circulated among
broad sections of government and Party officials and intellectuals. For example, chief of the propaganda department
of the Guizhow provincial committee of the CPC, Wang
Hsiao-chuan, said that the "dark days" experienced by China
were the result of certain mistaken guiding ideas, that the
"big leap" was a flop, that the general line was wrong, and
the people's communes were a bitter lesson. Deputy chief of
the propaganda department of the CPC Central Committee,
Chou Yang, in conversations with writers, described the
"big-leap" policy as ill-considered. Secretary of the Peking
city committee of the CPC, Teng To, wrote in the newspaper *Peiching wanpao* on November 26, 1961 about "boasters
who make much ado about nothing"; in his opinion, brags
believed they "could do anything. In the end they smashed
their heads against facts and were complete bankrupts".

Chinese readers justly interpreted these words as criticism
of those CPC leaders who had promised the people the
achievement of thousands of years of happiness within three
years.

The well-known Chinese economist Sun Yeh-fang, direc-
tor of the Institute of Economics under the PRC Academy
of Sciences, in 1961 made an appeal to restore the principle
of self-sustained operation of enterprises. Arguing against
disregard for material incentives he insisted on making
wider use of commodity-money relations in building socialism. Rector of the Higher Party School, member of the Central Committee of the CPC, Yang Hsien-cheng, stated that
the "big-leap" policy was the product of subjectivism and
voluntarism. These sentiments were shared by some CPC
leaders. Liu Shao-chi, in a speech on the occasion of the 40th
anniversary of the Communist Party of China in July 1961,
criticised those who believed that the Chinese revolution

could allegedly be directed relying on subjective views, desultory impressions or individual quotations borrowed from certain books.

Advocates of the special line certainly knew of these sentiments, but in that period they still did not dare to resort to open repression of opposition elements. It was evidently presumed that "stabilisation" of the economy would improve the situation and provide more favourable conditions for an offensive against the opposition.

In an effort to justify their claims to leadership in the world communist movement, Peking leaders, as far back as 1960, went ahead with propaganda on a growing scale of the "ideas of Mao Tse-tung" as the "pinnacle of theoretical thought in the modern epoch". Corresponding arguments were invented to support this allegation. An article in the Chinese press stated: "That contemporary China is the homeland of the ideas of Mao Tse-tung is not accidental. This has its deep-rooted historical and social causes. Similarly, in the 1840s Germany became the homeland of Marxism, and in the 20th century Russia became the homeland of Leninism."[1]

Propaganda of the "ideas of Mao Tse-tung" increasingly laid emphasis on the thesis that they were valid not only for China but also for the rest of the world. Peking "theoreticians" discarded in effect the earlier definition which described "the ideas of Mao Tse-tung" as a "combination of the universal truth of Marxism-Leninism with the concrete Chinese realities". Formerly, CPC leaders spoke of the "ideas of Mao Tse-tung" as the "investing of Marxism from its European form in its Chinese form", as "Chinese communism", whereas now this definition was regarded as insufficient. The national garments which CPC leaders had sought to put on Marxism in the past now became too small for the "ideas of Mao Tse-tung".

Ever wider currency was given to statements like this: "The ideas of Mao Tse-tung are Marxism-Leninism of the epoch of socialist revolution and socialist construction",[2] "the ideas of Mao Tse-tung are comprehensively developed

---

[1] *Shantung tahsüeh hsüehpao*, 1960, No. 1.
[2] *Sinkiang hungchi*, 1960, No. 6.

Marxism-Leninism of the epoch of proletarian socialist revolution",[1] etc.

All ideological work in China was focussed on propaganda of the "ideas of Mao Tse-tung", while works by the founders of Marxism-Leninism were actually banned. Chinese periodicals persistently advertised "works" of Mao Tse-tung, many of which oversimplified or distorted Marxism. This campaign came to a head in 1960 after the fourth volume of *Selected Works* by Mao Tse-tung had come off the press.

In the meantime, increasing emphasis was laid on nationalistic, great-power ideas in political education of China's population. The Chinese press began to elaborate intensively on the subject of China's exclusiveness, her crucial role in world history. Chinese newspapers and magazines printed numerous articles about the greatness of ancient China, quoted statements by ancient philosophers about the special stability of everything Chinese, about the Chinese having invariably remade foreigners in their own image, etc.

The Chinese press began striking clearly racialist notes, attempting to oppose one race to another. On February 4, 1961, *Kwangming jihpao* in an article entitled "Criticism of World History Without a World Character" maintained: "Until the 15th century, the peoples of Asia, i.e., the yellow race, had held the leading position in world history. After the 15th century this position was gradually won by the European nations, i.e., the white race." The authors predicted a comeback of the yellow race to its former "leading" position.

2. DEPARTURE OF THE CPC LEADERSHIP
FROM THE LENINIST PRINCIPLES
OF SOCIALIST FOREIGN POLICY

The failure of the policy of "three red banners" dashed the hopes of nationalistic elements to carry into effect their ambitious plans of aggrandizement by way of China's internal development, her "leap" forward to the position of the world's greatest power. They lost all faith in the possibility

---

[1] *Hsüehshu yüehkan*, 1960, No. 10.

for socialism to win in a peaceful economic competition against capitalism.

Whereas in the period of setting up people's communes the Maoists kept repeating that communism could be built within a matter of years ("three years of stubborn work—10,000 years of happiness," etc.), now they went to the other extreme, putting off the attainment of this goal to an indefinite future. It was asserted in Peking that "the final victory of socialism cannot be achieved within the lifetime of one or two generations. It can be achieved in full within the lifetime of five to ten generations or even after a longer period of time".[1] Thus, the nationalists in the CPC admitted their complete inability to cope with the breath-taking tasks of socialist construction, to lead the struggle of the Chinese working people for the final victory of socialism in their country.

This did not mean, however, that Chinese leaders had given up their nationalistic ambitions and claims to leadership. After their setbacks in the economic field they went about searching for new ways to attain their old objectives. They concentrated on foreign policy, seeking to prod a world revolution by war, to involve the world's leading powers—the USSR and the USA—in a mutually annihilating military conflagration and to build on their ruins "a new brilliant civilisation" where China would dominate thanks to the overwhelming numbers of her population.

It was declared in Peking that it was foolish to speak of building communism as long as imperialism existed and was relatively strong in the main regions of the world. Chinese leaders attacked the policy of peaceful coexistence pursued by the socialist countries in an effort to aggravate international tensions. At the same time, they sought to secure success for their policy at a minimum of risk for China herself, trying to keep away, insofar as possible, from the dangers involved in this policy.

The discrepancy between the slogans of Peking leaders and their practical actions in the field of foreign affairs became increasingly apparent. While declaring the need to fight imperialism on the principle of "sword against sword"

---

[1] *Jenmin jihpao,* July 14, 1964.

they actively sought, in fact, to achieve a normalisation of China's relations with the capitalist states to the detriment of China's co-operation with the socialist countries.

The departure of CPC leaders from the Leninist principles of foreign policy resulted in China's activities on the international scene being increasingly based on blackmail and bribery, all sorts of provocation, direct interference in the internal affairs of other countries, including socialist ones, ideological subversion of the fraternal parties, efforts to split the socialist community of nations and the world communist movement.

China's intensified activities on the international scene were largely motivated by the desire of the nationalists in the CPC to distract the Chinese people's attention from the catastrophic collapse of the policy of "three red banners", to establish their control over every field of life in China under the slogan of stepping up the struggle against imperialism and "modern revisionism".

In that period, China's foreign policy essentially boiled down to the following principles.

In relation to the socialist camp: to isolate the Soviet Union, to impose Chinese views on as many socialist countries as possible and ultimately to use the economic and political power of the socialist community to attain China's great-power, nationalistic goals.

In the field of relations with the national liberation movements: to separate them from the Soviet Union and other socialist states, from the international working class, to knock together a bloc of Afro-Asian countries and eventually to achieve hegemony over the countries which used to be colonial possessions of imperialism.

In relation to the communist movement: to isolate the CPSU, to undermine its prestige among the fraternal parties, to assert China's ideological and political platform as the general line of the international communist movement, and thereby to convert this movement into a tool of Peking's great-power strategy.

China's foreign policy was directed at frustrating the policy of peaceful coexistence, aggravating international tensions, bringing nearer a "decisive military battle with imperialism".

The departure of Peking leaders from the agreed common line of the socialist countries on the international scene became particularly glaring in the autumn of 1962 during the Caribbean crisis. At a time when Cuba was faced with a grave danger of invasion by US troops and the world was on the brink of a thermonuclear war, Chinese leaders made undisguised attempts to provoke a large-scale international conflict.

In the first stage of the crisis, between October 23 and 28, 1962, when the international situation was extremely tense, and it was particularly imperative to come out in a united front against the aggressive actions of American imperialism, CPC leaders abstained from active measures to support Cuba, as it was done by the USSR and other countries. Chinese leaders preferred to take up a wait-and-see attitude so as to say the last word whatever the outcome of the crisis.

After October 28, 1962, when the tension diminished, and a trend was in evidence toward ending the crisis, a clamorous campaign suddenly flared up in the PRC ostensibly in token of her determined support for the Cuban people's struggle in defence of their independence, sovereignty and dignity, Chinese propaganda emphasising quite unequivocally that the Soviet stand allegedly caused damage to Cuba. In the meantime, Chinese leaders, demonstrating their opposition to the settlement of the crisis through peaceful negotiations and pushing the USSR and Cuba to a path leading to a military conflict, attempted to prove by references to the developments in the Caribbean the soundness of their special views and to discredit the policy of peaceful coexistence. Anti-Soviet fabrications concerning the Caribbean crisis were circulated by Chinese representatives also within international democratic organisations and at various international meetings.

The true aims of the Maoists during the Caribbean crisis were to provoke an armed conflict between the Soviet Union and the United States and to warm their hands over this military conflagration. In this connection significant statements were made in the capitalist press. On November 7, 1962, the *New York Times* said ironically that Peking has long been prepared to fight to the last American and to the last Russian.

During the dangerous developments in the Caribbean, Chinese leaders failed to make any businesslike, constructive proposals for securing the interests of Cuba and preventing war. What is more, Peking, far from contributing to the settlement of the Caribbean crisis, exactly in those grim days opened hostilities on the Indian border, thereby creating another hotbed of international tensions. These actions were the best illustration of the actual designs of Chinese leaders. Taking advantage of the fact that the world's attention was riveted to the acute international conflict, Peking leaders attempted to implement their nationalistic plans.

In October 1962, Chinese troops under the pretext of acting in self-defence, made a 100-kilometre-deep invasion into areas controlled by India. In the prevailing situation Indian reactionaries launched an offensive against the democratic rights and freedoms of the working people. The progressive forces were subjected to repression. The Communist Party of India found itself in an extremely difficult position: it became the main target of fierce attacks by the reactionaries. The offices of democratic organisations were raided, and many Communists were arrested.

In view of the exacerbation of the Sino-Indian conflict, the United States and Britain immediately started arms supplies to India and sent their special missions there. The conflict threatened to grow from a local into an international one. The Soviet Union gave a warning against such a development. On October 25 and November 5, 1962, the newspaper *Pravda* published articles appealing to the belligerent countries to cease fire unconditionally and begin bilateral talks. CPC leaders, however, turned a deaf ear to the Soviet appeal and attempted to distort the Soviet stand, accusing the Soviet Union of a departure from proletarian internationalism in the Sino-Indian dispute.

Meanwhile, bourgeois propaganda raised an outcry about "the aggressive nature of world communism".

The imperialists, acting hand in glove with Indian reaction, made vigorous efforts to push India into the embrace of the West, while Chinese leaders by their warlike and irresponsible adventurist actions contributed to this in every way. The London *Times*, in an article entitled "China's Gains and Losses" published on November 22, 1962, said contentedly: "All Indian opinion has been outraged. ... The Chinese have pushed India closer to the west and to the United States, which is the particular quarter that affects China. The damage they have done to their own interests is immense. ... For thirteen years Chinese vituperation has isolated her from the west. For five years past, and never so violently as now, Chinese intransigence has been isolating her from the communist world. And now India is lashed and the effects are felt throughout Asia, Africa, and Latin America... but none of them in acknowledging Chinese power will therefore look more kindly on China."[1]

It was only the failure of attempts to dictate to India from the positions of strength and the prospects of a full-scale long war involving the United States, Britain and their allies of the aggressive blocs that somewhat sobered Chinese leaders: on November 21 a ceasefire and the withdrawal of Chinese troops to the positions they had occupied before the hostilities were announced.

The stand of Chinese leaders in the conflict with India caused great moral and political damage to the People's Republic of China, undermined the trust of the young national states of Asia and Africa in her policy. Many of these states in one way or another expressed their sympathies to India at the time of exacerbation of the Sino-Indian border conflict. More than 60 countries denounced China's actions.

In pursuance of their adventurist policy on the international scene Chinese leaders staked mostly on the use of the national liberation movement for their own purposes. CPC leaders believed that it would be easier for them to spread their pseudo-revolutionary theories in the developing countries, to recruit followers and take advantage of the upsurge in the anti-imperialist struggle of oppressed peoples to attain China's great-power goals.

The theoretical arguments of Peking leaders showed a definite scheme of using the national liberation movement in the drive toward realising their nationalistic ambitions. From the experience of the revolutionary struggle in China (first the seizure of power in rural areas, then the encirclement and capture of towns) Chinese leaders drew their glob-

---

[1] *The Times*, London, December 22, 1962, p. 13.

al formula of a world revolution: at first, to achieve the victory of the revolution in the underdeveloped countries ("world villages"), to cut off imperialism from Asia, Africa and Latin America, and then to destroy it for good. It goes without saying that China as a whole and Mao Tse-tung as its "leader" are assigned the role of leader of the entire worldwide revolutionary development.

The policy of Chinese leaders toward the national liberation movement assumed a strikingly obvious anti-Soviet character. Peking propaganda sought to play down the role of the Soviet Union on the international scene, to undermine its unity with countries waging a national liberation struggle against imperialism. While deliberately belittling the importance of the Great October Socialist Revolution for the development of the national liberation movement in the colonies and dependent countries, CPC leaders went out of their way to circulate the thesis on the first priority importance of the ideas of Mao Tse-tung for the success of this movement.

A textbook of history published by the Hofei Teachers' Training Institute in 1961 said: "The ideas of Mao Tse-tung are a new development of Marxism-Leninism in the conditions of revolution in the colonies and semi-colonies. The ideas of Mao Tse-tung are the only truth which has brought liberation to the Chinese people, as well as the only truth with the aid of which the peoples of the colonial and semi-colonial countries will liberate themselves. Therefore, the ideas of Mao Tse-tung are of exceedingly great importance not only for China, they also have universal significance for the world communist movement and the national liberation movements of the peoples of Asia, Africa and Latin America."

The Marxist-Leninist parties regard the collapse of the colonial system under the pressure of the national liberation movement as a historical phenomenon, second in importance to the formation of the world socialist system. Revising this assessment, Chinese leaders began to describe the national liberation movement as the main factor of struggle against imperialism, to play down the role of the world socialist community and the revolutionary movement of the working class in the capitalist countries. The journal *Hungchi*, theoretical organ of the CPC Central Committee, bluntly stated:

"The rise of the national liberation movement and the collapse of the colonial system constitute the main essence of our epoch."[1]

Peking propaganda beamed to countries of Asia, Africa and Latin America began to talk more and more openly about China as distinct from the socialist camp, as a result of which the interpretation of her unity with the developing countries acquired, in effect, an ambiguous and even racialist ring: China was opposed not only to the imperialist powers but also to the socialist community of nations. Frankly nationalistic motives were increasingly obvious in the propaganda and practical actions of Peking in Asia, Africa and Latin America. Speaking of the East, for example, Chinese leaders began to regard it as a purely geographical notion, drawing no class distinction between the working masses of the countries of this area and the exploiting elite. As a result, the slogans like "The peoples of Asia, Africa and Latin America, unite!", "The wind from the East prevails over the wind from the West" advanced by Chinese leaders were objectively opposed to the slogan of proletarian solidarity: "Workers of all countries, unite!"

The fallacy and ambiguity of these slogans were strikingly confirmed, in particular, by statements made in September 1962 by the prominent leader of Japan's Liberal-Democratic Party, Kenzo Matsumura, during his visit to China. At a reception in Peking attended by Chou En-lai and other Chinese leaders he made a speech, which was published in the Chinese press: "I believe this visit to be remarkable. This visit will help us to push the relations between our two countries step by step onto the path of relations which should exist between peoples of the same colour of the skin and the same system of graphic symbols. Premier Chou En-lai and Vice-Premier Chen Yi had many discussions with us at which it was acknowledged that the East remained the East after all, that Asians should change world history. We should draw closer together, to strengthen contacts between our peoples of the same colour of the skin and the same system of graphic symbols." In this speech Matsumura expressed what Chinese leaders themselves did not dare to declare openly.

---

[1] *Hungchi*, 1962, No. 1.

Advertising in every way their "vanguard role" in the
struggle against colonialism, CPC leaders in fact kept aloof
from the solution of practical problems of this struggle. It
is indicative that in 1960-1961, the PRC Government did
not support the actions of the Soviet Union and other socialist countries directed to abolishing the colonial system.

3. DIRECT ATTACKS OF THE MAOISTS
AGAINST THE IDEOLOGICAL POSITIONS OF THE CPSU
AND OTHER MARXIST-LENINIST PARTIES

The departure of the CPC leadership from the socialist
principles of home and foreign policies was accompanied by
stepping up its offensive against the ideological positions of
the Marxist-Leninist parties, its attempts to impose the anti-
scientific views and conceptions of Maoism on the world
communist movement.

In these circumstances the CPSU Central Committee took
steps to prevent the slide down of the CPC leadership onto
the path of an open ideological struggle against the fraternal
parties. Loyal to the principles of proletarian internationalism, the CPSU Central Committee persistently sought to discuss with the CPC leadership through intra-Party channels
in a comradely spirit all outstanding problems, and invariably expressed its firm confidence in the possibility to find
joint solutions useful for the common cause.

On April 5, 1960, the CPSU Central Committee and
the Soviet Government officially invited a Chinese Party
and government delegation led by Mao Tse-tung to pay a
friendly visit to the Soviet Union to help improve Sino-Soviet
relations.

However, this friendly offer of the CPSU Central Committee was not accepted by CPC leaders. What is more, they
stepped up their hostile activities against the CPSU and
other Marxist-Leninist parties.

At the end of April 1960, the Chinese press published
three articles timed to the 90th birth anniversary of Lenin
(later these articles were compiled in the collection *Long
Live Leninism!*). The articles levied criticism on the key
theoretical principles approved by the Communist and
Workers' parties in the Declaration of the Moscow Meeting

in 1957 and signed by CPC leaders in particular. The articles contradicted the conclusion in the Declaration that in the
present epoch world development was determined by the
struggle, progress and results of the competition between the
two opposite social systems—socialism and capitalism, that
the growing and consolidating world socialist system was
producing increasing influence on the international situation
in the interests of peace, progress and the freedom of nations.

Chinese leaders needed to play down the role of the world
socialist system to substantiate their conclusions on other
questions of principle as well.

One of the central ideas of the collection was as follows:
as long as socialism has not won on a worldwide scale, it is
allegedly impossible to prevent a world war. The collection
was pervaded with skepticism concerning the possibilities of
the world revolutionary forces. What is more, the collection,
in effect, peddled the idea that a new world war would have
favourable results for the peoples of the world. "The victorious people," it said, "will create on the ruins of destroyed
imperialism at an extremely fast rate a thousand times higher civilisation than under the capitalist system, will build
its truly beautiful future."[1] Thus, the question in point was,
in fact, the desirability of a world war.

In this collection Chinese leaders openly declared in the
face of the enemy—imperialism—the existence of differences
within the international communist movement on the cardinal problems of its strategy and tactics.

Seeking to preserve unity, the CPSU Central Committee
abstained until June 1960 from raising the question of the
contents of these articles as well as some public statements
by Chinese leaders made in a similar vein. The CPSU Central Committee believed that the differences which had aris-
en should be discussed at meetings between leaders of the
two parties. Therefore, the Soviet press abstained from
polemics.

In the beginning of 1960 Mao Tse-tung was again invited
to visit the Soviet Union. This was another opportunity to
hold constructive meetings and discussions between Chinese
and Soviet leaders. This time, too, Mao Tse-tung declined

---

[1] *Hungchi*, 1960, No. 8.

12*

the offer, showed no interest in contacts and no desire to see Soviet life with his own eyes. Later developments showed the true reasons for his refusal.

In response to the CPSU Central Committee's proposal motivated by a desire to preserve unity, the CPC leadership took another step, absolutely intolerable in the relations between fraternal parties, which could not be interpreted otherwise than as being openly divisive. Early in June, 1960, at a session of the General Council of the World Federation of Trade Unions held in Peking, Chinese leaders appeared before a large group of representatives of the fraternal parties with an exposition of their views on a number of key questions of principle, advancing propositions running counter to Marxism-Leninism.

This action, far from being supported by the Communists who attended the session of the WFTU General Council, met with their determined opposition. Then, CPC leaders took still another divisive step—they came out with criticism of the views of the CPSU and other fraternal parties both at meetings of the WFTU General Council and in a number of commissions attended by many members of parties other than Communist, as well as by trade union leaders having no party affiliation. Such actions were, in effect, a direct appeal to the World Federation of Trade Unions for a struggle against the views of the CPSU and other Communist parties on the key problems of modern world development.

CPC leaders also took vigorous measures in that period to win the support of Albanian leaders for their divisive actions.

At first, CPC leaders sought to create the impression that they had always tried to prevent a deepening of differences between the Albanian Party of Labour and the CPSU and to contribute to a normalisation of Soviet-Albanian relations. In fact, however, CPC leaders had taken a diametrically opposite stand. At all the stages of differences between the leaders of the APL and other parties the Mao Tse-tung group gave unequivocal support to Albanian leaders, bending every effort not to adjust but to exacerbate the relations of Albanian leaders with the CPSU and other Marxist-Leninist parties. At a time when all the Marxist-Leninist parties assessed the anti-Soviet line of Albanian leaders from positions of principle, CPC leaders seized every opportunity to emphasise their approval of this line.

On June 21, 1960, the CPSU Central Committee circulated to the fraternal parties a memorandum in which it convincingly exposed the untenability of the theoretical views of Chinese leaders, showed in full and, at the same time, in a comradely spirit, their obvious fallacy and possible harmful consequences.

The memorandum analysed facts which had been in evidence in the days of the session of the WFTU General Council in Peking, levied principled criticism on the wrong views of CPC leaders on a number of international issues. The memorandum was a response to attacks by Chinese leaders who had openly come out with biased criticism of the CPSU and other fraternal parties. The CPSU Central Committee expressed the hope that the Communist Party of China would take account of the interest of the entire socialist camp and the international communist movement, which are inseparable from the cause of building socialism in China.

On the eve of the 3rd Congress of the Rumanian Workers' Party there was a frank discussion at the CPSU Central Committee with the Chinese delegation heading for Bucharest, which was led by a member of the Political Bureau of the CPC Central Committee, Peng Chen. The purpose of this discussion was to consider disputed problems, again to show Chinese leaders the fallacy of their views and actions, to persuade them to act in Bucharest in a spirit of unity. Following directives from Peking, the Chinese delegation rejected the arguments of the CPSU Central Committee and continued to cling to the views CPC leaders had proclaimed at the WFTU General Council session in Peking.

In accordance with earlier agreement, a meeting of the fraternal parties of the socialist countries and a meeting of 51 fraternal parties of socialist and capitalist countries. were held in Bucharest on June 24-26, 1960.

At the first meeting it was acknowledged that the entire course of world development, the successes of the socialist camp, the international working-class and national liberation movement, the upsurge of the struggle for peace, the contin-

ued weakening of the imperialist forces fully confirmed the
correctness of the conclusions made in the Declaration and
the Peace Manifesto of the Moscow Meeting of Communist
and Workers' Parties in 1957. The participants in this Bucharest meeting agreed unanimously that the fundamental
provisions of the Declaration and the Peace Manifesto
remained fully valid.

The delegates with the exception of the Albanian representatives, showed a highly principled approach and adduced
facts illustrating the Chinese leaders' departure from the
principles of the Declaration and their attempts to substitute
their "Left" sectarian views for the ideology of scientific
communism.

The fraternal parties demonstrated their unity and cohesion also at the joint meeting of representatives of Communist parties of socialist and capitalist countries. Participants
in the meeting stated unanimously that the position and actions of Chinese leaders were detrimental to the struggle of
the revolutionary forces, sharply criticised CPC leaders for
their factional methods, denounced the behaviour of Chinese
representatives at the session of the WFTU General Council in Peking, the circulation of anti-Soviet publications by
Chinese offices abroad. Profound indignation was evoked by
the attempts of Peking leaders to brainwash representatives
of the fraternal parties visiting China in a spirit of their
divisive views.

When it became clear to Chinese leaders that their unseemly tactics had been exposed, they assumed the posture
of victims of injustice and declared that the meeting was
being conducted by undemocratic methods. This manoeuvre,
however, met with a determined rebuff.

At the final stage of the meeting, the question of issuing a
joint communique was raised on the initiative of a number
of parties. After long procrastination the delegation of the
CPC Central Committee signed the communique "for the
sake of unity", although it was an open secret to everyone
that this was a forced step—otherwise, CPC leaders would
have finally exposed themselves as factionalists and splitters.

The communique, signed by representatives of the Communist parties of all socialist countries, indicated that the

Communist and Workers' parties shall continue to strengthen the cohesion of the countries of the world socialist system and to preserve thoroughly their unity in the struggle for peace and the security of all nations, for the triumph of the great cause of Marxism-Leninism.

At the Bucharest meeting the fraternal parties unanimously declared that the leaders of the Communist Party of China should accept criticism of their views and actions and to draw the necessary conclusions from it in the interests of unity on the cardinal problems of strategy and tactics of the world communist movement.

The Bucharest meeting opened the way to overcoming the differences between the CPC leadership and the world communist movement. However, Chinese leaders did everything to prevent following this path. On June 26, 1960, on the closing day of the meeting, the CPC delegation distributed to all the Communist parties of the socialist countries a letter which deliberately distorted the character of the meeting. The letter alleged that the CPSU delegation "had violated the principle of consultations" by putting forward the proposal for issuing a communique. This allegation contradicted the facts, because actually the proposal for the meeting of the fraternal parties to adopt an agreed document, had been tabled by several fraternal parties. They justly emphasised the pressing need for such a document, which would declare support for the Moscow Declaration of 1957, the readiness of all the parties to observe its principles unflinchingly and would demonstrate the cohesion of the fraternal parties before the whole world.

In addition to this letter, Chinese leaders, in the editorials of *Jenmin jihpao* of June 29 and August 13, 1960, openly cracked down with unjustified criticism on the positions of the fraternal parties which had attended the Bucharest meeting.

CPC leaders also attempted to disseminate their anti-Soviet views among the Soviet people. They used for this purpose, in particular, the Chinese magazine *Druzhba* (Friendship) published in Russian and circulated in the Soviet Union. The magazine started publication of articles intended to brainwash Soviet readers in the spirit of Maoist ideas contradicting the line of the CPSU Central Committee and other

Marxist-Leninist parties. Propaganda material of the CPC leadership was also circulated throughout the Soviet Union by the Chinese Embassy in Moscow.

Such Chinese actions had nothing in common with the spirit of friendship and co-operation between the PRC and the USSR. Therefore, the Soviet Government had to take a number of measures to protect Soviet people from the barrage of unfriendly propaganda against the Soviet Union, to guard them against involvement in an unnecessary discussion on questions which were under consideration at the Central Committees of the CPSU and the CPC. After repeated warnings to the Chinese side Soviet authorities had nothing to do but to propose in July 1960 to end the publication of the Chinese magazine *Druzhba* (in Russian) and—on the principle of parity—the Soviet magazine *Sino-Soviet Friendship* (in Chinese). It was stated to the Chinese side that the material published in *Druzhba* magazine ran counter to documents of the international communist movement and that this contradicted not only the main principles on which the inter-state and inter-Party relations between the two countries were based, but also to the principles which the Chinese side itself had formulated for the magazine when beginning its publication.

Another step of CPC leaders adding to the deterioration of Sino-Soviet relations was the letter from the CPC Central Committee to the CPSU Central Committee of September 10, 1960. It contained another attack on the ideological positions of the CPSU and other Marxist-Leninist parties and a number of slanderous accusations against the CPSU. Views alien to it were ascribed to our party, and it was blamed for actions it had never committed.

The CPC Central Committee, ignoring the opinion of the fraternal parties unanimously expressed at the meeting in Bucharest, as well as in numerous resolutions adopted later, continued to uphold its mistaken line contradicting the principles of the Declaration and the Peace Manifesto of the 1957 Moscow Meeting. What is more, in this letter, CPC leaders, alleging demagogically that a temporary majority cannot turn untruth into truth and a temporary minority truth into untruth, frankly declared that it would further ignore the opinion of the fraternal parties and the entire world communist movement. Thereby Chinese leaders laid an open claim to monopoly possession of "ultimate truth" on all questions of Marxist-Leninist theory, the strategy and tactics of the world communist movement.

Seeking to sow within the world communist movement doubts as to the correctness of the theoretical views of the CPSU, to drive a wedge between our party and other fraternal parties, CPC leaders immediately went ahead with circulating this letter among the fraternal parties, using it for propaganda of their special views and for stepping up their attacks on the CPSU.

The letter was also widely discussed in local organisations of the CPC. Thus, while paying lip service to unity and cohesion with the CPSU and the Soviet Union, Chinese leaders in fact educated Chinese Communists in a spirit of open hostility towards them.

In September 1960, persistent efforts of the CPSU Central Committee to hold a meeting with representatives of the CPC were finally crowned with success: the CPC Central Committee accepted the invitation of the CPSU to hold negotiations. The meeting took place in Moscow between September 17 and 22, 1960.

This time, too, however, the Maoist leadership of the CPC remained loyal to its former line. No key members of it came to Moscow. The Chinese delegation was led by the General Secretary of the CPC Central Committee, Teng Hsiao-ping, and consisted of zealous advocates of the special creed of the CPC.

Keeping to the contents of the letter of September 10, 1960 and piling up new and new unfounded demands to the CPSU Central Committee, the Chinese delegation did its best to avoid a discussion of the main international issues, the strategy and tactics of revolutionary struggle, and raised instead a host of problems of secondary importance partly settled long ago.

The talks, which lasted five days, proved fruitless through the fault of the Chinese side. Moreover, they showed with striking clarity that Chinese leaders were deliberately expanding the range of their differences with the CPSU and other fraternal parties, staking on an exacerbation of the situation in the world communist movement.

The Moscow Meeting of Communist and Workers' Parties held in November 1960 was a milestone event in the struggle of the world communist movement for the unity and cohesion of its ranks on the principles of Marxism-Leninism. The wrong views and factional methods of CPC leaders were severely criticised at the meeting.

The discussion was imposed on the meeting by the CPC delegation itself. Challenging the Declaration of 1957, the Chinese delegates expressed, in particular, disagreement with the thesis that the international working class and the world socialist system play the decisive role in the world revolutionary development. All statements by Chinese delegates at the meeting were aimed at undermining the very foundation of the general line of the international communist movement, the principles of Marxism-Leninism.

Representatives of many fraternal parties showed in their statements that the fallacious and adventurist schemes of CPC leaders completely ignored the new historical situation which had taken shape in the world as a result of the radical change in the balance of power after the Second World War. The meeting denounced the factional activities of the CPC, as well as attempts to substantiate them "theoretically". It was emphasised that the splitting policy of Chinese leaders caused particularly great damage to the parties operating underground.

The Marxist-Leninist parties resolutely denounced the slander campaign of CPC leaders against the CPSU and unanimously reaffirmed their high assessment of its activities. The attempts of the Chinese delegation to oppose the CPSU to the other parties, to defame and calumniate it failed completely. Delegates from the fraternal parties declared unequivocally that the cause of the CPSU was inseparable from the communist movement, that the Party of Lenin was the centre of the international communist movement. The efforts of the Chinese delegates to undermine the prestige of the CPSU were interpreted as an affront not only to the CPSU but also to the entire international communist movement.

The Moscow Meeting of 1960 clearly demonstrated that on all problems revealing the departure of CPC leaders from the general line of the international communist movement the CPC delegation met with a resolute rebuff from the fraternal parties. Exposed to severe criticism, Chinese leaders accused the CPSU and other parties of organising a campaign of attacks and even a "crusade" against the CPC. This, however, was but another fabrication. The proceedings of the Meeting showed that the fraternal parties displayed exceptional patience and restraint in the discussions with the CPC delegation.

The threat of complete isolation compelled the Chinese delegation to resort to a manoeuvre and give up temporarily its attempts to impose its false conceptions on the international communist movement. In the face of unanimous criticism of the anti-Leninist views and subversive activities of the leadership of the CPC, its representatives had to sign the statement which rejected in fact the views of Chinese leaders hostile to Marxism-Leninism and denounced its factional activity.

The Meeting threw into salient relief the two ideological and political lines opposed to each other. The first is the line of the international communist movement which was upheld by the overwhelming majority of parties. This is a line of creative Marxism-Leninism, the unity and cohesion of the international communist movement on a basis of principle. The second is the nationalistic line of CPC leaders which was openly supported only by the delegation of Albanian Party of Labour, a line of departure from the general policy of the international communist movement, of increasing sectarian tendencies.

The fallacious anti-Leninist line of the Chinese and Albanian delegations suffered a complete fiasco. The allegation of Chinese propaganda about the victory of the Chinese line at the meeting of 1960 is an outrageous lie.

The CPSU Central Committee and the Soviet Government, immediately after the Moscow Meeting, took steps to improve Sino-Soviet relations. The CPC delegation led by Liu Shao-chi, which had attended the Meeting, was invited to make a tour of the USSR. In discussions with members of the delegation Soviet leaders emphasised the unchangeable line of the CPSU Central Committee and the Soviet Government toward unity with the CPC and the PRC, toward strengthening and developing in every way Sino-Soviet inter-Party and inter-state relations.

At that time, Chinese leaders in their public statements reaffirmed their devotion to Sino-Soviet friendship, hypocritically expressed their admiration for the achievements of the Soviet Union, the successes of its foreign and home policies. In a message of congratulation on the occasion of the 43rd anniversary of the Great October Socialist Revolution, Mao Tse-tung and other Chinese leaders said: "The great Soviet people led by the glorious Communist Party of the Soviet Union have achieved tremendous successes both in the implementation of the seven-year plan of comprehensive construction of communism and in the struggle for peaceful coexistence of states with different social systems and for preserving world peace. The Chinese people rejoice with all their heart and soul in these great successes of the fraternal Soviet people. The Chinese people will continue to march shoulder to shoulder with the Soviet people along the common path of building socialism and communism, struggle against imperialist aggression and for peace throughout the world. . . . The great friendship and unity of the peoples of China and the Soviet Union . . . express both the supreme interests of the peoples of China and the Soviet Union and the supreme interests of the peoples of the world."[1]

The newspaper *Jenmin jihpao*, commenting on the results of the visit to the USSR by the Chinese Party and government delegation, wrote on December 10, 1960: "The current visit by Chairman Liu Shao-chi has undoubtedly still more strengthened and developed the great friendship and unity of the peoples of China and the Soviet Union and inscribed a golden page in the history of Sino-Soviet friendship." "The Communist Party of China and the Chinese people," the newspaper said, "are firmly devoted to the principles of proletarian internationalism and regard it as their sacred duty to preserve and strengthen the great unity of China and the Soviet Union, the CPC and the CPSU. The Government and people of China invariably give their active support to the efforts of the Government and peoples of the Soviet Union to defend peace throughout the world, will always fight to the end alongside the Soviet Union for victory in the cause of defending universal peace and mankind's progress."

---

[1] *Pravda*, November 7, 1960.

In their 1961 New Year message of greetings to Soviet leaders, Mao Tse-tung and other Chinese leaders assessed this visit in similar terms. The message said, in particular: The recent state visit to the Soviet Union by a Chinese Party and government delegation led by Chairman Liu Shao-chi has further strengthened and developed the great time-tested friendship and unity of the peoples of China and the Soviet Union based on Marxism-Leninism and proletarian internationalism.

In January 1961, the 9th plenary meeting of the CPC Central Committee discussed the results of the Moscow Meeting of Representatives of the Communist and Workers' Parties. The plenary meeting heard and discussed the report of Teng Hsiao-ping on this question and adopted the resolution, which said: "The plenary meeting welcomes enthusiastically the great results achieved by the Meeting of Representatives of the Communist and Workers' Parties and fully approves of the Statement and Appeal to the Peoples of the World unanimously adopted at the Meeting. The Communist Party of China will fight with determination to carry into life the common tasks set out in the documents of the Meeting. The plenary meeting appeals to all Party members and the people of the whole country to carry aloft the great Marxist-Leninist banner of the Moscow Declaration of 1957 and the Moscow Statement of 1960; in the field of international affairs, to strengthen the unity with the Soviet Union, to strengthen the unity of the entire socialist camp and the unity of the international communist movement, to strengthen the unity of the working class of the whole world and the unity of all peace-loving and freedom-loving peoples, to struggle for new victories for the cause of world peace and mankind's progress."[1]

These statements evidence that nationalistic elements were still far from being in full control of the situation in the CPC leadership. After the failure of the "big leap" and great setbacks for China on the international scene they had to reckon with the opposition in the Party and country to their anti-Soviet divisive line, to camouflage it for the time being, to resort to all sorts of manoeuvres, waiting for an oppor-

---

[1] *Pravda*, January 22, 1961.

tune moment to start an offensive. Later developments demonstrated that as soon as the nationalistic group had consolidated its positions it resumed with renewed vigour its struggle against the socialist community and the world communist movement.

4. 22nd CPSU CONGRESS
AND INTENSIFICATION BY CPC LEADERS
OF IDEOLOGICAL STRUGGLE
AGAINST THE FRATERNAL PARTIES

The congresses of the Communist Party of the Soviet Union for their importance and influence on the world communist movement extend far beyond the framework of one party. They produce a deep impact on the direction and content of ideological and theoretical work of all the fraternal parties adhering to the principles of creative Marxism-Leninism. In view of this, a major goal of CPC leaders was to discredit the 22nd Congress of the CPSU held in October 1961.

CPC leaders sought to present this Congress as an ordinary event. Unlike the delegations of other fraternal parties which attended the Congress, the Chinese delegation was led not by the Chairman of the CPC, Mao Tse-tung, but by his deputy, Chou En-lai. Among the delegates was alternate member of the Political Bureau, Kang Sheng, an active advocate of the line toward exacerbation of Sino-Soviet relations.

In their efforts to disorganise the work of the 22nd CPSU Congress CPC leaders deliberately attached a special role to the so-called Albanian question. In his message of greetings to the Congress, the CPC representative, ignoring the elementary rules of courtesy, declared that the statements in the report of the CPSU Central Committee containing criticism of the splitting activities of Albanian leaders "cannot be regarded as a serious, Marxist-Leninist approach" and began in effect to lecture the Congress arrogantly, appealing to the audience to support the viewpoint of CPC leaders.

Thus, Chinese leaders took a step absolutely intolerable in relations between Marxist-Leninist parties. Declaring from the Congress rostrum their opposition to the report of the

Central Committee of the Party which had invited them, they again exposed before the whole world the differences between the CPC and the CPSU (while expressing hypocritical regrets on an open one-sided denunciation of some fraternal party since this did not strengthen unity or solved any problems) and unequivocally stated their claims to the role of orthodox supporters of Marxism-Leninism, of the supreme force cementing the unity of the socialist camp and all the fraternal parties. The statement of the leader of the CPC delegation at the 22nd CPSU Congress ran counter to the provisions of the Moscow Declaration of 1960 on the intolerability of any actions likely to undermine the unity of the international communist movement, as well as to the assurances of Chinese leaders themselves to the effect that the Chinese people would not permit any actions or statements detrimental to the unity of our two parties and countries.

Despite the unfriendly statement of the leader of the CPC delegation and the generally hostile attitude of the Chinese leadership to the 22nd Congress, the CPSU Central Committee displayed great patience and prevented the Congress from becoming an arena for inter-Party disputes. It stood its ground on matters of principle and firmly and consistently upheld the line toward the achievement of unity between the CPC and the CPSU and other Marxist-Leninist parties. This was conclusively demonstrated by the discussion the Soviet leaders had with the Chinese delegation, in which they explained the views of our party on the vital problems of today and emphasised its readiness to do everything to overcome differences. Nevertheless, Chinese leaders remained as unco-operative as before.

When the CPC delegation returned to Peking it was given a pompous welcome, in which Mao Tse-tung himself took part. It was called upon to demonstrate that the CPC leadership fully approved of the actions of the Chinese delegation at the 22nd CPSU Congress, that it had not renounced its views and would continue its struggle against the CPSU and other fraternal parties rejecting its wrong views and nationalistic claims.

During the 22nd CPSU Congress and immediately after its closure a broad anti-Soviet campaign was launched in the PRC. After returning to Peking Chou En-lai delivered a long report in which he described the 22nd CPSU Congress as "revisionist" and made a number of crude attacks against our party. At closed meetings and in certain localities at open meetings held in November and December 1961, secretaries of Party organisations made special reports on Sino-Soviet relations. They attempted to shift the blame for the difficulties experienced by the PRC in 1958-1960 on the Soviet Union. Fabrications were circulated to the effect that downtime at Chinese plants was due to a shortage of spare parts and equipment the Soviet Union had allegedly refused to sell to the PRC, that the Soviet Union demanded that China should immediately repay all Soviet loans and credits and that China had to give away foodstuffs to settle her debts, that the Soviet Union was unwilling to give her food aid, that the Soviet people did not care about their internationalist duty to the working people of other countries, etc.

Under the disguise of the demagogic slogan "the people will themselves find out what is true and what is not true" CPC leaders widely opened the door for bourgeois propaganda to China. Simultaneously, items containing truthful information about the life of Soviet people disappeared from the pages of the Chinese press.

The stepping up of the anti-Soviet policy caused concern and indignation among the Chinese people. This was said in numerous letters from Chinese citizens received by the Soviet Embassy and consulates in the PRC. A teacher of a secondary school in Hailar wrote on January 25, 1962: "Of late, deliberate statements and actions unfriendly towards the Soviet Union have been in evidence within the CPC. At first, the bulletin *Tsankao hsiaohsi* was used to lead people to the wrong path of slandering Soviet leaders. Now the matter is coming into the open, and pernicious fruits are ripening."

A similar picture was reported by a Chinese student. "...At present," he wrote on February 14, 1962, "there is a group of people who portray themselves as exemplary, genuine Marxist-Leninists. However, taking the cue from the capitalists, they curse the CPSU Central Committee and engage in double-dealing. While trumpeting for all to hear about their great feelings of friendship and fraternity, they treacherously deceive their people, pouring slander and malicious fabrications into documents and reports used for the training of cadres; they are waiting for an opportune moment to deal a strike, regarding the Soviet people as an enemy; they have no respect for the CPSU Central Committee. To us students of Kwangchow University this is painful and unbearable."

After the 22nd Congress of the CPSU, officials of the Party and government apparatus of the PRC held in Peking a number of special talks with diplomats from socialist countries in the course of which they tried to denigrate in every way the policy of the CPSU, to distort the decisions of the 22nd Congress and the CPSU Programme.

5. EFFORTS OF THE CPSU TO ELIMINATE IDEOLOGICAL DIFFERENCES BETWEEN THE CPC LEADERSHIP AND THE MARXIST-LENINIST PARTIES

Early in 1962 the CPSU took a new important step to check the process of exacerbation of Sino-Soviet relations. On February 22, the CPSU Central Committee in a letter to the CPC Central Committee expressed its concern about the way the relations between the two parties developed. The CPSU Central Committee acted on the premise that the cardinal interests of the socialist and communist cause demanded that our parties should rise above their differences and follow an agreed line on all matters of principle. In the situation prevailing it was important, above all, to encourage every step, that contributed to a normalisation of Sino-Soviet relations, without emphasising disputed problems. The CPSU Central Committee appealed for good will in the settlement of disputes, for an end to the unnecessary controversy on questions understood differently, for abstention from public statements likely to deepen rather than smooth out differences. It was particularly intolerable to extend the differences into the sphere of inter-state relations between the socialist countries, to their economic, political, military and cultural co-operation. The CPSU Central Committee reaffirmed the earlier Soviet proposals directed to developing Sino-Soviet relations in all main fields, expressed its readiness to resolve differences in a comradely spirit, without accumulating or increasing them.

The letter of the CPSU Central Committee gave CPC leaders an opportunity to make the differences between the CPC and the international communist movement a subject of comradely discussions and to provide conditions for a normalisation and successful development of Sino-Soviet relations.

In its reply of April 7, 1962, however, the CPC Central Committee rejected the proposals of the CPSU Central Committee and again digged up the notorious "Albanian problem" in an effort to use it for its anti-Soviet, splitting purposes.

Since the early days of breaking with the CPSU and other fraternal parties, Albanian leaders had been a mouthpiece and instrument of the splitting policy of Mao Tse-tung and his group. Numerous statements by Albanian leaders, articles in the Albanian press abounded in crude attacks on the CPSU and the Soviet Government. Statements by Albanian leaders in defence of the integrity of Marxism-Leninism, all their arguments adduced to show their independent views on the key issues of today had been fully borrowed from Peking leaders.

The setting up of the anti-Soviet alliance of Chinese and Albanian leaders, their union in a single opportunist bloc spearheaded against the CPSU was one of the first results of the practical implementation of the Peking leaders' splitting policy within the socialist camp and the world communist movement. There is no doubt that the splitters would not have dared to oppose the CPSU so brazenly, to oppose themselves to the entire world communist movement, if they had not been encouraged and fully supported by Peking. From the very outset this support was not only ideological but also material. Already the first anti-Soviet statements by the splitters at the 1960 Meeting of the Communist and Workers' Parties were generously rewarded by Chinese leaders. Later, this sort of encouragement camouflaged with the false slogans of "international fraternal assistance" became regular. During a certain time after the 1960 Meeting, Chinese leaders pretended to have taken up an objective attitude and appealed to the CPSU and the APL to find ways to rapprochement and elimination of differences in the interests of unity. This, however, was sheer hypocrisy. In fact, CPC leaders systematically incited Albanian leaders to deepen the split. The CPC Central Committee never appealed to APL leaders to seek ways to improve relations with the CPSU and other fraternal parties. On the contrary, Chinese leaders encouraged in every way the anti-Soviet campaign launched in Albania. Significantly, the bourgeois press wrote that Tirana was a "mouthpiece of Peking" even in its comments on the very first statements by APL leaders attacking the CPSU and the Soviet Union.

In that period the Maoists still did not dare to declare openly their hostility towards the CPSU. Therefore, they needed organisations through which to slander our party. Therefore Peking began to set up at a feverish pace various splitting groups within the world communist movement. The louder and the more scandalous the curses such groups made against the CPSU, the fouler and the more cynical their anti-Soviet fabrications, the greater was the support they received from Peking.

In the Chinese press and official statements by CPC leaders, leaders of dissentient groups were extolled as "great" and "staunch" Marxist-Leninists. On every occasion bombastic greetings interspersed with hypocritical epithets and fulsome praises were sent to them from Peking. In return, the dissenters took servile oaths of life-long allegiance and gratitude to Mao Tse-tung for his solicitude and support.

Stepping up their attacks on the CPSU Peking leaders accused it of a striving for "dictatorship" in the communist movement, a desire to impose its will on other parties. These slanderous accusations graphically showed how far CPC leaders had departed from the views they professed a short time ago. Indeed, only three years before *Jenmin jihpao* wrote: "The imperialists, referring to the fact that the socialist camp is led by the Soviet Union, accuse the Communist parties of all countries of being dependent on Moscow or slander the Communist Party of the Soviet Union on account of its alleged control of the Communist parties of other countries. Such absurdities do not deserve as much as a laugh from the Communists. Any genuine Communist has heartfelt respect for the Communist Party of the Soviet Union, the first strike force of the international proletariat, which has broken the chains of international capitalism, the Party

13*

which is now the first to rise to the summits of communism.... Only enemies of the proletariat and traitors to Marxism-Leninism can oppose with malicious intent the vanguard role of the Communist Party of the Soviet Union as the centre of cohesion of the international communist movement to the relations of equality and independence between the Communist parties."[1]

On May 31, 1962, the CPSU Central Committee in another letter to the CPC Central Committee gave a condign rebuff to the unscrupulous manoeuvres of Chinese leaders. The CPSU Central Committee re-emphasised the need to check the process of sliding down to a new round of heated debates and mutual recriminations, to rise above the existing differences, to strengthen the united front of struggle against imperialism. The CPSU Central Committee expressed its readiness to take another step to adjust the differences and to strengthen the unity of the two parties. Guided by these motives, the CPSU Central Committee abstained from dwelling on all the issues raised in the Chinese letter of April 7, 1962, although on some of them our party held a different view. The CPSU Central Committee deemed it unnecessary to answer all unfounded charges made by Peking leaders in direct or indirect form. It was emphasised at the same time that should need arise the CPSU Central Committee would give a detailed exposition of its views on all the problems raised in the letter of the CPC Central Committee.

Without confining itself to appeals for unity and cohesion, the CPSU Central Committee pointed out the need for a joint public rebuff to the most spiteful attacks of hostile propaganda, for a more effective exchange of information on foreign affairs and greater co-ordination of actions by the fraternal parties in international organisations. This was motivated by our party's sincere desire to put an end to differences and all sorts of misunderstanding, to restore unity between the CPSU and the CPC.

The new initiative of the CPSU Central Committee faced CPC leaders with this alternative: either to normalise relations with the CPSU or to cling to their old positions. And again, they showed no willingness to step on the right track.

---

[1] *Jenmin jihpao*, February 10, 1959.

The 10th plenary meeting of the CPC Central Committee late in September 1962 put forward the task of stepping up the class struggle at home and abroad, implying mostly an intensified anti-Soviet campaign.

6. NEW ATTACKS OF CHINESE LEADERS AGAINST THE MARXIST-LENINIST PARTIES

At the end of 1962, the Chinese press launched a new fierce attack on the ideological principles of the CPSU and the entire world communist and working-class movement. To attain its objectives it took advantage of the congresses of the fraternal parties held in that period: the 8th Congress of the Bulgarian Communist Party, the 8th Congress of the Hungarian Socialist Workers' Party, the 10th Congress of the Italian Communist Party, and the 12th Congress of the Communist Party of Czechoslovakia.

At first, the Chinese press sought to conceal from the public the fact that the splitting line of the CPC leadership had been exposed to sharp criticism at the congresses of the fraternal parties. In its interpretation, the Albanian Party of Labour was subjected to one-sided attacks at these congresses, while CPC leaders defended it and struggled to prevent a split.

When their hopes to hush up the actual facts were dashed, Chinese leaders finally threw off the mask of "defenders" of the APL and openly attacked the CPSU and other Marxist-Leninist parties. This attack was started by *Jenmin jihpao* in an editorial published on December 15, 1962 under the title "Workers of All Countries, Unite, Fight Our Common Enemy!"

Pushing to the foreground the question of "who began the quarrel" CPC leaders concealed the true reasons for their struggle against the CPSU and other fraternal parties.

They evaded discussion of the essence of the problems raised at the congresses of the fraternal parties. The Maoists also advanced the thesis that "a contrary current directed against Marxism-Leninism, against the Communist Party of China" had appeared within the international communist movement. In accordance with this thesis the differences between the CPC and the international communist movement were presented as a split within the international communist and working-class movement, while all the parties which had come out with criticism of CPC leaders were indiscriminately listed as elements of this "contrary current" and declared the "common enemy of the world proletariat". The CPC leadership concealed from the Chinese people the true alignment of forces within the international communist movement, the unanimous denunciation of their splitting activities practically by all parties.

The article in *Jenmin jihpao* of December 15, 1962, summed up, as it were, the results of the congresses of the four fraternal parties. However, it did not utter a word about the importance of these congresses, but only denigrated the activities of the fraternal parties and defended the special line of Chinese leaders. The nearly 70 fraternal parties represented at the 12th Congress of the Communist Party of Czechoslovakia were indiscriminately described as a "contrary current" in the world communist movement, because they had criticised the special line of CPC leaders and exposed their splitting activities.

The Chinese press intensively circulated the thesis on the possibility of restoration of capitalism in the socialist countries. In this way, CPC leaders systematically prepared the "theoretical" positions from which to levy criticism on the socialist countries and fraternal parties opposed to their special creed.

The character of writings by Peking "theoreticians" is eloquently illustrated by the fact that imperialist propaganda immediately and broadly exploited them for their anti-communist goals. The capitalist press readily reprinted Chinese material. For example, the US press published detailed summaries of all the main Chinese publications of this kind.

Thus, the common objectives of Maoist and imperialist propaganda in the ideological offensive against the positions of socialism, in the production and circulation of anti-Soviet fabrications became clearly manifest. This was illustrated by the following fact: as Peking stepped up its subversive ideological activities, offices of the US Information Agency in countries of Southeast Asia began reducing their staffs by dismissing personnel from among the local population. The dismissed declared that the Americans treated them as the "master would treat a dog which can no longer bark the loudest of all". "We are expelled because we can't curse the Soviet Union as loudly and strongly as it is done by Chinese leaders," they said.

Ideological brainwashing of the Chinese population in the spirit of the splitting anti-Soviet line of CPC leaders was continued in China on a still wider scale. In late December, 1962 and early January 1963, large conferences were held, which were addressed by CPC leaders.

Party political training was directed to educating the Chinese people in an anti-Soviet spirit. Lessons in the Party training system were based on slanderous material in which the Soviet people were depicted as "wholly and completely turned bourgeois", "fattened", "oblivious of the principles of proletarian internationalism", etc.

The Peking splitters started subversive activities among representatives of the fraternal parties employed in Chinese organisations (broadcasting studios, publishing houses, educational institutions, etc.), foreign students, members of foreign delegations visiting China.

7. REJECTION BY PEKING
OF THE CPSU CENTRAL COMMITTEE'S PROPOSALS
FOR ENDING OPEN CONTROVERSY

In a situation of stepped-up splitting activities by Peking leaders, the CPSU Central Committee undertook new efforts to end open controversy. Our party persistently sought to restore the relations of unity and cohesion between the CPC and international communist movement, to normalise and strengthen Sino-Soviet relations.

On January 3, 1963, in a discussion with the Chinese Ambassador Pan Tzu-li held at the CPSU Central Committee, the Soviet side re-emphasised that the CPSU was seeking to restore friendly Sino-Soviet relations and was prepared to do everything necessary to this end.

On January 7, 1963, the CPSU Central Committee appealed in *Pravda* for strengthening the unity of the communist movement to secure the triumph of peace and socialism. *Pravda* emphasised that differences between individual communist parties on this or that question had no deep-going roots in the social system of the socialist countries, had no objective foundation but were primarily subjective in character. "Therefore," *Pravda* wrote, "there is everything for overcoming the differences successfully. It is necessary to be guided by the supreme goals and interests of the international communist movement and seek ways towards rapprochement, ways towards co-operation and unity."

On January 16, 1963, at the 6th Congress of the Socialist Unity Party of Germany, the leader of the delegation of the CPSU Central Committee stated that the latter would consider it useful to end the polemic between the Communist parties, criticism of other parties inside any one party. This proposal, which was supported by many Marxist-Leninist parties, might have been the starting point for a gradual normalisation of relations between the CPC, on the one hand, and the CPSU and other fraternal parties, on the other.

However, the statement made at the Congress on January 18 by the representative of the CPC showed that its leadership had no interest in ending open controversy. The leader of the CPC delegation clung to the old positions of Chinese leaders and repeated attacks against the CPSU on questions at issue, including the assessment of the Caribbean crisis, the Sino-Indian border conflict, etc. The statement by the Chinese representative showed that CPC leaders wanted to turn the subject in such a way as to guard themselves against criticism while continuing their splitting activities and their attacks on the CPSU and other Marxist-Leninist parties.

Chinese leaders confirmed their negative attitude to the proposal for ending open controversy in a *Jenmin jihpao* editorial of January 27, 1963. This article, for the first time in the official Chinese press, contained direct slanderous attacks on the CPSU leadership and rejected the proposal of the CPSU Central Committee supported by the fraternal parties.

The Communist Party of the Soviet Union has never denied the usefulness of fruitful discussions within the ranks of Communists who are pursuing the same goals. Without comparing different opinions and points of view the successful development of the revolutionary movement is impossible. No differences or discontent with the behaviour of this or that party, however, can justify methods of struggle detri-

mental to the interests of the international communist movement. The deeper and the wider a party's understanding of
the objectives and tasks of the international working class,
the more energy it should display to secure that differences,
however grave, be discussed in a quiet and businesslike way,
without interfering with fruitful work, without disorganising
the revolutionary activities of the international working class.

The Marxist-Leninists not for a moment overlook the
main purpose of a discussion. This purpose is not to disso-
ciate the parties and to sow discord but, on the contrary, to
help strengthen their unity. The CPSU Central Committee
repeatedly emphasised that it is absolutely intolerable to use
methods alien to Marxism, such as distortion of viewpoints
discussed and expressed, deliberate falsification of the views
of opponents or ascribing to them opinions they have never
held, application of offensive labels, advancing of groundless accusations.

In all its activities the CPSU has invariably been guided
by the principle that criticism of erroneous views on the fundamental questions of Marxist-Leninist theory should reveal
the root causes of such mistakes and help correct them. It
seeks to promote in every way the cohesion of revolutionary
forces, to prevent their dissociation, separation or isolation
of this or that section of the international revolutionary
movement.

At the same time, the CPSU firmly upholds the view that
unity of the international communist movement cannot be
achieved through concessions and compromise deals on matters of principle. On the contrary, only consistent as well as
flexible implementation of a general line based on the principles of Marxism-Leninism, proletarian internationalism
can secure genuine unity.

The correctness of the theoretical conceptions of the Communist parties is tested and confirmed, above all, in their
practical activities. The CPSU firmly abides by Lenin's instruction to the effect that differences between political parties "are usually resolved not only by polemics over principles, but also by the course of political developments", and,
moreover, rather by the latter than the former.[1]

---

[1] V. I. Lenin, *Collected Works*, Vol. 9, p. 146.

Proceeding from these positions of principle, the CPSU Central Committee, in a letter to CPC leaders of February 21, 1963, again proposed an end to open controversy between the fraternal parties.

On February 26, 1963, i.e., within five days of the CPSU Central Committee's appeal for ending the controversy, *Jenmin jihpao* reprinted a foul anti-Soviet article from the Albanian newspaper *Zeri i Popullit* (The Voice of the People). This was followed by a series of Chinese own polemic articles attacking the general line of the Marxist-Leninist parties: "What Has Caused the Differences—Reply to M. Thorez and Other Comrades" (February 27, 1963); "Another Look at Comrade Togliatti's Differences with Us—On Some Major Problems of Leninism in Our Epoch" (March 1); "On the Statement of the Communist Party of the USA" (March 8); "A Mirror of Revisionism" (March 9).[1]

On March 9, 1963, the CPC Central Committee replied to the CPSU Central Committee's letter of February 21, 1963 by spewing out another series of dissentient anti-Marxist ideas. Chinese leaders hypocritically declared their willingness to end open controversy. The sole aim of such a statement, however, was to mislead the CPSU and other fraternal parties. This is evidenced if only by the fact that Chinese leaders began to insist stubbornly on publishing confidential correspondence between the CPC and the CPSU, which could not but lead to a continuation of open controversy. Nevertheless, at the insistence of the CPC Central Committee the letter of the CPSU Central Committee of February 21, 1963 and the letter of the CPC Central Committee of March 9, 1963 were published in China and the Soviet Union on March 14, 1963.

Insisting on publication of the letters, CPC leaders hoped for a propaganda success. The point is that the letter of the CPSU Central Committee was not intended for publication and therefore it did not contain a comprehensive exposition of the position of the CPSU on the disputed problems. The letter of Chinese leaders, however, was intended for publication in advance and couched in terms which distorted the line of the CPSU and embellished the position of their own.

---

[1] *Jenmin jihpao*, February 27, March 1, 8 and 9, 1963.

The Communists of the world, however, easily discriminated between right and wrong.

The press and radio of the PRC, even after March 9, 1963, continued on a growing scale their attacks on the Marxist-Leninist parties. Slanderous publications of the CPC were circulated not only in China but also abroad almost in all the main languages of the world. They were advertised as the "supreme truth" of Marxism-Leninism.

Distribution of slanderous anti-Marxist publications of CPC leaders became one of the main tasks of PRC Embassies and offices of the Hsinhua News Agency abroad. These activities caused deep indignation of the Communist parties and the progressive public.

A special agency set up under the PRC Government dealt with the publication and circulation of Chinese dissentient publications in foreign languages.

Chinese aircraft, trains, ships going abroad were lavishly supplied with such publications to be circulated free of charge. Not infrequently Chinese magazines posted to subscribers abroad were supplemented free of charge with slanderous articles with an indication that they were being sent "at readers' request".

8. SINO-SOVIET MEETING IN JULY 1963

In its letter of February 21, 1963, the CPSU Central Committee came forward with the initiative of holding a high-level bilateral meeting of representatives of the CPSU and the CPC to discuss all major problems of interest to both parties point by point. After an additional exchange of views the meeting was scheduled for July 5, 1963.

Shortly before the meeting, on June 14, 1963, CPC leaders published a document allegedly in reply to the letter of the CPSU Central Committee of March 30, 1963, pretentiously called "Proposal for the General Line of the International Communist Movement" (so-called 25 points).

In this document they further elaborated their old views on today's main problems of principle. While hypocritically declaring their loyalty to the Declaration of 1957 and the Statement of 1960 Chinese leaders made it clear that they were dissatisfied with the strategic line formulated at the international forums of Communist parties and raised the question of replacing this line by their fallacious platform. In the history of the international communist movement there had not yet been an instance of such unprecedented claims by one party to formulating arbitrarily a "general line" for the entire movement. This was a striking manifestation of the hegemonistic claims of the Maoists.

The letter of the CPC Central Committee of June 14, 1963, was obviously meant to aggravate the situation, unfavourable as it was, for holding a Sino-Soviet meeting. In view of this, the CPSU Central Committee deemed it unwise to publish this letter in the Soviet press at that moment.

However, Chinese propaganda depicted the position of the CPSU Central Committee, which was motivated by concern for unity, as an intention to "conceal" the views of Chinese leaders from the Communists, from the Soviet people. Taking the patience of the CPSU Central Committee for its weakness, Mao Tse-tung and his group, contrary to the rules of friendly relations between socialist countries, started with growing persistence to circulate illegally in Moscow and other Soviet cities through the PRC Embassy in the USSR the letter of the CPC Central Committee of June 14, 1963 printed in Russian in a mass impression. Chinese Embassy officials personally distributed copies of the letter to various offices in Moscow and other cities, delivered them by post, circulated them from flat to flat and carried them to Leningrad, Kiev, Odessa, Dubna, and other Soviet cities.

Under these circumstances, on June 27, 1963, the USSR Ministry of Foreign Affairs in a note to the PRC Embassy again demanded an immediate end to the unprecedented practice of illegal circulation in the Soviet Union by officials of the Embassy and other Chinese citizens of the letter of the CPC Central Committee of June 14, 1963. The note also declared that the further stay in the Soviet Union of three Embassy officials and two other Chinese citizens, who had been the most impudent in violating the universally accepted standards of relations between socialist states and between countries in general and who had crudely infringed upon the sovereignty of the Soviet Union, was undesirable.

When the meeting between representatives of the CPSU and the CPC was in progress Chinese leaders took a number of steps to complicate negotiations.

On July 7, i.e., on the second day of the meeting, a mass rally was held in Peking, at which official speakers supported the provocative actions of Chinese Embassy officials in Moscow and the Chinese research students expelled from the Soviet Union for illegal circulation of anti-Soviet publications. Fomenting among the Chinese people unfriendly feelings towards the Soviet Union Chinese authorities again and again attempted to prove their right to violate the sovereignty of our state and the standards of international relations.

On July 9, the CPSU Central Committee in a special statement pointed out that such actions of Chinese leaders endangered Sino-Soviet relations.[1] Despite these unfriendly actions the CPSU will continue to make every effort to avoid an aggravation of existing differences and overcome the difficulties in the relations between the CPC, on the one hand, and the CPSU and other Marxist-Leninist parties, on the other.

Chinese leaders, however, continued to put up new obstacles in the way of normalising Sino-Soviet relations. On July 10, 1963, the CPC Central Committee issued a statement fully justifying the actions of the Chinese citizens expelled from the Soviet Union for the circulation of anti-Soviet publications and, in effect, attempted to arrogate the right to interfere in Soviet internal affairs.

The frankly unfriendly actions of CPC leaders, their stubborn efforts to distort the position of our party compelled the CPSU Central Committee to publish on July 14, 1963 a letter of the CPC Central Committee of June 14, 1963, and give it a proper assessment. Simultaneously, the CPSU Central Committee published an open letter to the Party organisations, all Communists of the Soviet Union.

The open letter of the CPSU Central Committee presented the true picture of Sino-Soviet relations and showed who was to blame for the difficulties which had arisen in the world communist movement. At the same time, this document was pervaded by a sincere desire for normalising Sino-

---

[1] *Pravda,* July 9, 1963.

Soviet relations, for strengthening the unity of all revolutionary forces. "The Central Committee of the CPSU," the
open letter pointed out, "with a full sense of responsibility
declares to the Party and all Soviet people that we have
done and will do everything in our power to strengthen unity
with the Communist Party of China, to consolidate the world
communist movement under the banner of Lenin, to promote
the cohesion of the countries of the world socialist system, to
give effective assistance to all peoples fighting against colonialism, to further the cause of peace and secure the triumph
of the great ideals of communism throughout the world."[1]

The open letter of the CPSU Central Committee met with
full support and unanimous approval of the Marxist-Leninist
parties. On July 19, 1963, the newspaper *Trybuna Ludu*,
organ of the Central Committee of the Polish United Workers' Party, stated in an editorial: "We fully share the viewpoint of the CPSU concerning the history of differences between the CPC, on the one hand, and the CPSU and the international communist movement, on the other. We completely agree with the description of the essence of these differences given in the letter of the CPSU Central Committee
and with the denunciation of the hostile and slanderous attacks by the CPC leadership on the Communist Party of the
Soviet Union. We believe that the appeal of the CPSU Central Committee to the Chinese comrades to step on the path
of eliminating differences and strengthening genuine unity
between our parties on the principles of Marxism-Leninism,
proletarian internationalism is correct and well-grounded."

The Central Committee of the Communist Party of Czechoslovakia, in connection with the publication of the open
letter of the CPSU Central Committee, issued a statement
which said in particular: "The letter of the CPSU Central
Committee fully coincides with the opinion and line of our
Party. Therefore, the Central Committee of the Communist
Party of Czechoslovakia is in complete agreement with its
conclusions and the action of the Party of Lenin which contributes in supreme degree to consolidating the Marxist-
Leninist unity of the international communist movement.
Our party is highly appreciative, above all, of the fact that

---

[1] *Pravda*, July 14, 1963.

the letter of the CPSU Central Committee contains a consistent reflection and principled defence of the ideas, which are the common programme of all Communists in the struggle of the working people of the world for peace and communism."[1]

Similar statements were issued by many other Communist and Workers' parties. The Political Bureau of the Central Committee of the Communist Party of Germany declared its full agreement with the open letter of the CPSU Central Committee of July 14, 1967. The Political Bureau emphasised that the letter completely conformed to the spirit of the Declaration and Statement of the Moscow meetings of 1957 and 1960 and that it was a new important contribution to the unity of the world communist movement and its cohesion on the principles of Marxism-Leninism and joint decisions.

The 12th plenary meeting of the Central Committee of the Communist Party of Mexico held in mid-July 1963 also expressed its full accord with the open letter of the CPSU Central Committee. The resolution adopted by the plenary meeting pointed out the fallacy of the stand taken by the leadership of the Communist Party of China on problems of crucial importance for developing and intensifying the struggle of the Communists, the working class and the peoples of the whole world for the triumph of peace, for national liberation, for socialism.

The strategic plans of the anti-Sovietiers in the CPC provided for an escalation of the political struggle against the Soviet Union. Therefore, the prospect of reaching any agreement between the CPC and the CPSU frightened the Maoists. In order to thwart a normalisation of Sino-Soviet relations, Peking leaders continued to provoke differences. Nevertheless, despite the tense situation in which the Sino-Soviet meeting was held, the CPSU Central Committee did everything in its power so that the meeting could help overcome the differences between the CPC and the CPSU, to achieve unity and cohesion between our countries.

At the meeting the Soviet delegation made concrete proposals with a view to eliminating differences, developing cooperation between the Soviet Union and the PRC in all

---

[1] *Pravda,* July 22, 1963.

spheres. It proposed to examine the question of widening trade exchanges, scientific and technological co-operation and other economic relations between the two countries, expressed itself in favour of discussing the prospects for developing economic relations and co-operation over a long period, signing a long-term trade agreement in the interests of the two countries and the entire socialist community, exchanging information on trade and currency policy on the world market.

The Chinese delegation left all these proposals without an answer.

On July 20, 1963, the bilateral meeting was suspended at the request of the CPC without yielding any positive results.

The Central Committee of the CPSU deemed it necessary to take all measures to prevent any further exacerbation of Sino-Soviet relations during the interval in the negotiations. For this purpose, the Soviet side again made a proposal to end the publication of articles, statements and material, as well as the broadcasting of programmes containing mutual criticism and thereby to contribute to an improvement of the atmosphere for a successful continuation of the bilateral meeting and for preparing an international conference of representatives of the Communist and Workers' parties.

For its part, the CPSU Central Committee expressed its readiness to undertake a corresponding commitment in case of reaching agreement on this issue. The CPC leadership, however, rejected this proposal as well, although there could be no doubt about its usefulness among all who really desired a normalisation of Sino-Soviet relations.

Loyal to its unflinching line toward the attainment of unity between the CPSU and the CPC on the principles of Marxism-Leninism, the CPSU Central Committee, even at the time of actual disruption of the bilateral talks by the Chinese leadership, did not miss the slightest opportunity to direct the development of Sino-Soviet relations along the path of normalisation. This was again demonstrated by the talks with the CPC delegation on the eve of its return to Peking. It was again declared to the Chinese representatives that our party sincerely strove to overcome differences and that in approaching the solution of this task the CPSU was invariably guided by the interests of socialism and communism.

9. EXACERBATION OF SINO-SOVIET INTER-STATE RELATIONS

Since the time CPC leaders launched their attacks on the ideological positions of the CPSU they began to extend more and more often their ideological differences with our party to the sphere of Sino-Soviet inter-state relations. Under the camouflage of the slogan "lean on your own resources" in an effort to fence off the Chinese people from the renovative ideas of the CPSU and other Marxist-Leninist parties, to efface from their minds friendly feelings for the Soviet Union, Chinese leaders began to curtail co-operation with the Soviet Union in all major fields.

In 1960, guided by political considerations, Chinese organisations abstained from the official commissioning of many enterprises built with Soviet assistance.

Although the Soviet Union had handed over to China a quantity of scientific and technical documents seven times that it had received from her, since the latter half of 1960 the conditions created in the PRC for systematic study of her scientific and technical achievements and her experience in economic development became intolerable. The office of the Soviet Embassy counsellor for economic affairs was refused subscription for 20 industrial, agricultural and scientific and technical journals, as well as for 209 periodicals on science and technology, economics and finance; all of them were withdrawn from sale. Officials of Soviet offices in Peking were practically forbidden to visit Chinese public libraries.

The Soviet Union, however, continued to send to the PRC industrial-economic, agricultural, scientific and technical journals, technical information bulletins, the bulletin of the USSR Academy of Sciences, abstracts journals, press information and other similar literature.

In 1960, the Chinese side by its provocative actions faced the Soviet Government with the necessity to recall Soviet specialists from the PRC. This decision was taken under the pressure of circumstances artificially created by the Maoists.

The first groups of Soviet specialists had been sent to China at the request of the CPC Central Committee as far back as August 1949. As Sino-Soviet co-operation widened, the number of Soviet specialists increased, so that 1,600 people worked in China in August 1960. In the course of the "big leap" accompanied by a sharp increase in elements of conceit and nationalistic arrogance, a contemptuous attitude to Soviet know-how became more and more common in China. Facts evidencing Chinese mistrust in Soviet specialists were increasingly frequent.

On February 3, 1960, the PRC Vice-Premier, Li Fu-chun, was handed in a memorandum from the Soviet Embassy counsellor on economic co-operation concerning violations of technological requirements in the operation of boilers at thermal power stations in China and the intolerability of making unwarranted changes in Soviet technical documents at the Harbin boiler-making plant. On February 8, 1960, the Deputy Minister of the Oil Industry Liu Feng, was notified about violations of technical standards in the assembly of technological equipment at the Lanchow oil refinery. On March 25, 1960, the PRC Vice-Premier, Po I-po, was handed in a memorandum on violations of process charts and technical instructions in the operation of equipment at the Anshan, Wuhan, Pao-tow and Hsiengtan metallurgical complexes. On April 2, Po I-po was notified about violations of the requirements of Soviet design and technical documents in the construction and assembly of a number of thermal power stations.

However, neither managers of enterprises nor heads of ministries and government departments, or the CPC leadership as a whole paid heed to the well-grounded recommendations of Soviet specialists. This was nothing less than a deliberate attempt to discredit Soviet know-how, to challenge the aims of Soviet technical and economic assistance to China. In other words, the question of Soviet specialists became an acute political issue.

Soviet specialists began to be regarded with suspicion, were subjected to surveillance, their personal belongings were searched and letters addressed to them censored.

What is more, since the spring of 1960 Chinese organisations started brainwashing Soviet specialists in a spirit of opposition to the policy of the CPSU. This caused legitimate indignation of Soviet people working in the PRC. Soviet authorities repeatedly called attention to such developments and insistently requested that normal conditions be provided for the work of Soviet specialists. Chinese authorities, however, ignored these requests.

Later developments demonstrated clearly that the Chinese leaders who had taken to the path of anti-Sovietism sought pretexts for fomenting feelings of hostility towards the Soviet Union within the Party and people. They were least of all concerned about the immense damage they caused to the national interests of the Chinese people, China's economy, by ruining the relations of fraternal co-operation between China and the Soviet Union.

The provocative actions of the Maoists made it impossible for Soviet specialists to stay in China any longer. On July 16, 1960, the PRC Ministry of Foreign Affairs was handed in a note about the recalling of Soviet specialists commissioned to work in China. When taking this decision, the Soviet Government took account of the fact that during the years of people's power the PRC had raised her own national personnel many of whom were trained at institutions of higher learning and enterprises in the Soviet Union. As far back as 1958 and in later years, Soviet leaders repeatedly raised the question of reducing substantially the number of Soviet specialists who could be effectively replaced by young Chinese personnel educated in the Soviet Union. As shown by developments, CPC leaders had their ulterior motives for declining these proposals.

While expressing themselves against the withdrawal of Soviet specialists, Chinese leaders in fact took no constructive steps to normalise the situation. This was evidenced if only by the fact that the reply to the Soviet note about the recalling of specialists was not handed in to the Soviet Embassy in the PRC until July 31, i.e., a fortnight after the PRC Ministry of Foreign Affairs had been informed of the beginning of withdrawal of specialists. The sole purpose of the note of the PRC Ministry of Foreign Affairs was to mislead public opinion at home and abroad and depict China as an innocent victim. In contravention of all standards of international relations Chinese authorities officially declared their right to continue political brainwashing of Soviet people in a spirit of blatant anti-Sovietism.

The allegation of Chinese leaders that the withdrawal of Soviet specialists was the cause of failures in the Chinese

14*

economy and necessitated a revision of its development programme is absolutely untenable.

It will be recalled that Chinese industry fulfilled the plan for the second quarter-year of 1960 by less than 90 per cent; consequently, failures in fulfilling the plans had been in evidence long before the withdrawal of Soviet specialists. They were the direct result of the policy of "three red banners".

Indeed, the recalling of Soviet specialists could have no effect on the coal, oil, timber, consumer goods and other industries and agriculture, where a small number of specialists worked in 1960: for example, 3 in the coal industry, 7 in the oil industry, 2 in the farm machine-building industry, 3 in the Ministry of State Farms and Virgin Lands, 1 in the Ministry of Agriculture and in the forest economy respectively. It will be recalled, however, that it was precisely in the coal, timber, consumer goods and other industries and particularly in agriculture that the biggest failures took place.

The Soviet Union repeatedly expressed its willingness to return Soviet specialists to China, if normal conditions were provided for their work. This was stated in particular in November 1960 to the Chinese delegation which had arrived in Moscow for the Meeting of Representatives of the Communist and Workers' Parties, the delegation of the CPC Central Committee which attended the 22nd Congress of the CPSU in October 1961, the delegation of the CPC at the meeting in July 1963, in the letter from the Central Committee of the CPSU to the Central Committee of the CPC on November 29, 1963. The Chinese leadership, however, ignored these proposals.

In 1960, the Chinese side, for the first time in 11 years, failed to fulfil its obligations to the value of 310 million rubles under the protocol for mutual goods deliveries and even refused to sign contracts on a number of commodity items. The turnover of Sino-Soviet trade decreased by 19 per cent from the 1959 level. Soviet exports to China fell by 14 per cent, and imports, by 23 per cent. On China's initiative the conclusion of a long-term trade agreement between the Soviet Union and China was put off for an indefinite period.

On October 31, 1960, the Chinese Government made a statement, in which it demanded a sharp reduction in the volume of operations under all the agreements and protocols for economic, scientific and technical co-operation with the Soviet Union. The Chinese side refused to fulfil in 1960 its obligations for goods deliveries to the Soviet Union in connection with a revision of her economic development plan allegedly due to severe natural disasters and the withdrawal of Soviet specialists from China.

The Soviet Government rejected the Chinese grievances as artificial and unfounded. In a statement of December 17, 1960, the USSR Minister of Foreign Trade gave an exhaustive answer to all questions raised in this connection and pointed out the need for developing trade and economic relations between the Soviet Union and China on a basis of friendship and comradely co-operation.

At the talks held from February to June 1961 on economic, scientific and technical co-operation, which culminated in the agreement of June 19, the Chinese representatives, ignoring the interests of their people, rejected further Soviet assistance in the construction of 89 industrial and 35 other projects to the total value of 1,100 million rubles. For the period 1961-1967, the Soviet Union kept on to its commitments to give China technical assistance in building only 66 projects of key importance for the development of the civilian and particularly the defence industries. Agreement was also reached on Soviet technical assistance in building new projects (a gas pipeline, a semi-conductor factory, etc.). As a result, in 1961 Soviet deliveries of complete plant and equipment to China reduced to one-fifth of the 1960 volume.

At the talks in February-June 1961 Chinese representatives no longer dared to motivate curtailment of economic co-operation with the Soviet Union by references to the withdrawal of Soviet specialists, evidently being aware of the absurdity of such an excuse. Adducing arguments to support their proposals, they pointed out the following reasons:

"First, Soviet assistance has been effective in providing China with the foundation of modern industry and technology; therefore, in the future the building and designing of the majority of projects will be carried out by China's own

means to ease Soviet efforts to help her. However, China
will need Soviet aid on projects she will be unable to design,
build and equip with her own facilities.

"Second, the CPC Central Committee and the Chinese
Government have decided to concentrate on the building of
key projects, cutting down the total number of capital construction projects and projects not on the list of priorities
so as to implement more effectively the principle of building socialism in China: 'To build better, more, faster and
more economically'. Construction will be continued in China
on a vast scale and at a fast rate.

"Third, natural disasters which hit agriculture during the
past two years have caused certain difficulties in the balance
of payments; therefore, China hopes to provide conditions
for more favourable co-operation between her and the Soviet
Union by reducing the number of projects being built with
Soviet aid."[1]

This explanation appeared quite plausible, and it did not
rule out the continued development of Sino-Soviet economic relations. The Soviet Government could not but reckon
with the arguments of the leadership of the PRC, which had
found herself in a difficult situation. On the Soviet initiative the communique on the talks indicated the willingness
of both parties to continue their co-operation. "The two
parties," the communique said, "have summed up the results
of the work over the past few years and concluded that the
economic, scientific and technical co-operation between the
USSR and the PRC based on the principles of proletarian
internationalism, equality and fraternal mutual assistance
has been fruitful."[2]

Two months after signing the agreement of June 19, 1961,
on August 15, the Chinese Government announced another
reduction in equipment deliveries from the Soviet Union,
motivating this again by difficulties experienced by the PRC.
The CPSU Central Committee and the Soviet Government
again accepted the explanations of the Chinese side and
agreed to defer deliveries of complete plant and equipment
to China regardless of the fact that the bulk of it (to the

---

[1] *For Unity in the International Communist Movement*, Documents
and Records, Moscow, 1964, pp. 208-209 (in Russian).
[2] *Pravda*, June 23, 1961.

value of tens of millions of rubles) was in the process of manufacturing or had been ordered from third countries and could not be used in the Soviet national economy.

This, however, was not the end of the matter. Early in December 1961, the Chinese side declared its complete refusal to import Soviet complete plant and equipment in 1962-1963. Thus, in less than half-a-year the PRC Government unilaterally revised the terms of operating agreements and contracts on three occasions, ignoring the damage caused by such practices to Soviet enterprises handling Chinese orders.

It is perfectly clear that the main reason for the actions of the PRC Government was not economic difficulties but political considerations issuing from the general line of the CPC leadership towards exacerbating Sino-Soviet relations. This alone was the true motive for the Chinese Government's decision to suspend for two years all industrial projects being built with Soviet technical assistance regardless of the degree of their readiness for commissioning and the quantity of equipment supplied. Suffice it to say that some of these projects were of paramount importance, and only a small quantity of completing equipment was needed to put them into operation. Chinese leaders even ignored the fact that a delay in commissioning such projects would inevitably have an adverse effect on the further integrated development of individual industries.

The purpose of this operation of Chinese anti-Sovietiers came to light later when excursions of Chinese and even foreigners to suspended projects were arranged to demonstrate the Soviet Union's "betrayal" of China and efforts to influence by economic pressure the ideological positions of the CPC. The masterminds of these provocations knew well enough that it would be difficult to expose their lies, because all questions of Sino-Soviet economic co-operation were settled through confidential inter-governmental channels. Using unscrupulous means, Peking leaders fabricated the fable that it was not themselves but the Soviet Union that was to blame for the disastrous state of the Chinese economy, the starvation and misfortunes experienced by the Chinese people.

The agreement of June 19, 1961 envisaged the possibility to commission Soviet engineers and technicians to work in

China. However, despite the acute need of many Chinese organisations for technical aid and repeated allegations of Chinese officials about the damage caused to China by the withdrawal of Soviet specialists the PRC Government throughout 1961 requested only on two occasions to commission specialists: four specialists to help assemble equipment at the Sanmenxia hydropower project and seven specialists to train airmen for agricultural aviation. Both these requests were satisfied.

Chinese propaganda stopped mentioning Soviet assistance to the PRC. In 1961, the Chinese press did not publish a single report on the commissioning of projects built with Soviet aid.

As is known, scientific and technical co-operation between the Soviet Union and China, which assumed a vast scope in earlier years, was tantamount in fact to gratuitous Soviet aid to the PRC. This was an expression of the Soviet Union's truly internationalist attitude to the People's Republic of China, which had just embarked on the path of technological progress. In the period 1950-1960, China received from the Soviet Union extremely valuable scientific and technical documents and trained with Soviet assistance research personnel and designers capable of handling many scientific and technical problems on their own. After attaining definite successes in economic development, CPC leaders, ignoring the national interests of the Chinese people, arrogantly declared that the PRC was no longer in need of developing scientific and technical exchanges with the Soviet Union.

In October 1960, the Chinese side unexpectedly put forward the proposal for revising the earlier Sino-Soviet agreements on scientific and technical co-operation, as well as for cancelling all the commitments assumed under them. In this connection two agreements were signed in June 1961 instead of the former seven: the inter-governmental agreement of June 19, 1961 and the agreement between the Academies of Sciences of the USSR and the PRC of June 21, 1961.

As a result of the revision of these agreements the obligations of the contracting parties were markedly reduced at the request of Chinese authorities.

The Chinese side sought to obtain from the Soviet Union mostly secret information in various fields of up-to-date, primarily military, technology. At the same time, Chinese organisations avoided exchanging with the Soviet Union their experience in those fields of science and technology, where the PRC had made achievements. For example, they refused to carry out joint tests of Soviet samples of equipment, apparatus, instruments and materials under tropical climatic conditions, to acquaint Soviet specialists with their experience in cultivating Chlorella algae under field conditions, to continue the operations of a joint paleontological expedition in Chinese territory, etc.

In view of the difficult food situation in China, the Soviet Union on its own initiative relieved her of her arrears in 1961 under unfulfilled obligations for food deliveries in 1960 and abstained from purchasing in China almost all of the foodstuffs which had been traditional items of Chinese export to the Soviet Union until 1961. The Soviet Union also gave China great assistance by loaning her 300,000 tons of grain and flour in the spring and summer periods difficult for China. In view of the acute shortage of foreign exchange in the PRC the Soviet Union agreed to buy from her 1,000 tons of silver to be paid for in hard currency.

In the latter half of 1960, the Chinese side exhibited a distinct trend toward curtailing cultural exchanges with the Soviet Union. Chinese purchases of Soviet films reduced. In 1960, Chinese organisations rejected 19 films offered by the Soviet Union, including the "Ballad of a Soldier", "Lullaby", etc. Characteristic changes also took place in the field of book exchange. Advertising of Soviet books was ended. Even such editions as the *Biography of V. I. Lenin* were withdrawn from sale. The number of Soviet books reprinted in the PRC was sharply reduced. In 1960, they came out in about 6 million copies as compared with 23,234,000 copies in 1958.

On the whole, the scale of cultural exchanges between China and the Soviet Union reduced in 1961 to an all-time low since the establishment of the PRC. On the Chinese initiative, sections on co-operation in the field of the press and book publishing, public health and journalism, direct contacts between Soviet and Chinese cultural institutions were left out of cultural exchange programmes. Exchanges in the fields of cinematography, broadcasting, television, higher and public education were curtailed particularly drastically.

After October 1961, the Chinese side, in contravention of the existing agreement, unilaterally ended the transmission of recordings of Soviet broadcasts and completely deleted them from programmes.

In 1961, Chinese imports of political literature and fiction from the Soviet Union continued to decline, falling roughly by more than half as compared with 1960. A similar situation developed in the field of re-publication of Soviet books in Chinese. In 1958, more than 5,000 Soviet books were reprinted, whereas in 1961 the figure dropped to less than 400 and in the field of socio-political literature, in particular, to 22.

The activities of the Sino-Soviet Friendship Society were gradually wound down. In 1961, its branches in the provinces and large cities practically ceased to operate, confining themselves to occasional work connected with national holidays and anniversaries.

The unfriendly position of the Chinese leadership was also strikingly demonstrated by its attitude to such an epoch-making event as man's first space flight carried out in the Soviet Union on April 12, 1961. In an attempt to play down the importance of this outstanding accomplishment of the Soviet people, the CPC leadership abstained from congratulating the CPSU Central Committee and the Soviet Government on the occasion of Yuri Gagarin's exploit.

After 1960, when Chinese leaders went over openly to implementing anti-Soviet policy, they began evading stubbornly high-level contacts through party and government channels. In 1961, under the pretext of economic difficulties they postponed the visit to the PRC by the President of the Presidium of the USSR Supreme Soviet who had been officially invited by the PRC Chairman in December 1960. These difficulties, however, did not prevent the visits to China in 1961 by the King of Nepal, the Queen of Belgium, the British Field Marshal Montgomery and other foreign statesmen.

The curtailment of economic and cultural co-operation with the Soviet Union was an expression of the Maoists' general policy of undermining China's relations with the socialist countries, of breaking away from the socialist community. In 1961, the turnover of Chinese trade with the socialist countries of Europe, with the exception of Albania, sharply reduced from the level of 1959. China's trade with Czechoslovakia diminished to one-fourth, with Hungary to less than one-third, with the GDR to almost one-third, with Poland to one half, etc. The total volume of Chinese foreign trade reduced from 14,000 million yuan in 1959 to 8,000 million in 1961 almost exclusively at the expense of turnover with the socialist countries. Chinese leaders began to reject deliveries even of equipment manufactured in the socialist countries to Chinese orders, although in many instances it was to be supplied on credit. The PRC completely terminated information exchange with the socialist countries on economic problems, the world market situation, etc.

The reversal of China's policy of economic co-operation with the socialist countries had negative consequences both for the latter and, above all, for China herself, caused definite damage to the interests of the world socialist system. Chinese leaders, however, ignored this fact and the line towards developing all-round co-operation between the socialist countries laid down in the Statement of the Meeting of the fraternal parties in 1960.

While winding down economic co-operation with the socialist countries, Peking leaders were widening China's trade with the capitalist world. Chinese organisations started purchasing in capitalist Europe the goods and equipment they could have obtained from the socialist countries at greater advantage. For example, in 1960-1961 China bought from Britain aircraft, tractors, motor vehicles, etc. Her trade with Japan, the FRG, Italy substantially increased in that period.

10. THE LINE OF THE CPC LEADERSHIP TOWARD BUILDING UP TENSIONS ON THE SINO-SOVIET BORDER

The development of friendship and good-neighbourly relations between the Soviet Union and the People's Republic of China was largely facilitated by the absence of mutual territorial claims and border conflicts. In the Treaty of Friendship, Alliance and Mutual Assistance signed four and a half months after the proclamation of the PRC the Soviet Union and China solemnly declared their intention to base their relations on the principles of "mutual respect for state sovereignty and territorial integrity".

During the first ten years of existence of the PRC the Sino-Soviet border was one of friendship and good-neighbourly relations. The population of border areas maintained broad intercourse, carried on lively trade and cultural exchanges, applied joint efforts to solve economic problems, to fight natural disasters. Soviet authorities permitted Chinese to make hay, procure firewood, fish and engage in other economic activity in a number of areas in Soviet territory. Comradely relations developed between Chinese and Soviet border guards.

Disputes which arose at the border were invariably resolved in an atmosphere of mutual understanding and courtesy.

Leaders of the CPC and the PRC on no occasion declared the existence of any territorial disputes between China and the Soviet Union, nor did they ever call in question the legitimacy and justness of the Sino-Soviet border. On the contrary, CPC leaders repeatedly stated that after the October Revolution the Soviet state had based its relations with China on the principles of equality and respect for the sovereign rights of the Chinese people. Speaking at the Seventh Congress of the CPC in 1945, Mao Tse-tung noted that the Soviet Union was the first country to have renounced the unequal treaties and concluded new equal treaties with China. He repeated this statement on December 16, 1949 during his visit to Moscow.

The present Sino-Soviet border formed centuries ago along the natural boundaries dividing the territories of the Soviet Union and China. It was legally enforced in a number of treaties operating to this day. In the early fifties, the Soviet Union, at the request of China, handed over to her complete sets of topographical maps indicating the border line. After examining the maps, the Chinese authorities made no comments on the border line, and it was abided by in practice.

The first statements about outstanding territorial and border problems between China and the Soviet Union were made in China in 1957 by bourgeois Rightist elements who had risen in opposition to the Communist Party. Significantly, CPC leaders who gave a rebuff to attacks from the Right left unanswered their territorial claims to the Soviet Union. As later developments showed, this silence was deliberate.

After the nationalists within the CPC had changed over to an open struggle against the Soviet Union, they began to aggravate deliberately the situation on the Sino-Soviet border, advancing territorial claims to the Soviet Union, and using them to foment nationalistic, anti-Soviet sentiments in China.

In the summer of 1960, China provoked a border conflict in the area of Buz Aigyr, where Chinese stock-breeders deliberately violated the Soviet border and intruded into Soviet territory. Defying the demands of Soviet border guards, the Chinese citizens refused to return to China. They would not go back even when winter came. Naturally, Soviet authorities had to take care of supplies of all requisite goods to Chinese peasant trespassers. When asked by Soviet border guards why they were unwilling to return to China now that they had no feed for their cattle the chairman of a people's commune who was among the Chinese peasants admitted that they had crossed into Soviet territory under direct orders of Chinese authorities and were afraid to come back without their permission.

In later years, violations of the Sino-Soviet border from the Chinese side became systematic. In the period 1961-1962, a few thousand violations were reported. If it were not for the patience of Soviet border guards, they might have developed into large incidents.

The Maoists attempted to provide a "theoretical base" for their territorial claims to the Soviet Union and other neighbouring countries by distorting world history in a frankly nationalistic spirit. It was not fortuitous that nationalism became the keynote of social sciences in that period. It was from the angle of nationalism that generally known historical facts were revised, the role of historical figures was reassessed and emperor conquerors were glorified.

In February 1962, the Peking magazine *Mintsu tuantse*, in an article under the title "Sinkiang's Historical Ties with China", peddled the idea that in the past China's Western region had extended far beyond the borders of the present-day Sinkiang and that, according to reliable evidence available, the Western region was divided at the time first into 36 and later into 50-odd principalities incorporating the present-day Sinkiang, Kashmir, the northern border region of Afghanistan, the Soviet areas of Kokand, Kazakhstan, Northwestern Khorezm, the areas along the northern coast of the Black Sea as well as of the present-day Iran.

Chinese historians obsessed by great-power ambitions went out of their way to extoll the activities of Genghis Khan, ascribing to him a progressive role in the history of China and forty other states. The predatory conquests of Genghis Khan and his successors were described as being little short of a blessing to the peoples enslaved by his hordes. The *Lishih yenchiu* magazine, in an article commemorating the 800th birth anniversary of Genghis Khan, alleged that his conquests had opened for the peoples of subjugated countries a wider world to live and work in, a more advanced culture to learn from.

These views are in striking contrast to the conclusions of Marxist-Leninist historiography. ". . . Marxist scholars," writes the President of the Academy of Sciences of the Mongolian People's Republic, B. Shirendyb, "on the other hand, regard the wars of Genghis Khan and his successors as predatory, piratical and reactionary. Any attempt to revise the Marxist assessment of the wars of conquest by invaders and enslavers—khans and noyens (feudal nobility. —*Authors*.)—is a complete retreat from the basic principles of historical materialism and brings grist to the mill of aggressors, imperialists, revanchists and chauvinists, of all the forces eager to seize foreign territory."[1]

Seeking to exacerbate Sino-Soviet relations, CPC leaders attempted to take advantage of the events following the mass crossing of inhabitants of Sinkiang province into the Soviet Union in the spring of 1962.

---

[1] *Maoism Through the Eyes of the Communists,* Moscow, 1970, p. 102.

This was not an accidental intrusion but the result of grave mistakes of the CPC leadership in domestic policy, the hardships experienced by the population, the extreme measures in implementing the policy toward ethnic minorities. CPC leaders, however, attempted to shift the blame for the consequences of their actions on the Soviet Union. Chinese officials made contradictory statements to explain the causes of the incident. At first, a Vice-Minister of Foreign Affairs of the PRC described it as an "accident", whereas later notes of the PRC Ministry of Foreign Affairs changed over to allegations about subversive activities of Soviet authorities.

Besides native inhabitants of Sinkiang, many immigrants from Russia and the Soviet Union (Kazakhs, Uigurs, Russians, etc.) became victims of the anti-socialist national policy of Chinese leaders. The Presidium of the USSR Supreme Soviet, by its decrees of November 10, 1945 and January 20, 1946 granted Soviet citizenship to about 120,000 such persons and issued them with Soviet certificates of residence abroad. However, for various reasons the majority of immigrants had not obtained such papers, although under Soviet legislation they remained Soviet citizens.

In the early years of the PRC the attitude of Chinese authorities to Soviet citizens in Sinkiang was favourable on the whole. As anti-Soviet tendencies in China's policy grew, however, this attitude changed radically. Soviet citizens permanently residing in Sinkiang were discriminated against in matters involving property, legal and other status, expelled from government offices and enterprises and persecuted more and more vehemently. Officials of Chinese institutions openly subjected Soviet nationals to maltreatment and violence and denied them elementary human rights. Early in 1962, the Sinkiang authorities ended the issuance of exit visas to Soviet citizens willing to return to their homeland.

All this caused the exodus of people driven to desperation from Sinkiang. Between April 22 and June 1962, 67,000 people illegally crossed the border into the Soviet Union.

Chinese officials accused Soviet authorities of having "received" Chinese trespassers. In this connection, the Soviet Government in a memorandum to the Chinese Government denied these charges as unfounded, stating that the border

had been trespassed from the Chinese side before the eyes
of Chinese authorities who were obliged to take timely steps
to prevent these massive violations.

Ignoring obvious facts, Chinese leaders went ahead with
making new artificial charges against the Soviet Union. The
memorandum of the PRC Ministry of Foreign Affairs of
August 30, 1962 stated in part that Soviet authorities had
"prepared and organised the massive crossing of the border",
that Sinkiang was threatened with "serious subversive activities" by the Soviet Union, etc.

On September 19, 1962, the Soviet Government in a note
to the PRC Ministry of Foreign Affairs set out its views on
the issue of massive migration of Sinkiang residents across
the border and rejected the Chinese accusations of the Soviet
Union as slanderous. The PRC Government withheld a reply
to the Soviet note for a long time, and it was not before
July 18, 1963, at the time of the Sino-Soviet meeting, that
it made a statement to the effect that personnel of Soviet
offices in Sinkiang had allegedly carried out "subversive
activities against the PRC". In this statement an attempt was
made to shift on the Soviet Union the blame for the exodus
of Sinkiang residents, as well as for the bloodshed in the
town of Kuldja in the spring of 1962 when Chinese authorities staged organised massive raids against non-Han ethnic
minorities, in which many people were killed. The statement reaffirmed demands for forcible repatriation of all
refugees to China and reaffirmed the Chinese Government's
refusal to send over its representatives to carry out explan-
atory work among the refugees.

The provocative fabrications of the Chinese authorities
were conclusively laid bare in the Soviet Government's
note of October 31, 1963. The Soviet Government reaffirmed
its willingness to resolve in a spirit of friendship and co-
operation all disputed problems, including those involved in
the exodus of people from Sinkiang.

In the end, the Chinese authorities themselves were
compelled to reckon with the desire of Soviet nationals and
persons who were born in Russia to go to the Soviet Union.
In September 1962, the PRC Ministry of Foreign Affairs
requested the Soviet Government to facilitate entry to the
USSR by a summary procedure for applicants. To meet

this request, the Soviet authorities temporarily introduced a no-visa procedure of entry to the USSR from China by Soviet citizens and members of their families. Between October 15, 1962 and May 1, 1963, more than 46,000 persons left Sinkiang for the Soviet Union. This again demonstrated the untenability of the Chinese allegation concerning the efforts of Soviet authorities to "persuade Sinkiang residents to cross into the USSR".

Nevertheless, the Chinese authorities undertook a series of provocative actions against personnel of the Soviet consulates in Sinkiang, including forcible detention, searching of diplomats, etc. The local societies of Soviet citizens were banned and their leaders arrested on false charges of "anti-government activities" and violation of Chinese laws.

In that situation, the Soviet Government decided to close down the Soviet General Consulate in Urumchi and the consulate in Kuldja. At the request of the Chinese authorities this was followed by the closure of a branch of the Soviet Trade Delegation at Urumchi and by the recalling of Soviet foreign trade officials from the border stations of Horgos and Turugart.

Provocations like those in Sinkiang were repeated in other areas of China. In September 1962, the Chinese authorities in Harbin placed under seals all the premises and property belonging to the local society of Soviet citizens, while members of its board and officials in the city and neighbouring areas were arrested. They were subjected to humiliating interrogation and physical violence, and two of the detainees died in prison. Wholesale searches were carried out in their homes. Soviet nationals were faced with absurd charges of illegal activities. The Soviet General Consulate in Harbin was blocked by police.

As it might be expected, the efforts of Chinese authorities to create in Harbin a situation by which they could support their allegations of Soviet nationals' subversive activities proved of no avail. The promises of Chinese authorities to present factual evidence confirming the charges made against Soviet citizens and offices remained unfulfilled because no such facts had ever existed.

Under the circumstances, the Soviet Government in September 1962 closed down the Soviet General Consulates

in Harbin and Shanghai, and later the branches of the Soviet
Trade Delegation in the cities of Dairen, Shanghai and
Kwangchow, the agencies of the all-union association
"Sovfrakht" at the Chinese railway stations of Manchuria
and Tsining.

As CPC leaders persisted in their anti-Soviet line the
conditions of work for the Soviet Embassy in China increasingly deteriorated, too. Chinese leaders began to evade meetings with Soviet representatives even on important matters
raised on instructions from the CPSU Central Committee
and the Soviet Government.

11. ANTI-SOVIET CAMPAIGN IN CHINA
OVER THE MOSCOW PARTIAL NUCLEAR TEST BAN TREATY

Immediately after the break-off of the Sino-Soviet meeting in July 1963 Chinese leaders launched another anti-
Soviet campaign. This time they chose as the pretext for
their attacks on the CPSU and other Marxist-Leninist parties
the treaty on banning nuclear weapons tests in the three
media signed by the governments of the Soviet Union, the
United States and Britain in Moscow on August 5, 1963.
The Chinese side on three occasions—on July 31, August 15
and September 1, 1963—published official statements concerning the Moscow treaty. The PRC leadership opposed
the treaty: it refused to join it and cracked down on the
Soviet Union and the CPSU with unprecedented vehemency.

In their government declarations, Chinese leaders went to
the length of monstrous lies, accusing the Soviet Union of
pursuing a policy of alignment with the forces of war for a
struggle against the forces of peace, with imperialism for
a struggle against socialism, with the United States for a
struggle against China, with reaction in various countries for
a struggle against the peoples of the whole world, etc. All
this unbridled slander was taken up by the Chinese press.
In the summer of 1963 *Jenmin jihpao* alone published more
than 500 anti-Soviet items.

Peking's statements concerning the Moscow treaty touched
on many key issues of today: war and peace, peaceful
coexistence of states with differing social systems, etc.
However, neither the official documents of the PRC Govern-

ment nor the broad propaganda campaign developed on their basis in the Chinese press had anything in common with a businesslike discussion of these issues. They were master-minded by people seeking to discredit at all costs the CPSU and the Soviet Union, to deepen the split in the world com-munist movement, to undermine the unity of the anti-imperialist forces. Aware of the vulnerability of their ideo-logical positions, the Maoists wanted to turn the discussion on the current issues of principle into a petty squabble, an angry exchange of empty words.

In their attacks on the Moscow treaty Peking leaders deliberately ignored the fact that its conclusion was the first real, even if limited, success in the struggle that the peoples, the Communists of the whole world had been waging for years against the danger of nuclear war. Far from dulling the vigilance of working people against the intrigues of imperialism, as was alleged by Chinese propaganda, this success inspired the fighters for peace, strengthened their belief in the possibility to force the imperialists to conces-sions. The peoples of the world saw the practical importance of the treaty in that it would put an end to contamination of the atmosphere with radioactive fallout (strontium-90, cesium-137, etc.) posing a formidable health hazard to the living and future generations of men.

Chinese leaders' allegations to the effect that the conclu-sion of the Moscow treaty would undermine the defence capability of the socialist community were absolutely unten-able. The treaty imposed identical obligations on all the signatory powers, so that none of them would enjoy unilat-eral military advantages.

The Maoists were opposed to the treaty above all because of their desire to obtain nuclear arms at any cost in order to attain their great-power objectives. In a statement of September 1, 1963, Peking leaders frankly declared that despite China's economic difficulties they were determined to develop her own nuclear weapons even if this would take 100 years.

The Maoists were not worried by the fact that prolifera-tion of nuclear arms would inevitably cause a chain reac-tion, with the result that the atomic carcinoma would spread throughout the world and increase the danger of nuclear war many times over. The Chinese line played into the hands, above all, of the West German militarists and revanchists.

The PRC's government statements concerning the Moscow treaty made it clear that the Chinese Government, ignoring its duty as an ally, abusing the relations of mutual trust between the socialist countries, had taken to the path of divulging confidential documents and information relating to the defence capability of the countries of the socialist community, and, moreover, presenting facts in a biassed, distorted form. In this connection, the Soviet Government had to declare that after such actions by the PRC Government hardly anyone would believe in the sincerity of its assurances and entrust to it information important for defence. Naturally, the Soviet Government added that it would draw its conclusions on this score.

Attacking the Moscow treaty, Chinese leaders opposed not only the Soviet Union and the CPSU but also the agreed position of the overall majority of the socialist countries, world public opinion. The collective opinion of the socialist countries on the issue of ending nuclear tests was expressed in the resolution of the meeting of First Secretaries of the Central Committees of the Communist and Workers' parties and heads of government of the Warsaw Treaty member-states held in August 1963.

The fraternal Marxist-Leninist parties on all the continents approved of the treaty, assessing it as an important result of the line consistently pursued by the international communist movement to strengthen the forces of peace and progress. At the same time the Communist and Workers' parties resolutely denounced the Peking leaders' stand in relation to the Moscow treaty.

Referring to the Maoists' attacks against the CPSU and the Soviet Government in connection with the treaty, the secretariat of the Australian Communist Party emphasised that the Party rejected and denounced these statements by Chinese leaders as the most harmful and irresponsible affront to the peace forces waging a long and difficult struggle to prevent nuclear war.[1]

---

[1] *Pravda*, August 11, 1963.

The meeting of representatives of the Communist parties of Denmark, Finland, Norway and Sweden held in Copenhagen on August 16-17, 1963, declared in its communique: "Representatives of the four Communist parties acknowledge that the struggle waged for years by the socialist countries and all peace forces throughout the world has now culminated in an important achievement—a partial ban on nuclear weapons tests. This ban prevents contamination of the atmosphere and is the first and most important step in the direction of international détente.... The meeting seriously regrets the rejection of this treaty by the Communist Party of China."[1]

The slanderous anti-Soviet attacks by Chinese leaders were given a determined rebuff. In August and September 1963, the Soviet Government published statements exposing the anti-Soviet motives of the CPC leaders' attitude to the Moscow treaty and the harm they did to the cause of peace and socialism.[2]

While repulsing the anti-Soviet attacks of Chinese leaders the CPSU Central Committee and the Soviet Government displayed patience and goodwill to normalise Sino-Soviet relations. In a statement of September 21-22, 1963, the Soviet Government again appealed to the CPC leadership to end the controversy and expressed its willingness to use every opportunity to adjust differences.

The Soviet Government emphasised the intolerability of extending ideological differences between parties to the relations between socialist states and using them to foment nationalism and chauvinism, distrust and discord between nations.

The anti-Sovietiers in the CPC, however, pushed ahead along this slippery path. Their attempts to undermine the Soviet people's moral and political unity, trust in their party and its leaders became even more impudent and undisguised. Chinese propaganda material on the issue of the Moscow treaty was exploited for this purpose. The Maoists resorted to direct violations of law and order to circulate such material in the Soviet Union. This was exemplified by the

---

[1] *Pravda*, August 23, 1963.
[2] *Pravda*, August 4, 21, September 21, 22, 1963.

events at the Soviet border station of Naushki on September 7, 1963, when Chinese passengers on a train from Peking behaved outrageously in response to the confiscation by Soviet customs officials of anti-Soviet publications forbidden to be taken to the USSR. They delayed the train departure, made a row at the railway station, insulted Soviet officials and even attempted to fight them.

On the same day, the Soviet Ministry of Foreign Affairs reported this unprecedented fact to the PRC Embassy in Moscow and lodged a protest against the riotous conduct of Chinese citizens. The Ministry stated that it expected Chinese authorities to take action immediately to end violations of law and order by Chinese citizens at the station of Naushki.

Ignoring the demands of Soviet authorities, the Chinese train crew, as well as Chinese passengers, continued to obstruct the train departure, throwing up stop signals and pulling braking cocks. As a result, over 100 Soviet and foreign passengers had to board another train to Moscow and depart after four and a half hours' delay.

Outrages committed by Chinese citizens at the Naushki station were punishable under Soviet criminal law. However, guided by a desire to prevent an exacerbation of Sino-Soviet relations the Soviet Government abstained from prosecution of the Chinese offenders and merely expelled them from Soviet territory.

It was natural to expect Peking to take measures to prevent the recurrence of such incidents undermining Sino-Soviet relations. The Maoists, however, took advantage of the events at the station of Naushki to fan another anti-Soviet hysteria in China.

Upon their return to China the Chinese citizens who had rioted at the Naushki station were given a rousing welcome at meetings where these cynical hoodlums were lauded as martyrs in the struggle for the integrity of Marxism-Leninism.

Early in September 1963, the CPC leadership undertook another offensive against the CPSU and the Soviet Union. *Jenmin jihpao* and *Hungchi* published a series of foul anti-Soviet articles which were presented as replies to the open letter of the CPSU Central Committee of July 14, 1963.

In these articles, for the first time since the emergence of differences with the CPSU, Chinese leaders expressed in plain words what they had earlier talked of figuratively, as a rule, and openly came out with shameless slander of all external and internal policies of the CPSU and the Soviet state. Following in the steps of the Trotskyites, employing their methods and tricks, the Maoists attempted to oppose the Soviet people, the Soviet Communists to the leadership of our party and country. The Peking press and radio called on the Soviet people to fight against the CPSU Central Committee and the Soviet Government. For the blatancy of its attacks on the CPSU and other Marxist-Leninist parties, Chinese propaganda caught up with anti-Soviet, anti-Communist fabrications of reactionary imperialist circles.

Throwing away the Declaration and the Statement worked out collectively by the Communist and Workers' parties and signed by the CPC delegations, Chinese leaders opposed to them their own "platform", which boiled down, in effect, to denial of the decisive influence of the world socialist system on the course of social development, a contemptuous attitude to the struggle of the working class in the capitalist countries, efforts to oppose the national liberation movement to the world socialist system and the international working class movement, adventurism in foreign policy and a desire to preserve the "cold war" atmosphere, sectarianism and putschism in questions of revolution, defence of the cult of the individual denounced by the communist movement, justification of factional struggle within the communist movement.

In this way, the Maoists brought their differences with the international communist movement to a level where they actually grew into differences on all the key problems of modern world development.

Peking leaders gained approval for their anti-Soviet line at the fourth session of the National People's Congress held from November 17 to December 3, 1963. The Congress met behind closed doors. However, even the extremely scant information published in the Chinese press shows that the session from beginning to end was keynoted by a frankly anti-Soviet atmosphere. Chinese leaders used the rostrum of the supreme legislative body of the PRC for unbridled slander of the Soviet Union. They attempted to shift the blame for the economic difficulties in the PRC on "Soviet authorities" and thereby to "substantiate" and "justify" their so-called line of "leaning on one's own resources", a line of renouncing co-operation with the Soviet Union, of stepping up splitting, subversive activities within the socialist camp.

The main political outcome of the session was the official approval by the supreme legislative body of the PRC of the Chinese leadership's policy of disrupting the relations of co-operation with the Soviet Union.

12. CPSU CENTRAL COMMITTEE'S EFFORTS TO CHECK THE EXACERBATION OF SINO-SOVIET RELATIONS

The anti-Soviet line of the CPC leaders assumed an increasingly dangerous character. It extended steadily to all the spheres of relations between the two countries, entailing grave consequences for the socialist community and the world communist movement. Resolute steps were necessary at least to retard at first the further development of this line. Our party took such steps without hesitation.

On October 25, 1963, the Soviet Union again proposed an end to open controversy. The Soviet press unilaterally ceased publication of material exposing the great-power policy of CPC leaders.

CPC leaders completely ignored the cessation of open controversy by our party, describing it cynically as a "trick", a "ruse", etc. The Chinese press concealed the proposals of the CPSU Central Committee from the Chinese readers and continued publication of anti-Soviet items. More than 200 such items were published in November and December 1963 in *Jenmin jihpao* alone.

Despite the anti-Soviet campaign in the PRC unprecedented in scope and persistence, the CPSU Central Committee on November 29, 1963 sent to the CPC Central Committee a letter once again proposing an end to open controversy, as well as joint elaboration and implementation of measures to adjust differences and normalise Sino-Soviet relations. Particular concern of the CPSU Central Committee was caused by the extension of ideological differences to inter-state relations, to practical policy, which tended to under-mine the friendship and cohesion between the peoples of the socialist community, to weaken the anti-imperialist front, to divert the efforts and attention of the fraternal parties from solving the pressing tasks of socialist construction, from the struggle against imperialism.

This time, too, the CPSU did not limit itself to appeals for unity but put forward concrete proposals.

In view of the fact that the next five-year plan for 1966-1970 was being drawn up in the Soviet Union, and the third five-year plan in China, the CPSU Central Committee pro-posed a discussion of the opportunities for developing trade and other relations between the two countries and provision for corresponding measures in their economic plans.

The letter expressed willingness to widen Sino-Soviet scientific and technological co-operation and cultural ex-changes.

Of great importance was the CPSU Central Committee's proposal for friendly consultations to specify the border line along individual sections and thereby to eliminate the causes of tension on the Sino-Soviet border.

The CPSU Central Committee also pointed out the need for creating conditions favourable to an improvement of relations between the two parties and for avoiding any steps likely to aggravate difficulties within the world communist movement. The CPSU was clearly aware of the fact that to overcome differences was a difficult matter requiring much work and time. It was important, however, to advance in this direction step by step, to display Leninist concern for strengthening the unity of the world communist movement on the principles of Marxism, to prevent any actions under-mining unity and to repulse attacks by factionists and dissenters.

CPC leaders withheld an answer to the letter of the CPSU Central Committee for three months (until February 29, 1964); all their actions, however, evidenced their unwilling-ness to accept any proposals for normalising Sino-Soviet relations.

13. ATTACKS BY CPC LEADERS AGAINST THE CPSU
ON THE ISSUE OF PREPARATIONS
FOR A MEETING OF FRATERNAL PARTIES

The increasingly intensive splitting activities of CPC leaders
within the world communist movement made it more and
more imperative to convene an international meeting of
Communist and Workers' parties.

The proposal for calling such a meeting had been advanced
by several fraternal parties (of Indonesia, New Zealand,
the DRV, Sweden, Great Britain) as far back as late 1961-
early 1962. The CPC leadership, in a letter to the CPSU of
April 7, 1962, supported this idea but frankly intimated its
desire to raise the "problem of Soviet-Albanian relations"
as the central subject of discussion. Chinese leaders patently
intended to exploit this problem to prevent the international
meeting of Communists from promoting the unity of the
socialist community and the world communist movement and
to use it for aggravating the existing differences.

The CPSU invariably stood for a collective discussion of
vital problems of the world communist movement, and it
gave its full support to the proposal for calling a meeting
of all fraternal parties. However, the CPSU Central Committee in its reply letter of May 31, 1962 objected to making the problem of Soviet-Albanian relations the main
subject of discussion at the meeting. The CPSU Central
Committee emphasised that, as shown by experience, preparations for such a meeting required, above all, a profound
and comprehensive analysis of the current international
situation and coordination in a spirit of collective decisions
of the basic tactics of the world communist movement at the
present stage. On the question of creating an atmosphere
favourable to the meeting, the CPSU Central Committee declared that this should evidently imply, above all, the ending
of direct and indirect attacks against the fraternal parties and
abidance by the principles of proletarian internationalism in
relations between parties in the interests of their cohesion
and unity.

In a new letter to the CPC Central Committee of February
21, 1963, the CPSU Central Committee again declared that
the CPSU and many other fraternal parties had invariably

been in favour of calling the meeting, because adequate reasons for this were in evidence. The meeting should discuss the common tasks of the struggle against imperialism and its aggressive plans, for the further development of the national liberation movement, for the cohesion and all-round development of the world socialist community and for increasing its influence throughout the world, for strengthening the unity of the communist movement.

The CPSU Central Committee proposed a bilateral meeting between representatives of the CPSU and the CPC which in addition to handling the problems of Sino-Soviet relations, could greatly contribute to preparations for the meeting of Marxist-Leninist parties. Many fraternal parties linked the question of calling their international conference with a favourable outcome of the Sino-Soviet meeting. This meeting held in Moscow between July 5 and 20, 1963, however, was made fruitless by the hard line of CPC leaders.

Early in 1964, the leaderships of the fraternal parties were informed of the CPC leaders' opposition to the proposals of the CPSU for adjusting differences in the international communist movement and for ending open controversy. Since the CPC leaders had flatly rejected the proposals of the CPSU Central Committee and stepped up their splitting activities and the anti-Soviet campaign, the CPSU Central Committee was compelled to resume publication of material explaining its position, which was maliciously distorted by Chinese leaders, and exposing the Maoists' true aims in the world communist movement.

Aware of the exceptional importance of this matter, the CPSU Central Committee decided to examine in detail the situation brought about by the splitting activities of the Maoist leadership of the CPC which were causing tremendous damage to the unity of the fraternal parties, the revolutionary and national liberation struggle of the peoples. The plenary meeting of the CPSU Central Committee held in February 1964 heard and discussed M. A. Suslov's report "On the Struggle of the CPSU for the Unity of the International Communist Movement" and adopted a resolution on this issue.[1]

---

[1] *Pravda*, April 3. 1964.

Having noted that the Communist Party of the Soviet Union had recently taken new steps towards overcoming or at least mitigating at first the differences of the CPC leadership with the CPSU and other fraternal parties, towards strengthening economic and political co-operation between the USSR and the PRC, the plenary meeting of the CPSU Central Committee acknowledged that the CPC leadership had not responded to this initiative, had failed to end the open controversy but, on the contrary, had stepped up its campaign against the general line of the world communist movement.

Under the camouflage of professions of loyalty to Marxism-Leninism and verbiage about the struggle against imaginary revisionism, the Maoists had launched an attack against the main theoretical and political principles guiding the world communist movement today.

The resolution of the plenary meeting of the CPSU Central Committee stated that the Chinese leaders, who had departed on all the main issues of strategy and tactics from the Leninist line of the world communist movement, had proclaimed their own line in which petty bourgeois adventurism and great-power chauvinism merged into one. CPC leaders adopted, in effect, the Trotskyite methods of struggle against the Marxist-Leninist parties, knocking together in various countries factional groups of their supporters. They sought to impose their special ideological platform on the entire socialist camp and the world communist movement, on international democratic organisations.

At the same time, the resolution of the plenary meeting emphasised that although the Chinese leaders had gone far in their splitting activities, the plenary meeting of the CPSU Central Committee, which placed the interests of unity of the world communist movement above anything else, expressed its willingness to continue to apply efforts towards a normalisation of relations between the CPSU and the CPC.

While obstructing in every way the efforts of the fraternal parties to put an end to open controversy, Chinese leaders at the same time stubbornly interfered with preparations for a new international forum of Communists of all countries.

The CPC Central Committee insisted, in effect, on deferring the convocation of an international meeting of fraternal parties to an indefinite future date. Referring to the need for a great deal of preparatory work it declared bluntly that this work would possibly take four to five years or more.

CPC leaders also attempted to exaggerate the procedural questions involved in calling an international meeting of Communist parties, challenging the decision of the Moscow meeting of 1957, which had invested the CPSU with the functions of calling conferences of Communist and Workers' parties upon consultations with them. Chinese leaders sought to push into oblivion Mao Tse-tung's statement at the 1957 meeting to the effect that it was imperative to recognise the CPSU as the sponsor of such conferences.

On July 30, 1964, the CPSU Central Committee circulated a letter to all the fraternal parties. Referring to the explicit desire of the overall majority of the fraternal parties, the letter said that it was time preparations were started for calling an international meeting of Communists and proposed that an editorial commission of representatives of 26 Communist parties meet in Moscow in December 1964. The CPSU Central Committee emphasised that the meeting should serve to strengthen the unity of the world communist movement. Its purpose was not to stigmatise or ex-communicate somebody from the communist movement and the socialist camp, apply insulting labels or make unfounded charges against anybody.

The CPSU Central Committee's proposals met with broad support within the world communist movement. The Peking leaders, however, ignored this fact. On August 30, 1964, the CPC Central Committee, with the same intransigence as in its letter of July 28, 1964, rejected all the proposals for calling an international meeting of Communists and flatly refused to take part in the work of the editorial commission.

The stand taken by the CPC leaders on the question of calling an international meeting of Communists graphically illustrated their line towards a disruption of relations between the Communist Party of China and the world communist movement. Chinese leaders had already displayed their contempt for these relations before. In 1963, CPC representatives withdrew from the editorial board of the *World Marxist Review*, a collective theoretical and informational organ of the Communist and Workers' parties. One of the motives for this step was, by all accounts, to deprive Chinese Communists of an objective source of information about the activities of the international communist movement.

14. CONTINUED FOMENTING BY CPC LEADERS OF ANTI-SOVIETISM IN CHINA

Having rejected the constructive programme of normalising Sino-Soviet relations proposed by the CPSU, the Maoists went ahead with their anti-Soviet activities. Since September 1963 mass-scale political training in China was based on the so-called replies to the open letter of the CPSU Central Committee of July 14, 1963. These replies, which contained malicious fabrications about our party and country, were studied even in secondary schools. A letter received by the Soviet Embassy from Chinese students read: "It was stated at political lessons before that the Soviet Union was our elder brother, that we must follow the Soviet example in every field, learn Soviet experience, etc., whereas now the directly opposite stand has been taken. Who was formerly called a friend and teacher is now cursed in the worst of words. What was formerly called assistance is now called exploitation."

The anti-Soviet campaign was raised to a still higher pitch in connection with the publication in the Chinese press in May 1964 of letters exchanged by the Central Committees of the CPSU and the CPC. Reports alleging that the Soviet Union intended to break off diplomatic relations with China and even to declare war on her were read to factory and office workers.

French tourists who visited China in the summer of 1964 reported: "The villages we visited have radio, and residents listen to broadcasts directed against the USSR from morning till night. Sometimes one could see newspapers which carried nothing except items critical of the Soviet Union. The Chinese in general publish a lot of anti-Soviet literature and supply it to all tourists. Anti-Soviet publications can even be found in WCs."

By deception, intimidation, direct repression, the Maoists managed to involve more and more government, party and public organisations in the anti-Soviet campaign.

In June 1964, the 9th National Congress of the Young Communist League was held in Peking in an atmosphere of attacks against the CPSU and the Soviet Union.

CPC leaders did not abandon their hope to organise anti-Soviet propaganda directly in Soviet territory, and to this end systematically undertook actions amounting to interference in the Soviet Union's internal affairs. Despite repeated verbal and official protests from the USSR Ministry of Foreign Affairs, the PRC Embassy in Moscow did not desist from its attempts to circulate in Soviet institutions, public organisations and among individuals an information bulletin published by the Embassy in Russian to disseminate views hostile to our party. Anti-Soviet publications continued to be smuggled into the USSR from China. Within a few months of 1964 more than 11,000 copies of such material were sent at private addresses from China to the Soviet Union, sometimes even to schoolchildren.

In an effort to spread their malicious fabrications about the Soviet Union as widely as possible, Peking propagandists grossly violated international agreements and regulations for the use of special-purpose wavebands intended for aviation, the merchant marine, radiotelephone and radiotelegraph communications. Peking conducted its anti-Soviet broadcasts even on wavebands set aside for distress signals, which seriously interfered with the operation of aircraft and merchant ships of the Soviet Union and other countries.

On February 22, 1964, the USSR Ministry of Foreign Affairs lodged with the PRC Embassy in Moscow a note of protest against these illegal actions of Chinese authorities. The PRC Government, however, ignored the note. The subversive activities of Chinese radiostations against the Soviet Union assumed an ever wider scope.

An important goal of the Maoists in stepping up anti-Soviet propaganda was to distract the Chinese people's attention from the difficulties at home, to intimidate them and obscure the true causes of China's difficulties caused by the fallacious home and foreign policies of Peking leaders. The economic situation of the PRC in 1964 continued to remain grave. The budgetary appropriations for economic development hardly reached their 1957 level.

In 1964, from 13 to 17 kilograms of cereals per person was handed out in towns, rice and flour accounting for only one-third or at best a half of the total ration, the remainder consisting of batata (sweet potato), millet, maize, sorghum. The overwhelming majority of manufactured goods were sold in very limited quantities to special coupons issued according to the size of earnings. For example, a family earning 60 yuan was entitled to three coupons, whereas two coupons were required for purchasing, say, 100 grams of tea.

The economic difficulties caused profound discontent with the policy of Peking leaders. This was confirmed, in particular, by letters from Chinese citizens which occasionally reached the Soviet Union through the screens of Chinese censors. One of them, which was sent to Radio Moscow in May 1964, said: "It is with a feeling of indignation and pain that we watch the consequences of Mao Tse-tung's zigzags. We see that the violation of objective economic laws has ruined China's economy, while the ideas of communism are being discredited in the eyes of the Chinese people."

Progressive members of Chinese society clearly realised that the anti-Soviet policy was an inalienable component of the general anti-popular line of the CPC leadership. In April 1964 Peking University became a scene of student unrest caused by circulation of slanderous anti-Soviet leaflets in Chinese. Students made this inscription on the title pages of these lampoons: "An honest Chinese can't believe this." Students' hostels were searched, all "suspects" were placed under surveillance and many of them arrested.

15. CHINESE PROVOCATIONS
ON THE SINO-SOVIET BORDER

In 1963-1964, violations by the PRC of the Sino-Soviet border became increasingly frequent. In 1963 alone, more than 4,000 such violations were reported, the number of Chinese civilians and servicemen involved in them being in excess of 100,000.

Chinese trespassers refused as a rule to obey the legitimate orders of Soviet border guards to leave Soviet territory. Far from taking steps to prevent incidents, Chinese authorities encouraged local residents to cross the border and settle in individual areas of Soviet territory, evading meetings with Soviet border authorities to adjust conflicts.

Violations of the border by Chinese citizens were committed with the connivance and even on direct instructions from Chinese authorities. The following fact is an example in point. One of the trespassers detained in 1963 was found to have instructions of the People's Committee of Heilunkiang Province which said in particular: "When our fishermen visit the disputed islands on the Amur and Ussuri rivers for fishing in their waters Soviet border guards often demand that our fishermen should leave them. We propose to continue fishing off the disputed islands and tell Soviet border guards that the islands belong to China, and it is they, not we, that violate the border.... Our fishermen should be on no account removed from these islands. We presume that in view of the friendly relations between our states, the Soviet authorities will not use force to expel our fishermen from the islands."[1]

Chinese servicemen and civilians began to show unfriendliness or open hostility to Soviet border guards. On May 3, 1964, for example, forty Chinese trespassers with two tractors crossed the border near the village of Bakhty and started ploughing up a field in Soviet territory. When told by Soviet border guards to leave Soviet territory, they responded with acts of hooliganism, shoving the guards, driving tractors into their way, etc.

Chinese authorities artificially aggravated the situation by concentrating in border areas army units and large contingents (of 100,000 men and more) of the so-called labour army, beginning the construction of large military state farms which were, in effect, army camps. Since early 1964 "regular units" of people's volunteers began to be formed in border areas to guard the border, as well as to maintain a "state of emergency" in populated localities along it.

Local residents in border areas were organised into groups headed by public security officers. A strip of territory up to 200 kilometres wide abutting on the border was proclaimed

---

[1] *Pravda*, September 22, 1963.

a "no entry zone". All persons suspected of friendliness towards the Soviet Union or having relatives in the Soviet Union were evicted from this zone to the Chinese hinterland.

Unbridled anti-Soviet agitation was carried out among the population of border areas and fabrications were spread about Soviet preparations for a war against China, about illegal Soviet seizure of Chinese territory, and the idea that the border with the Soviet Union was a frontline of China's defence was peddled insistently.

The Soviet Government invariably held the opinion that no territorial disputes existed between the Soviet Union and China, that the Sino-Soviet border had a firm foundation in treaties and that any revision of it was absolutely intolerable. At the same time, the Soviet Government repeatedly proposed consultations on the question of specifying the Sino-Soviet borderline in individual sections to rule out any cause for misunderstanding. The first proposal had been made as far back as 1960. The Chinese side, however, stubbornly evaded consideration of this proposal.

In November 1963, the Chinese leaders finally accepted the Soviet proposal for holding a meeting on the border issue. The wording of the Chinese reply, however, clearly revealed a desire to evade the problems the Soviet Union sought to discuss at the forthcoming meeting and to use it not for adjustment but for exacerbation of border conflicts.

A note of the PRC Ministry of Foreign Affairs of November 19, 1963 stated that all along the length of the Sino-Soviet border there were many issues that needed discussion. The Chinese side declined the proposal for publication in the press of a joint announcement on the forthcoming meeting, referring to difficulties in reaching agreement on the wording.

Also worthy of note was the fact that on the eve of the meeting Peking leaders had made fierce slanderous attacks against the Soviet Premier's message to the world's heads of government and state of December 31, 1963, on a peaceful settlement of territorial and border disputes, which met with a broad international response and support. On April 26, 1964, *Jenmin jihpao* wrote that "the proposal for renunciation of the use of force in settling territorial disputes and border issues is another fraud" called upon to serve the interests of the imperialists.

The Sino-Soviet meeting began in Peking on February 25, 1964. The Soviet delegation was led by a plenipotentiary representative in the rank of Deputy Minister, P. I. Zyryanov; the Chinese delegation, by the Deputy Minister of Foreign Affairs, Tseng Yung-chüan.

The Soviet delegation tabled constructive proposals for specifying within the shortest possible time the Sino-Soviet borderline in individual disputed sections. The solution of this problem would have greatly contributed to the maintenance of friendly relations between the two nations.

The Chinese leaders, however, persisted in their territorial claims. In the article "On the Statement of the Communist Party, USA" published in *Jenmin jihpao* on March 8, 1963 the treaties signed in their time between China and Russia and defining the existing Sino-Soviet borderline were described as "unequal". On July 10, 1964, Mao Tse-tung in a talk with a Japanese delegation declared: "Some 100 years ago the area east of Lake Baikal became Russian territory, and since then Vladivostok, Khabarovsk, Kamchatka and other areas have been part of Soviet territory. We have not yet submitted our claims on this account." Chinese official representatives threatened to think of other ways to solve the territorial dispute and declared their intention to restore their historical rights.

On August 22, 1964, the Sino-Soviet consultations on border questions were broken off. It was agreed in principle to resume them in Moscow on October 15, 1964. Despite repeated reminders from the Soviet side, however, the PRC Government evaded a resumption of consultations for years.

16. SINO-SOVIET ECONOMIC, SCIENTIFIC, TECHNICAL AND CULTURAL CO-OPERATION IN 1962-1964

Toward the end of 1962, Sino-Soviet business relations had reached an all-time low in every field. The volume of economic co-operation between the two countries in 1962 was roughly equivalent to 5 per cent of the 1959 volume. Supplies to China of Soviet equipment, materials, technical facilities and documents reduced to 41-42 million rubles as against 428 million rubles in 1960, i.e., more than 90 per cent. Supplies of complete plant and equipment amounted to 7.8-8 million rubles as compared with 336.5 million rubles in 1959, a reduction to less than 97.5 per cent.

Early in 1964, the Soviet Union proposed to the PRC talks to specify the volume and range of equipment China wanted to receive from the Soviet Union over and above the amount provided for in the letter of May 13, 1962. The Chinese side refused to negotiate the matter, referring to the difficulties in compiling the PRC economic development plan. This, however, did not prevent China from widening economic relations with the capitalist countries, where she bought equipment, including that for oil refineries and chemical plants for which she had deferred equipment imports from the USSR by two years. In 1963, the PRC signed contracts for complete plant and equipment deliveries to chemical industry enterprises with firms of Britain, Denmark, Italy, the Netherlands and France.

In contrast to this, the Soviet Union firmly abided by its commitments. In 1964, it continued supplies to China of equipment and materials for 31 industrial projects under existing agreements.

While winding down deliberately economic relations with the Soviet Union, the CPC leadership continued a campaign of slander of our country, playing down the importance of Soviet aid in every way. In a letter to the CPSU Central Committee of February 29, 1964, it attempted to reduce Sino-Soviet economic co-operation exclusively to trade which was allegedly carried on terms disadvantageous for the PRC.

In an effort to discredit Sino-Soviet economic co-operation, the Maoists did not stop at direct frauds. In April 1964, for example, they demonstrated to representatives of the diplomatic corps at the Wuhan plant a deliberately disassembled Soviet machine tool, assuring the audience that it had been supplied unfit for operation and could not be used for work. When a representative of Soviet external economic organisations in Peking expressed willingness to go to the plant to examine the case on the spot Chinese authorities, aware of the danger of being exposed as liers, did not issue a permit for this trip. In another case, Peking masters of anti-Soviet propaganda showed foreigners not far from Wuhan a score of broken down Soviet locomotives, explaining that they had allegedly been sold by the Soviet Union without spare parts, with defects and at a very high price. In May 1964, the PRC Minister of Foreign Affairs in an interview with Norwegian, Dutch and West German correspondents of bourgeois newspapers slanderously declared that the Soviet Union had been plundering China, selling her equipment and machines at twice the world market price.

The curtailment of scientific and technical exchanges with the Soviet Union caused great damage to the development of science and technology in the People's Republic of China. Peking leaders, however, were not concerned about it. They deliberately sacrificed the interests of scientific and technical progress in China to their anti-Soviet objectives.

The turnover of Sino-Soviet trade in 1963 reduced 20 per cent (to 540 million rubles) from 1962 to the level roughly equivalent to that of 1950. The Soviet Union's share in Chinese foreign trade fell to 23 per cent as against 29 per cent in 1962 and 50 per cent in 1959.

In spring 1964 talks were held in Peking on the turnover of Sino-Soviet trade for the current year. They were held in an atmosphere of difficulties artificially created by the Chinese side. PRC representatives refused to sell the Soviet Union commodities it had been interested in and which for years had been traditional items of Chinese export to the USSR. For example, tin exports in 1964 reduced to 1,000 tons as against 22,000 tons in 1957, while deliveries of zinc, beryllium and spodumene concentrates were stopped altogether. At the same time, the Chinese side persistently sought to impose on the Soviet delegation goods the Soviet Union was not interested in and which the PRC was unable to market in other countries.

As noted above, since 1961, the Soviet Union, in view of the difficult economic situation of the PRC, abstained from purchases of foodstuffs from her. At the trade talks in 1964, however, the Chinese representatives were especially persistent in seeking a Soviet consent to imports of foodstuffs from China. They did not stop at crude pressure and blackmail, alleging that a Soviet refusal would be tantamount to assuming the responsibility for cutting down Sino-Soviet trade and threatened to withdraw from the negotiations. The provocative character of these actions soon came into the open. Peking propaganda started spreading fabrications at home and abroad to the effect that the PRC was exporting to the Soviet Union "hundreds of thousands of tons of meat products", although in reality in 1964 China supplied to the Soviet Union a little more than 40,000 tons of meat products, including tinned meat.

At the same time, the Chinese side reduced in 1964 purchases in the Soviet Union of a number of items of traditional Soviet export to China. Needless to say, all this led to a further reduction of the turnover of Sino-Soviet trade.

Cultural co-operation between the Soviet Union and the PRC developed in similar fashion. In 1962, its volume was roughly 30 per cent below that of 1961. The Chinese side sought to play down in every way the political import of Soviet undertakings. For example, at the talks in 1962 it declined the Soviet proposal for holding in China an exhibition of political posters dedicated to V. I. Lenin and stubbornly insisted on replacing it with an exhibition of toys. The Soviet Union increased its import of Chinese printed matter approximately 150 per cent as compared with the 1961 level. Chinese organisations, however, curtailed their orders of Soviet publications, particularly of those on socio-political subjects, fiction, and literature for children. Purchases in the Soviet Union of works by the founders of Marxism-Leninism reduced almost 50 per cent as compared with 1961 and of socio-economic and socio-political publications, by one third. All in all, Soviet book, gramophone record and postage stamp exports to China fell 20 per cent from 1961.

On Peking's initiative contacts between public organisations were also wound down. CPC leaders began to enlist Chinese cultural workers on a wide scale to implement their nationalistic, anti-Soviet policies. They demanded that writers and artists, actors and musicians should step up the struggle against "Soviet revisionism". Implementation of such directives led to a further reduction of cultural exchanges between the PRC and the Soviet Union.

Since the autumn of 1963 Chinese undergraduates and research students in the Soviet Union began to organise, on instructions from Peking, political discussions at lectures on social sciences and, when given a rebuff, they, upon new instructions, refused to attend lectures and pass examinations in Marxism-Leninism and other social sciences.

On May 13, 1964, the PRC Embassy in Moscow made an official statement to the USSR Ministry of Foreign Affairs slandering the curricula of Soviet institutions of higher learning and Soviet instructors and raising the question of optional attendance of lectures and examination in socio-political subjects for Chinese students. Thereby the Chinese side grossly violated the Sino-Soviet agreement of August 9, 1952, which envisaged that all the rules for undergraduate and research students of corresponding educational institutions of the USSR should apply to Chinese students.

The purpose of this action was to prevent Chinese students from acquaintance with Marxist-Leninist theory, to place them on a niggardly diet of "Mao Tse-tung's ideas" and thereby to poison the minds of this section of youth with the venom of nationalism and anti-Sovietism.

Chinese organisations refused to attend scientific conferences, symposiums, meetings held in the Soviet Union. In 1963, the USSR Academy of Sciences forwarded to Chinese scientists 23 invitations; however, the latter took part only in eight conferences and meetings and refused other invitations under the pretext of being "busy with current work". At the same time, the Chinese side stubbornly avoided inviting Soviet scientists to similar conferences held in the PRC.

Already at that time, impudent attempts were made to use cultural exchanges to undermine the moral and political unity of the Soviet people, to impose on cultural and art workers of our country, on members of Soviet delegations visiting China anti-Marxist views, to spread malicious fabrications about the CPSU, its internal and foreign policies. For example, in 1962, during the visit to Wuhan by a delegation of the Ukrainian branch of the Soviet-Chinese Friendship Society leading executives of the Sino-Soviet Friendship Society attempted to make members of the delegation denounce Soviet foreign policy, foisted on them anti-Soviet literature published in Russian in the PRC. Similar provocations were carried out against the Soviet writers V. N. Sobko and S. P. Zalygin who visited China in 1962, the composers Dankevich and Ilyin, the Lezghinka Dance Company, the delegation of Soviet architects, to mention but a few. Needless to say the Maoist provocateurs received a condign rebuff from Soviet representatives. Such actions, however, could not but have an extremely adverse effect on the development of Sino-Soviet cultural exchanges.

Guest tours of the Soviet Union by Chinese performers were often used by the Maoists for anti-Soviet propaganda and all sorts of provocation. This can be illustrated by the example of the Chinese People's Army Company which visited the Soviet Union in 1963. Numerous leaders of the company who accompanied it on its tour of the USSR, Chinese Embassy officials and correspondents of the Hsinhua News Agency, tried to arrange anti-Soviet meetings during intermissions, distributed slanderous publications denigrating our party and country in theatres, hotels, wherever they went.

At the same time, in that period Chinese authorities still did not want to end completely Sino-Soviet cultural exchanges, intending to use them for ideological subversion of our party. Pursuing their selfish goals they even agreed to widen the programme of cultural co-operation with the Soviet Union in 1964. The later activities of the Chinese side fully exposed the ulterior motives of the Maoists.

During the stay of Soviet delegations in China in 1964, they were being intensively brainwashed in a spirit of opposition to the policy of the CPSU and the Soviet Government and persuaded to approve in one form or another of the ideological concepts of Mao Tse-tung and his followers. This was the case, for example, with the teams of Soviet fencers and volleyball players who visited China in May 1964. Soviet athletes were given "warm receptions" at which bombastic speeches were made about friendship between the Chinese and Soviet peoples. They were asked to convey to Soviet people kind regards and friendly feelings from the Chinese, persuaded to tell about the "triumph of Mao Tse-tung's ideas" to their relatives and friends, were given numerous gifts to win their favour and were followed everywhere by photographers taking pictures of friendly handshakes, joint outings and "friendly talks" between Soviet and Chinese athletes.

At the same time, Chinese authorities took steps to prevent genuine contacts between Soviet representatives and Chinese people. The following case may be adduced as an example in point. In 1964, the Soviet Army Song and Dance Ensemble was on a visit to China. Its members were actually under police surveillance. Walkie-talkies were used by Chinese agents to transmit instructions like these: "Seven Russians are talking in a passage near room No. 5. Listen to what they are talking about"; "A group of dancers have finished a rehearsal ahead of schedule and are leaving. Follow them!"; "Attention, first post, Russians are going out. Remove spectators from the entrance."

During its stay in the PRC the company was deprived of the possibility to mingle with audience even in the foyers of concert halls. Chinese representatives who followed the company used physical force without ceremony to push Soviet performers behind the scenes when they wanted to go to the foyer to meet the public.

The atmosphere of hostility to anything Soviet being created by the Maoists caused indignation and protests of Soviet people visiting the PRC. Characteristically, between January and July 1964 not a single application for a visit to China was received by the Soviet travel agency Intourist from Soviet citizens. As a result of the unfriendly attitude of official Chinese authorities to the Soviet Union and Soviet citizens visiting the PRC, the Soviet tourist agency was compelled to declare to the Chinese Foreign Tourist Company in August 1964 that it was unable to continue tourist exchanges with China.

17. INTENSIFICATION BY PEKING LEADERS OF ANTI-SOVIET ACTIVITIES ON THE INTERNATIONAL SCENE

A major component of the anti-Soviet line of CPC leaders was the struggle against our party and country on the international scene.

Dissentient groups set up by Peking in different countries actively engaged in anti-Soviet propaganda abroad. When forming these groups, the Maoists did not stop at slander, bribery, blackmail in relation to unstable elements. They willingly enlisted in the ranks of fighters against "modern revisionism" any political adventurers if the latter opposed the CPSU and other Marxist-Leninist parties. Therefore, pro-Chinese groups have come to include Trotskyites, anarchists, political adventurers, immoral persons, agents of police and imperialist intelligence services. In their search for allies in the struggle against the Soviet Union the Maoists got in touch even with whiteguard émigrés.

For example, Chinese representatives set up close contacts with Ukrainian nationalists in Canada and bought from them a large consignment of anti-Soviet literature in 1963-1964. For their part, the whiteguard scum, who sensed in the Maoists their kin in spirit and proneness to anti-Soviet provocation, extended their dirty hand to them. For example, the émigré rug *Vilne Slovo* (Free Voice) published in Canada appealed in the summer of 1964 for siding actively with Maoist China against communist Moscow and proposed to the Ukrainian nationalists an alliance with the Maoists for a joint struggle against the common enemy.

The same coincidence of ideological positions was revealed between the Maoists and the Trotskyites of the 4th International, who even sent the CPC Central Committee an open letter bluntly declaring that since the day of its foundation the 4th International had been waging a struggle against the ideas opposed by Peking today and supported the latter's stand. The international secretariat of the 4th International welcomed the discussion started by the Maoists in the world communist movement and called on the Chinese leaders to develop it.

The foreign policy line of the PRC hostile to the Soviet Union became clearly manifest in the splitting activities of the Maoists in the developing countries, in particular, in the efforts undertaken by Peking in 1964 to prevent the Soviet Union's participation in the Second Afro-Asian Summit Conference.

The Maoist leadership of the CPC had long been undermining relations between the Soviet Union and the countries of Asia, Africa and Latin America. At a session of the executive committee of the Afro-Asian Solidarity Organisation in December 1961 the Chinese representative declared that "only the anti-imperialist popular organisations of Asia,

Africa and Latin America rather than organisations of other regions" can initiate and prepare a solidarity conference. He insisted that the Soviet Union should not send its delegates to it.

At the preparatory meeting for the Afro-Asian conference of journalists in Jakarta in 1962 the Chinese delegation opposed full participation in the conference of representatives of the Soviet Central Asian republics. The Maoists took a similar stand at other international conferences.

At the Afro-Asian Solidarity Conference in Moshi in 1963, the leader of the Chinese delegation frankly told Soviet representatives: "We regret your coming here at all. You are not needed here. This is an affront to the Afro-Asian solidarity movement. . . . You may do whatever you like, but we will oppose you." The Chinese delegates sought to persuade Afro-Asian representatives that since Russians, Czechs, Poles were white, they should not be trusted, they would always find a common language with the American Whites, while the peoples of Asia and Africa had specific interests and must set up their separate associations.

To attract to their side representatives of the developing countries in international democratic organisations, CPC leaders widely resorted to unscrupulous means. One of the participants in the 6th session of the Afro-Asian Solidarity Council held in Algeria in March 1964 reported that the Chinese delegation had promised him a large sum of money for casting a vote in its favour. When he asked on which issue he was to support the Chinese viewpoint he was told that he need not know that but should simply raise his hand.

In April 1964 in Jakarta representatives of 22 Afro-Asian states discussed the question of preparations for the Second Afro-Asian Summit Conference. The delegates of India and Ceylon proposed that the Soviet Union, which invariably gave tremendous aid to Afro-Asian peoples, should attend the conference by all means. This initiative, however, was categorically opposed by the Chinese delegation, which threatened to leave Jakarta, if India and Ceylon did not withdraw their proposal.

Seeking to separate the Soviet Union from the Asian and African states, Chinese leaders went to the length of absurd allegations to the effect that it is not an Asian country. In

a statement of May 5, 1964, the Soviet Government remind-
ed the Peking leaders that the Soviet Union accounted for
a good 40 per cent of Asian territory, its Asian part was
almost twice the area of all of China and as large as to
accommodate China, India, Indonesia, Pakistan, Burma and
Japan put together.

The question, however, was not one of Chinese leaders'
ignorance of geography. Denial of obvious facts was needed
by the Maoists to cause alienation between the Soviet Union
and the Afro-Asian countries. In an effort to disunite the
states and peoples upholding the cause of peace and national
independence, the nationalists in the CPC more and more
often emphasised the racial distinctions as the decisive factor
in defining common political interests and the possibility of
joint actions on the international scene. Speculating on their
thesis about racial affinity the Maoists peddled the idea that
people with a different colour of the skin could not understand each other and act hand in hand, even if they had
common objectives and a common enemy. What is more,
they insidiously implanted suspicions in relation to many
peoples of the socialist countries, simply because they were
white.

To prevent the Soviet Union from participating in the
Second Afro-Asian Solidarity Conference special Chinese
emissaries toured Afro-Asian countries, seeking to convert
their leaders to anti-Sovietism. When the CPC leadership
saw that the majority of these countries did not support its
views, it went as far as to torpedo the conference, thereby
demonstrating its full contempt for the interests of Afro-
Asian nations and its readiness to take any action to impose
its will upon them.

Peking leaders attempted to undermine the Soviet Union's
economic ties with the countries of Asia, Africa and Latin
America, to distort and denigrate the motives of Soviet assistance to them, declaring that it was "detrimental to their
economic and political interests".[1]

Peking's attempts to exacerbate relations between the
Soviet Union and the developing countries proved futile.
The prestige of the Soviet state, our party among the peo-

---

[1] *Jenmin jihpao,* October 22, 1963.

ples of Asia, Africa and Latin America steadily grew, because it was invariably supported by practical deeds.

At the same time, Chinese leaders by their practical actions in relation to the countries of the Third World exposed themselves as unprincipled politicians ready to make up with the most extreme reactionaries to attain their great-power chauvinistic objectives. While proclaiming its slogans of struggle for the liberation of oppressed nations, Peking carried on lively trade exchanges with the South African Republic, the most abominable specimen of a colonialist and racialist regime. In the period from 1961 to 1963, trade between the PRC and the SAR increased tenfold.

18. DENUNCIATION
OF THE DIVISIVE LINE OF CPC LEADERS
BY THE COMMUNIST AND WORKERS' PARTIES

The changeover of the CPC leadership from the policy of Sino-Soviet friendship to an open struggle against the CPSU and the Soviet Union was accompanied by a radical reorientation of the entire foreign policy of the People's Republic of China. In the process of this revision the gulf between the PRC and the revolutionary forces steadily deepened, and her rapprochement with the pro-imperialist forces on the international scene became increasingly closer. The divisive line of Peking leaders caused growing indignation in the countries of the socialist community, in the international communist movement and in the ranks of fighters for national liberation, within the progressive circles of the world public.

This line, hostile to the cause of peace and socialism, was denounced without reservations in the resolutions and documents of the Communist parties of the socialist countries. The Central Committee of the Communist Party of Czechoslovakia, in a statement of July 21, 1963, underscored that the actions of the CPC leadership against the world socialist system could not be described otherwise than splitting and adventurist.

On June 12, 1964, the Central Committee of the Mongolian People's Revolutionary Party sent the CPC Central Committee a letter emphasising that the splitting, subversive activities of Chinese leaders caused tremendous damage to the unity of the socialist community and the world communist movement, diverted the attention and forces of Communists and the working class from the struggle against imperialism, created new obstacles to achieving the victory of socialist and national liberation revolutions in various countries.

The Central Committee of the Socialist Unity Party of Germany, in a statement of April 23, 1964, noted that the brainwashing of China's population in a malicious, anti-Soviet spirit grossly contradicted the principles of proletarian internationalism.

The March 21, 1964 plenary meeting of the Central Committee of the Bulgarian Communist party pointed out that Mao Tse-tung and his group had extended ideological differences to the inter-state relations with the socialist countries, that co-operation between the PRC and other member-states of the socialist community had sharply reduced through the fault of the Chinese. The disastrous divisive line of Chinese leaders in relation to the socialist countries, as well as their attempts to interfere in the internal affairs of member-states of CMEA, was condemned indignantly in the resolution of the Central Committee of the Hungarian Socialist Workers' Party published on April 3, 1964.

The policy of the CPC leadership was exposed to severe, uncompromising criticism at the 4th Congress of the Polish United Workers' Party held in June 1964. It was noted in the report of the PUWP Central Committee that the behaviour of the CPC evidenced that it had started a dispute with other parties and advanced its separate platform not in search of the truth or in an effort to achieve an agreed position of all parties but in order to divide them.

The Communist parties of other countries denounced with equal determination the departure of CPC leaders from the principles of Marxism-Leninism and proletarian internationalism.

"The Chinese leaders' attitude towards the policy pursued by our party and other fraternal parties," said the statement of the Political Bureau of the French Communist Party, "shows, in effect, that they ignore the contribution of the working class, the Communist parties of the capitalist countries to the common cause of the world revolutionary movement and have full contempt for it."[1]

The General Secretary of the Central Committee of the Communist party of Chile Luis Corvalan wrote: "All the activities of CPC leaders in circulating their false conceptions against the will of the Central Committee of the Communist parties and governments of the socialist countries are an open defiance of the principles of mutual respect and comradeship which determine relations between parties and between socialist states."[2]

CPC leaders did not pay heed to the voice of those who, guided by the interests of peace and socialism, came out against their divisive, subversive line. Increasingly subjugating the Party and country to their rule, the Maoists continued to tread their old path.

[1] *Pravda,* July 23, 1963.
[2] *Pravda,* September 6, 1963.

CHAPTER VII

SINO-SOVIET RELATIONS
ON THE EVE
OF THE "CULTURAL REVOLUTION"

The relatively brief period from October 1964 to August 1966 holds a special place in the history of Sino-Soviet relations in the 60s.

At that time, the situation on China's home scene was characterised by a sharp exacerbation of contradictions which had been developing in hidden form for a long time, and in the autumn of 1966 came to a head in the so-called cultural revolution. The basis for the political crisis which affected all the spheres of life of Chinese society was the growing contradiction between the anti-socialist line of the foreign and home policies pursued by the ruling clique in the CPC and the interests of China's socialist development. In the period under review, the Maoists and the forces they leaned upon were still unable to give an open battle to their opponents. What is more, they had to reckon with the opposition and at times to retreat until an opportune moment for a decisive counterattack. The strife between different factions within the Chinese leadership left an imprint on the situation in China and resulted in strange zigzags in her internal and foreign policies.

On the whole, however, the group of nationalists in the CPC began to exert a growing influence on Sino-Soviet relations. In a situation of flagrant violation of socialist democracy, complete break with the Leninist principles of party life, Chinese Communists were unable to resist effectively the crude pressure of the Maoist leadership which resorted to physical suppression of dissidents. The Maoists managed to pursue and even to fortify their line towards an open political struggle against the Soviet Union, which became an important condition for preparing the "cultural revolution". Anti-Sovietism became a major component of its political programme.

As for the Soviet Union, the period under review witnessed the continued efforts of our party to return the PRC to the path of friendship and co-operation with all socialist countries, to the positions of proletarian internationalism.

In October and November 1964 discussions were held at the CPSU Central Committee with party and government delegations of Bulgaria, Hungary, the German Democratic Republic, the Democratic Republic of Vietnam, the Korean People's Democratic Republic, Cuba, Mongolia, Poland, Rumania, Czechoslovakia, Yugoslavia. During the discussions, the CPSU Central Committee reaffirmed the immutability of the general line laid down by the congresses of the CPSU and proclaimed in its programme, and expressed its views concerning the further promotion of the unity and cohesion of the socialist community.

These discussions helped specify the positions of the fraternal parties on questions of mutual interest and stimulated their joint efforts towards solving vital and urgent problems and strengthening unity.

By pursuing a principled and flexible policy the CPSU sought to secure, on the one hand, unity of action in practice, a coordinated policy of the socialist countries on issues involving the vital interests of world communism; on the other hand, to secure a wide field for initiative, independence of each socialist country, consideration of its specific interests.

The CPSU Central Committee persistently strove to secure a situation where, even with specific positions held by certain parties on ideological issues, all the parties would come out in a united front against imperialism, because the fastest way to strengthen the unity of the international communist and working class movement is to take practical joint actions against the common enemy.

1. SINO-SOVIET TALKS IN NOVEMBER 1964

After the October 1964 plenary meeting, the CPSU Central Committee took a series of new important steps intended to create a situation favourable to normalising relations between the CPSU and the CPC, between the Soviet Union and the People's Republic of China. The CPSU Central Committee proceeded from the principle that despite the ideological differences it was necessary to work for the unity of practical actions, primarily in the struggle against imperialism, to develop inter-state relations. The CPSU, which was supported by other Marxist-Leninist parties, unilaterally ended criticism in the press of the views and actions of Chinese leaders, which opened up prospects for resuming direct contacts between the Central Committees of the CPSU and the CPC.

This, however, did not satisfy CPC leaders. They attempted to bring pressure to bear on the CPSU to force it to abandon its positions of principle, the general line of the world communist movement mapped out collectively by the fraternal parties at the Moscow meetings of 1957 and 1960. Significantly, on the day when the CPC Central Committee was informed of the decisions of the October plenary meeting of the CPSU Central Committee, the first atom bomb was exploded in China. Thereby Peking seemed to make clear its intention to base its relations with the Soviet Union on "positions of strength".

The atom bomb test in China was used for the continued fanning of nationalistic passions among her population. Whereas shortly before the test Peking propaganda had stinted no effort to depict nuclear weapons as a "paper tiger", now it began boasting about China's sharply increased power and influence on world developments.

The Chinese press openly called on the CPC to step up its struggle for winning the commanding positions in the world communist movement. On October 17, 1964, *Jenmin jihpao* wrote that the moment had come for the CPC to raise the banner of revolution to an unprecedented height.

For tactical considerations, in the early days after the October plenary meeting of the CPSU Central Committee,

CPC leaders tuned down their most vehement anti-Soviet statements. For some very brief time, Chinese propaganda in its attacks on our party and country did not call the CPSU and the USSR by name but used such terms as "modern revisionists", "a certain great power", etc. However, it was clear not only to the Chinese population drilled by the Maoists but also to foreigners what Peking leaders meant by these provocative labels. Practically, Chinese leaders not for a moment stopped their anti-Soviet activities. Chinese foreign trade organisations continued wholesale marketing of anti-Soviet publications printed in China in various languages to foreign capitalist firms at the Kwang-chow export goods fair.

Publication of anti-Soviet material was not interrupted in the Chinese press practically for a single day.

Chinese diplomatic missions abroad went on with their anti-Soviet activity. PRC missions in Prague, Luxembourg, Geneva, Bamako continued to distribute literature hostile to our country. Anti-Soviet publications were sent from Peking to the FRG, France, and other countries.

Newspapers and magazines published by pro-Peking groups abroad were used for anti-Soviet propaganda as before. For example, the *Resurrection* magazine published in Greece with the aid of Chinese money (its first issue came off the press early in November 1964) printed articles containing malicious anti-Soviet fabrications. An active anti-Soviet campaign was carried on by the pro-Peking newspaper *Ludu* published in Burma. Chinese radio continued anti-Soviet broadcasts in several foreign languages, beamed, in particular, to African countries.

PRC representatives at meetings of the executive bodies of the World Federation of Trade Unions and the Women's International Democratic Federation, hardly caring to mask their slanderous anti-Soviet attacks, spoke of the "foreign policy line of a certain state, whose leadership had gone bankrupt with it", the "capitulatory line of a certain great power", and that the conclusion of the Moscow treaty banning nuclear tests in the three media was "a great fraud" by which the nuclear powers wanted to "perpetuate their monopoly and bind hand and foot all countries and peoples struggling for peace", etc.

17*

Despite the unscrupulous manoeuvres of Peking, the CPSU Central Committee and the Soviet Government invited a PRC party and government delegation to attend the celebration of the 47th anniversary of the Great October Socialist Revolution so as to use contacts at top level for exploring ways to normalise Sino-Soviet relations.

On November 5, the Chinese delegation led by Chou Enlai, arrived in Moscow. On the same day, Chinese newspapers printed photographs of an atom bomb explosion in the PRC as if to give another reminder of the CPC leadership's intention to proceed from the "positions of strength" in its relations with the Soviet Union.

The plans the Chinese delegation brought to the USSR could also be judged by the character of functions held in China on the occasion of the 47th anniversary of the October Revolution. On November 6, at a solemn meeting in Peking dedicated to this date, slightly camouflaged attacks were made against the home and foreign policies of the CPSU. An editorial in *Jenmin jihpao* of November 7 attempted to oppose the Soviet people to the leadership of the CPSU and the Soviet State, the revolutionary traditions of the Soviet working people to their constructive activities today.

The behaviour of the Chinese delegation in Moscow fully exposed its plan: by using direct and crude pressure to dislodge the CPSU from its positions of principle, by using petty grievances and blackmail to store up "facts" illustrating the "unfriendly" attitude of the CPSU to the CPC, to carry out under the slogans of "bankruptcy of modern revisionism" and "victory of Mao Tse-tung's ideas" the brainwashing of the leaders of other fraternal parties and countries who had arrived in Moscow, to sow new seeds of discord in the socialist community and the world communist movement.

The Chinese side brazenly demanded that the CPSU revise its policy based on the resolutions of the 20th, 21st, and 22nd congresses, the CPSU Programme, the documents of the Moscow meetings of 1957 and 1960, adopt Mao Tsetung's ideas, accept the Chinese "25-point" programme as its theoretical basis, etc. While insisting on a revision of the CPSU policy as an indispensable prerequisite for normalising Sino-Soviet relations, the CPC leaders not only wanted to subordinate the Communist Party of the Soviet Union to their influence but also to clear the way towards establishing their supremacy in the socialist community and the world communist movement.

Naturally, all these attempts suffered a complete fiasco, because the political line of the 20th, 21st and 22nd congresses and the Programme of the CPSU express the will of all party members, all Soviet people. As for Sino-Soviet relations, the position of the CPSU has always been clear on this issue: for considerations of principle, the CPSU and the CPC should proceed in their relations from what unites them, not from what separates them; the problem consists essentially in the necessity to begin normalising the situation despite differences. The CPSU has repeatedly emphasised that conditions should be provided for a calm and businesslike discussion of disputed issues of principle, which takes time and effort.

CPC leaders continued to decline the proposal for ending open controversy. What is more, they declared that if the CPSU followed its programme, Peking would not stop its political struggle against the CPSU. The CPSU proposal for carrying on the dispute within the framework of a comradely discussion was also categorically rejected.

The CPC delegation also evaded consideration of concrete measures to promote the cohesion of the anti-imperialist front. Chinese representatives replied with vague declarations to the proposal for consultations on the question of ways and means of waging the struggle against imperialism in the prevailing international situation, and in view of the character of modern warfare, and other factors. At the same time, one could clearly see the striving of the CPC leadership to interfere with the policy of peaceful coexistence, to aggravate the international situation, particularly the relations between the Soviet Union and the United States.

The Chinese side showed no desire to discuss the problem of Sino-Soviet inter-state relations and advanced no positive proposals for normalising them.

The Soviet side came forward with a new initiative, proposing a new high-level meeting of CPSU and CPC representatives as soon as the Chinese leadership was ready for that to exchange views on a number of problems, to restore confidence between our parties and countries and to strengthen their unity. The Soviet side expressed its consent to hold this meeting either in Moscow or in Peking, openly or behind closed doors. The CPC leaders, however, failed to accept this proposal also.

Before its departure from Moscow, the Chinese delegation again demonstrated its unwillingness to normalise relations with the Soviet Union and its intention to continue attacks against the CPSU and other fraternal parties. On the insistence of the Chinese delegation a paragraph saying that the sides had agreed to continue contacts between the CPSU and the CPC in the interests of strengthening the unity of the international communist movement on the principles of Marxism-Leninism and proletarian internationalism was deleted from the press release on the meetings of CPSU and Soviet government leaders with the PRC party and government delegation.

On November 14, 1964, the delegation, which had returned to Peking, was given a deliberately pompous welcome in which all Chinese party and government leaders led by Mao Tse-tung took part. This welcome was to demonstrate the full solidarity of the Chinese leadership and Mao Tse-tung personally with the actions of the delegation which had obstructed a constructive discussion and stemmed the process of normalising relations begun on the initiative of our party.

Upon the delegation's return from Moscow even the slightest symptoms of a relative and unstable truce practically disappeared. Chinese leaders gave up their hypocritical stance of peace makers and soon fully reverted to their positions of open hostility towards the CPSU and the Soviet Union.

On November 21, 1964, the journal *Hungchi* published an editorial comparable in its embittered anti-Sovietism and hostility to the CPSU to the former, most vehement Chinese attacks on the CPSU and the Soviet Union. The article advanced in ultimatum form the following demand: the CPSU should renounce its general line without reservations and adopt the ideological platform and political line of Mao Tse-tung and his group. This alone, in the opinion of its authors, would make a normalisation of Sino-Soviet relations possible. *Hungchi* cracked down on the basic programme principles of the CPSU, on the foreign and home policies of our state.

The article contained numerous attacks against the CPSU and its leaders, against the Soviet people as a whole. CPC leaders made monstrous statements about the "degeneration of Soviet society", the "collapse of the Soviet economy", "degradation of Soviet culture", the "sway of capitalistic forces in the USSR"; they accused the Soviet state of "complicity with American imperialism", etc. This statement in *Hungchi* was followed by a series of new open attacks on the CPSU. On November 26, 1964, *Jenmin jihpao* published a message of greetings from the CPC Central Committee to the 9th Congress of the Communist Party of Japan, which was interspersed with slanderous anti-Soviet statements.

Seeking to create the impression that Peking's anti-Soviet policy met with broad support in other countries, the Maoists repeatedly used their favourite method: they inspired anti-Soviet statements by their supporters abroad and then passed these outrageous lies for the voice of world public opinion.

CPC leaders again used for their anti-Soviet propaganda the supreme body of power in the PRC—the National People's Congress which went into session in Peking on December 20, 1964. Premier Chou En-lai made a report on the activities of the PRC Government. He repeated the threadbare provocative allegations of the Maoists about the sudden and treacherous abrogation by the Soviet Union of hundreds of agreements and contracts, presented in distorted form the question of withdrawing Soviet specialists and ending equipment deliveries from the Soviet Union to China, slanderously accused our country of subversive activities in Sinkiang, hinted at the "restoration of capitalism" in the USSR, etc. The speaker harped on the false thesis that the difficulties in relations between the PRC and the Soviet Union had to be blamed on the latter. The speeches of other Chinese leaders who took the floor at the session of the National People's Congress also contained anti-Soviet attacks.

In the latter half of November 1964, PRC representatives resumed with renewed vigour their attacks on the Soviet Union in international democratic organisations. Chinese delegations made anti-Soviet statements in the Executive Committee and at the 8th Congress of the International Union of Students in Sofia, at the Vietnam Solidarity Conference in Hanoi, in the Presidium of the World Council of Peace in Berlin, at the 47th session of the Executive Bureau of the World Federation of Trade Unions, in the international preparatory committee of the 9th World Festival of Youth and Students, at an Afro-Asian economic seminar. Ignoring the vital tasks of struggle against imperialism and colonialism, for promoting peace, they focussed their criticism exclusively on the Soviet Union. Peking leaders described the USSR as enemy No. 1, attacked Soviet foreign policy, spread allegations to the effect that the Soviet Union was seeking to make international organisations adopt a position of refusal to fight imperialism, to turn them into a blind tool of its "revisionist" policy on the international scene.

2. CPC LEADERS THWART THE EFFORTS
OF THE CPSU CENTRAL COMMITTEE
AND THE SOVIET GOVERNMENT
TO NORMALISE SINO-SOVIET INTER-STATE RELATIONS

After the November meeting in Moscow, the CPSU Central Committee and the Soviet Government, despite hostile statements by CPC leaders, took concrete steps to normalise Sino-Soviet inter-state relations. The Soviet side made an attempt to restore confidential exchanges of foreign policy information with the PRC. For this purpose, corresponding material was repeatedly handed over to Chinese leaders between November 1964 and January 1965. The Soviet Government, in the Soviet Premier's message of December 28, 1964, supported the proposals of the PRC for calling a conference of heads of state to discuss the problem of banning and eliminating nuclear weapons put forward in Chou En-lai's letter of October 17, 1964.

The Soviet Union also complied with the PRC Government's requests connected with the discussion of the issue of restoration of China's legitimate rights in the United Nations. Soviet representatives actively opposed the efforts of hostile forces to raise the so-called Tibetan problem at the 19th session of the United Nations General Assembly.

Soviet organisations proposed resuming an active exchange of delegations with the PRC under cultural co-operation programmes and within the framework of friendship societies. Such exchanges had also been curtailed through the fault of the Chinese side. After the October plenary meeting of the CPSU Central Committee delegations of workers of Soviet cultural and educational institutions, writers, art workers, activists of the Soviet-Chinese friendship society, etc., went to China. However, these and other positive Soviet steps were not reciprocated by Chinese organisations.

On November 21, 1964, in response to the Soviet Government's opinion, expressed by the Soviet Ambassador, on the Soviet Union's participation in the forthcoming Second Afro-Asian Conference, the PRC Deputy Minister of Foreign Affairs, Liu Hsiao, declared that the PRC was against Soviet participation. On January 14, 1965, the PRC Ministry of Foreign Affairs officially confirmed this stand. Propaganda against the Soviet Union's participation in the conference and attempts to discredit its foreign policy were one of the main objectives of the Afro-Asian tour of the PRC Minister of Foreign Affairs, Chen Yi, in November and December 1964.

In mid-January 1965, Chinese leaders made a statement which purpose was to drive a wedge between the Soviet Union and Japan and thereby improve relations between the PRC and Japan. On January 17, 1965, Chen Yi, in an interview with a member of the Japanese Diet, emphasised that China had repeatedly advised the Soviet Union to return the Kurile Islands, including their northern part, to Japan and that at present this opinion remained unchanged.

In connection with Chen Yi's interview involving the question of territorial integrity of the USSR and the inviolability of its borders and containing other statements unfriendly to the Soviet Union, the USSR Ministry of Foreign Affairs on January 29, 1965 requested explanations about what had given cause for such statements. The Chinese authorities, however, evaded a reply.

Since the end of November 1964, Chinese leaders again began to add heat to the border dispute and to carry on propaganda of their territorial claims to the Soviet Union.

3. NEW CONSTRUCTIVE STEPS OF THE SOVIET UNION

Early in February 1965, a Soviet delegation, led by member of the Presidium of the CPSU Central Committee, Chairman of the USSR Council of Ministers Alexei Kosygin, paid a visit to the Democratic Republic of Vietnam and the Korean People's Democratic Republic. The CPSU Central Committee decided to take advantage of the stopover of the Soviet delegation in Peking for a new initiative to normalise Sino-Soviet relations and continue contacts with Chinese leaders.

During its two stopovers in Peking the Soviet delegation had meetings and talks with leaders of the CPC and the PRC, Mao Tse-tung in particular. It became clear from the outset that Chinese representatives had no constructive proposals for a joint discussion. And again the Soviet delegation displayed the initiative, raising important problems for an exchange of views.

The situation in Indo-China was discussed in view of the US escalation of aggression in this area. The Soviet side pointed out that the US military involvement in South East Asia was a formidable threat to universal peace and emphasised the need for coordinated efforts by the socialist countries to assist the Vietnamese people.

The Chinese leaders, while acknowledging the Soviet Union's important contribution to the Vietnamese people's struggle against the US aggression, failed to make any constructive proposals for aiding the Vietnamese people. What is more, statements were made in China to the effect that the Vietnamese would defeat the aggressors themselves without any foreign assistance, that casualties from US air raids on towns and villages in the Democratic Republic of Vietnam could be ignored. On March 22, 1965, *Jenmin jihpao* wrote in an editorial: "The more bombs dropped by the USA, the stronger the militant will of the Vietnamese people." The Soviet delegation opposed this view and declared that the socialist countries should do everything possible to defend the fraternal Vietnamese people against the US imperialist aggression.

The Chinese leaders declined the Soviet proposal for a joint statement by the DRV, the PRC, the USSR and the KPDR and other socialist countries to expose the violation by the United States of the 1954 Geneva agreements which guaranteed the independence and security of the Democratic Republic of Vietnam and provided for the withdrawal of all foreign troops from Indo-China. They motivated their disagreement by references to differences between the CPC and the CPSU.

Chinese leaders stubbornly emphasised their determination to wage a relentless struggle against the ideological positions of the CPSU and other Marxist-Leninist parties. They reaffirmed persistently their categorical objections to ending open controversy.

The Soviet side explained to the Chinese leaders that the conference of the fraternal parties on the question of preparations for an international meeting of Communists in March 1965 would have the character of consultations and offer favourable opportunities for the participation of CPC representatives. CPC leaders, however, strongly opposed the calling of a consultative meeting in whatever form, as well as an international meeting of Communist and Workers' parties within the coming few years. They alleged that no such meeting could be held within 4 to 5 years, as the CPC Central Committee had officially declared in its letter to the CPSU Central Committee of May 7, 1964, and even in 8 to 10 years.

Chinese leaders again rejected the proposal of the CPSU Central Committee for holding a high-level bilateral meeting between representatives of our parties to discuss all disputed problems, saying that the time for such consultations had not yet come.

The Soviet delegation also initiated an exchange of opinion on the problems involved in developing inter-state relations between the USSR and the PRC. On this issue, too, the Chinese leadership took an evasive stand.

4. PROVOKING BY PEKING LEADERS
OF A FURTHER EXACERBATION
OF SINO-SOVIET RELATIONS

The constructive programme of the CPSU directed to normalising Sino-Soviet relations placed in a difficult situation those Chinese leaders who stubbornly and deliberately resisted the attainment of this goal. To justify and reinforce their line, they resorted to new crude anti-Soviet actions. These tactics were thrown into striking relief, by the anti-Soviet provocative actions of Chinese students organised by the Maoists in Moscow on March 4, 1965.

For these provocative actions Chinese students acting on instructions from Peking took advantage of the demonstration of Soviet and foreign citizens against the US aggression in Vietnam in front of the US Embassy.

Chinese students, who mingled with the demonstrators, called out anti-Soviet slogans, accused the CPSU of refusing to help the DRV, of a collusion with imperialism, committed acts of hooliganism against Soviet militiamen, instigated Soviet people to come out against the policy of the CPSU and the Soviet Government. The demonstrators gave a condign rebuff to the provocateurs. Then the masterminds of this shameful riot fabricated the lie about Chinese students in Moscow having been beaten up, subjected to bloody reprisals, etc.

The Maoists launched a new anti-Soviet campaign in connection with the events on March 4. A mass manifestation of Chinese citizens under anti-Soviet slogans was staged before the Soviet Embassy in Peking on March 6, 1965. During these outrages demonstrators shouted "Get out!" and hurled onto the Embassy grounds numerous "letters of protest" written after a single crib and containing violent curses and threats against the Soviet Government and the CPSU. Then the Chinese press was brought into action. Between March 5 and 20 it published 25 reports on "bloody atrocities against Chinese students in Moscow" cooked up by the Hsinhua News Agency.

Meetings were held at Chinese institutions and enterprises, where anti-Soviet material was read out, appeals were made for a relentless struggle against the CPSU, and the Soviet people were denigrated in every way. The mass meetings organised in Peking and other Chinese cities on March 19 were used for the same purpose.

Chinese leaders attempted to involve in their anti-Soviet campaign even international democratic organisations. At a meeting of the bureau of the World Federation of Democratic Youth, which was in progress in Budapest at the time, the PRC representative tabled a proposal for sending to the Soviet Government on behalf of the federation a message of protest against the "discrimination" against Chinese students enrolled in Soviet higher schools. This provocation, however, was repulsed with determination. The bureau of the WFDY unanimously decided to ignore the information and draft message submitted by the Chinese representative.

The anti-Sovietiers in the CPC also chose as a pretext for new attacks against the CPSU and the Soviet Union the consultative meeting of representatives of 19 fraternal parties. In the article "On the March Meeting in Moscow" published in *Jenmin jihpao* on March 23, 1965, CPC leaders brazenly demanded that the CPSU publicly renounce the decisions of the 20th, 21st and 22nd congresses and the Programme of the CPSU and even promise "never to repeat such mistakes", and give up its policy of peaceful coexistence. They went as far as to qualify their differences with the CPSU and the international communist movement as "differences between the two opposing classes—the proletariat and the bourgeoisie" and declared that they would continue their struggle "as long as the classes and the class struggle will exist in the world".

Chinese leaders openly came out for a continuation of the controversy. In an article of March 23 they declared that the open polemic "should be ceased not for a day, not for a month, not for a year, not for a hundred, a thousand and even ten thousand years. If we do not complete it in nine thousand years, we shall carry on criticism for ten thousand years". The Maoists exerted themselves to carry such declarations into effect. Since the October plenary meeting of the CPSU Central Committee to the end of March 1965, the Chinese national newspapers alone published more than 150 anti-Soviet articles made to the order of Peking leaders and more than 90 similar items concocted by their stooges abroad.

In March 1965 the Chinese publishing house *Jenmin jupan-cheh* brought out in Chinese and foreign languages the collection "On the Polemic over the General Line of the International Communist Movement" which included the most malicious anti-Soviet articles published in the PRC since September 1963.

To increase tensions in Sino-Soviet relations, Peking stepped up its provocative activities on the Sino-Soviet border. Since the end of March attempts to seize individual areas of Soviet territory became more frequent. During fifteen days in April 1965, the border was violated on twelve occasions, with over 500 Chinese civilians and servicemen being involved.

Violations of the border became more and more impudent. For example, on April 11, 1965, about 200 Chinese civilians escorted by Chinese servicemen ploughed up an area of Soviet territory, using eight tractors. Having come up against a cordone of Soviet border guards Chinese soldiers at the command of their officer attempted to force their way through it, committing violent and insulting actions.

To justify their policy of anti-Sovietism, Peking leaders sought to create the impression in China and abroad that the Soviet Union was allegedly pursuing a policy unfriendly towards the PRC, conducting an anti-Chinese campaign, etc. To confirm this fabrication the Maoists twisted facts, crudely falsified them and lied shamelessly. The visit to the USSR by any statesman of a capitalist country was immediately interpreted by Peking as evidence of the Soviet Union's collusion with imperialism for a struggle against China, and every publication about China in the Soviet press, regardless of its contents, was described as an attack against the great Chinese people.

The slanderous fabrications of Peking leaders, however, failed to distort the clear and definite policy of the Soviet Union towards China. This policy was reaffirmed at the plenary meeting of the CPSU Central Committee in September 1965. The First Secretary of the CPSU Central Committee, Leonid Brezhnev, in his speech at the plenary meeting on September 29, declared definitely that the Soviet Union would "consistently search for ways to adjust differences, strengthen friendship and co-operation between the Soviet and Chinese peoples, between our parties and countries".

Far from reciprocating this statement, Peking leaders did their best to put up new obstacles in the way of normalising Sino-Soviet relations. Their divisive anti-Soviet platform was set out in all frankness in an editorial published on November 11, 1965 by *Hungchi* and *Jenmin jihpao*.

Before the publication of this article CPC leaders, referring to differences with the CPSU, had usually stated: "What divides us is only one finger of the ten", "we have a little quarrel and a great unity". Now they finally threw off the chance to overcome differences and flatly announced that there was between the CPC and the CPSU only what disunited them and none of what could unite them; there was what opposed them to each other and none of what they could have in common. The article proclaimed the task of breaking with the CPSU and other Marxist-Leninist parties politically and organisationally.

Chinese leaders made the most wanton attacks against all that had been done by the CPSU Central Committee after the October 1964 plenary meeting in the field of home and foreign policies.

After the publication of the article of November 11, the Chinese side again stepped up its attempts to interfere in the Soviet Union's internal affairs with a view to provoking actions against the CPSU Central Committee and the Soviet Government. CPC leaders more and more openly and crudely violated Article 5 of the Sino-Soviet treaty of friendship and mutual assistance, which made it incumbent on both states to observe the principles of mutual respect for state sovereignty and noninterference in each other's internal affairs.

The Maoists attempted to smuggle anti-Soviet publications into the Soviet Union. In 1963, 11,000 copies of anti-Soviet books and pamphlets were sent to Soviet offices, organisations, and individuals from China, whereas in 1965 this figure rose to about 45,000. To avoid inspection by Soviet government agencies, various tricks were employed: anti-Soviet pamphlets were hidden between pages or placed into the covers of other books, including books for children, shoved in different places in carriages of the Peking-Moscow express, etc.

The Chinese Embassy in Moscow continued to be the centre of circulation of anti-Soviet publications and provocative rumours among Soviet people. In 1966, the Embassy began to circulate illegally the magazine *China Builds* in Russian. The USSR Ministry of Foreign Affairs had to make a corresponding representation on this matter to the Chinese Embassy.

On November 29, 1965, the CPC Central Committee was handed in a letter from the CPSU Central Committee which pointed out definitely the disastrous character of the divisive line of the Chinese leadership, the harm it caused to the Sino-Soviet relations, the socialist community, the struggle against imperialism, for liberating the peoples from the burden of exploitation, for building a communist society. The letter contained proposals aimed at setting a limit to the exacerbation of Sino-Soviet relations.

Chinese leaders reacted to this expression of goodwill towards the unity of our parties and peoples on the part of the CPSU Central Committee with new hostile attacks. On November 29, 1965, at a reception in the Albanian Embassy in Peking, the Premier of the PRC State Council, Chou Enlai, made crude anti-Soviet statements. Unbridled anti-Soviet propaganda was continued in China by every means: in the speeches of party and government leaders, in the press, in broadcasts, etc.

On January 7, 1966, the CPC Central Committee gave an official reply to the letter of the CPSU Central Committee of November 29, 1965. The Chinese letter reiterated slanderous and irresponsible charges against the CPSU and the Soviet Union, attacked the CPSU Programme, Soviet foreign and home policies, repeated over and over again groundless allegations about "Soviet-American collaboration in the name of domination of the world", distorted the Soviet Union's stand on the Vietnam problem in every way.

All this evidenced that the forces hostile to Sino-Soviet friendship had consolidated their positions in the CPC leadership still more.

As the hostile policy of Chinese leaders towards the Soviet Union and other socialist countries took shape, their special position on the Vietnam problem also became increasingly obvious.

While declaring for all to hear their determination to defend the Vietnamese people against the US aggression, Chinese leaders, in fact, repeatedly intimated to Washington that these bellicose statements were intended merely for propaganda. As reported by the American journalist Edgar Snow, Mao Tse-tung, in an interview granted him early in 1965, said that he did not believe in the United States' intention to extend hostilities to North Vietnam and, therefore, China had no reason for entering the war on the side of the DRV. Mao Tse-tung stated that the Vietnamese could very well cope with their problems themselves.

In October 1964, the United States extended its aggression directly to the territory of the Democratic Republic of Vietnam, beginning systematic bombing raids on its towns and villages. These developments faced the socialist countries with the urgent problem of increasing their aid to the embattled Vietnamese people. Peking leaders, however, obstinately interfered with the solution of this problem. Chinese propaganda attempted to denigrate the Soviet Union's stand on the Vietnam problem, to distort the genuine aims of Soviet policy in relation to the Vietnamese people's heroic struggle. The Chinese press deliberately withheld publication of any facts testifying to the Soviet people's unconditional denunciation of the US aggression in Vietnam and the Soviet Government's efforts to help the Vietnamese freedom fighters by every possible means.

Naturally, the attempts of Chinese propaganda to deny the Soviet Union's great contribution to the Vietnamese people's struggle against the US aggression were doomed to failure from the outset. The Vietnamese freedom fighters knew well that it was precisely the Soviet Union that supplied them with missiles, artillery and other modern weapons, ammunition, radio engineering facilities, motor vehicles, ships, industrial equipment, foodstuffs, medicines. The Vietnamese leadership highly assessed this assistance and emphasised its prime importance for strengthening the defence capability of the DRV.

In February 1965, the CPSU Central Committee and the Soviet Government appealed to the CPC Central Committee and the PRC Government for assistance in implementing urgent measures to supply Soviet military aid to the DRV. Unexpectedly this request was opposed by Peking.

Seeking to assist the Vietnamese people, the Soviet Union repeatedly requested the Chinese leadership to discuss joint measures to be taken in defence of the security of the DRV. The Soviet side repeatedly proposed a top-level meeting of representatives of the DRV, the PRC and the USSR, emphasising that any venue convenient for all participants in such a meeting would be accepted by the Soviet Union. Peking leaders stubbornly opposed these Soviet proposals, thereby demonstrating their divisive line and unwillingness to co-operate on the most vital problems.

Peking leaders took a similar stand in relation to the proposals of other socialist countries for coordinating efforts to assist the Vietnamese people.

The stand of the Chinese leadership on the Vietnam problem graphically demonstrated that the Maoists were ready to sacrifice the interests of the Vietnamese people's national liberation struggle and to jeopardise the cause of socialism in Vietnam for the sake of their divisive line and anti-Soviet objectives.

In connection with the 23rd Congress of the CPSU our party came forward with a new initiative to normalise Sino-Soviet relations.

Attaching to the 23rd Congress of the CPSU great importance in the cause of strengthening the unity of the socialist community and the world communist movement the CPSU Central Committee invited a delegation of the Communist Party of China to attend the Congress. From the Congress rostrum the CPSU Central Committee reaffirmed its readiness to hold a top-level meeting at any time with CPC leaders to discuss existing differences and find ways to overcome them on the principles of Marxism-Leninism. This policy of the Central Committee was unanimously approved by the Congress.

In its resolution on the report of the CPSU Central Committee, the 23rd Congress declared: "The Congress approves the activities of the CPSU Central Committee and the concrete measures directed to adjusting differences with the Communist Party of China on the principles of Marxism-Leninism.

"The Congress expresses its confidence that our parties, the peoples of our countries will ultimately overcome difficulties and march shoulder-to-shoulder in the struggle for the common great revolutionary cause."

Despite all this, the Chinese leaders took an openly hostile stand against the 23rd Congress of the CPSU and stepped up their struggle against the CPSU and the Soviet Union.

In a letter to the CPSU Central Committee on March 22, 1966, the CPC leaders rudely refused the invitation to send a delegation to the 23rd Congress.[1] Instead of paying heed to the appeals of the CPSU supported by representatives of the overall majority of the Marxist-Leninist parties who attended the Congress, Chinese leaders cracked down on the supreme forum of the Communist Party of the Soviet Union with malicious slander. This disgraceful campaign was ushered in by Chou En-lai's speech at a 100,000-strong rally in Peking on April 30.

The refusal of CPC leaders to attend the 23rd Congress completed the process of full disruption by them of all contacts with the CPSU through inter-party channels.

Simultaneously the Maoists broke off all relations between the Young Communist Leagues of the two countries. On May 13, 1966, the Central Committee of the Chinese Young Communist League published its reply to the invitation of the Central Committee of the Soviet Young Communist League of March 1966, categorically rejecting it and making attacks against the CPSU and the Leninist Young Communist League.

The stand taken by the CPC leaders in relation to the 23rd Congress reflected the Maoists' general line towards isolation of the Communist Party of China, Chinese Communists from the Marxist-Leninist parties. In 1966, CPC representatives refused to attend the congresses of seven fraternal parties: of Finland (January), India (January-February), the Soviet Union (March-April), Czechoslovakia (May-June), Mongolia (June), Bulgaria (November), Hungary (November-December). In January 1967, CPC representatives failed to attend the 18th Congress of the French Communist Party.

In their statements at the 23rd CPSU Congress, leaders of the fraternal parties sharply criticised the anti-Sovietism of Peking leaders, described the tremendous damage they caused to the common revolutionary cause by their irresponsible slanderous attacks on the CPSU and the Soviet Union.

---

[1] *Jenmin jihpao*, March 24, 1966.

The First Secretary of the Central Committee of the Hungarian Socialist Workers' Party, János Kádár, stated from the rostrum of the 23rd Congress that a principled, comradely attitude to the Soviet Union had always been the touchstone of internationalism. There had never been nor would there ever be anti-Soviet communism. This statement was enthusiastically supported by representatives of the fraternal parties.

5. SINO-SOVIET ECONOMIC AND CULTURAL RELATIONS IN 1965-1966

In 1965, the PRC Government radically revised the character of economic relations between the Soviet Union and China, proposing that they should be developed in the future not on an inter-governmental but on a ministerial basis, i.e., it deliberately played down their political importance and also curtailed them to a minimum.

On April 21, 1965, the PRC Government declared its full cancellation of all work on projects envisaged in the agreement between the USSR and the PRC of June 19, 1961, which provided for Soviet technical assistance (including designing, delivery of materials, equipment and technical documents) in the construction of 66 large industrial enterprises. Thereby the Chinese side refused to resume economic co-operation between our countries and blocked the main path to its possible development.

Soviet supplies of complete plant and equipment to China in 1965 diminished to less than one hundredth of their level in 1959.

At the trade negotiations in the spring of 1965, the PRC representatives declined many proposals of the Soviet side for increasing the turnover of Sino-Soviet trade. China was deliberately reorienting her foreign trade primarily on the capitalist markets. For example, Chinese tin exports to the capitalist countries grew to 6-7 thousand tons, and those to the Soviet Union, diminished to 500 tons. All this led to a 7-per cent-reduction in the volume of Sino-Soviet trade in 1965 as compared with 1964, so that it fell to a mere 375.5 million rubles. Since 1966 trade became the only form of Sino-Soviet economic relations, but it also reduced considerably—to less than 300 million rubles.

This was the result not only of the anti-Soviet policy of Peking leaders but also of the general line towards disruption of China's economic co-operation with the socialist community. The share of the socialist countries in China's foreign trade fell in 1966 to 25 per cent from 68 per cent in 1959. Over the period, the share of the capitalist countries in Chinese foreign trade grew to 75 per cent.

Throughout 1966, the Soviet side took steps to remove any pretexts for a further exacerbation of inter-state relations, to find ways to solve at least isolated problems. In March 1966, a regular meeting of the mixed Sino-Soviet commission on border river shipping was held in Khabarovsk on a Soviet initiative and in February of the same year Soviet and Chinese representatives had a meeting in accordance with the agreement on joint protection of forests against fire.

The volume of Sino-Soviet scientific and technical co-operation in 1965 diminished to a mere fraction of a hundredth as compared with 1959. Soviet organisations' inquiries were declined even on a number of non-secret subjects (study of experience in the operation of iron tube casting units, processes of pressing and long storage of maize, information on up-to-date technical facilities for vegetable oil and fat storage, etc.).

In November 1966, the 15th session of the Sino-Soviet commission on scientific and technical cooperation took place. Its proceedings again demonstrated the obvious unwillingness of the Chinese side to extend scientific and technical exchanges with the Soviet Union. As a result, the total number of obligations assumed by both sides reduced more than by half as compared with that adopted at the preceding session.

In 1966, scientific co-operation between the Academies of Sciences of the Soviet Union and China was also curtailed. The Soviet side was allowed to send to the PRC only one research worker for the study of one problem instead of 11 scientists for work on seven problems as envisaged in the plan.

China sent to the Soviet Union 11 research workers for work on 3 problems instead of 20 scientists for work on 6 problems.

In April 1966, the PRC Academy of Sciences made an unfriendly step, declaring the "refusal" of two Chinese scientists to accept the title of member of the USSR Academy of Sciences. Needless to say, this "refusal" was the result of crude political pressure. Suffice it to recall that by that time even business correspondence of Chinese scientists with their Soviet colleagues began to be regarded by Chinese authorities as a grave political crime. Such qualification entailed definite practical consequences: in the years of the "cultural revolution" thousands of Chinese research workers were subjected to brutal repression only because they had studied in the Soviet Union or subscribed to Soviet scientific publications.

Demonstrating their hostility to the Soviet Union, Chinese organisations in the spring of 1966 refused to accept medicines and vitamins sent by the Soviet Red Cross to areas of the PRC hit by a destructive earthquake.

The Soviet draft programme of cultural co-operation with the PRC in 1965 provided for an expansion of cultural exchanges by approximately 25 per cent as compared with 1964. Because of opposition from the Chinese side this programme was not adopted in full.

The programme of cultural co-operation between the Soviet Union and China in 1966 was signed in Moscow in June after numerous delays and difficulties created by the Chinese side. For the volume of planned exchanges, this was the smallest programme throughout the history of Sino-Soviet relations.

Actually in 1966 only delegations of health workers were exchanged, and the Peking Song and Dance Company gave guest performances in the Soviet Union. Its programme was obviously intended to demonstrate the greatness of "Mao's ideas". The Soviet side repeatedly expressed its willingness to send to China art companies and groups of specialists; however, in December 1966, the Chinese side proposed that these visits be put off until 1967 without specifying concrete periods. The Soviet proposal for co-operation in the field of broadcasting and television was rejected.

It is easy to see why the Maoists so stubbornly frustrated co-operation between the mass media of the PRC and the Soviet Union. They feared like hell truthful information about Soviet realities, the successes of communist construction in our country, and the crimes of the Maoists who caused unprecedented suffering to the Chinese people and destroyed their socialist gains one after another. It was precisely this fear of the truth, a desire to prevent their black deeds from being made public that motivated the measures taken by Peking authorities, unheard of in civilised society, against foreign correspondents. They were forbidden not only to leave Peking but even to go about town, to read newspapers and advertisements on house walls, to speak to Chinese; they were constantly exposed to abuse by official authorities and even manhandled by crowds of hungweipings instigated by Maoists. Workers of the press, broadcasting and news agencies of the socialist countries evoked especially bitter hatred of the Maoists. They were placed in the most difficult situation, deliberately terrorised by provocative accusations of illegal activities, banned access to information sources.

Implementing these practices, the PRC Ministry of Foreign Affairs on December 16, 1966 demanded the recalling from China within ten days of three Soviet correspondents whose only "guilt" was truthful coverage of the developments in China.

The Maoists continued to use cultural exchanges for their anti-Soviet goals. Numerous cases were uncovered of Chinese tourists, members of various delegations, students, attempting to gather secret information in the USSR. In July 1966, the Soviet Ministry of Foreign Affairs lodged an official protest with the Chinese Embassy in Moscow over the fact that Chinese servicemen enrolled in a Soviet military academy had photographed secret material on military installations and handed over photographs to the Chinese Embassy.

By contrast, the Soviet Union regarded the development of cultural exchanges with the PRC as an important field of cultural intercourse, promoting mutual understanding and friendship between the Soviet and Chinese peoples. In 1966, solemn meetings were held in the Soviet Union to mark the 16th anniversary of the Treaty of Friendship, Alliance and Mutual Assistance between the Soviet Union and China and many red-letter days in Chinese life—the 17th anniversary of the People's Republic of China, anniversaries of Chinese revolutionaries and cultural figures, in particular, Sun Yat-sen, Lu Hsin, Mao Tun, Wen Yi-to. In Irkutsk, one of the streets was named after Sun Yat-sen on the occasion of his birth centenary.

In 1966, cultural co-operation between the PRC and other socialist countries was also sharply curtailed. The Chinese side even refused to sign programmes of cultural co-operation with Bulgaria, Poland, the GDR, Mongolia, and Czechoslovakia for 1967.

Chinese authorities continued their policy of renunciation of collective forms of co-operation with the socialist countries. In the summer of 1965, the PRC unilaterally withdrew from the Joint Nuclear Research Institute at Dubna. On April 17, 1965, the PRC was handed in a proposal for participation in joint exploration of outer space by the socialist countries (letter from the Soviet Premier to the Premier of the PRC State Council of April 14, 1965). This and other proposals, however, were ignored in Peking.

In 1966, the Chinese side unilaterally withdrew from the agreement of April 21, 1956 on co-operation of the USSR, the DRV, the PRC, and the KPDR in commercial fishing and other research in the Western Pacific.

CHAPTER VIII

SINO-SOVIET RELATIONS
IN THE LATTER HALF OF THE 60s

In the latter half of 1966, the Maoist leadership of the CPC launched an all-out attack on the socialist gains in China, openly broke with the principles of Marxism-Leninism in its internal and foreign policies. At the eleventh plenary meeting of the CPC Central Committee held in August 1966 it announced the task of implementing the so-called cultural revolution spearheaded against the foundations of socialism in the PRC.

The eleventh plenary meeting took place in a situation where the Maoists had already disorganised the party ranks, removed the leading cadres opposed to the Mao Tse-tung line. On the eve of the plenary meeting the journal *Hungchi*, which was placed under Maoist control warned threateningly that all those opposed to the ideas of Mao Tse-tung whatever posts they might hold and whatever prestige enjoyed would be ousted.

The eleventh plenary meeting adopted two documents: the "Resolution on the Great Proletarian Cultural Revolution" and a communique. The communique specially emphasised that the plenary meeting had held its proceedings under the direct leadership of Mao Tse-tung. The plenary meeting admitted that the "cultural revolution" had met with resistance and described it as strong and stubborn enough.

The eleventh plenary meeting issued instructions for setting up everywhere "cultural revolution" groups and committees, conferences of "cultural revolution" representatives, as well as other "mass organisations". These new organisations were invested with broad powers, their actions were not limited by law, and they were responsible only to Mao himself.

As it became known later, at the eleventh plenary meeting Mao Tse-tung made public his appeal "Fire at the Headquarters", which was a signal for beginning the ruining of party bodies from top to bottom.

The developments in the PRC at the time of the "cultural revolution" had a direct bearing on Sino-Soviet relations and resulted in their further sharp deterioration. Intensified struggle against the CPSU and the Soviet Union became one of the major directions of activity of Peking leaders in the course of the "cultural revolution".

1. SOURCES OF THE "CULTURAL REVOLUTION"

The "cultural revolution" was not an unexpected turn in the policy of the Maoists. Although it was officially proclaimed by the eleventh plenary meeting of the CPC Central Committee, in fact it took its origin from an earlier period and was a concentrated expression of the deep-going political crisis the PRC had been plagued by for a number of years as a result of the disastrous policy of the present CPC leaders.

As pointed out above, after the collapse of the adventurist policy of "three red banners" (new general line, "big leap", and people's communes) the Maoists were compelled to resort to the so-called adjustment in order to improve the situation in the country. The pivot of the PRC Government's economic policy in that period was the line of "agriculture—the basis for the entire national economy" proclaimed by the ninth and tenth plenary meetings of the CPC Central Committee held in January 1961 and September 1962 respectively.

However, the "adjustment", which failed to restore the basic principles of socialist economic management, could not lead the PRC economy out of its critical condition. The line of "agriculture—the basis for the entire national economy" retarded China's economic development in general, and in individual industries (machine-tool building, ferrous and non-ferrous metallurgy, etc.) resulted in a reduction of production or at least in considerable idle capacities. In 1965, the last year of the "adjustment", the total industrial output was still 26 per cent below the 1959 level. A decline in labour enthusiasm was to be noted everywhere, and demands were made at enterprises for reducing the plan targets, while the quality of products sharply deteriorated. Even the official Chinese press published appeals for relaxing efforts.

The rise in agricultural production was, as before, restrained by the extremely low level of mechanisation. At the end of 1965 there were only 100,000 tractors in rural areas, whereas the country needed at least 1.2-1.5 million tractors. Not more than 10 per cent of all arable land, mostly on farms managed by the army, was ploughed up by machines. The grain harvest in the years of the "adjustment" hardly reached the level of 1957 (180-185 million tons). This meant that the per capita annual grain production was 12 per cent below the average in the first five-year plan period and 20 per cent below the level before the anti-Japanese war. In 1965, the total grain harvest was much below the level which was to be attained as far back as 1962 (250 million tons) under the draft project of the second five-year plan adopted by the Eighth National Congress of the CPC in 1956. Since the end of 1960 China began to import from abroad an average of 5-6 million tons of grain annually, which was equivalent to about 30 per cent of the value of all Chinese imports.

The economic difficulties entailed a sharp exacerbation of the struggle in the CPC over the question of ways to develop the country. During this struggle the contradictions between the two groups in the Party leadership became increasingly acute. One of these groups was for using rational methods to develop the national economy with due regard for the experience of the socialist countries; the other, directed by Mao Tse-tung, categorically rejected the international experience in building socialism and came out for voluntaristic methods of economic management, for whipping up the rates of economic development.

The Maoist line was opposed by Chinese Communists loyal to the Marxist-Leninist views. At the same time, Mao's adventurist policy evoked growing discontent also among many of his former followers who, while remaining at the nationalistic positions in general became increasingly aware of the futility of his policy. This made the struggle within the CPC leadership especially bitter.

In 1964-1965, the Maoists opened a methodic offensive against those who threatened their domination. This offensive was carried on along the lines of further curtailing party and government democracy, militarising the life of society and enhancing the role of the army, fanning nationalistic passions, bringing the cult of Mao to a still higher pitch.

Already in that period one of the central targets of Maoist attacks was the intelligentsia which was capable of realising the disastrous character of the internal and foreign policies of the Mao group better than the other sections of the Chinese population. The movement was intensified among the intelligentsia for the so-called adjustment of the style with the purpose of making it accept the Maoist line without reservations. The first victim of the "cultural revolution" was the progressive part of the intelligentsia in the Party membership. Mao Tun, a world-famous writer, was dismissed from the post of Minister of Culture. The leaders of all professional unions were also ousted. It will be no exaggeration to say that in 1964-1966 the cream of the Chinese intelligentsia was declared politically untrustworthy and subjected to repression, ranging from humiliating chastising, dismissal and exile to rural areas to corporal punishment. As admitted by *Jenmin jihpao* in October 1966, 160,000 intellectuals had been exiled to rural areas for re-education by labour over the previous 18 months.

Simultaneously, the Maoists started the struggle against the progressive cultural heritage of other nations. They cracked down upon the works of such great men of world culture as Shakespeare, Rabelais, Stendhal, Balzac, Romain Rolland, Beethoven, Mozart, and others. Peking dogmatists attempted to justify their attacks on classical works of literature and art with hypocritical concern for revolutionary criteria. For example, Beethoven's Ninth Symphony was denounced on the grounds that it had been produced and performed for the first time before the publication of the Communist Manifesto. Balzac was accused of "advertising the bourgeois theory of humanity" in his narration of father Goriot's love for his daughters. On account of the operas "Carmen", "La Traviata", "Eugene Onegin", the ballets "Swan Lake",

"Giselle", it was declared that they "poisoned and depraved the working people", etc.

In the campaign of destroying culture launched by the Maoists one of the main targets was Soviet literature. Works by A. Tolstoi, M. Sholokhov, K. Simonov, I. Ehrenburg, A. Korneichuck and many other Soviet prose writers and poets were declared "harmful" and "subversive" and subject to destruction. Anyone who dared to read them was persecuted as a political criminal.

Marxism-Leninism proclaims that it is impossible to build socialism without wiping out ignorance, backwardness, illiteracy. As is well known, in the early years of Soviet power when the civil war had not yet ended in the country, Vladimir Lenin made this appeal: "Study, study, study!" He regarded it as a first priority task of the builders of socialism to assimilate and critically assess everything of value in the more than 2000-year-long history of human thought and culture. He demanded that the store of culture, knowledge and technology accumulated by capitalism, historically necessary for us, be turned from an instrument of capitalism into an instrument of socialism. The founder of the world's first socialist state repeatedly emphasised that "we must take the entire culture that capitalism left behind and build socialism with it. We must take all its science, technology, knowledge and art. Without these we shall be unable to build communist society".[1]

These instructions of Lenin's are fully valid for China where the implementation of a genuine cultural revolution is an urgent necessity, where down to the present time more than 300 million people are illiterate.

As one of the basic means to distract the Chinese people's attention from difficulties, to keep them in submission the masterminds of the "cultural revolution" employed propaganda campaigns in preparation for the so-called revolutionary war. The aim of these campaigns was to enhance the role of the army in the country's life, to speed up militarisation of the economy, to introduce an army drill order, to justify the low standards of living of the people. The following episode is an example in point. In the summer of

---

[1] V. I. Lenin, *Collected Works*, Vol. 29, p. 70.

1965, a Chinese delegation visiting the Soviet Union was invited for a discussion to the Moscow City Soviet where the delegates were told about the vast-scope housing construction in the Soviet Union. After hearing the report Chinese delegates expressed their surprise with the spending in the Soviet Union of large funds on such "trifles" as housing and declared: "We in the PRC do not build housing, we prepare the people for revolution."

While carrying out militarisation of the economy and pushing the army to the key positions, the nationalists in the CPC took measures in advance to free the army from party and people's control and to turn it into an obedient tool of their military bureaucratic dictatorship.

In the period 1959-1965, the best politically educated and active part of the officers' corps was expelled from the army. In May 1965, the so-called revolutionisation of the armed forces was carried out: military ranks and insignia were abolished under the pretext of "strengthening the ties between commanding officers and the masses". In reality, the aim was to reduce the role of the numerous veteran officers promoted during the national liberation and revolutionary war who sided with the opponents of the Maoists. Simultaneously, propaganda was intensified of the slogan of the priority of politics, implying Mao's "ideas" in every field, including military work. Criticism was levied upon those who insisted on improving the professional training of the army, its technical equipment and ignored the work in educating officers and men in a spirit of loyalty to the "ideas of the great helmsman". Under the smoke screen of this "revolutionisation", a new wave of purges swept the army.

The so-called revolutionisation of the army was, in effect, preparation for militarising the country's social life as a whole to be carried out under the same slogan. In 1964-1965, political departments staffed with army officers were set up at enterprises and offices. In other words, it became possible for the army to influence directly the activities of enterprises and offices, which facilitated the transition to the "cultural revolution" on a nationwide scale.

Uncertain of their ability to keep their positions with the aid of the army alone, the nationalists in the CPC stepped up their activities in undermining the moral and political unity of the Chinese people. Under the slogan of exacerbation of the class struggle they made intensive efforts to set one layer of Chinese society against another. Workers, peasants, soldiers and intellectuals were intimidated at every step at work and at home with the spectre of restoration of capitalism in China, the intrigues of the class enemies.

To suppress dissidents in 1964-1965, in addition to corrective labour in special camps, so-called courtyard education was introduced; a system of spying on neighbours by neighbour's regular secret reports, constant chastising of every one suspected of disloyalty to the "great helmsman" were effected. Other forms of "re-education" that became widespread were "meetings of struggle" with all those present obliged to denounce the suspect, presentation of the "family history", describing all the "sins" and criticising every misdemeanour ever committed by its members.

To brainwash the Chinese population the cult of Mao Tse-tung was used on a growing scale. Chinese propaganda sought to surround Mao with the halo of a man of genius—wise, great, infallible, farsighted, etc. His "ideas" were described as food and weapons, a compass and a beacon for the Chinese people. The Chinese revolution was depicted not as an objective historical process but as the handiwork of Mao Tse-tung, as his "brainchild".

The low cultural level of the bulk of China's population, the domination of petty bourgeois psychology, the strong vestiges of feudalism and patriarchal traditions enabled the masterminds of the "cultural revolution" to impose their dogmas on the masses with comparative ease, and then to pass them for slogans of the masses themselves. Illiterate or semiliterate people systematically subjected to ideological indoctrination were infected with fanatical faith in a semi-god leader, and this made it very difficult for them to sober from this mystical craze.

For all their efforts, however, the leading group in the CPC were unable to consolidate their positions decisively. Among the leading Party cadres and within the broad Party membership discontent with their policy continued to increase, while local party and government bodies on their own initiative restored the order which had existed before

the "big leap" and the "people's communes", and the prestige of central authority in peripheral areas was weakening
in threatening proportions. Without fearing intimidation and
repression, Chinese men of letters produced works which in
figurative form caustically derided the cult of Mao Tse-tung
and exposed his "ideas" to scathing criticism.

The domination of the ruling clique was threatened not
only by the growing discontent within the country but also
by its grave setbacks on the international scene.

The Maoists failed in their efforts to break up the socialist
community. The nationalists in the CPC succeeded in foist-
ing their fallacious principles on none of the socialist countries except Albania. Contrary to the intrigues of Chinese
leaders the striving for cohesion and unity, for further developing all-round co-operation tended to grow within the
socialist community.

The great-power policy of Peking leaders failed to meet
with any substantial support in the world communist movement. Peking's attempts to establish its hegemony over it
proved futile. The overall majority of the fraternal parties
resolutely rejected the Maoists' anti-Leninist foreign policy
platform. By their practical daily revolutionary struggle, their
theoretical work the fraternal parties proved conclusively
that the views of CPC leaders ran counter to the vital interests of the peoples fighting against imperialism and colonialism, for peace, democracy, national liberation, socialism,
and communism.

The Chinese leaders' designs in relation to the national
liberation movement also proved of no avail. The great setbacks for those sections of the national liberation movement
which blindly followed Peking's instructions alerted the
governments of young national states, revolutionary democratic parties and helped them to see through the true aims
of the Maoists.

The failure of the Maoists' attempts to make the Afro-
Asian countries take up a negative attitude to the Moscow
treaty on banning nuclear weapons tests in the three media,
the frustration of their hopes to lead the Afro-Asian countries at the Second Afro-Asian Conference, the forced aban-
donment of their plans to set up a "revolutionary United
Nations", the collapse of their plans to thwart the Tashkent

Conference convened for a peaceful settlement of the Indo-Pakistan conflict which broke out in 1965—all evidenced that the foreign policy platform proposed by Chinese leaders met with no support in the Afro-Asian countries.

Peking leaders failed to knock together an exclusive bloc of South-East Asian states under the aegis of the PRC, which they advocated vigorously in 1964-1965. The Peking-Jakarta axis (the core of the planned bloc) failed to be created. After the events of September 30, 1965, the relations between the PRC and Indonesia sharply deteriorated almost to the point of complete disruption.

Year after year the PRC increasingly lost its prestige as a socialist state. On all the key issues of international politics its line proved to be in sharp contrast to the common stand of the socialist countries, the communist movement, all anti-imperialist forces.

Thus, towards the beginning of 1966 the crisis of both the home and foreign policies of the Mao Tse-tung group had come to a head. Seeking to avoid complete bankruptcy, the Maoists launched the so-called cultural revolution, hoping to create more favourable conditions for implementing their anti-socialist policy at home and abroad.

As long as the Communist Party of China, the bodies of people's government, the trade unions, the Young Communist League, and other mass organisations of working people operated in China the Maoists were unable to divert the country from its socialist path. The ruling clique was faced by these alternatives: either to retreat and accept defeat or to try and destroy this political superstructure, to carry out a coup d'état and establish a military bureaucratic dictatorship, thereby securing the conditions for their undivided rule. As is known, the Maoists chose the second alternative.

The chief obstacle in their way was the Communist Party of China.

The Maoists realised, of course, that the struggle against the Communist Party would not be an easy matter. They were aware of the fact that its veteran cadres had been trained not only on Mao Tse-tung's articles and speeches but were also familiar with Marxist-Leninist theory; despite the prolonged anti-Soviet campaign they continued to be favourably disposed towards the Soviet people, the CPSU and could not be taken in by fabrications about the Soviet Union's collusion with the United States and about the restoration of capitalism allegedly taking place in the Soviet Union. These cadres were also aware of the importance of culture for building socialism, of the need to attain the heights of modern science and technology; they saw better than others the disastrous consequences of the refusal to emulate the experience in socialist construction accumulated by the fraternal parties. Therefore, the ruling elite had no confidence in the party activists, in the workers and peasants; moreover, it feared the party and the people lest their hidden discontent grow into open actions against its policy.

The Maoists found support for their anti-socialist line in the army, which was declared "the most loyal and obedient instrument of the great helmsman". They also pinned their hopes upon the school youth and students who had been brought up in the spirit of Maoist ideas, had a vague and distorted idea of socialism, of Marxism-Leninism, of the developments in China and the rest of the world. A fairly great role was played by the Maoists' cynical designs to use emotionality and vacillations inherent in young people, their dissatisfaction with their status in society, their ambitions. The fact that the greater half of the student youth in China came from bourgeois or petty bourgeois families was also important.

Gangs of hungweipings formed of young people became a strike force for routing party organisations. What is more, young people without party affiliation, mostly of petty bourgeois origin, who had distinguished themselves in the riots, were proclaimed by the Maoists as the cream, the most advanced, the most conscious part of the Chinese people, and it was made incumbent on party veterans, veteran workers, outstanding scientists and art workers to learn from them and emulate their actions.

The emergence on the political scene of gangs of hungweipings backed up by the army and state security agencies opened one of the most tragic pages in the history of post-revolutionary China. The ruling clique officially sanctioned mass outrages in the capital and the provinces which grew into a veritable reign of terror, manhandling and murders of opponents of the Maoists, acts of vandalism against cultural values, destruction of the remnants of socialist legality, law and order.

Things were brought to a head by the exacerbation of contradictions between members of Mao Tse-tung's entourage and his possible successors. As a result of conflicts within the CPC leadership, the position of the PRC Chairman, Liu Shao-chi, was seriously undermined, and the secretaries of the CPC Central Committee, Peng Chen, Lu Ting-yi and Lo Jui-ching were deposed. Instead of them Mao's wife, Sung Ching-ling, his closest associates, Kang Sheng, Chen Po-ta, and others came to the foreground. It was precisely these people who directed the indiscriminate purges, the reshuffling of the entire party and government apparatus.

The Maoists made short work of their opponents and rivals with sadistic brutality, subjecting them to tortures and humiliating their dignity in every way.

More than two thirds of the members of the CPC Central Committee elected by the Eighth National Congress, the overwhelming majority of leading executives of central government departments, provincial and town committees of the CPC, leading ideological workers, leaders of professional unions, administrators and leading members of the faculty of institutions of higher learning and research institutions, many high-ranking generals were purged.

Simultaneously, the ruling elite steered its course towards undermining the state institutions of people's power. The National People's Congress and its Standing Committee were completely paralysed. More than a half of the deputies of the National People's Congress and the members of its Standing Committee were victimised by repression. Without knowledge of the National People's Congress and in contravention of the Constitution the PRC Chairman, Liu Shao-chi, was suspended from office. The elected bodies of people's government in the provinces were dissolved. Military control was established over the State Council of the PRC, its offices and ministries. Most of the Vice-Premiers of the State Council of the PRC, chiefs of chanceries and Ministers were deposed.

2. ANTI-SOVIETISM—KEYNOTE
OF THE "CULTURAL REVOLUTION"

From the very outset a major distinctive feature of the "cultural revolution" was its clear-cut anti-Soviet orientation. The eleventh plenary meeting of the CPC Central Committee held in August 1966 endorsed all the anti-Soviet measures implemented by the Maoists in the preceding four years, acknowledged open criticism against the CPSU as absolutely correct and indispensable and also approved of all the main anti-Soviet articles published by the editors of *Jenmin jihpao*, *Hungchi*, and other anti-Soviet publications. The plenary meeting proclaimed the task of dissociating definitely from the CPSU and other Marxist-Leninist parties and bringing the struggle against them to the end.

After the eleventh plenary meeting of the CPC Central Committee, the anti-Soviet campaign in the PRC, broad enough as it was, flared up with renewed intensity. The street in Peking on which the Soviet Embassy is located, became a scene of wanton riots. On August 20, 1966, it was renamed "Struggle Against Revisionists" street. All the houses, fences, even pavements and driveways were daubed with anti-Soviet slogans calling for the defeat of the CPSU and the Soviet Union, destruction of all things Soviet. Hungweiping leaflets on house walls near the Soviet Embassy contained threats against Soviet people like this one: "When the time comes, we shall skin you, pull out your tendons, burn your corpses and commit your ashes to the wind."

On August 29, an anti-Soviet manifestation was staged in front of the Soviet Embassy, which continued without a break until the night of August 30. At a meeting which preluded these mass outrages the so-called message to the people of the country was read out, announcing that "the Soviet Union is our mortal enemy".

During the "cultural revolution" monuments symbolising friendship between the peoples of the Soviet Union and China were defiled or destroyed. Among them were the monument to Alexander Pushkin, the Sino-Soviet friendship monument in Shanghai, etc. Soviet citizens having permanent residence in China were attacked by hoodlums, searched, beaten up. and subjected to indignities.

On September 1, 1966, the Soviet press published an announcement under the title "In the Central Committee of the CPSU", which pointed out that the decisions of the eleventh plenary meeting of the CPC Central Committee had officially confirmed the intention of the CPC leadership to go ahead with its special policy, opposing it to the Marxist-Leninist line jointly worked out by the fraternal parties at the meetings of 1957 and 1960, and declared that the Chinese leadership was again provoking a sharp deterioration of relations between the Soviet Union and China. The CPSU Central Committee qualified such actions and statements as a step rendering a particularly great service to imperialism and reaction and pointed up the responsibility of the leadership of the CPC and the PRC for their refusal to wage a joint, coordinated struggle against imperialism and reaction, for their incessant attempts to split the communist movement, the socialist community and to weaken the anti-imperialist front. The CPSU Central Committee, loyal to its principled policy, declared that despite the difficulties created by the CPC leadership the Communist Party of the Soviet Union would continue to pursue a policy of strengthening friendship with Chinese Communists, with the multi-millioned Chinese people, to uphold with determination the general line of the world communist movement, the principles of Marxism-Leninism, proletarian internationalism.

On September 20, 1966, Chinese authorities announced the decision of the PRC Government to suspend for one year foreign students enrolled in Chinese institutions of higher learning and demanded that Soviet students leave China within 10 to 15 days. The Soviet students were compelled to return to the Soviet Union. On the principle of reciprocity Chinese undergraduates and research students in the Soviet Union were also suspended. Simultaneously the Soviet Union expressed its willingness to consider a resumption of student exchange on the basis of reciprocity as soon as the Chinese side was ready for this.

CPC leaders made use of the return of Chinese students from the Soviet Union to whip up anti-Soviet hysteria in China. At the end of October 1966, another anti-Soviet demonstration was held in front of the Soviet Embassy in Peking. On October 27, the USSR Ministry of Foreign Affairs, just as on August 26, lodged a note of protest against it; however, Chinese authorities continued to encourage rioting in front of the Soviet Embassy. The riots went on even on November 7, 1966, the date of the 49th anniversary of the Great October Socialist Revolution.

Peking propaganda sought to convince everybody, young and adult alike, that the Soviet Union was allegedly a foe of China and pursued a hostile and even aggressive policy against her, that the PRC was threatened with intervention not only by the imperialist powers, but, above all, by the Soviet Union. Chinese leaders also came up with public statements about the possibility of a military conflict between the PRC and the Soviet Union. For example, on September 29, 1965, the PRC Foreign Minister, speaking at a press conference before 400 Chinese and foreign journalists specially invited to Peking from Hongkong, Macao, and other places, declared that if China were attacked by the United States, the "modern revisionists" would coordinate with the latter their operations in the North. Since then, the "threat from the North" became a staple item of Chinese propaganda spearheaded against the Soviet Union. The Chinese population was indoctrinated to believe that if the United States attacked China, the Soviet Union would immediately occupy her North East provinces, that the Soviet Union was one of the dangerous friends without whom China felt more secure, that Russian missiles might fly from Moscow to Peking. The Chinese were told over and over again that even the slightest feeling of favour for the Soviet Union was tantamount to treason.

Seeking to foment anti-Sovietism, the masterminds of the "cultural revolution" employed the services of the arch-reactionary circles of old China. For example, they offered a broad rostrum for the anti-Soviet statements of the ex-President of Kuomintang China, Li Tsung-jeng, the blood-stained suppressor of the Chinese people's revolutionary movement, who had returned to the PRC from exile and was given a warm welcome by the Maoists on his arrival in Peking.

Chinese authorities organised an outrageous anti-Soviet provocation against the Soviet motorship *Zagorsk* in the port of Dairen. On December 8, 1966, when she was leaving harbour, the Chinese pilot on board the ship suddenly gave a command, which, if it were obeyed, would result in her collision with the breakwater, grave damage and, possibly, sinking. Naturally, the master refused to obey the command and steered her safely past the harbour gate, where she promptly cast anchor as demanded by the pilot. However, the ship was immediately boarded by armed Chinese guards and port officials, who detained her and attempted to break into the chart-house to seize maps and ship documents.

It was not before December 28 that the motorship was permitted to sail off.

Besides anti-Soviet outrages in China herself, Peking leaders sought to organise similar riots against Soviet missions in other countries: Cambodia, Egypt, Syria, France.

The period after the eleventh plenary meeting of the CPC Central Committee witnessed a renewal of hostile Chinese activities along the Soviet border. Early in October 1966, Chinese army units appeared at the Pamir section of the Soviet border for the first time and started photographing Soviet territory. Numerous gangs of hungweipings kept arriving in the border areas. People's volunteers under the command of Chinese army officers carried out military exercises on the banks of border rivers, simulated attacks in the direction of the Soviet border, crossings of the river Amur by storm, etc.

Simultaneously, the Chinese leadership made efforts to adapt the "cultural revolution" to the goals of interfering in the Soviet Union's internal affairs and subversive activities against it. Speaking at a military academy in October 1966, the PRC Minister of Foreign Affairs declared: "The cultural revolution directed personally by Chairman Mao Tse-tung is a major initiative in the communist movement, a great beginning in the socialist revolution. It has produced a deep impact on the Soviet Union, the countries of Asia, Africa, and Latin America. We should turn the great cultural revolution towards the USSR. Eventually the day will come when hungweipings will appear on Moscow streets."

Peking propaganda sought to create the impression that the Soviet people supported the "cultural revolution" and were prepared to emulate it, that they already regarded Mao Tse-tung as their "leader". On November 16, 1966, in a report on another anti-Soviet rally in Peking, the Hsinhua

News Agency alleged, for example, that the Soviet people "see light and hope for the future in the greatest leader of the revolutionary peoples of the whole world, Chairman Mao Tse-tung".

Peking loudly announced that the "cultural revolution" which was in progress in China should be extended to the whole world. Hungweiping publications earnestly put forward the task of remaking the universe with the aid of the ideas of the "great helmsman", of staging a great revolutionary spectacle not only on the home scene but on the international scene as well.

3. GROWING DIFFICULTIES IN THE "CULTURAL REVOLUTION" AND A HARDENING IN THE ANTI-SOVIET LINE OF CHINESE LEADERS

In 1967, the "cultural revolution" came up against new obstacles which showed that the Maoists had failed to attain their targets at one fling, within a brief space of time.

The "cultural revolution" resulted in a general decline of the national economy and aggravated the economic crisis in the PRC. It undermined industrial and agricultural production, reduced government revenues, dislocated the transport services. It involved a tremendous loss of working time, unproductive spending of huge material and monetary resources. Not less damage to the national economy was caused by disorganisation of the management bodies, repression of experienced managers and economists, the apparatus of state administration.

Only the defence industry, primarily its sectors manufacturing missiles and nuclear weapons, were in a privileged position. From the very outset they were placed under rigid control of the army and were safeguarded against excesses which accompanied the "cultural revolution". According to Western press estimates, the PRC's military spending in 1967 exceeded investment in industry roughly fourfold and was larger than all investments in the national economy put together (in 1966, military expenditure was 14-16 thousand million yuan).

The total output of Chinese industry diminished by 15 per cent in 1967. The output of coal, which accounted for 90 per cent in the country's fuel balance, fell by 40 per cent, electricity, by 30 per cent, steel, by 25-30 per cent. Premier Chou En-lai publicly admitted that some price in production had had to be paid for the "cultural revolution".

At first, the "cultural revolution" did not affect the villages. However, since the end of 1966 its disorganising influence began to be clearly felt in agriculture as well. Between January and March 1967, peasants began to seize illegally and share among themselves, products in public possession, to loot food stores, to slaughter publicly owned livestock.

During the spring sowing season of 1967, Peking leaders, who had no trust in the organisation of peasants and cadres in rural areas, were compelled to send regular army units there to supervise field work.

Stoppages in industry and the transport services, disorganisation of trade resulted in cutbacks in food supplies to towns and cities. At the end of 1966, prices of some foodstuffs (rice, pork, tomatoes, cucumbers) were raised. In addition to rations for bread, rice, vegetable oil, sugar, cotton fabrics, footwear, tobacco, rations for meat, vegetables, fuel, kerosene were introduced. Special coupons were issued even for visits to a bathhouse.

The political situation in the PRC in 1967 was characterised by a general weakening of central authority, increased anarchy, intensified feuds between gangs of hungweipings and tsaophans, a more bitter power struggle within the ruling clique.

Towards the autumn of 1967, armed clashes had spread to almost all the areas of the country. Whereas in the earlier period mostly young people were involved in them, now masses of working people joined in.

The developments in China exposed the true essence of the "cultural revolution" as one thoroughly hostile to the interests of the Chinese people, to the causes of socialism and directed to undermining China's friendship and co-operation with the Soviet Union and other socialist countries.

The falsity of the Maoist pseudo-revolutionary slogans became increasingly obvious, and the adventurist plans and intentions of the ruling elite, its efforts to divert China from her socialist path by every means at its disposal were more and more clearly realised both in China and abroad. Speaking at an electoral meeting on March 10, 1967, Leonid Brezhnev said that the "legend about the 'proletarian cultural revolution' is merely a crude camouflage for a policy alien to Marxism-Leninism", that "it looks more like suppression of the socialist revolution" and a "reactionary military coup d'état."[1]

Faced by an extreme exacerbation of the internal political crisis, the masterminds of the "cultural revolution" again attempted to improve their positions by stepping up the policy of anti-Sovietism. They sought by further fomenting anti-Soviet hysteria to distract the Chinese people's attention from the formidable internal problems, to stir up nationalism in China, and to consolidate warring factions on its basis. The ultimate aim of this policy was to stabilise the situation, to give a respite to the ruling elite, enabling it to wipe out the last pockets of opposition and move onwards towards their cherished goals.

Peking leaders were no longer capable of fomenting anti-Soviet sentiments in China by means of propaganda alone. Malicious anti-Soviet propaganda repeating endlessly the same primitive fabrications about the CPSU and the Soviet Union ceased to impress the Chinese population. In view of this, the masterminds of the "cultural revolution" resorted to other means of stirring up anti-Soviet feelings in China. They organised a series of crude provocations in Soviet territory and against Soviet offices in China.

These provocations were started by a riot of Chinese students and Chinese Embassy officials in Moscow's Red Square on January 25, 1967. They impudently violated the rules of visiting the Lenin Mausoleum, kicked up a fight with Soviet citizens in Red Square. The Chinese hoodlums were openly instructed by the first secretary of the Chinese Embassy.

Presently it became clear that the provocation in Red Square was not a routine episode in the series of anti-Soviet acts of the CPC leadership. Already on the next day, Chou

---

[1] *Pravda*, March 11, 1967.

En-lai and Chen Yi, in a cable on behalf of Mao Tse-tung and Lin Piao, approved of the violations of law and order by Chinese students in Moscow and expressed their enthusiastic support for them. On January 28, the PRC Embassy in Moscow organised a so-called press conference on the issue of the "manhandling" of Chinese citizens in Red Square. At the conference, Chinese diplomats went out of their way to produce anti-Soviet lies addressed to capitalist pressmen. Soliciting the aid of imperialist propaganda in attacks against the CPSU and the Soviet Union, the sponsors of the conference even presented material evidence to the audience: Chinese students and Embassy officials made up to look like beaten victims.

This fraud, however, was so crude and primitive that it was not taken up even by Western anti-Sovietiers. Exposing it, member of the Central Committee of the Belgian Communist Party Claude Renard, who had witnessed the acts of hooliganism by Chinese students in Red Square, wrote in the *Drapeau rouge* weekly on February 3: ". . . I insist categorically that there is nothing in common between the incidents I saw as a chance witness and the 'information' later given by Chinese authorities. . . .

"On that day I had the impression that I witnessed incidents which, though regrettable, of course, were, nevertheless, of secondary importance. The way they were later presented by Peking is another evidence of the fact that the group now in control of the Communist Party of China uses the most unscrupulous means to maintain the nationalistic and anti-Soviet fanaticism it has made the pivot of its policy."[1]

The Maoists also used the Chinese crew of the Peking-Moscow express for all sorts of provocations in Soviet territory. Members of the crew attempted to smuggle anti-Soviet publications into the USSR, deliberately violated Soviet railway regulations.

All in all, in 1967 Chinese authorities organised 40 anti-Soviet provocations in the transport services, in particular, 17 on railways, 15 on airways, 8 on seagoing and river ships.

---

[1] *Pravda,* February 5, 1967.

In this connection, the USSR Ministry of Foreign Affairs and corresponding Soviet government departments made 18 protests to Chinese authorities.

In China herself anti-Soviet actions were carried out even more brazenly.

The riot of Chinese citizens in Moscow's Red Square on January 25, 1967, was a signal for organising new outrages in front of the Soviet Embassy in Peking. They had been planned and prepared in advance and began already on the next day, January 26.

This time, the anti-Soviet demonstrations around the Embassy assumed a particularly wide scale and malicious character. They continued round the clock for almost a fortnight. Soviet citizens on the Embassy grounds were literally tortured by incessant noise: loudspeakers installed round the Embassy kept on bellowing day and night. From January 26 to February 13 no Soviet newspapers or magazines were delivered to the Embassy. Chinese personnel left the Embassy, declaring that they went on strike. When they were informed that the Embassy no longer needed their services, they attempted to force their way back to their working places. On February 3, they broke into the Embassy's consular department and demanded their reinstatement in an ultimatum form. For almost 24 hours they forcibly kept the chief of the consular department in his office, threatening him with physical violence.

On January 29, the USSR Ministry of Foreign Affairs lodged a resolute protest against the anti-Soviet riots in front of the Soviet Embassy and on behalf of the Soviet Government demanded that the Embassy be safeguarded against hostile demonstrations interfering with its normal activities and threatening the security of its personnel.

However, the riots in front of the Soviet Embassy did not cease. In view of this, the Soviet Government decided to recall from Peking the families of officials of the Soviet Embassy, the Trade Delegation, the Office of the Economic Counsellor, and the TASS office.

On February 2, the Soviet Premier Alexei Kosygin, in a letter to Premier Chou En-lai, raised the question of security of the families of Soviet officials on their way home from Peking.

The PRC leadership failed to secure normal conditions for the departure of Soviet citizens. On the contrary, with the connivance and encouragement of Chinese authorities, the departure of Soviet women and children from Peking took place in a situation of brutal violence and abuse, infringement of the basic standards of international law and morality.

On February 5, when the Soviet citizens leaving for home and workers of the Soviet Embassy and the Embassies of other socialist countries in the PRC arrived at Peking airport they were surrounded by a crowd of hungweipings and tsaophans. Interspersing anti-Soviet slogans and cynical curses with chants of quotations from works of Mao Tse-tung, the rampant hoodlums terrorised the defenceless people during eight hours. The outrages continued when they were boarding the plane. Hungweipings lining both sides of their way hit children and women in the face, in the legs, tugged them by the hair.

Similar scenes were repeated during the departure of the next groups of Soviet citizens.

Describing the departure from China of the families of Soviet workers, the Italian newspaper *La Stampa* reported that the outrageous, unprecedented acts of hooliganism of the Red Guards against the Soviet Union definitely went beyond all limits. They appear as absolutely intolerable to all foreigners living in Peking. One cannot escape the impression that the Mao Tse-tung Government wants to force the USSR to break off also its official relations with China and at the same time seeks to foment fanatical hatred of the Soviet Union in the country. The newspaper noted that the Soviet citizens had demonstrated an exemplary presence of mind and dignity amidst this disorderly howling mob ready to commit any outrage. Women and men, small babies in their arms, stood with their heads proudly raised amidst the roaring crowd.

The Maoists' anti-Soviet provocations were sternly condemned by the Communist and Workers' parties.

The fraternal parties unanimously noted that the anti-Soviet actions of CPC leaders served the interests of imperialism. On February 27, 1967, the newspaper of the Argentinean Communist Party, *Nuestra Palabra*, wrote: "...Mao is resolved to show to the whole world that nobody is more anti-Soviet, anti-Marxist and anti-Leninist than he is, and has succeeded in doing so. Yankee imperialism must be thankful to him in the supreme degree: naturally, it is not accidental that the yankees have undertaken their new bombing raids over Vietnam precisely at the height of an all-out anti-Soviet campaign by Chinese leaders. The aggressive anti-Sovietism of the clique in question is a great gift to the imperialist aggressors."

In addition, during the "cultural revolution" Chinese authorities organised numerous hostile acts against the missions of other socialist countries in the PRC. On April 29, 1966, the wife of the first secretary of the GDR Embassy in China was attacked and seriously wounded. On August 28, 1966, the GDR military attaches in China and the DRV, their wives and children were assaulted and battered. Hungweipings also attacked a Polish Press Agency correspondent in the PRC. Violent demonstrations were also held in front of the Embassies of Bulgaria and Hungary in the days when the fraternal parties of these countries met in congress (November and December, 1966).

During the riots in front of the Soviet Embassy in Peking in January and February 1967, as well as during the departure of the families of Soviet Embassy officials from China, Chinese authorities committed hostile acts against Embassy officials of Bulgaria, Hungary, the GDR, Mongolia, Poland, Czechoslovakia, the Korean People's Democratic Republic. On January 26, 1967, hungweipings attacked two Czechoslovak diplomats and damaged a vehicle of the Czechoslovak Embassy. On February 5, groups of young fanatics perpetrated acts of violence against the Polish Ambassador in China and Polish Embassy officials who accompanied him while Chinese police looked on. The crowd held the Polish diplomats for several hours, cursing them in foul language, while the Ambassador's car carrying the Polish state flag was smeared with paint and glued over with posters bearing abusive inscriptions. On the same day, the Ambassadors of Mongolia, the GDR, Hungary, Bulgaria, Czechoslovakia were subjected to crude insults. Hungweipings attempted to overturn the car of the Bulgarian deputy trade counsellor carrying his family and threatened to shoot them.

On August 9, 1967, a heinous provocation was committed against Mongolian representatives in Peking. A group of hungweipings overturned the car of the Mongolian Ambassador in China and set it on fire. The driver, a Mongolian citizen, was roughly manhandled and arrested. On the same day, a crowd of hoodlums broke into the Embassy of the Mongolian People's Republic and committed outrages there.

The line towards aggravating Sino-Soviet relations to a maximum was not limited to organising outrages in front of the Soviet Embassy in Peking. In 1967 Chinese authorities committed provocations against Soviet representatives in China literally times out of number. An especially heinous provocation was perpetrated against the Soviet motorship *Svirsk* in the port of Dairen in August 1967.

All in all, about 80 crude outrages were committed in China against the Soviet Embassy, other Soviet offices, Soviet personnel and members of their families on the instigation and direct orders of the ruling clique in 1967.

The total number of large-scale anti-Soviet provocations perpetrated in 1967 was in excess of 200. The scope of this criminal activity can be illustrated by the fact that over 90 protests and other statements were sent to the Chinese authorities in one year.

The stepped-up provocative activities of Peking leaders were also expressed in the more frequent and widened Chinese violations of the Sino-Soviet border. All Chinese violations of the border without exception had been planned and prepared in advance after a uniform pattern. Here is an example in point. Early in February 1967 a lorry packed by Chinese drove onto a Soviet island on the river Ussuri. Soviet border guards ordered the trespassers to leave Soviet territory. The latter, however, many of them drunk, armed themselves with sticks and iron bars and attempted to fight the border guards. Half an hour later, new groups of Chinese in fur coats covering military uniforms emerged from concealment on the Chinese bank. The Chinese shouted curses at Soviet border guards, tried to drive them back and move into the depth of Soviet territory swinging iron bars, axes, and poles. Simultaneously they battered one of their own men, placed him on a stretcher, and a photographer providently included in their group took pictures of this "victim of atrocities" of Soviet border guards.

The anti-Soviet line of Peking leaders was expressed with striking clarity also in the days of celebrating the 50th anniversary of the Great October Revolution. This jubilee, which was marked by all revolutionary forces as an epoch-making event was exploited by Peking leaders for stepping up their wanton anti-Soviet campaign. In those days, *Jenmin jihpao*, which had become a mouthpiece of the "cultural revolution", regularly set aside full pages for slanderous attacks on the Communist Party of the Soviet Union, its domestic and foreign policies, attempted to denigrate all the accomplishments of the Soviet people during the heroic fifty years of their history. Fearing an improvement in Sino-Soviet relations, the Peking ruling clique rudely refused to send a PRC delegation to Moscow to attend the celebration of the 50th anniversary of the October Revolution. By this it demonstrated again that it had nothing in common with the Chinese working people who are vitally interested in strengthening friendship and co-operation with the Soviet people.

However, the masterminds of the "cultural revolution" were unable to quench the people's feelings of friendship for the Soviet people, who had carried out the October Revolution. This was strikingly, demonstrated by numerous letters Chinese working people, bypassing all the obstacles put up by Kang Sheng's censors, sent to our party, their Soviet brothers during the anniversary days.

"We Chinese Communists," said a letter from a group of CPC members sent from Kwangchow, "with boundless joy and enthusiasm convey our greetings, our most sincere congratulations and best wishes to the great Communist Party of the Soviet Union, the Soviet Government and the heroic Soviet people. The October Revolution showed the proletariat, the working people and the oppressed nations the way to liberation. The Soviet Union's experience over the past fifty years, the tremendous successes of its home and foreign policies have proved that the CPSU correctly and scientifically applies Marxist-Leninist theory to raise and solve these problems. This is a model for Communists, for internationalists, which has been approved of by all Communists and all progressive mankind and has instilled revolutionary confidence in the working people of the whole world. . . ."[1]

The CPSU Central Committee received a stirring letter from a group of Chinese intellectuals which said in particular: "Neither today nor in the future, under no circumstances will it be possible to obliterate from the minds of the Chinese people the image of the Soviet Union as the stronghold of world communism, a friend of the Chinese people. In today's intolerable situation, the Chinese people are unable to express their true attitude to their Soviet friends but we beg you to believe that the heart of the Chinese people belongs to you forever."

In connection with the celebration of the 50th anniversary of the Great October Socialist Revolution the CPSU reaffirmed the immutability of its internationalist policy towards China.

In his report dedicated to the 50th anniversary of the October Revolution, Leonid Brezhnev stated: "We believe that the current developments in China are a historically transient stage in her development. We are confident that the cause of socialism will win in the People's Republic of China despite all difficulties."

4. THE 12th PLENARY MEETING
OF THE CPC CENTRAL COMMITTEE.
A NEW STAGE IN THE POLICY LINE OF PEKING LEADERS

In 1968, the anti-Soviet policy of the masterminds of the "cultural revolution" was further developed.

Propaganda hostile to the CPSU and the Soviet Union assumed an increasingly wide scale in China. During 1968, *Jenmin jihpao* alone published more than 600 lengthy articles containing wanton slanderous attacks on the CPSU and the Soviet Union.

In late March and early April 1968, Chinese authorities perpetrated a crude provocation against the Soviet tanker *Komsomolets Ukrainy* which had arrived in the port of Wampu (near Canton) with a cargo of goods intended for the embattled Vietnam.

---

[1] *Pravda*, November 24, 1967.

On the night of April 3, an armed Chinese party boarded the ship, intending to seize the ship documents, arrest the captain and the mate. The attackers tore off cabin doors, damaged bulkheads, broke hatches in the stern structure, cut off the aerial and the through telephone line, and smashed the ship radio. They wrested the arms of Soviet seamen and beat them up. Eleven crew members sustained severe bodily injuries. The ship master was led away and thrown into jail. During this outrageous provocation the tanker crew displayed courage and reserve. In protest against the captain's arrest the crew declared a hunger strike.

On March 31 and April 3, the Soviet Government sent strongly worded protests to the PRC Government, demanding that measures be taken to ensure the release and safety of all members of the crew and the lifting of the ban on the ship's departure from Wampu. The Soviet Government underscored that all the responsibility for the grave consequences of the acts of violence against the tanker and her crew rested with the PRC Government. As a result, the Chinese authorities were forced to release the captain of the Soviet ship on April 4 and permit her to leave port.

The anti-Soviet line of the Maoists created intolerable conditions for Soviet nationals living in China. Since the beginning of the "cultural revolution" they were openly subjected to crude violence and persecution. Their property was illegally seized, they were evicted from their homes, thrown out of jobs, expelled from educational institutions, forbidden to keep up correspondence with their relatives in the USSR and to apply to the Soviet Embassy. Many Soviet nationals were arrested, the Chinese authorities withholding from the Soviet Embassy information about such facts.

The hatred of the masterminds of the "cultural revolution" for the CPSU, which staunchly upheld the ideas of Marxism-Leninism, was expressed, in particular, in their abstaining from marking the 98th birthday of Lenin, the 150th birthday of Karl Marx, the 51st anniversary of the October Socialist Revolution. Anti-Sovietism is one of the facts testifying to the Peking leaders' break with Marxism-Leninism.

At the height of the offensive of the internal and foreign counter-revolution in Czechoslovakia in August 1968, Peking landed in one camp with the West German revanchists and other reactionaries, with Right-wing rivisionists. Simultaneously, the Maoists launched a campaign of malicious slander in connection with the measures of the five fraternal countries to help the Czechoslovak people defend socialism in their country. Peking leaders began vehement propaganda of the thesis that the socialist camp as such no longer existed and, consequently, there could be no question of any common interests of the socialist community.

Proceeding from this position the Maoists intensified their attacks against the collective organisations of the socialist countries in an effort to destroy them. They circulated slanderous fabrications to the effect that the Warsaw Treaty and the CMEA, which guarantee the security and successful development of the socialist states, were allegedly used for the "restoration of capitalism in the countries of Eastern Europe". In a message to Enver Hoxha of September 17, 1968, Mao Tse-tung openly called for the struggle against the Warsaw Treaty and the Council for Mutual Economic Assistance. In the same message he announced that Peking was entering a "new historical period of struggle" against the CPSU and the Soviet Union.

The Peking ruling clique did not desist from their attempts to implant in the minds of the Chinese people the idea of possible armed conflicts between the USSR and the PRC. Chinese leaders began to take a direct part in fanning the anti-Soviet hysteria. On October 30, 1968, Premier Chou En-lai declared at a state reception that anything, including an attack on China could be expected from the Soviet Union.

The masterminds of the "cultural revolution" exerted themselves to get approval for their anti-Soviet policy at the 12th plenary meeting of the CPC Central Committee held in October 1968.

The 12th plenary meeting of the CPC Central Committee ushered in a new stage in the development of the political situation in China. It was not fortuitous that the Maoists, who had routed the Communist Party and done everything they could to discredit it, turned their minds to the CPC and even decided to call a plenary meeting of its Central Committee. They were compelled to do this by the extremely dangerous situation they had met with in the course of the "cultural revolution".

The masterminds of the "cultural revolution" soon realised their inability to rule the country during a long period without a mass political party. The CPC leadership had failed to organise an efficient state administration, to set up a stable system of new government with the aid of the army, hungweipings and tsaophans. At the same time, the ruling clique was afraid of remaining alone, face to face with the army, whose role had sharply increased. The Peking leaders who had usurped power were also worried by the continuing discontent among the Party cadres and millions of rank-and-file Communists. A resumption of the activities of the CPC was also necessary to perpetuate the results of the "cultural revolution" and to use the Party's name to cover up the crying injustices and lawlessness accompanying the suppression of its opponents.

Peking leaders also needed the Party's name for considerations issuing from the tasks of their divisive activities in the international communist movement. For all their propaganda bravado, Chinese leaders feared the consequences of the denunciation and criticism of their anti-party activities by the international communist movement. Since they persisted in their complete denial of the Party's role, they found it difficult to join into an independent movement various pro-Peking and renegade groups which had landed in an extremely absurd situation as a result of the routing of the CPC.

Under the pressure of all these circumstances, the Chinese ruling clique, already since the end of 1967, started broad activities to set up a Maoist party which would inherit the prestige of the Communist Party of China and be an obedient tool of the anti-popular policy of "cultural revolution". For the sake of camouflage, this work was carried out under the slogan of "streamlining and reorganising" the party, although it was openly declared in effect that the goal was to establish a qualitatively new political organisation.

The composition of the Communist Party was to be changed essentially. "Streamlining and reorganisation" were accompanied by a massive purge of the Party, a check upon the loyalty of every former member of the CPC, expulsion of all those who had displayed any hesitations or doubts about the current leadership of the PRC and its policy, had failed to take an active part in the "cultural revolution", had not proved their allegiance to anti-Sovietism. Simultaneously, measures were taken to infuse the party with "fresh blood" from among the most zealous Maoists. The directives on "streamlining" the Party contained instructions for giving priority in admission to the Party to activists from among hungweipings and tsaophans.

The 12th plenary meeting of the CPC Central Committee was held in a situation of complete disregard for the CPC Charter and the basic standards of party life. Suffice it to say that by the time of calling the plenary meeting of the 173 members and alternate members of the CPC Central Committee more than 130 had been discredited and subjected to repression. The damage caused to the Central Committee was so tangible, and the Maoists' demand for obedient executors of their line so acute that people who were not members of the Central Committee and even of the Party were invited to take part in the plenary meeting for the sake of a quorum.

All the documents of the 12th plenary meeting were pervaded with fierce anti-Sovietism. They officially confirmed the line of waging an open struggle against the CPSU and the Soviet Union. The communique of the plenary meeting and the draft of the new CPC Charter approved by it demonstrated that the Chinese ruling clique had made their anti-socialist, anti-Soviet policy the basis for the long-term home and foreign policy programme of the PRC.

5. ARMED PROVOCATIONS OF CHINESE AUTHORITIES ON THE SOVIET BORDER IN MARCH 1969

Implementing the continuous escalation of anti-Sovietism, Peking leaders organised an armed provocation on the Sino-Soviet border on the river Ussuri in March 1969.

On the night of March 2, a specially trained Chinese army unit of about 300 officers and men crossed the Soviet border and invaded Damansky island. On the morning of March 2 it was joined by another party of 30 armed soldiers. Reinforcements and weapons, including an anti-tank gun battery, mortars, grenade launchers and large-calibre machine-guns had been concentrated on the Chinese bank in advance.

When Soviet border guards approached the Chinese trespassers to order them to leave Soviet territory, as repeatedly done before, the Chinese soldiers opened fire without warning and mowed down the Soviet border guards at pointblank range. Simultaneously another group of Soviet border guards was fired on from an ambush on the island and from the Chinese bank.

The Soviet border guards assumed a combat order and jointly with reinforcements from a neighbouring frontier post courageously repelled the attack and expelled the trespassers from Soviet territory.

The armed provocation undertaken by the PRC had been planned and thoroughly prepared in advance. Abandoned Chinese firearms and military equipment, field telephones, wire lines leading to Chinese territory, mortar shell stabilisers, splinters of shells and grenades, etc., were found at the site of the battle. As a result of the bandit attack organised by Chinese authorities 31 Soviet border guards were killed and 14 wounded.

On March 14 a group of armed Chinese soldiers made another attempt to infiltrate Soviet territory. On the next day, a large Chinese unit supported by artillery and mortar fire from the Chinese bank attacked Soviet border guards. The aggressors were driven back from the island.

The armed provocation on the Sino-Soviet border had been undoubtedly planned as a multi-purpose action. It was used by the masterminds of the "cultural revolution" to step up nationalistic and chauvinistic hysteria in the PRC in order to deal new blows to their opponents and reinforce their rule.

It was not accidental that the armed conflict on the Sino-Soviet border was organised in the period of completing preparations for the Ninth Congress of the CPC. By fanning anti-Soviet hysteria and chauvinistic passions the Maoists sought to secure a situation where they could get approval by the Congress for their anti-Soviet great-power line as the general line of Chinese foreign policy.

The stepping up of anti-Soviet hysteria in China and attempts to use the armed provocation on the Sino-Soviet border to discredit the USSR on the international scene also. served the tasks of intensifying the subversive activities of the Maoists against the socialist community and the world communist movement. One of the immediate aims of Peking leaders was to hamper and frustrate the efforts to call an international meeting of representatives of Communist and Workers' parties, preparations for which had entered their final stage.

At the same time, the armed provocations of Chinese authorities along the border with the Soviet Union created favourable conditions for Peking's new moves in its unprincipled political flirtation with imperialist states. Organising criminal attacks on the Sino-Soviet border, the Chinese ruling clique made advances, as it were, to the extreme imperialist reaction and showed its willingness to collaborate with it.

The provocation on the Sino-Soviet border was an important part of the Maoists' effort to speed up a radical revision of the foreign and home policies of China and to turn her, in fact, into a force openly hostile to the socialist countries.

The armed provocations of Chinese authorities on the Sino-Soviet border were indignantly condemned by the entire Soviet people. Mass meetings of protest swept the length and breadth of the Soviet Union. The people stigmatised the provocateurs, expressed readiness to give a crushing rebuff to their encroachments on the sacred borders of our homeland.

The working people of Bulgaria, Poland, Hungary, the GDR, and other socialist countries declared their solidarity with the Soviet people.

The Chinese provocations played into the hands of international imperialism, and evoked profound concern of the Communists and progressive forces all over the world. The Marxist-Leninist Communist and Workers' parties, progressive world public opinion strongly denounced them.

Determined, as it was, to repulse any armed provocation by Chinese authorities, the Soviet Union, nevertheless, remained loyal to its unflinching line towards a normalisation of relations with the PRC, on the Sino-Soviet border issues in particular. This line was strikingly demonstrated in the Soviet Government's statement of March 29, 1969.

The statement proved conclusively the groundlessness of Chinese leaders' claims to Soviet territory supported by excursions into history and references to the allegedly unequal character of the treaties defining the present Sino-Soviet border.

In their attempts to justify their territorial claims to the Soviet Union Peking leaders went to the length of declaring themselves heirs to Genghis Khan, describing him as a Chinese emperor. Such chauvinistic falsifications of history had been ridiculed in his time by Lu Hsin. In 1934, he wrote: "At twenty I heard that when 'our' Genghis Khan conquered Europe, it was 'our' golden age. Only at 25 did I learn that in reality during our so-called 'golden age' the Mongols conquered China and we became slaves. In August this year I thumbed through the pages of three books on the history of Mongolia to specify some historical facts and only then did I learn that before conquering the whole of China, the Mongols had conquered 'Rus', invaded Hungary and Austria. At that time, Genghis Khan was not yet our khan. Indeed, the Russians had been enslaved before us, so it was for them to say: 'When our Genghis Khan conquered China, our golden age began.' "[1]

It is in place to recall another statement by the great Chinese writer, a revolutionary and an internationalist, which was addressed to the imperialists, and sounds like a direct accusation of the provocateurs who organised bandit attacks on Soviet border guards. In 1932, in an article entitled "We Will Not Be Taken In Again", Lu Hsin wrote: "We are against an attack on the Soviet Union. We seek to destroy the dark forces attacking it whatever sweet speeches they may make, whatever mask of justice they may put on. This is our only path in life and no other!"

After proclaiming the PRC the Chinese Government repeatedly reaffirmed its commitment to respect Soviet state sovereignty and territorial integrity as laid down in the Sino-Soviet Treaty of Friendship, Alliance and Mutual Assistance signed in February 1950. Article 5 of the Treaty provides for observance of the principles of mutual respect for state sovereignty and territorial integrity. The same commitment is contained in the joint Sino-Soviet government

---

[1] Lu Hsin, *Collected Works*, Vol. 6, Peking, p. 109.

declaration of October 12, 1954 and in the joint Sino-Soviet statement of January 18, 1957.

As noted above, in the early fifties, at China's request the Soviet Union handed over to her complete sets of topographical maps indicating the border line in accordance with Russo-Chinese treaties. At that time, the Chinese authorities made no comments on the border line indicated on the maps, and it was abided by in practice.

After the conclusion of the Sino-Soviet Treaty of Friendship, Alliance and Mutual Assistance the two sides organised joint exploration and use of the rivers Amur and Ussuri. The population of both countries maintained friendly relations, developed trade, cultural and other exchanges. In 1951, a Sino-Soviet agreement was signed on the rules of shipping on the rivers Amur, Ussuri, Argun, Sungari and Lake Hanka and on the provision of navigation facilities on these waterways. In 1956, a Sino-Soviet agreement was concluded on the joint comprehensive use and exploration of the river water resources of the Amur basin.

Soviet and Chinese border guards maintained friendly co-operation, resolving disputed problems in a businesslike and good-neighbourly spirit. No conflicts or misunderstandings were in evidence all along the border. Such a situation had existed until the PRC leadership entered upon the path of exacerbating Sino-Soviet relations.

It was not accidental that Chinese leaders opposed the very principle of a peaceful settlement of border disputes. They came out with rude attacks on the Soviet Government's proposal of December 1963 for signing an international agreement on the renunciation by states of the use of force in settling territorial disputes and border issues. It is indicative that Chinese leaders were infuriated by the efforts of the Soviet Union and other countries towards a peaceful settlement of the armed conflict between India and Pakistan which broke out in 1965. The Tashkent Declaration which put an end to this conflict became an object of slander in Peking. Down to the present time Chinese leaders ignore India's initiatives in proposing an adjustment of the Indo-Chinese border dispute.

By contrast, the Soviet Government after the very first Sino-Soviet border incidents expressed its willingness to reach a settlement by means of bilateral consultations. This position was reaffirmed in the Soviet Government's statement of March 29, 1969[1].

In its statement on March 29, the Soviet Government again proposed a resumption in the near future of consultations on border issues started in Peking in 1964. Guided by its invariable desire to ensure lasting peace and security, to develop friendship and co-operation with the Chinese people, the Soviet Government emphasised the need to take practical measures without delay to normalise the situation on the Sino-Soviet border. It called on the PRC Government to abstain from any actions along the border likely to cause complications, to adjust differences arising in a quiet atmosphere.

On April 11, 1969, the USSR Ministry of Foreign Affairs, in a note to the PRC Ministry of Foreign Affairs, proposed a resumption of consultations between plenipotentiary representatives of the Soviet and Chinese governments and expressed its readiness to begin them in Moscow on April 15, 1969 or at any other time in the near future convenient for the Chinese side.

On April 14, 1969, in response to the note of the USSR Ministry of Foreign Affairs of April 11, the Chinese side declared that the Soviet proposals concerning adjustment of the situation on the border were under examination and would be answered in due time. However, both the practical actions of Chinese authorities directly on the border and the general political line of the Chinese leadership, far from losing their anti-Soviet orientation assumed an increasingly hostile character.

6. ANTI-SOVIETISM, A MAJOR COMPONENT OF THE POLITICAL PROGRAMME OF THE 9th CPC CONGRESS

The armed provocations on the Sino-Soviet border were a sort of a prelude to the 9th Congress of the CPC held in Peking between April 1 and 24, 1969. It assembled in a situation of further aggravation of the internal political crisis

---

[1] *Pravda,* March 30, 1969.

in the country, as well as intensified factional strife within the Maoist camp itself. To distract the Chinese people's attention from setbacks in China's home and foreign policies, the CPC ruling clique decided to hold the congress in an atmosphere of chauvinistic and anti-Soviet hysteria.

The Ninth Congress took place in a situation of complicated factional struggle; on the whole, however, the Maoists succeeded in imposing their line upon it.

The Congress summed up the results of the "cultural revolution" and outlined the policy of the Chinese leadership for the coming few years.

In the Party Charter, the Ninth Congress of the CPC gave its official endorsement to the cult of Mao Tse-tung, and laid down principles which were to secure the triumph of "Mao's ideas" for a long period ahead. The Charter says that Mao Tse-tung is the "leader of the Party". As the basic standard of party life, the Ninth Congress put forward devotion to Mao Tse-tung.

The directives of the Ninth Congress on the issues of China's internal development were aimed at making her a militarist bureaucratic state geared to implementing an adventurist, great-power policy on the international scene. The Congress did not even attempt to outline a positive programme of economic and social development, of improvement of the people's standards of life. Instead, it put forward the task of carrying on a continuous revolution, preparing for war, preparing for starvation. The Peking ruling clique absolved itself in advance from the responsibility for a worsening of the living standards of the working people, for the collapse of the national economy, for adventures in foreign policy.

The report to the Congress grossly distorted the picture of modern world development: the imperialist states and all the socialist countries opposed to the Peking line were put on the same footing. The latter were proclaimed "revisionist" or "social-imperialist" and placed in the category of forces hostile to revolution. This differentiation was based not on a class analysis but merely on the attitude of this or that country to the policy of Peking leaders. The Congress declared, in effect, that the socialist countries were China's enemy No. 1.

Anti-Sovietism was put at the basis of the foreign policy line mapped out by the Ninth Congress of the CPC. The new Charter endorsed it as the Party's official policy. The report to the Congress emphasised that at present a new "historical" period of struggle against our party and country began, outlined the task of setting up an international anti-Soviet front, reaffirmed territorial claims to the Soviet Union, again made references to "unequal treaties", seizures of Chinese territory, presented a false picture of Sino-Soviet border incidents. The report attempted to distort the meaning of Soviet government statements in the 1920s concerning the Sino-Soviet border and alleged that the Soviet Union had not fulfilled its promise to return everything that "was seized from China" by the tsarist government.

Speakers at the Ninth Congress of the CPC crudely slandered Soviet realities and called for open interference in the internal affairs of the Soviet Union and the CPSU.

The policy in the field of Sino-Soviet relations formulated in the report fully contradicted the Sino-Soviet treaty of 1950. The Peking leadership showed no signs of interest in co-operating with the Soviet Union or in normalising Sino-Soviet relations. The Congress failed to advance a single constructive proposal to this effect.

7. DETERMINED OPPOSITION
TO THE DIVISIVE, ANTI-SOVIET LINE OF PEKING
AT THE INTERNATIONAL MEETING
OF FRATERNAL PARTIES

The anti-Soviet line of Peking leaders is a major component of their struggle against all the revolutionary forces of today. For a long time, the Maoists sought to present the matter in such a way that they had differences only with the CPSU. By this trick they attempted to camouflage the fact that the position of the Peking leaders was hostile to the entire world revolutionary movement. In time, however, it became obvious that the Maoists were waging a struggle against all the Communist parties. As far back as 1967, in an article on the meeting of European Communist and Workers' parties at Karlovy Vary, the Maoists openly described as their implacable enemies and "cliques" such biggest contingents of the world communist movement as the Communist and Workers' parties of Hungary, the German Democratic Republic, Poland, Bulgaria, Italy, France, Britain, Spain, Finland, and other countries. At the Ninth Congress of the CPC the Maoists went as far as to declare the socialist community and the world communist movement "non-existent" at all. They came out against the Warsaw Treaty, the impregnable shield and guarantee of the security of the socialist countries, the bulwark of peace in Europe; against the Council of Mutual Economic Assistance which has become a major instrument of mutually advantageous co-operation between the fraternal nations. Peking leaders have long been organising and financing factional, divisive activities in the communist movement, direct provocations against the lawful leadership of the Marxist-Leninist parties, and implanting large and small groups of their supporters.

The Peking leaders' policy of struggle against the socialist community and the world communist movement, their anti-Soviet divisive activities were strongly condemned at the Moscow Meeting of Communist and Workers' Parties in June 1969.

In the process of preparations for the meeting, the CPSU and other parties made persistent efforts to draw the Communist Party of China into this work. The CPC Central Committee was sent invitations to attend all conferences held in preparation for the meeting; it was informed in advance of the course of preparations for the meeting, and was offered an opportunity to examine all documents to be discussed at the world forum of Communists.

Peking leaders, however, stubbornly clung to their position of hostility to the international meeting of Communist and Workers' parties and rudely refused to attend it. Thereby they again demonstrated their hostility to the ideas of unity of all Communists, all revolutionary forces in the struggle against imperialism.

The calling of the meeting evoked extreme irritation in Peking, because this fact alone showed the futility of the Maoists' designs to isolate the CPSU and other parties which staunchly and consistently upheld their Marxist-Leninist principles. The meeting forcefully confirmed the key trend of

development of the world communist movement—the
strengthening of the unity and cohesion of its ranks.

The meeting adopted the Main Document, "Tasks at the
Present Stage of the Struggle Against Imperialism and United
Action of the Communist and Workers' Parties, and All Anti-
Imperialist Forces". It contained a profound and comprehensive analysis of the world situation, which fully disproved
the distorted views of this situation presented in the report to
the Ninth Congress of the CPC. None of the 75 Communist
parties which took part in the meeting supported at least
some of the ideas the Peking leaders sought to impose on the
revolutionary forces.

The meeting unanimously adopted an address on the occasion of the Lenin birth centenary. This strikingly demonstrated the loyalty of the Communist and Workers' parties
to Marxism-Leninism, their determination to continue the
struggle under the banner of scientific communism, their ir-
reconcilability towards attempts to substitute the "ideas of
Mao Tse-tung" for Marxism-Leninism.

Peking propaganda raised hue and cry about the meeting
in a helpless effort to distort its objectives and tasks, to belit-
tle the historical significance and interfere with the circulation of its documents. Peking leaders described the slogan
of unity of action against imperialism proclaimed by the
Marxist-Leninist parties as a "threadbare flag" and the idea
of alliance between the international working class and the
peasantry as a "stale commodity".

No matter how Peking leaders rant and rave it remains a
fact that the anti-Marxist platform and the subversive divisive policy of the CPC, its anti-Soviet line in particular, were
strongly condemned at the international forum of Communists.

Speakers from the fraternal parties directly linked the importance of criticism and exposure of Maoism with the task
of strengthening the unity of the world communist movement.

The meeting listened with great attention to the speech
of the leader of the Soviet delegation, the General Secretary
of the CPSU Central Committee, Leonid Brezhnev, who gave
a profound and convincing analysis of the anti-Leninist principles of the Maoist leaders, their divisive line and great-
power foreign policy.

The leader of the Soviet delegation dwelt in detail on the principled stand of the CPSU and the Soviet Government in relation to China, a stand based on long-range prospects and an awareness of coincidence of the vital interests of the Soviet and Chinese peoples.

The meeting acknowledged the betrayal of Marxism-Leninism by the present Chinese leaders, the thorough hostility of Maoism to Marxist-Leninist theory, emphasised the extremely disastrous character of the Chinese leaders' line of struggle against the socialist community, reported numerous facts of crude interference by CPC leaders and their stooges in other countries in the internal affairs of the fraternal parties.

The subversive divisive activities of Peking leaders and their agents in the national liberation movement were also exposed to stern condemnation in the statements made at the meeting. Speakers said, in particular, that these activities boiled down to direct complicity with imperialism in its struggle against the revolutionary forces.

The Maoists' anti-Marxist thesis of the inevitability of a new world war was subjected to scathing criticism. Acceptance of this thesis, speakers emphasised, would be tantamount to giving up the struggle for securing in the interests of all the peoples the most favourable conditions for a settlement of the main conflict of our epoch—the conflict between socialism and capitalism, to distrusting the strength of the socialist system, the international working class, and the national liberation movement. Speakers at the meeting also proved conclusively the untenability of the Maoists' allegations to the effect that there were only two alternatives in the question of the possibility of a world war: either the war will lead to a revolution or the revolution will prevent a war.

The meeting stigmatised the anti-Soviet policy of Chinese leaders as direct support for imperialism, as open treason to the principles of Marxism-Leninism and proletarian internationalism. "The anti-Soviet line imposed by the Mao Tse-tung group on the Chinese People's Republic," the meeting indicated, "denudes the anti-imperialist declarations of Chinese leaders of all content. For one cannot fight against US imperialism and simultaneously direct blows against the

Soviet Union, the main bastion of the anti-imperialist front. The most high-sounding anti-American slogans are empty words if accompanied by a hate campaign against the Soviet Union."[1]

The armed provocations of Chinese authorities on the Sino-Soviet border evoked profound indignation among participants in the meeting.

The plenary meeting of the CPSU Central Committee held late in June 1969, on hearing and discussing Leonid Brezhnev's report "On the Results of the International Meeting of the Communist and Workers' Parties", declared that the CPSU would wage uncompromising struggle against the anti-Leninist principles of the present leaders of China, against their divisive policy and great-power nationalistic line, that it would do everything necessary to protect the interests of the Soviet people, builders of communism, against any encroachments.

At the same time, the resolution of the plenary meeting emphasised that the vital interests of the Soviet and Chinese peoples coincided, that the CPSU would continue its efforts to preserve and encourage friendly feelings, which the Soviet people had for the Chinese people, and which the Chinese people undoubtedly had for the Soviet Union and other socialist countries.

8. THE MEETING BETWEEN
THE SOVIET AND CHINESE PREMIERS IN SEPTEMBER 1969

Early in July 1969, a session of the USSR Supreme Soviet discussed the international situation and Soviet foreign policy.

It was reaffirmed at the session that the policy of the Soviet state in relation to China had invariably been based on the line towards the restoration and development of Sino-Soviet friendship. It was also declared that the Soviet side was ready to have talks with Chinese leaders without any preliminary conditions on a wide range of problems of mutual interest to facilitate progress in this direction.

---

[1] *International Meeting of Communist and Workers' Parties, Moscow 1969,* Prague, 1969, p. 103.

Peking leaders, however, stubbornly ignored the Soviet proposals for normalising Sino-Soviet relations. What is more, on July 8, 1969, they made another effort to aggravate tensions on the Sino-Soviet border. On that day Chinese authorities organised an armed attack on Soviet river-ship crews, in which two Soviet citizens were killed.

The USSR Ministry of Foreign Affairs made a strong protest against this new provocation and demanded that the PRC Government punish those responsible and take measures to prevent a recurrence of such incidents. The note stressed that to safeguard its legitimate rights the Soviet side was compelled to take additional measures against Chinese violations of the Soviet state borders endangering the security and lives of Soviet citizens.

Late in July 1969 the Soviet Government proposed a Sino-Soviet meeting to discuss the key problems of Sino-Soviet inter-state relations, to exchange views on ways to ease tensions between the two countries, in particular, the question of trade, economic, scientific, technical and cultural exchanges.

The PRC State Council evaded an answer to this initiative. The extremist part of the Peking ruling clique, which seeks to perpetuate China's stand of irreconcilable hostility to the Soviet Union, continued its efforts to exacerbate relations with the Soviet Union, resorting to direct armed provocations on the border.

An obstacle in the way of implementing these plans was the meeting between the Soviet Premier Alexei Kosygin and the Premier of the PRC State Council, Chou En-lai. This meeting was held on a Soviet initiative in Peking on September 11, 1969, when Alexei Kosygin was on his way home from a visit to the Democratic Republic of Vietnam.

During the meeting, some problems of Sino-Soviet relations were discussed. The exchange of views was continued in official correspondence. The main result of the meeting was the resumption of talks on the border issues in Peking in 1969.

The Soviet Union attached crucial importance to the talks with the PRC on the border issues. On October 27, 1969, Leonid Brezhnev, speaking at a Soviet-Czechoslovak friendship meeting, stated: "There is no lack of goodwill on the

Soviet side. We stand for a settlement of border and other disputes between the USSR and the PRC on a stable and just basis, in a spirit of equality, mutual respect and consideration of the interests of the two countries. If the Chinese side also displays goodwill this will undoubtedly become possible."[1]

The Soviet side did everything necessary to create an atmosphere favourable to the progress of the talks: criticism of the policy of CPC leaders was ended in the press, and measures were taken to contribute as much as possible to normalising the situation on the Sino-Soviet border, to solving outstanding problems in a spirit of goodwill, through consultations. The Chinese side pursued the opposite line. Shortly before the talks were opened, on October 7 and 8, the PRC Government had published statements reiterating its earlier groundless allegations to the effect that the Russo-Chinese treaties defining the present border between the USSR and the PRC were unequal and attempting to blame the Soviet Union for the aggravated situation on the Sino-Soviet border. They slandered our party and country and said that the contradictions between China and the Soviet Union were irreconcilable contradictions of principle and that the struggle between them would continue for a long time.

When the talks were opened, anti-Soviet propaganda was whipped up in China. In the days when the delegations started discussions, anti-Soviet pamphlets in Chinese, Russian and other languages were put on sale in government bookshops. They contained vicious attacks on and territorial claims to the Soviet Union, deliberately distorted historical facts relating to the Sino-Soviet border, and alleged provocatively that the Soviet Union was hatching up plans of conquest of Chinese territory, etc.

Chinese cinema theatres resumed the showing of so-called newsreels exciting feelings of hostility and hatred towards the Soviet people. Anti-Soviet photographic displays were arranged in shop windows, in parks and other public places, and slogans were put up such as "We'll smash your heads, drain your blood and bury you". Such slogans were published even in official organs of the Chinese press.

---

[1] *Pravda*, October 28, 1969.

Since the autumn of 1969, a campaign of preparations for war was started in China. This campaign which was continually instigated by provocative warnings about the danger of attack on the PRC by the Soviet Union, spread literally throughout the country and pervaded its entire political and economic life. Preparations for war were proclaimed the cardinal goal of economic development in China. Mass-scale evacuation of industrial plants to the hinterland was started, reserves of foodstuffs, medicines and other supplies were being built up. The population of towns and rural areas was mobilised to build fortifications, bomb shelters and hideouts in the event of a state of siege. Air alarms were frequently called to simulate enemy air raids on China.

While creating an atmosphere of war hysteria in the country, the Maoists sought to prevent a slackening of anti-Soviet sentiments in connection with the Sino-Soviet talks on the border issues, to dash the hopes of the Chinese people for a normalisation of relations between our countries, to suppress the growing political strife, to rally as wide sections of the population as possible in the face of the imaginary Soviet threat, to justify the economic difficulties, to create an excuse for the continued military build-up. All this served in the final analysis to strengthen the bureaucratic dictatorship in China.

The spirit of brazen militarism advertised by Maoist propaganda, the attempts of Chinese leaders to place under arms almost the entire population of the country, the rabid campaign of hate against other peoples caused indignation of the world progressive public.

To justify its war preparations, Peking gave currency to the absurd fabrication that the PRC was allegedly under military pressure from the Soviet Union. Chinese propaganda intensively spread provocative lies about Soviet plans to attack China, about large-scale exercises of the Soviet Army. The situation on the Sino-Soviet border was deliberately misrepresented, allegations were made about Soviet troop concentrations there, etc.

On March 14, 1970, a TASS statement published in the Soviet Union gave the lie to these attempts to cast aspersions on Soviet policy towards China. "...Such fabrications," the statement said, "have absolutely no basis in fact. Anticommunist propaganda uses them to hamper the Sino-Soviet talks now in progress in Peking, to create the pretext for stepping up tensions in Sino-Soviet relations. The Soviet armed forces fulfil their routine duties and improve their military skill within the framework of ordinary plans and programmes, reinforcing the defences of the Soviet Union throughout its territory".

The TASS statement stressed that a desire to normalise Sino-Soviet relations, to develop co-operation, restore and strengthen friendship between the peoples of the two countries had invariably been the basis for the policy of the USSR and its government.

However, the campaign of "preparations for war", measures to implant the spirit of militarism, instigative anti-Soviet propaganda continued unabated in China. Statements about the "Soviet threat" to China of an obviously provocative character were used by Peking leaders for their unseemly purposes. They were nothing but attempts to bring pressure to bear on the USSR, to blackmail it with the threat of military force and to coerce the Soviet Union into concessions in the talks on the border issues. These attempts, however, were in vain.

9. SINO-SOVIET ECONOMIC RELATIONS IN 1967-1969

In the latter half of the 60s, the Chinese implemented measures which shut all the channels of China's economic and inter-state co-operation with the Soviet Union and the majority of other socialist countries.

On June 24, 1967, China announced her withdrawal as of January 1, 1968 from the agreement signed by the governments of the USSR, the PRC and the KPDR on July 3, 1956, on co-operation in saving human lives and rescuing ships and aircraft in distress at sea. This was the third multilateral agreement between the socialist countries from which the PRC withdrew.

In 1967, the PRC continued its sabotage of the multilateral agreements between socialist countries on international freight and passenger railway services, stepped up its splitting activities in the Committee of the Conference of Ministers of the Railway Co-operation Organisation in an effort to paralyse its work. The Chinese also took a stand against the

Organisation of Socialist Countries on Electrical and Postal Communications (multilateral agreement of 1957).

Ignoring two requests from the Soviet authorities, China forbade transit across Chinese territory of cargoes of foodstuffs and medicines for Soviet specialists in the DRV. On June 9, 1967, the Chinese officially cancelled the agreement on flights of Soviet specialists to the DRV over Chinese territory. Under the protocol for 1967 the turnover of Sino-Soviet trade was set at 228 million rubles, which was 58 million rubles less than the actual turnover in 1966. In fact, however, it amounted to only 96 million rubles, i.e., reduced almost to one third as compared with 1966. The Soviet Union dropped to 14th place in China's foreign trade.

China's trade with other socialist countries sharply diminished in 1967. As compared with 1966, the goods turnover between the PRC and the member-states of CMEA fell from 528 million rubles to 313 million.

In 1967, no plans of cultural and scientific exchanges and co-operation within the framework of friendship societies and tourist organisations were signed by the USSR and the PRC for the first time. Soviet authorities expressed their willingness to continue a delegation exchange within the framework of friendship societies, if Chinese authorities guaranteed safety to Soviet visitors. They also proposed that photographs, literature and other material dedicated to the 50th anniversary of the Great October Socialist Revolution be sent to China. All these proposals, however, were either declined or ignored.

A similar situation developed in the field of tourist exchange.

In 1968, no trade protocol was signed through the fault of the Chinese side for the first time after 1949, and trade between the Soviet Union and China was carried on on the basis of contracts for individual commodity items. The actual trade exchanges in 1968 diminished by 10 per cent from 1967, amounting to 86 million rubles.

In 1969, the Soviet Union made several proposals for a re-activation of Sino-Soviet economic ties, in particular for an expansion of trade in 1969, for an increase in the turnover of Sino-Soviet trade in 1970 by 150 per cent as compared with 1969, for a resumption of border trade.

The Chinese authorities ignored them all. In 1969, Sino-Soviet trade diminished by 41 per cent from 1968, amounting to only 51 million rubles, i.e., it was at the lowest level in the history of trade relations between the two countries.

In December 1969, the PRC announced the cancellation of the 1965 Sino-Soviet government convention on quarantine and control of agricultural pests and diseases.

A vivid expression of the Soviet policy of good-neighbourly relations and co-operation with China is the fact that work in educating the people in a spirit of friendship with the Chinese people, respect for their glorious history and revolutionary accomplishments has not ceased in the Soviet Union for a single day. Wide and fruitful activities are being carried out by the Soviet-Chinese Friendship Society. It regularly sponsors functions dedicated to milestone events in the life of the Chinese people, solemn meetings to celebrate the anniversaries of outstanding leaders of the national liberation movement in China, Chinese Communist internationalists, world-famous Chinese cultural figures and men of letters, to mark red-letter days in the history of Sino-Soviet friendship and co-operation. Over the past few years, the Society has celebrated the birth centenary of the great Chinese revolutionary democrat, Sun Yat-sen; the 80th birth anniversary of Li Ta-chao, one of the founders of the CPC; the 70th birth anniversary of the prominent Chinese Communist internationalist Tsü Chiu-po; the 80th birth anniversary of the father of modern Chinese literature, Lu Hsin; the 60th birth anniversary of the well-known Chinese author, Chou Li-po; the 70th birth anniversary of the outstanding scientist and author, Cheng Chen-to; the 1200th birth anniversary of the Chinese humanist, a classic of Chinese literature, Han Yün; the 40th anniversary of the death of the well-known CPC leader, Peng Pai; the 60th birth anniversary of the Chinese poet, Yin Fu. These dates were marked by public meetings in Moscow's House of Friendship with the Peoples of Foreign Countries. The national newspapers published commemorative articles on the life and work of these outstanding representatives of the Chinese people.

Under the rubric "In the Soviet-Chinese Friendship Society" Soviet broadcasts beamed to China and the *Soviet Union* and *Soviet Woman* magazines published in Chinese invariably inform their readership of the practical implementation of the policy pursued by the CPSU and the Soviet Government to develop and strengthen friendship with the Chinese people, of the broad involvement of the Soviet public in carrying out this policy. For example, a number of items under this rubric were devoted to the Institute of Oriental Languages under Moscow University, which trains sinologists, to Moscow's boarding schools No.11 and No.14 where pupils learn Chinese, to the Department of Sinology at the Institute of Orientology under the USSR Academy of Sciences, where a large body of Soviet researchers work on the problems of Chinese history, literature and art.

The Second All-Union Conference of the Soviet-Chinese Friendship Society which took place in January 1969 heard and discussed the report of its Vice-President, Corresponding Member of the USSR Academy of Sciences, S. L. Tikhvinsky, elected a new board, and set the guidelines for the society's further activities.

The Institute of Far Eastern Studies under the USSR Academy of Sciences makes an important contribution to the study of the problems of sinology and to dissemination of information about China. Over the past few years its research workers have issued a number of monumental works on China.

The invariably friendly attention to China, propaganda of the ideas of friendship and co-operation between the Soviet and Chinese peoples are all elements of the Soviet Union's Leninist foreign policy towards the PRC.

CHAPTER IX

SINO-SOVIET RELATIONS
IN THE EARLY 70s

1. SOME ASPECTS
OF CHINA'S HOME SITUATION AND FOREIGN POLICY
AFTER THE "CULTURAL REVOLUTION"

The Maoists did not declare officially the completion of the developments in the PRC in the context of the so-called "cultural revolution". What is more, according to the essence of the declaration repeatedly made in Peking the "cultural revolution" must be continuous or periodical in character. Such statements are not accidental. They show that the Maoists have far from succeeded in attaining all the objectives they pursued in beginning the "cultural revolution".

Nevertheless, since the early 70s, the development of China's home situation and foreign policy entered a specific new period which has come to be known in publications about China as the post-"cultural revolution" period. For all the conventionality of this definition, this period is truly characterised by a number of essential distinctions which have a direct bearing on Sino-Soviet relations in particular.

In the early 70s, the Chinese leadership took a number of measures inside the country to stabilise and strengthen the regime created by the "cultural revolution". At the same time, it had to resort to manoeuvres, to revise some of its former principles, to denounce the worst outrages of the "cultural revolution".

An important role in the development of the home situation was played by the "September crisis" of 1970, which culminated in the removal from China's political scene of a group of generals led by Mao Tse-tung's "heir apparent", Lin Piao. As demonstrated by later developments, the conflict between Mao and Lin Piao had deep-going roots. Besides purely personal and subjective factors, as well as an unprincipled power struggle, they consisted in a difference of approach, interpretation and methods of implementing the main political directives of the Ninth Congress of the CPC. As is known, the resolutions of the Ninth Congress were keynoted by anti-Sovietism. However, one part of the Maoist ruling clique held an anti-Soviet position based on a wrongly interpreted "national interest" of China, and combined the struggle against the USSR with a simultaneous confrontation with the USA, which continued its occupation of Taiwan and waged war in direct proximity to China's southern frontiers. The other part, led by Mao Tse-tung and Chou En-lai, intended to use anti-Sovietism for a "switchover" to the West and, above all, for a reorientation of Chinese foreign policy on rapprochement with the United States. It was on these issues that the struggle which led to the "September crisis" broke out.

An important role in reinforcing Lin Piao's positions could have been played by the session of the National People's Congress scheduled for September 1971, which was to approve the new draft Constitution providing for the legal enforcement of Lin Piao's status as Mao Tse-tung's successor. This speeded up developments, compelling the opposing groups to come over to more determined action. Mao Tse-tung again took the upper hand in the grapple that followed.

Since the end of October 1971, Mao and his followers began to bring to the notice of the population their version of the "case of Lin Piao" which was given an anti-Soviet interpretation.

The September crisis had far-reaching consequences. It undermined trust in the resolutions of the Ninth Congress of the CPC. The ouster of many leading generals and the beginning of purges in the army evoked the opposition of wide strata of high-ranking officers promoted to key positions with Lin Piao's support. The new split in the Maoist ruling clique had a demoralising effect on the Maoists inside China and abroad and added to the feelings of uncertainty about the stability of the Maoist regime among China's population.

It will be recalled that it was not the first time that Mao Tse-tung resorted to cruel repression of his political opponents. In the 40s, he made an attempt to oust such outstanding leaders of the Chinese revolution as Chang Wen-tien, Wang Ming, and others. In the 50s, Political Bureau member Kao Kang was liquidated, and another Political Bureau member, Peng Teh-huai was purged.

In the 60s, a large number of Political Bureau members, including Liu Shao-chi, Peng Chen, and others, were also purged. Significantly, many of them had at one time been praised as "Chairman Mao's most loyal disciples".

The ouster of Lin Piao and, somewhat earlier, one of the main ideologists of the "cultural revolution", Chen Po-ta, dealt a heavy blow to the ideological and political positions of the Maoists as a whole. Peking was compelled to withdraw from circulation and even to disavow many documents which for years had been regarded as fundamental material explaining "Mao's ideas" and policy.

In their struggle against Lin Piao and his supporters, Mao and Chou took advantage both of discontent at grassroots level with the promotion of army leaders to key party and government posts (the view that "the General Staff of the Chinese Army has substituted for the CPC Central Committee" was current among broad strata of party cadres) and the rivalry among army generals, particularly between those who served in the centre and those in the provinces. What is more, the objective requirements of economic development necessitated replacement of army generals appointed to government posts and found to be incapable of managing the economy by skilful veteran executives. This circumstance was exploited for the expulsion of Lin Piao's supporters from the party and administrative bodies.

However, the Maoists are aware of the fact that the army continues to be the sole real support of their power. In view of this, they have taken steps to reinforce their positions in the Chinese Army. In January 1973, the PRC State Council and the Military Council of the CPC Central Committee published an appeal to the army "to observe in exemplary fashion the political principles and laws of the Party and State". This was followed by the study within army units of a document of the CPC Central Committee containing instructions on comprehensive criticism and analysis of the activities of every serviceman.

The "September crisis" was followed by a new approach to cadres censured during the "cultural revolution". According to a new directive, veteran workers who had committed errors but admitted them and undergone re-education, were to be reinstated. The process of "reinstatement" served to intensify the internal strife. Persons who rose to prominence on the crest of the "cultural revolution" see in this process a danger to themselves and try to hold it back as hard as they can. The military are also alerted, because they are worried by the prospects of a further infringement of their influence as a result of reinstatement of veteran cadres. In this contradictory situation the Maoists dodge and resort to intricate compromise deals. The Chinese press, while speaking of the need to value veteran cadres, their experience and know-how, simultaneously emphasises that consolidation of veteran cadres is possible only on the basis of the Mao Tsetung line. Reinstated cadres are mainly appointed to managerial and technical jobs and with rare exceptions are not admitted to responsible political jobs for the time being.

The realities of the situation, the need to solve urgent practical problems, as well as to limit the influence of the military has compelled the Maoists to take steps to enhance the prestige of the party in society. Chinese propaganda has begun to lay special emphasis on the importance of centralised leadership of the party and points out that the party must direct all affairs, the army affairs in particular. The blame for playing down the role of the party in the recent past is laid upon Lin Piao.

The Maoists also seek to enlist the services of the trade unions, youth, women's and other public organisations. The provincial congresses of trade unions and conferences of the youth league in 1973 were held under the slogans of the Ninth CPC Congress and advanced the task of implementing the line charted by Chairman Mao.

The restoration of a number of former elements of the social mechanism by no means implies a change in the essence of the Maoist regime. On the contrary, it means the use by the Maoists of new methods to reinforce this regime. Indeed, it is to this purpose that all the activities of the newly-established public organisations are subordinated. All the main attributes of military bureaucratic dictatorship are pre-

served in China. The political power is, as before, held by
Mao Tse-tung and a handful of his closest associates leaning on the army, the machinery of repression, militarism and
the cult of Mao.

Ideological and political work in China is carried out in
conformity with the directives of the Ninth CPC Congress.
Political education boils down to the study of "Mao Tse-
tung's ideas", while individual works of Marxist-Leninist
classics are used only to prove that Mao Tse-tung has allegedly protected and developed this doctrine. For a number
of years not a single remarkable work of literature or art
has been produced in the PRC. Only a small number of
higher schools closed during the "cultural revolution" have
been reopened. Admission to reorganised higher schools is
limited due to a shortage of applicants capable of qualifying
and the absence of curricula.

The Chinese leadership seeks to convince the Chinese population and public opinion abroad that China's home scene
is quiet, that the people work enthusiastically like a well-
organised team, that production is expanding in all sectors
of the economy. Actually, however, the home political situation remains unstable. In the country, particularly in the
army, the influence of Lin Piao's supporters is still strong,
and many people do not understand the reasons for steep
turns in policy. There is discontent with new directives among
a part of veteran military officers and favourites of the "cultural revolution".

The objective laws of development of the socialist economy, difficulties constantly plaguing Peking in the economic
field, exhaustion of the country's resources by exorbitant
military expenditures—all face the Chinese leadership with
the need to take, contrary to the Maoist conceptions, certain
measures characteristic of the methods of management used
before the "cultural revolution". The unscientific concepts of
Maoism in the field of economics, which have become widespread in China, are in some areas actually opposed by
practical measures which comply to a certain extent
with the objective laws of economic development. Appeals for improving the organisation of production, the
training of skilled workers, engineers and technicians are
more and more often published in the Chinese press. At

many industrial enterprises control over product quality and observance of process charts, economic self-sufficiency and labour protection have been restored. Redundant manpower in some sectors of industry is being reduced by redistributing manpower resources and sending workers to help agriculture. Measures are taken to expand enterprises, introduce rationalisation proposals and study foreign experience.

In implementing its line of "walking on two legs" the Chinese leadership continues its policy of broad utilisation of local resources for the development of small- and medium-sized enterprises. But now account is taken of the sad experience of the "big leap" when products of such enterprises were unusable because of their poor quality, so more advanced machinery is supplied to them.

Wages in industry are paid in accordance with categories awarded to workers depending on their qualifications and working record. The application of material incentives, however, is limited. The piece-rate system, bonuses and extra pay, for overtime work in particular, have not been restored. The size of wages within every category is not dependent on the quantity and quality of work of a given employee. The press publishes contradictory instructions concerning the place material incentives must hold among other forms of encouragement.

Certain measures have been taken to raise production efficiency in agriculture. In contrast to industry, however, agriculture is wholly based on the principle of "leaning on one's own resources", and no large investments are made in it. The rural areas remain a major source of funds for building up China's military-industrial potential. Arduous manual labour prevails here as before. The income of a member of a commune is directly dependent on his political loyalty rather than on the quantity and quality of his work.

In 1971, for the first time after 1959, the PRC published official statistics on her steel output (21 million tons) and her grain output (246 million tons). To estimate the real worth of these figures, it will be recalled that as far back as 1960, i.e., more than ten years ago, the capacity of modern steel plants in China was equivalent to 18 million tons. As for grain, its production in China in the late 60s was about 200 million tons. It is hard to tell how the output announced in 1971 was attained since the area of arable land has not grown, the material and technical facilities of agriculture have not improved, and the exaction of surplus product from rural areas has not been reduced. China which was a grain-exporting country before, has now begun to import grain in quantity. Grain consumption in China continues to be strictly rationed, and bread rations are still smaller than in 1955.

The inconsistency with which amendments are made in the PRC economic policy in the post-"cultural revolution" period has led to a situation where China's economy develops in the absence of clear-cut directives, and leading cadres are absolutely disoriented. In today's China elements of the former methods of management can be encountered occasionally, as well as Maoists' instructions in abridged or unabridged form. Obviously no stable economic development can be secured on this contradictory and flimsy basis. The Maoists' attempts to "amend" their own directives cannot substitute for a scientifically grounded management of the national economy. Developments strikingly demonstrate the Maoists' inability to put forward a well-balanced positive programme of China's socio-economic development. What is more, they have proved unable to perform even current economic planning on a nationwide scale.

In the early 70s the Chinese leadership considerably stepped up its activities in the field of foreign policy. Over the three years after October 1970 the number of states maintaining diplomatic relations with Peking grew from 50 to 91. The 26th session of the UN General Assembly restored the rights of the PRC in this organisation. Important changes have taken place in China's relations with the United States, the capitalist countries of Europe, many states of Asia, Africa and Latin America. The economic and trade ties of the PRC have widened.

The exit of the PRC from the international isolation she found herself in as a result of the "cultural revolution" is attributable to a number of circumstances. The first of them is directly connected with the struggle the Chinese working people have waged for years against imperialism, with the consistent and determined support for this struggle, for the Chinese people's just demands by the Soviet Union and other socialist countries, the international anti-imperialist forces. Another contributing factor was the fact that the imperialist circles considered it useful for themselves to achieve rapprochement with the Maoists so as to employ them in the struggle against the world revolutionary movement. On the other hand, the crisis of the foreign policy principles of the "cultural revolution" period compelled the Maoists to modify and revise the tactics they used to achieve their strategic objectives. They sought to gain time to strengthen their positions at home and abroad and then to go ahead with their efforts to attain their long-range global objectives on this stronger foundation.

The activation of Peking's foreign policy activities was attended with efforts to lend them more flexible forms and methods, to adapt them to modern political realities. Chinese leaders began to advertise in every way their "love of peace", their desire to develop relations with various countries, and to declare for noninterference in the internal affairs of other states, for peaceful coexistence, for a peaceful settlement of disputes, etc.

At the same time, Chinese leaders did not relax their efforts to secure already at the current stage the recognition of China as a great power, and by aid of their conception of struggle against the "hegemony of two superpowers" to assume leadership of the national liberation movement, the developing countries and other "small- and medium-sized" states (including capitalist and some socialist states), to undermine as much as they could the international positions of states Peking regarded as its enemies. Also, the struggle against the Soviet Union and its allies remained a first priority task, whereas confrontation against the United States was, in effect, removed from the agenda. Chinese leaders made strenuous efforts to step up splitting activities against the socialist community, the communist and national liberation movement by employing more refined techniques, to undermine by using a differentiating approach the relations between the socialist countries, and set them at loggerheads.

To facilitate the attainment of their objectives, the Maoists sought to maintain and, insofar as possible, to step up tensions in the relations between nations, above all, between the Soviet Union and the United States, between the Soviet

Union and Japan, as well as between each of these states and other countries. While posing as a peacemaker protecting small nations, Peking sought, in fact, to frustrate the efforts of the socialist states to strengthen peace and achieve détente. Chinese leaders opposed the socialist countries' proposals on the issues of disarmament, banning nuclear weapons tests, strengthening European security, setting up a collective security system in Asia. However, they were intent on removing existing and emerging hotbeds of war danger away from China's own frontiers.

The Chinese leaders' practical activities on the international arena strikingly confirmed the conclusion of the Meeting of Communist and Workers' Parties in June 1969 that their foreign policy had broken, in fact, with proletarian internationalism, lost its class socialist content, that Peking leaders were merely giving lip service to the struggle against imperialism while actually helping it by direct and indirect means, and that for the imperialists Peking's foreign policy orientation was but a trump card in their political game against world socialism and the liberation movements. Developments conclusively show, however, that despite the special stand of the CPC leadership, the negative effects of its divisive activities can be substantially mitigated and prevented by coordinated actions of the socialist countries and the Marxist-Leninist parties. For all the efforts of imperialism and anti-communism to turn Peking's policy to their advantage, they have been unable to check the process of change in the alignment of forces on the international scene in favour of socialism, democracy and peace. The realities of life again and again corroborate the indisputable fact that the world socialist system has the decisive bearing on international politics. The growing power and unity of the socialist community, the continuous consolidation of its positions are unquestionable. The constructive efforts of the fraternal parties to develop relations with states in various regions, to promote détente, to support the peoples fighting for freedom and independence—all evoke profound sympathy of the peoples of the world for the foreign policy line of the socialist countries firmly adhering to the positions of Marxism-Leninism.

2. PEKING'S OPPOSITION
TO A NORMALISATION OF SINO-SOVIET RELATIONS

After the meeting between the Soviet and Chinese Premiers in September 1969 and the opening of Sino-Soviet talks
on the border issues, signs of a situation favourable to an
improvement in Sino-Soviet relations were clearly in evidence. The Soviet Union vigorously strove to achieve progress
in this field.

In October 1970, in accordance with an earlier arrange-
ment, the Soviet Union sent its Ambassador to Peking. In
November 1970, a Chinese Ambassador arrived in Moscow.
This exchange was an important step on the way of developing inter-state relations between the two countries. In 1970,
the turnover of Sino-Soviet trade fell to an all-time low. To
remedy this situation, the Soviet side made constructive
efforts at the trade talks held in November 1970. At the end
of the talks a bilateral trade agreement was signed for the
first time after a long interval. Systematic activities in disseminating ideas of Sino-Soviet friendship were continued in
the Soviet Union. An important step in this field was the
"Lenin and China" anniversary conference which the Soviet-
Chinese Friendship Society held in Moscow in February 1970
on the occasion of the Lenin birth centenary. The conference was attended by activists of the Society, members of the
Soviet public, prominent Soviet generals and specialists who
had helped the Chinese people in their revolutionary struggle and the building of a new society. Speakers at the conference emphasised the immense importance of Lenin's ideas
for the national liberation and revolutionary struggle of the
Chinese people and adduced vivid examples of friendship
and co-operation between the People's Republic of China
and the Soviet Union in the struggle for peace and socialism,
against imperialism.

During 1970, the Society also held soirees dedicated to the
1200th death anniversary of the great Chinese poet Du Phu,
the 75th birthday of the remarkable Chinese artist Hsu Pei-
hung, the 45th anniversary of the anti-imperialist and anti-
feudal revolution in China, and a number of other functions.

The Soviet Government took steps to organise an exchange
of information with the PRC Government on international

problems of interest to both sides. Such information was submitted by the Soviet Union unilaterally; Peking failed to reciprocate this move.

At a regular session of the United Nations General Assembly in November 1970, the Soviet Union, as before, took a determined stand in favour of restoring the PRC to its lawful seat in the United Nations immediately and for expelling the representatives of the Chiang Kai-shek regime. A positive resolution on this issue was stalled by opposition from the United States and its allies. The Americans forced the UN General Assembly into accepting the proposal for the issue of restoring the PRC to her seat in the United Nations to be decided by a two thirds majority of votes. The debate over the question of restoration of the PRC's rights in the United Nations again showed who was the true friend of the Chinese people and who sought to use relations with the PRC in fact against the interests of her people.

The anti-Sovietiers in Peking obviously felt ill at ease at the sight of a prospect for improving Sino-Soviet relations, fearing lest a revival of friendship and co-operation between the PRC and the USSR remove the pretext for implanting militarism and justifying the people's low standards of living in China. This time, too, the Maoists attempted to shift on the Soviet Union the blame for all their failures and setbacks for their home and foreign policies.

On January 1, 1970, the leading organs of the Chinese press published a common editorial entitled "Towards the Great Seventies", setting out the basic guidelines for Chinese foreign policy in the decade to come. The highlights of the article were wanton anti-Soviet attacks. The Maoist strategists openly declared that they regarded the struggle against the USSR as their central long-range target.

Ignoring repeated Soviet statements giving the lie to allegations about the so-called threat to China from the North, Peking went on spreading provocative fabrications to this effect. On Soviet Army Day Peking leaders did not permit Soviet Embassy officials to lay wreaths on the graves of Soviet officers and men who gave their lives for the Chinese people's freedom and were buried in China. A *Pravda* correspondent was denied an entry visa to the PRC. The Chinese official press published numerous items designed to show not only to the people of China but also to foreign "friends" of Peking that it did not intend to normalise relations with the USSR.

In April 1970, the Soviet people and all progressive mankind celebrated the birth centenary of the leader of the world's working people, Vladimir Lenin. On the occasion of this red-letter day, the Soviet Union received messages of congratulation from all over the world. Representatives of all the sections of the revolutionary movement, world public opinion expressed their admiration for the remarkable achievements of the socialist state founded by Lenin. The world acknowledged its respect for the great party of Lenin, which follows the path mapped out by Lenin with the same determination and consistency as under the personal guidance of its founder and leader.

In Peking, however, the Lenin birth anniversary was used as the pretext for wanton anti-Soviet actions. Peking leaders published a series of articles slandering Lenin's homeland, the party he founded, the Soviet people.

In his report dedicated to the Lenin birth centenary, the General Secretary of the CPSU Central Committee, Leonid Brezhnev, emphasised that the only right way to follow in developing relations between China and the Soviet Union, between China and other socialist countries was the path outlined by Lenin, a path of joint struggle against the dark forces of imperialist reaction, for the victory of the sacred cause of socialism and communism.

As for the Soviet Union, Leonid Brezhnev said, it was resolutely determined to uphold socialist internationalism, to restore good relations between socialist countries whenever they were disturbed, and was always ready to co-operate in this field. The Soviet Union's firm and consistent policy was also reaffirmed in the speeches Leonid Brezhnev, the Soviet Premier Alexei Kosygin, and the President of the USSR Supreme Soviet, Nikolai Podgorny, made at electoral meetings in June 1970.

This clearly formulated friendly policy of the Soviet Union in relation to China failed to meet with a favourable response in Peking.

In an interview with a correspondent of the Japanese newspaper *Asahi Shimbun* on January 3, 1971, the Soviet

22*

Premier Alexei Kosygin, dwelling on the prospects for improving Sino-Soviet relations, emphasised that on the Soviet side there was no lack of goodwill for resolving all existing disputes between the Soviet Union and China on the principles of equality, mutual respect and consideration of each others' lawful interests. The Soviet Premier noted, however, that a normalisation of relations could be achieved only when both sides took steps in this direction.

The Soviet Union took a series of constructive steps testifying to its goodwill and desire to develop good-neighbourly relations with China. On January 12, the Soviet press published a report about the forthcoming session of the National People's Congress and the progress of preparations for it. On January 18, the Soviet Premier Kosygin received in the Kremlin the Chinese Ambassador, Liu Hsin-chuan and had a discussion with him. The Soviet-Chinese Friendship Society stepped up its activities in disseminating the ideas of friendship between the two countries. On March 4, the Society, jointly with the Institute of Orientology and the Institute of Far Eastern Studies under the USSR Academy of Sciences, held a soiree dedicated to the great Chinese poet, Li Po. On April 30, the Society sponsored a soiree on the occasion of the 60th birthday of the famous Chinese composer Neh Erh. The function was attended by Chinese Embassy officials.

The Soviet side displayed willingness to acquaint Chinese representatives with the situation in the Soviet Union. More often than not, however, even such initiatives met with opposition or indifference. Peking obviously preferred to collect information about the Soviet Union from other, foul sources distorting the true state of affairs, slandering the Soviet people, their Communist Party and state. On March 11, for example, the Chinese Ambassador was invited to a discussion between the Soviet Vice-Premier, Chairman of the USSR State Planning Committee, N. K. Baibakov, and Ambassadors from the socialist countries on problems connected with the draft directives of the 24th CPSU Congress on the USSR five-year economic development plan for 1971-1975. The Chinese Ambassador, however, ignored the invitation. On March 12, the Press Department of the USSR Ministry of Foreign Affairs sponsored at the Central Club of the USSR

Journalists' Union a press conference of the editors and writers of the newspaper *Socialist Industry* for correspondents from the socialist countries and organs of the communist press of capitalist countries accredited in Moscow. Hsinhua News Agency correspondents invited to attend the conference ignored the invitation, too.

The hostile policy of the Chinese side towards the Soviet Union was evidenced by a series of other facts in early 1971. The New Year editorials in three leading party press organs were interspersed with vicious anti-Soviet statements. In its first issue in 1971 the journal *Hungchi* opened a special rubric for slanderous anti-Soviet items.

Not only the Chinese press but also Chinese government leaders never missed a chance to make an anti-Soviet statement. For example, Premier Chou En-lai, in an interview with a Japanese delegation led by A. Fujiyama, declared his support for the territorial claims of Japan's reactionary circles to the Soviet Union.[1]

Chinese leaders again demonstrated their hostility towards the Soviet Union in connection with Soviet Army Day. In February 1971, as in the past, the Chinese authorities declined the Soviet Embassy's request for permission to Soviet diplomats to visit the cities of Harbin, Wuhan, Shenyang, Lushun and Dairen on Soviet Army Day to lay wreaths on the graves of Soviet servicemen killed in the war for the liberation of the Chinese people. This refusal, which was an affront to millions of Soviet people, was clearly motivated by a desire to aggravate Sino-Soviet relations.

A serious move called upon to put up obstacles in the way of normalising Sino-Soviet relations was the malicious anti-Soviet article published by Peking leaders on the occasion of the centenary of the Paris Commune. This glorious anniversary, which was celebrated by all progressive forces under the slogan of struggle for the unity of revolutionary ranks, was used in Peking for divisive purposes, for attacks on the Communist Party of the Soviet Union waging a determined and consistent struggle for carrying into life the great ideals of the Paris Commune.

---

[1] *Asahi Shimbun*, March 4, 1971.

3. THE 24th CPSU CONGRESS
ON SINO-SOVIET RELATIONS

The undeviating policy of the Communist Party of the Soviet Union to normalise and develop relations with China was vividly embodied in the decisions of the 24th CPSU Congress held from late March to early April 1971. The Congress met in a situation of remarkable successes for the home and foreign policies of the CPSU. It summed up the results of the Soviet people's heroic work in the period after the 23rd CPSU Congress and outlined the tasks for the coming period. The Congress was attended by representatives of the overwhelming majority of the world's Communist and Workers' parties. This was an expression of the profound respect of the international communist movement for the party of Lenin, for the Soviet State he founded. In their statements at the Congress, envoys of the fraternal parties expressed their admiration for the Soviet people's accomplishments in building communism under the leadership of the CPSU.

In the report made at the Congress by the General Secretary of the CPSU Leonid Brezhnev on behalf of its Central Committee the problem of Sino-Soviet relations was given special place. The speaker said that in the period under review the CPSU Central Committee and the Soviet Government had been doing everything in their power to secure a normalisation of relations with the People's Republic of China. By the time of calling the 24th CPSU Congress definite progress had been made in this direction. As a result of the Soviet initiative certain signs of such normalisation were in evidence: a meeting between the Soviet and Chinese Premiers, the opening in Peking of talks between Soviet and Chinese government delegations on the settlement of border disputes, the exchange of Ambassadors, the signing after a long interval of a trade agreement, and a certain increase in the turnover of Sino-Soviet trade. After mentioning these facts, Leonid Brezhnev stated: "These are useful steps. We are prepared to go ahead in this direction."

At the same time, the 24th CPSU Congress acknowledged that the anti-Soviet line in Peking's propaganda and policy was continued, that the policy hostile to the Soviet Union had been endorsed in the decisions of the 9th Congress of the CPC.

The 24th CPSU Congress expressed its sincere concern for a normalisation of Sino-Soviet relations. This testified to the fact that the CPSU, its Central Committee, the Soviet Government had a keen sense of responsibility for the destinies of the two nations, an interest, motivated by internationalist feelings, in the restoration of friendship and cooperation between them. In his report, Leonid Brezhnev specially emphasised that the efforts to sow discord between China and the Soviet Union were absurd and harmful, the more so as the imperialists were stepping up their aggressive actions against freedom-loving peoples. It was perfectly obvious that this situation imperatively demanded unity, joint actions of all anti-imperialist and revolutionary forces. Naturally, the fomenting of animosity between such states as the Soviet Union and China could only hamper the attainment of these goals. Leonid Brezhnev said that the CPSU and the Soviet Government were firmly convinced that an improvement of relations between the Soviet Union and the People's Republic of China would answer their vital, long-term interests, serve the cause of socialism, the freedom of nations, and peace. "Therefore," the CPSU General Secretary said, "we are prepared to contribute in every way not only to normalising relations but also to restoring good-neighbourly relations and friendship between the Soviet Union and the People's Republic of China and we are confident that this will eventually be achieved."

Leonid Brezhnev's pronouncements were enthusiastically supported by other speakers at the Congress. Envoys of the Communists of Byelorussia and Uzbekistan, the Maritime Territory in the Far East and Lithuania, the Sverdlovsk Region and Moldavia, other republics, regions and territories of the Soviet Union unanimously expressed their full support for the policy of the Leninist Central Committee towards China and spoke of the need for normalising Sino-Soviet relations. They emphasised that the anti-Soviet policy of Chinese leaders merely played into the hands of the common enemy of the Chinese and Soviet peoples—imperialism, which had an interest in fomenting enmity between them. Soviet Communists educated, as they were, by the Leninist party in a spirit of proletarian internationalism, spoke of their sincere feelings of friendship towards the Chinese people and expressed their confidence in the ultimate restoration of good-neighbourly relations and friendship between the Soviet Union and the People's Republic of China.

The 24th CPSU Congress approved the principled Leninist policy and constructive steps of the CPSU Central Committee and the Soviet Government to normalise Sino-Soviet relations. It pointed out that in a situation where Chinese leaders came forward with their separate ideological and political platform, incompatible with Marxism-Leninism and directed to a struggle against the socialist countries, to splitting the international communist movement and the entire anti-imperialist movement, the CPSU Central Committee took the only correct stand, one of upholding consistently the principles of Marxism-Leninism, of promoting in every way the unity of the world communist movement, of protecting the interests of the socialist homeland. The Congress resolutely rejected the slanderous fabrications of Chinese propaganda about the policy of the CPSU and the Soviet State. At the same time, the Congress declared in its resolution that the CPSU was in favour of normalising relations between the Soviet Union and China, of restoring good-neighbourly relations and friendship between them.

The policy of the Soviet Union in relation to China was given a high assessment by the representatives of foreign Marxist-Leninist parties who spoke at the Congress. "The attitude to the CPSU and the Soviet Union," the First Secretary of the Central Committee of the Polish United Workers' Party, Eduard Gierek, said in his speech, "is the most dependable, time-tested criterion of one's true attitude to the unity of the socialist and anti-imperialist forces." The speaker stressed that those clinging to anti-Soviet positions caused grave damage both to the common cause of socialism, peace and freedom and to the vital interests of their parties and peoples. The same idea was emphasised by the First Secretary of the Central Committee of the Socialist Unity Party of Germany, Erich Honecker in these words: "The attitude to the CPSU and the Soviet Union has always been the touchstone of every progressive man and woman." Envoys of other fraternal parties stressed their determination to oppose any attempts to undermine the unity of the revolutionary forces with the Communist Party of the Soviet Union.

The line of the 24th CPSU Congress in relation to China met with full support at the congresses of the Communist and Workers' parties of Bulgaria, Czechoslovakia, Mongolia, Poland, the GDR held soon after its closure. At the 16th Congress of the Mongolian People's Revolutionary Party, its leader Yumzhagiin Tsedenbal, stated that the Chinese leaders' policy of warlike nationalism and anti-Sovietism had resulted in China's break with the socialist countries, armed provocations against the Soviet Union, the homeland of Lenin. This policy radically contradicted the interests of the revolutionary struggle of the peoples, the vital interests of the Chinese people in particular.[1]

The 24th CPSU Congress clearly outlined the way to normalising Sino-Soviet relations. The Peking leaders, however, again opposed this initiative. Ignoring the goodwill displayed by our Party, they persisted in their hostile policy towards it.

4. IMPLEMENTATION OF THE POLICY
OUTLINED BY THE 24th CPSU CONGRESS

After the 24th CPSU Congress, the Soviet Union consistently and firmly implemented the policy charted by the Congress in relation to the People's Republic of China, one of normalising and developing Sino-Soviet relations. It was pointed out at the Congress that an expansion of trade between the Soviet Union and China would promote their relations in other fields. Premier Alexei Kosygin, in his report to the Congress on the Directives for the USSR five-year economic development plan for 1971-1975, said that the Soviet Union had taken a series of steps to develop trade with China; the progress made in this field, however, was far below the actual potentialities of the two countries. Premier Kosygin went on to say that in the coming few years the Soviet Union would continue its efforts to develop trade exchanges with China on the basis of equality and mutual advantage. In keeping with this line, the Soviet Union had

---

[1] *Pravda*, June 8, 1971.

taken steps to widen trade with China with the result that its volume in 1971 grew more than threefold since 1970.

The Soviet Union continued its efforts to secure the restoration of the lawful rights of the People's Republic of China in the United Nations. At the 26th session of the United Nations General Assembly in October 1971, the Soviet representative voted for her admission to the United Nations. In an article devoted to restoration of the PRC to her lawful seat in the United Nations, the newspaper *Pravda*, organ of the CPSU Central Committee, expressed the hope that the admission of the PRC to this international organisation would contribute to effective implementation of the principles of the United Nations Charter, to strengthening universal peace and the security of nations. Speaking at the plenary session of the United Nations General Assembly, the Soviet Ambassador to the United Nations, Yakov Malik, welcomed the PRC delegation which had come to take part in the 26th session of the United Nations General Assembly.

The Soviet Union took a favourable stand on the issue of participation of PRC representatives in international conferences and congresses held in the Soviet Union. For example, Chinese authorities were handed in material for the 23rd International Congress on Apiculture to be held in Moscow between August 27 and September 2, 1971. The Chinese refused to attend the congress. In the Soviet Union, public meetings were held to mark such red-letter days in the history of China as the 50th anniversary of the CPC and the 22nd anniversary of the PRC. On the occasion of the 50th anniversary of the CPC, the Central Board of the Soviet-Chinese Friendship Society, jointly with the Institute of Far Eastern Studies under the USSR Academy of Sciences, sponsored a solemn meeting at Moscow's International Friendship House. This event was also the subject of a conference held under the auspices of the Institute of Far Eastern Studies, the Institute of the International Working-Class Movement, and the Institute of Orientology under the USSR Academy of Sciences. The newspaper *Pravda* and the journal *Communist* published articles commemorating the 50th anniversary of the Communist Party of China.

Unfortunately, no signs of willingness to improve relations with the Soviet Union were shown by the Chinese side. On

July 1, 1971, a policy article was published in China on the occasion of the 50th anniversary of the CPC. Its authors took advantage of this memorable date in the history of the Communist Party of China for making hostile statements against the CPSU and the Soviet State.

After the 24th CPSU Congress, anti-Soviet propaganda in China, far from ceasing, assumed a wider scale. Chinese propagandists left no stone unturned in seeking pretexts for their anti-Soviet attacks. The Chinese press and statesmen viciously slandered the Soviet Union in connection with its stand on the Indo-Pakistani conflict. In pursuit of their anti-Soviet objectives Peking leaders fell to harping at length on the theme of "superpowers". They are trying to draw a parallel between the Soviet Union, which is the leading anti-imperialist force, and the United States, which is the citadel of imperialism.

In this context the assessment of the theory of "superpowers" by the US Communists, who are waging revolutionary struggle on the American scene, merits special attention. In June 1971 Gus Hall, General Secretary of the Communist Party, USA, wrote:

"Is the role of the Soviet Union and US imperialism the same in the Mid-East, in Africa, in Latin America? They are at the opposite dialectical poles. One is the main force of oppression and exploitation, the other the main outside force of support to the forces of liberation and freedom. To speak about them in general terms as 'superpowers' is a service to US imperialism."[1]

After the PRC's rights in the United Nations had been restored, Peking leaders went out of their way to use this international organisation for the anti-Soviet purposes. The very first steps of the PRC delegation to the United Nations General Assembly demonstrated the Chinese leaders' intention to pursue in the United Nations their policy of anti-Sovietism and splitting the progressive forces.

The policy of the Peking leadership hostile to the Soviet Union was resented by those who favoured friendship between the Soviet Union and China and evoked malicious joy of the imperialists. Meanwhile, the consistent implementation of the

[1] *New Times*, No. 30, 1971.

line mapped out by the 24th Congress of the CPSU made it increasingly clear that it was Peking's opposition alone that stood in the way of normalising Sino-Soviet relations. The frankly hostile actions of Maoist leaders graphically demonstrated their unwillingness to develop friendly relations with the Soviet Union.

5. NEW SOVIET CONSTRUCTIVE STEPS

In 1972, the Soviet people celebrated the 50th anniversary of the Union of Soviet Socialist Republics. In that memorable year the Soviet working people made new progress in all the fields of communist construction. The 50th anniversary of the USSR was also marked by the Soviet Government's vigorous efforts in pursuing its Leninist foreign policy, in the field of Sino-Soviet relations in particular.

The Soviet Union's principled policy in relation to China was reaffirmed in the speech the CPSU General Secretary, Leonid Brezhnev, made at the 15th USSR Congress of Trade Unions. He emphasised that the CPSU consistently upheld the principles of Marxism-Leninism, strengthened in every way the unity of the world communist movement, defended the interests of the socialist homeland. Referring to official Chinese statements to the effect that Sino-Soviet relations ought to be based on the principles of peaceful coexistence, the CPSU General Secretary said: "If Peking is unwilling to go further than that in relations with a socialist state, we are prepared at the present moment to develop Sino-Soviet relations on such a basis, too."

Leonid Brezhnev stressed that the Soviet Union not only declared such readiness but was translating it into a language of clearly-worded and constructive proposals for a settlement of border issues, for improving relations on a mutually beneficial basis.

All the experience in developing Sino-Soviet relations clearly evidenced that the Soviet Union did everything necessary for improving these relations. All the blame for the lack of progress in this direction rested entirely with the Peking leaders.

Guided by its principled view that a normalisation of Sino-Soviet relations would meet the interests of all the countries and peoples, the Soviet Union invariably regards this issue as one of international importance. Seeking to facilitate China's participation in solving crucial world problems the Soviet Government offered the PRC Government assistance in matters connected with the signing of some international agreements. For example, in a note delivered to the Chinese Government it was informed of the opportunity to sign in Moscow the international convention on responsibility for damage to space vehicles and the convention on banning development, production and stockpiling of bacteriological (biological) and toxin weapons and on their destruction. Pursuing its line of opposition to détente and to promotion of peace the Chinese Government abstained from signing these conventions.

This striking contrast between the Soviet Union's constructive stand and Peking's opposition to it was shown by many other facts. On July 17, the PRC Ministry of Foreign Affairs was handed in a copy of the Soviet Foreign Minister Andrei Gromyko's letter to the United Nations Secretary General concerning the proposal of several countries for a revision of the United Nations Charter. On August 18, the PRC Ministry of Foreign Affairs was given a copy of the letter from the USSR Ministry of Foreign Affairs to the United Nations Secretary General on the issue of calling a world disarmament conference, and on September 19, a copy of the letter on the renunciation of the use of force in international relations and on banning the use of nuclear weapons for all time. On each occasion, the Chinese Government demonstrated its frank anti-Sovietism. In December the PRC Embassy in Moscow was tendered a note of the USSR Ministry of Foreign Affairs on the forthcoming signing by all states of a convention on prevention of sea pollution with wastes and other obnoxious matter. China refused to send her representatives to the signing ceremony.

The Chinese press marked the beginning of the New Year 1972 in its traditional style. The New Year editorial in *Jenmin jihpao* contained rude attacks against the Soviet Union and set the guidelines for carrying on the struggle against it. Far from subsiding, anti-Soviet propaganda in China tended to grow in scope. At the same time, one could note a falling-off in the vehemency of Chinese criticism of imperialism.

Items exposing the aggressive essence of American imperialism were vanishing from the Chinese press.

Early in 1972, an unexpected interest in archaeology became manifest in China. A number of lengthy articles were published on this subject. Even a cursory acquaintance with these articles, however, was enough to see their clear-cut anti-Soviet objectives. Archaeology was used by Peking as yet another means of attacking the Soviet Union as well as supporting China's territorial claims to neighbouring countries.

On July 15, 1972, a *World Atlas* containing quite a few slanderous anti-Soviet fabrications was put on sale in Peking. According to its authors, Russia had been pursuing a policy hostile to China since antiquity. It was nothing but an attempt to stir up anti-Russian sentiments among the Chinese people and depict Russia as China's ages-old enemy. The *World Atlas* was not a press article but a monumental edition intended for years-long use, and inasmuch as its Peking editors had decided to furnish it with anti-Soviet material, it might be concluded that they had in mind long-range anti-Soviet objectives.

Even in a pamphlet dedicated to the proletarian song *Internationale* enough space was set aside for malicious anti-Soviet fabrications. One would think the story of making this song was the right occasion for speaking about strengthening the international solidarity of the revolutionary forces in the struggle against imperialism. In Peking, however, it was thought of as an occasion for slandering the world's first socialist state, the main stronghold of the world revolutionary movement.

Peking propaganda also exploited a number of other events for its anti-Soviet statements. For example, material published on the occasion of the 45th anniversary of the People's Liberation Army of China was presented in a spirit of hostility to the Soviet Union. The same purpose was pursued by an article commemorating the 23rd anniversary of the PRC. Its authors went to the length of describing the Soviet Union as a "more dangerous" enemy of China than the imperialist states.

The Chinese delegation in the United Nations continued to use its rostrum for spreading slanderous anti-Soviet fabrications. An example in point was the statement of the PRC delegation at a meeting of the Second Subcommittee of the United Nations Committee on Peaceful Uses of the Seas and Oceans in July 1972.

The following fact shows how far Peking was carried away by its policy of hostility towards the Soviet Union. In February 1972, the Chinese press reprinted an item from Hongkong's newspaper *Hsingtao jihpao* saying that Mao Tse-tung regarded the USSR as "China's chief enemy".

In 1972, China was visited by President Nixon of the United States. On this occasion, Peking again demonstrated its unfriendly attitude to the Soviet Union. The following fact is indicative. Hundreds of correspondents from various countries arrived in the PRC to cover the US President's visit. Only correspondents of the Soviet News Agency TASS and the Novosti Press Agency were not granted entry visas in good time.

It has long become clear to the world that Peking's curses addressed to imperialism are a mere propaganda verbiage without any practical actions behind it. Even at the height of the "cultural revolution" when the Maoists' ultra-Left phraseology was brought up to its climax, it coexisted quite peacefully with their acceptance as useful of the remnants of imperialist colonial possessions on Chinese soil, with their tolerance of piratic acts of US aircraft and warships against the PRC, with their evasion of involvement in the joint efforts of the socialist countries to aid the Vietnamese people struggling against the US aggression. On the whole, this stage may be described as a kind of neutrality displayed by Peking in the confrontation between the imperialist and anti-imperialist forces, and camouflaged with loud declarations which already at that time were often tantamount to complicity with imperialism. After the "cultural revolution" the Maoists proceeded to the next stage, one of setting up broad and ramified contacts with the leading capitalist states. The process of radical reorientation of China's foreign policy entered a new stage.

Needless to say, the widening of China's foreign relations is in itself a perfectly legitimate and natural process. It has been facilitated in no small measure by the consistent and determined support for the Chinese people's just demands by the Soviet Union and other socialist countries, the progressive international forces. Another contributing factor has been the use of more flexible forms and methods in Peking's stepped-up foreign policy activities in the period after September 1972, its better adaptation to the modern political situation. In contrast to earlier years, Peking has begun to advertise its "love of peace", and willingness to develop relations with various countries, to avow the principles of peaceful coexistence and noninterference in the internal affairs of other states.

In the eyes of Peking, however, the chief means of adjusting relations with the imperialist states is anti-Soviet policy. The activities of Chinese leaders on the international scene increasingly acquire the character of global opposition to all foreign policy acts of the Soviet Union. Peking leaders seek to furnish this policy with a "theoretical" basis. A policy article published in three leading organs of the Chinese press on the occasion of the 23rd anniversary of the PRC declared that the Soviet Union, on which the authors tried to paste the dirty label of "social imperialism", was "more deceptive than imperialist powers of the old type and hence more dangerous". In other words, Peking leaders, now through their official mouthpiece, declared the Soviet Union, in effect, their "enemy No. 1".

The Chinese leadership opposed all of the Soviet Union's proposals directed to solving crucial world problems. This was thrown into striking relief by the line the PRC delegation pursued at the 27th session of the United Nations General Assembly. The Chinese representative vehemently opposed the Soviet initiative in calling a world disarmament conference, declaring outright that "it's better not to hold such a conference". At the same time, Peking took a stand against the existing international agreements on disarmament. Chinese leaders openly came out for carrying on nuclear tests, emphasising China's determination to go ahead with improvement of her nuclear arms. Peking defiantly ignored all the protests against China's nuclear tests in the atmosphere and denied, not caring to adduce any proofs, the obvious harm these tests were bound to cause in the densely populated Asian continent.

The Soviet-American agreements on strategic arms limitation went against the grain with Peking leaders. These agreements were welcomed throughout the world as a major contribution to improving the international atmosphere, as a long step on the way to solving one of the most crucial problems of today. Peking, however, attempted not only to play down the importance of this achievement but also to distort its true meaning and purpose. Ignoring the voice of reason and generally known facts, the Chinese leadership sought to depict the Soviet-American agreements on strategic arms limitation as ". . . the beginning of a new stage in the nuclear arms race".

The Soviet proposal for renunciation of the use of force in international relations and banning the use of nuclear weapons for all time, submitted to the 27th session of the United Nations General Assembly, met with a broad and favourable response throughout the world. Only two delegations in the United Nations—of the USA and the PRC—openly opposed the Soviet initiative. The Chinese delegates displayed special zeal in their attacks against the new Soviet move to strengthen peace and international security. In accordance with their Maoist logic, they alleged that acceptance of the Soviet proposals for renunciation of force and banning nuclear weapons for all time would mean a "betrayal of the peoples of the world".

Peking fiercely attacked the Soviet moves aimed at easing international tensions and strengthening world peace. The Chinese leaders were particularly outraged at the prospects of calling an all-European conference on security and cooperation. At the same time, Chinese leaders made no bones about their sympathy with the Common Market, regarding it as a tool of struggle against the Soviet Union and the East European socialist countries. The Chinese press expressed the hope for "greater unity and joint opposition to threats and interference" allegedly endangering this monopoly association from the outside. Spelling out the true meaning of such Chinese statements, the West German newspaper *General-Anzeiger für Bonn und Umgegend* wrote that "Peking is openly in favour of a strong Western Europe, economically as well as militarily".

Peking did not desist from its efforts to aggravate the situation in the Middle East and on the South Asian Subcontinent. Speaking at a session of the United Nations Gen-

eral Assembly on October 3, 1972, the Chinese representative
went to the length of declaring that the Soviet Union was
"more dangerous than an open enemy" to the Arab countries.
In the same speech he stated that the "turmoil on the South
Asian Sub-continent continued because of the Soviet Union's
interference".

While pushing ahead along their anti-Soviet path, the
Peking leaders simultaneously demonstrated their special
favour to the leading imperialist powers. In an interview
with *The Times* editor on October 13, 1972, Chou En-lai
said that if one were to choose, the United States should be
given preference to the so-called socialist system of Russia.

Chinese leaders' declarations of love for American imperialism did not remain empty-worded. Peking sought to prove
them by practical deeds. In the summer of 1972, Chou En-lai,
in a discussion with US congressmen, pleaded, in fact, that
the United States should not withdraw from the Pacific area
or other regions of the world.

To win the favour of the reactionary forces on the international scene, Chinese leaders are ready to assist any of their
anti-Soviet actions. Peking even went as far as to support and
encourage the territorial claims of the revanchist circles
to the Soviet Union.

The activities of the Chinese leadership on the international arena made it increasingly clear that its foreign policy
had broken with proletarian internationalism, lost its socialist class content, that all of the Maoists' anti-imperialist
declarations were no more than empty verbiage. If Peking
leaders clash occasionally with the imperialist circles, it hap-
pens only when their great-power chauvinistic plans are at
stake.

The plenary meeting of the CPC Central Committee held
from late August to early September 1972, endorsed the anti-
Soviet line of the Peking leadership. After the meeting, attacks of Chinese propaganda against the CPSU and the
Soviet Union, as well as Peking's anti-Soviet activities on the
international scene assumed an even wider scale. Referring
to the state of Sino-Soviet relations in his speech on November 30, 1972, Leonid Brezhnev said that the true source of
China's strained relations with the Soviet Union lay in the
capital of China herself, in her leaders' own policy aimed at

aggravating relations between states, splitting the socialist community and the anti-imperialist forces.

In December 1972, the Soviet people solemnly celebrated the golden jubilee of their country: the 50th anniversary of the Union of Soviet Socialist Republics. In a report on this occasion, Leonid Brezhnev paid special attention to the state of Sino-Soviet relations. Speaking at a joint solemn meeting of the CPSU Central Committee, the Supreme Soviets of the USSR and the Russian Federation, he reaffirmed the Soviet Union's principled policy vis-à-vis China. He noted that Peking's current policy of confrontation against the Soviet Union was bound to have grave negative consequences. This policy was unnatural for relations between socialist countries. It was directed against the interests of both the Soviet and Chinese peoples. It was also detrimental to the cause of world socialism, interfered with the liberation, anti-imperialist struggle, and was incompatible with the interests of peace and the security of nations.

Leonid Brezhnev again exposed the hypocrisy of statements about the Soviet threat to China. He recalled that since 1969 the Soviet Union had repeatedly come forward with proposals for clearly worded, firm and permanent commitments to be assumed by the two countries to rule out an attack by one on the other. These proposals, however, had been invariably declined by the Chinese side. By way of specifying its proposals the Soviet Union offered China to sign a treaty on renunciation of the use of force. To put this proposal on a practical basis, the Soviet side on January 15, 1971 submitted to the Chinese a draft of the treaty, which stated in plain words that "the High Contracting Parties shall not use against each other armed forces employing any type of weapons, including (a) conventional; (b) missiles; (c) nuclear". It would seem that Peking leaders, who make frequent allusions to the mythical "Soviet threat", should take a favourable view of such a treaty; in fact, however, they refused to conclude it. One can hardly imagine more conclusive evidence to the effect that all of Peking's statements about the "Soviet threat" are false from A to Z. The Soviet Union again declared unequivocally that it had neither territorial nor economic claims to China.

Leonid Brezhnev expressed his profound confidence that

23*

the objective interests of the peoples of the Soviet Union and China, the laws of history would ultimately prevail over the subjective political distortions and that Sino-Soviet friendship would be restored. We want China to be a prosperous socialist power, he said, to struggle jointly with her for peace, against imperialism.

6. ENFORCEMENT BY THE MAOISTS OF THEIR ANTI-SOVIET LINE AT THE 10th CPC CONGRESS

The Peking leaders turned a deaf ear to the new initiative presented in Leonid Brezhnev's report on the occasion of the 50th anniversary of the USSR. Moreover, the beginning of 1973 saw a further intensification of Peking's propaganda hostile to the Soviet Union. In January 1973, the Chinese newspapers *Jenmin jihpao* and *Kwangming jihpao* alone published 37 anti-Soviet articles.

This line was pursued in the later period. Peking leaders exerted themselves with particular fervour to oppose the implementation of the Peace Programme advanced by the 24th CPSU Congress, to check the trend of change from the "cold war" towards a stable and lasting peace. The April 1973 plenary meeting of the CPSU Central Committee, in the resolution on its foreign policy activities, emphasised that the PRC leaders' stubborn struggle to undermine the unity of the socialist countries and the world communist movement, opposition to the efforts of the peace-loving nations seeking to achieve a relaxation of international tensions, Peking's anti-Soviet line were harmful to the cause of peace and world socialism. The plenary meeting reaffirmed the determination of the CPSU to pursue further the policy outlined by the 24th CPSU Congress in relation to China.

Chinese propaganda went on harping on its old theme of the "Soviet threat" to China. This lie was readily caught up by those interested in an aggravation of Sino-Soviet relations. For example, in May 1973 obviously inspired rumours became current in the United States concerning its alleged intercession in behalf of China, which saved her from a preventive Soviet nuclear strike in 1969. In this connection, on

May 31, 1973, the Soviet Embassy in Washington made a statement for the press, to the effect that it had been authorised to declare that allegations about the threat of a Soviet attack on China were a blatant lie. No such threat had ever existed nor did it exist today, the statement stressed.[1]

Without confining itself to explaining its stand, the Soviet Union took constructive steps to create conditions favourable to a normalisation of Sino-Soviet relations. In June 1973, the PRC Government was approached with a proposal for signing a Sino-Soviet non-aggression treaty and handed in a draft of it. Simultaneously, the Soviet side proposed a high-level meeting between Soviet and Chinese delegations in Moscow or Peking.

This new important Soviet initiative, which knocked whatever sand was left from under fabrications about the threat to China from the North, was not reciprocated by Peking. Anti-Soviet propaganda in China went on with increasing intensity. By the end of August 1973 it reached the climax of vehemency. One of the causes of such developments soon came into the open: between August 24 and 28 the Maoists held the 10th CPC Congress, for which they needed an atmosphere of anti-Soviet hysteria.

The 10th Congress of the Communist Party of China which is described by the Maoists as China's ruling party was shrouded in mystery. This was a striking illustration of the extremely complicated situation which had developed on China's home scene following the crack-down on Lin Piao and his supporters, in September 1971, of the existence of deep-going contradictions and differences within the Maoist clique itself, and an aggravation of the ideological and political crisis of Maoism. The Congress was called upon to take the heat out of the situation and stabilise it, to fix the new balance of power in the leadership of the Party and country, to reaffirm Mao's authority and endorse the home and foreign policy guidelines he had set during the "cultural revolution". Special emphasis was laid on unconditional approval of the "cultural revolution" and the line of the 9th CPC Congress. As shown by documents of the 10th Congress, it completely

---

[1] *Pravda*, June 2, 1973.

ignored the problems of economic and cultural advance, and failed to put forward any constructive programme of China's further development.

The foreign policy guidelines approved by the 10th Congress are striking evidence of the fact that China's foreign policy has become still less anti-imperialist in its content and even more hostile to the cause of peace and socialism. To begin with, the 10th CPC Congress openly took a stand against the joint line of the socialist countries and all progressive forces towards securing a relaxation of international tensions and promoting universal peace. To this line the Maoist Congress opposed its line of encouraging "colossal upheavals on the earth", describing them as "good rather than bad" events. In the main report to the Congress the speaker called in question the possibility of strengthening international security, depicted the people's struggle for peace as a fruitless and hopeless affair doomed to setbacks and defeats. "Détente," the report said, "is a transient and superficial phenomenon, while 'colossal upheavals' will continue in the future." By advancing this slogan, which is equally pessimistic and provocative, the Maoists challenge all peace forces, oppose themselves to the worldwide movement for peace, to all people of goodwill, make an apology for violence, excuse the imperialist policy of aggression and war. It follows from the Maoist slogan that international upheavals are inevitable and desirable, which is a direct service to the ultra-reactionary imperialist circles which have not abandoned their hopes of starting a new world war.

In the Peking leaders' designs the chief means of stirring up "colossal upheavals", i.e., international conflicts, is to provoke a war between the Soviet Union and the United States. The 10th CPC Congress gave prominence to the old Maoist thesis on the "conspiracy between the two superpowers". This lie is used by Chinese propaganda to interfere, on the one hand, with the favourable development of Soviet-American relations, to hold back the Soviet Union from taking steps in this direction by accusing it falsely and demagogically of a "collusion with imperialism" and, on the other hand, to knock together, under the slogan of struggle against the "two superpowers", a motley bloc of various states headed by China and actually called upon to become a tool for implementing Peking's hegemonistic plans on the world arena.

The 10th CPC Congress reaffirmed the divisive, subversive policy of the Maoists in relation to the socialist community, the world communist movement, and the national liberation movement. The Congress demonstrated its opposition to the unity and cohesion of the revolutionary forces and the Peking leadership's intention to make them serve its selfish ends.

The Congress fully dispelled whatever doubts were left about the fact that anti-Sovietism was the core of Peking's foreign policy, the keynote of all Maoist activities on the international scene. Now their declarations to the effect that they regarded the Soviet Union as their chief enemy were made not in propaganda publications but from the Congress rostrum, in the report of the CPC Central Committee. The Maoists seek to give a theoretical substantiation for their anti-Soviet policy. The documents of the 10th Congress spurn the principle of class analysis of the international situation, misrepresent the alignment of forces on the world arena and the main contradictions in the world. Distorting the essence of the present epoch, juggling with Lenin's theory of imperialism, the Maoists seek to place the Soviet Union among the imperialist states. They have already frankly defined their attitude to the Soviet Union as a "leading imperialist power" and describe their anti-Soviet policy as the key trend of anti-imperialist struggle. This allows them to justify their actions against the Soviet Union, even when acting in alliance with the most reactionary forces, to knock together a pro-Chinese bloc that could be used in particular, to bring pressure to bear on the United States in bargaining over political issues.

The very first steps of Peking on the international scene after the 10th CPC Congress showed graphically that the policy guidelines it had proclaimed really make the basis of China's practical actions in the field of foreign affairs, that the Chinese leaders stubbornly seek to carry into effect their plans and intentions hostile to the cause of peace and socialism.

One of the most important world events soon after the 10th CPC Congress was the 4th summit conference of the non-aligned countries held in Algiers in September 1973. The Chinese leaders went out of their way to impress their authority on the conference and make it serve, above all, their anti-Soviet objectives. They displayed special fervour in opposing discussion in Algiers on the issue of calling a world disarmament conference proposed by the Soviet Union. In Chinese propaganda material circulated among the delegates the Soviet policy in relation to the developing countries was qualified as a policy of "sweet words" and "a stab in the back", and Soviet aid to them, as a "bait".

Neither the Maoist conceptions on the key world problems nor the subversive anti-Soviet line of Peking were supported at the conference in Algiers. In particular, the Peking leaders' hopes for antagonising the non-aligned states to the Soviet Union by the fake slogan of struggle against the "superpowers" were dashed. A number of speakers to the conference described China herself as a "superpower" and an "ultra-nationalist state". The documents adopted by the Algiers conference showed that on most issues of principle the positions of non-aligned countries differed from those of Peking leaders. In contrast to the Maoist doctrine of two "superpowers", the conference clearly stated in its political declaration that the "main reality of today is the confrontation of the peoples against colonialism, neo-colonialism and imperialism". The conference also declared its support for such moves—constantly under intense fire from Peking—as détente and the settlement of European problems, the appeal for general and complete disarmament, in particular, for banning the use and testing of nuclear weapons, support for a world disarmament conference, etc.

Significantly, the capitalist press, commenting on the results of the 4th summit conference of the non-aligned countries in Algiers, had to acknowledge that at this forum delegations openly supporting China turned to be in an obvious minority.

The ulterior motives of the foreign policy guidelines of the 10th CPC Congress were exposed in full at the 28th session of the United Nations General Assembly which opened in September 1974. The proposal of the Soviet delegation to place on the agenda of the session as a matter of urgency the question of reducing by 10 per cent the military budgets of the permanent members of the UN Security Council, and diverting a share of the funds thus saved to assist the developing countries evoked a broad and favourable response among the delegates. Such a reduction would be a long step towards ending the arms race and a major contribution to strengthening peace and international security, would release huge resources for civilian construction and for greater assistance to the developing countries. The Chinese delegation, however, far from supporting the Soviet proposal motivated, as it was, with sincere concern for mankind's welfare, opposed its discussion at the General Assembly session. The leader of the Chinese delegation bluntly declared from the rostrum of the General Assembly: "Is it truly possible to reduce military budgets?... We believe it's better to end such empty talk, and the sooner, the better." Not surprisingly, the Peking representative was unable to support his obstructionist statement with any coherent arguments. The only motive he adduced was to the effect that it was allegedly impossible to estimate military budgets, because, as he said, "to study this problem alone, a commission would have to be set up, which would work for many years".

One could, of course, be surprised at the fact that the Peking leaders cannot afford to spend time on the settlement of such a crucial problem as arms reduction, one that is vital to the interests of all countries. It is perfectly obvious, however, that the Maoists' motive is by no means their fear of difficulties in estimating military budgets. It is widely known in the world that military appropriations account for over-one third of China's budget, and it was Peking's desire to continue this exorbitant spending that was the true motive for the Chinese delegation's opposition to the Soviet proposal at the 28th session of the UN General Assembly.

The Chinese representative's statements at the session on other international issues also shed ample light on the character of the foreign policy outlined by the 10th CPC Congress. Peking vehemently attacked the Soviet-American agreement on the prevention of nuclear war, which was welcomed by progressive world opinion as one contributing to a radical amelioration of the international climate. The Chinese leaders do not desist from their attempts to put up obstacles in the way of the conference on security and co-operation in Europe, where for the first time in history all the European states, the United States and Canada have had a round-table meeting to work out jointly measures that may help secure a peaceful life for the peoples of Europe in a historically foreseeable future. Ignoring the vital interests of the Asian peoples, the leader of the Chinese delegation cracked down on the Soviet proposal for setting up a collective security system in Asia, resorting again to the ridiculous allegation to the effect that the Soviet Union (which borders on China over a length of thousands of kilometres) is not an Asian country. Just as at the previous session of the UN General Assembly, the Chinese delegate obstructed the admission of the Republic of Bangladesh to the United Nations, revealing once again the hypocrisy of his statements in support of the national liberation movement and the developing countries.

A striking example of the Maoists' betrayal of the interests of the embattled peoples is Peking's stand in relation to the counter-revolutionary coup in Chile. Far from coming out in support of Chile's revolutionary democratic forces or denouncing the fascist junta, the Chinese leaders offered the latter a friendly hand, recognising the anti-popular regime it had established in Chile.

That Peking's foreign policy is detrimental to the interests of the national liberation movement was made strikingly clear by the developments connected with the continued Israeli aggression in the Middle East and the outbreak of hostilities there in October 1973. The Chinese leadership abstained from giving effective assistance to Egypt and Syria. In the meantime, it took advantage of the new flare-up in the Middle East crisis for attacks on the Soviet Union, which sided unhesitatingly with the Arab nations.

Peking leaders have long deserted the ranks of the movement in support of peace and international security. They deigned no answer to an invitation to attend the World Congress of Peace Forces held in Moscow in October 1973, withheld their support for its appeals and resolutions and took, in effect, hostile stand in relation to this largest international forum of peace supporters.

Peking's continued efforts to step up its anti-Soviet policy after the 10th CPC Congress have laid bare the hypocrisy of Chinese leaders' statements at the Congress that Sino-Soviet disputes on issues of principle should not interfere with a normalisation of relations between the two countries on the basis of the five principles of peaceful coexistence. In reality, Peking's policy towards the Soviet Union exemplifies a blatant violation of these principles.

The Soviet Union displayed calmness and reserve in the face of the anti-Soviet orientation of the 10th CPC Congress. The Soviet policy in relation to China is, as before, based on the principles formulated by the 24th CPSU Congress. Referring to the 10th CPC Congress Leonid Brezhnev declared in his speech in Tashkent on September 24, 1973 that the Soviet Union had invariably and consistently come out for normalising relations with China, and more, for restoring Sino-Soviet friendship. This would meet the interests of both the Soviet and the Chinese peoples, and, on a broader plane, would serve the cause of peace, socialism and progress. The CPSU General Secretary reaffirmed that the Soviet Union had no territorial claims to China and sought to base its relations with her on the principles of respect for sovereignty, equality, noninterference in each other's internal affairs.

The plans of those who hope to benefit by the present strained relations between the Soviet Union and China are nearsighted and irresponsible. It is quite obvious that an aggravation of tensions between the Soviet Union and China and conflicts between them would cause damage not only to their own interests but to those of other states as well. Therefore, genuine champions of peace and international security have invariably been in favour of normalising Sino-Soviet relations and denounced attempts to prevent this.

The position set out by Leonid Brezhnev showed the profound concern of Soviet leaders for a normalisation of Sino-Soviet relations, their keen sense of responsibility for the destinies of the two nations, the cause of socialism and peace throughout the world.

AFTERWORD

The study of the history of Sino-Soviet relations in the period 1945-1973 inevitably leads one to draw this conclusion: friendship and co-operation between the Soviet Union and China meet the vital interests of their peoples and serve the cause of peace, democracy and socialism throughout the world. At all the stages of China's modern history, assistance and support from the Soviet Union were invariably a crucial factor of the Chinese working people's national liberation and revolutionary struggle. Each time Sino-Soviet relations became closer, China's revolutionary forces consolidated their positions, the progressive movement was given additional impetus, reaction had to beat a retreat. And, conversely, a weakening of China's links with the Soviet Union had an extremely adverse effect on the political climate in China, kept down revolutionary enthusiasm, facilitated the growth of nationalistic trends, opened for domestic reaction the way to conspiracy with imperialism.

The Soviet Union's assistance to China's revolutionary forces retained its vital importance after the proclamation of the People's Republic of China in 1949. The transition from the bourgeois-democratic stage of revolution to its socialist stage in China with her relatively small and politically fragmented industrial proletariat required special conditions for strengthening the leading role of the working class and increasing the proportion of workers in the Party membership. The relative weakness of the political positions of the working class on the home scene could be and was